THE
BARBARIANS
OF
ASIA

THE
BARBARIANS
OF
ASIA

Stuart Legg

DORSET PRESS
NEW YORK

This edition published by Dorset Press,
a division of Marboro Books Corporation,
by arrangement with Farrar, Straus & Giroux.
1990 Dorset Press

ISBN 88029-534-1

Printed in the United States of America

M 9 8 7 6 5 4 3 2 1

Contents

List of Maps

I
Journey Through Inner Space

Beyond this flood a frozen Continent
Lies dark and wide; beat with perpetual storms
Of Whirlwind and dire Hail, which on firm land
Thaws not, but gathers heap, and ruin seems
Of ancient pile; all else deep snow and ice: the parching air
Burns frore, and cold performs th'effect of Fire.
                                    — MILTON, *Paradise Lost*

T HE bell in Moscow station spoke once, announcing an
      imminent departure. Throughout the crowd on the plat-
form heads were slowly bared in preparation for last farewells.
Swinging himself on board the train, an Englishman, John
Foster Fraser by name, observed the scene. He noted the big,
solemn men heavily embracing each other, bestowing on big,
solemn brothers the customary parting kiss on the lips. His
eye caught the movement of white-sleeved arms and gold
shoulder-straps as a group of young officers laughed and shouted
to their friends below. He saw a blond lad in a private's uniform
standing rigidly to attention while a tiny old woman repeatedly
clutched and kissed the breast of his tunic.

The bell sounded again. All aboard. At the windows of the
next car Fraser saw a row of round, vacant faces beneath mops
of matted hair: peasants, emigrating from an old world to a
new. They stared down at their piano-legged, kerchief-headed
wives on the platform. And their wives, red-eyed but motionless, stared back. Like men and women, they seemed conscious
that a moment of crisis had arrived: but like animals, were
powerless to mark it by word or sign.

The bell clanged for a third and last time. Imperceptibly,

the long train began to move. Then, as if aware of the interminable journey ahead, it jerked almost to a stop again; shuddered in seeming indecision; and at last, in monstrous effort, gathered way. From the moving windows, along the whole length of the platform, people crossed themselves. The mail train for Siberia was leaving. The time was 3 p.m. The date, Thursday, 22 August 1901.

Ten years before, the Grand Duke Nicholas, heir apparent to the reigning Tsar Alexander III, had landed at Vladivostok after a round of official visits abroad. Among the ceremonial duties awaiting him was that of inaugurating, as his father's representative, the building of the Great Siberian Railway. And on 31 May 1891, while a bitter wind swept down from the north over the huddled roofs of the drab, slummy town that Vladivostok then was, the Tsarevich duly tipped a barrow of sticky spoil on to the site scheduled for the most easterly embankment of the longest railway in the world.

Expert foreign opinion remained sceptical of the colossal project. Russia, part civilized, part brute, was planning to construct a railway across the best part of a hemisphere. She was setting out to lay some 6,000 miles of permanent way through steppe and forest, over huge rivers and treacherous marshes, through formidable mountains; across some of the most difficult engineering country imaginable, where much of the terrain was frozen the year round; across tracts scarcely inhabited except by primitive tribesmen, where labour of any kind was hard to find and skilled labour non-existent; where there were no means of bringing in materials save along potholed, mud-choked tracks; where the ferocious winters must bring work virtually to a standstill for months on end. And even if it was completed, this most improbable of undertakings could only culminate in 'rusty streaks of iron through the vastness of nothing to the extremities of nowhere'.

The Trans-Siberian was indeed born in adversity. On some sections, so little was known of soil and climate that engineers had to rely for critical data on the yarns of oldest inhabitants. On others, routings based on hasty, optimistic surveys had to be abandoned as unforeseen difficulties came to light. Contractors refused to bid for work in regions so remote that no one could estimate the risks; or if they did, proved ineffective or

went bankrupt. Mile upon mile of permanently frozen ground
had to be blasted loose with dynamite or slowly thawed out
with countless wood fires burning simultaneously. In winter
it sometimes became almost impossible to obtain water from
rivers frozen solid to the bottom. In summer floods demolished
works already half completed. Droughts reduced food supplies
to dangerous levels. Epidemics deprived the working force of
precious men and animals. Chinese coolies, drafted in, were
found unable to use that basic Chinese invention, the wheel-
barrow. Delays deepened while committees in St Petersburg
argued whether bridges should be built of steel or timber. Nearly
everything that could go wrong went wrong, and on a gargantuan scale.

Yet much went right. Rails for the section through the forests
of mid-Siberia duly arrived from Britain via the Arctic Ocean
and the Yenisei river. Masons and metalworkers for the Far
Eastern division, as well as materials and rolling stock, safely
made the long voyage from Odessa round India to Vladivostok.
Where no other labour was available, provincial governors
provided convicts. By the turn of the century, less than ten
years after the windswept little ceremony at Vladivostok, the
greater part of the Trans-Siberian was open to traffic.

True, it could hardly be called a railway of the highest standards. Embankments showed a disturbing tendency to wash out,
cuttings to collapse, couplings to break. Locomotives had a habit
of coming to involuntary rest, often miles from the nearest
station. Enginemen and passengers commended themselves to
God as they approached certain bridges. And although passenger
trains seemed providentially immune from total disaster, the
ponderous rumbling crash of freight wagons piling up in heaps
along the trackside rolled across the Siberian landscape so
frequently as to excite little remark. None the less – and with
the exception of a short voyage across Lake Baikal – it was
possible, by 1900, to travel continuously by rail from Moscow
to an unheard-of place called Sretensk, lying on the Shilka
river to the north-east of Mongolia. From here to Khabarovsk
on the Amur, a matter of 800 miles, there was still a gap; and
this section of the journey was done by river steamer. At
Khabarovsk another train was waiting to take the weary
traveller southward down the valley of the Ussuri, just east

of the Manchurian frontier, to Vladivostok and the Sea of
Japan.

Before the railway, to travel overland from European Russia
to the Pacific had meant a journey of up to a year along the
Trakt, the old Siberian post-road. It was performed behind
teams of shaggy ponies, in summer in a *tarantas,* a kind of
cart without springs in which you lay almost prone, trying to
sleep, insulated by layers of straw, mattresses and pillows; in
winter in a sledge, when your body was additionally swathed
in furs and several pairs of felt and leather boots. The incessant
jolting was so appalling that you refrained from speech lest
you should bite off a piece of your tongue. Your driver, well
fortified with vodka, took rickety bridges at full gallop so that
you would be across before they had time to collapse. A smash-
up could land you with the certainty of a night out in wild
country at sub-zero temperatures, possibly with a broken limb.
The post-houses stank, crawled with vermin, and could sometimes offer little but boiling water from a samovar, from which
you made your own tea. Nor could you be sure of horses the
next morning, or the morning after; for officials of every degree
– and they were legion – had prior claim. Such a journey was
seldom undertaken by Russians, except for compelling reasons.
Few foreigners could contemplate it.

The Trans-Siberian Railway, even in its uncompleted state,
reduced to days the crossing of the greatest continent on earth.
For Westerners, it was suddenly possible to penetrate the vast,
mysterious Eurasian land-mass in a lounge suit or a dress, with
leisurely stop-overs, and at very moderate cost. Indeed, the price
of a first-class fare from Moscow to Vladivostok, including
sleeper, was about $58, or £12. And if you could not afford the
weekly *train de luxe* leaving each Saturday evening, or if you
preferred to rough it, there was a mail train every afternoon.
There was, perhaps, no great initial rush to book. Mournful
steppe horizons, monotonous infinities of rock and fir and distant white-toothed ranges, were not to everybody's taste.
There was doubt about the actual degree of *luxe;* about the
lounges and libraries, dining-cars with tanks of live fish, baths
and showers, gymnasia and hairdressing saloons with which, the
publicity insisted, the expresses would be equipped. Russian
reality might be different. There were second thoughts, too,

about venturing into regions of such sinister repute. 'The very
word Siberia is one to make the blood run chill. It smells of
fetters in the snow. You hear the thud of the knout on the
shoulders of sickened men. For generations, to whisper Siberia
in the ear of a Russian has been to make the cheek blanch.'

Yet there were, both in Europe and America, a number of
determined spirits eager for the new experience. There was
Fraser, the English journalist we have already met, disdaining
first-class comfort in favour of closer contact with Russians in
the slower mail. There was the lively Annette Meakin with her
elderly, intrepid mother – probably the first Englishwomen to
make the trip. From America came Michael Myers Shoemaker,
a writer of travel books, and the Rev. Dr Francis E. Clark with
his wife and small son. There was Jonas Stadling, a Swedish
explorer, bent on the rescue of a balloonist who had disappeared
in the Arctic regions; and E. W. Pfizenmayer, a German arch-
aeologist on his way to excavate a mammoth found in north-
eastern Siberia. Their names strike no special chord now. But
they and others like them were the first 'ordinary people' from
the outside world – professional men and tourists, as distinct
from the handful of hardened travellers who had endured the
rigours of the *Trakt* – to glimpse the immensities of northern
Asia. Though they made the journey at different times during
the opening years of the present century, they shared a common
sense of adventure and wrote down what they saw. To go with
them is to see through their eyes sights and spaces that were
almost as strange and novel then as those opening to the astro-
nauts of today.

They watched the afternoon sun firing the cupolas of Moscow
as the city faded in the distance. Then they turned to settle
down for the first stage of their journey across the woods and
pastel fields of eastern Russia, past slow rivers and identical
untidy villages clustered round the domes of great churches.
Annette Meakin found herself entranced by the solid, ornate
appointments of the *train de luxe*. She could be snug in private
or expansive in public as the mood took her. In her coupé there
was a galaxy of buttons and switches: one bell to summon the
car attendant, another to call the waiter from the buffet; there
were silk-shaded reading lamps on the table and above the bed. Or

she could stroll to the dining-car, where at one end stood a Bech-
stein piano, vases of flowers and ferns, and a bookcase filled with
novels, albeit in Russian. On the wall here, beside the normal
pictures of the Tsar and the Empress, was a less familiar por-
trait: that of an alert, strong face with hair brushed back from
a high forehead and a tufted goatee beard. This was Prince
Khilkov, who, as Minister of Communications, had been responsible for much of the construction of the Trans-Siberian.
He was the antithesis of the usual Tsarist aristocrat-minister.
He had studied engineering in England and America, then
worked his way up in the Russian railway service. Easy and
friendly in manner, he described himself as 'a sort of blacksmith'; and was wont to add, possibly with his recent labours
in mind, 'What's the good of worrying?' And here, chatting in
French with a young Russian lady, Miss Meakin received an
indication of the nature of the journey she had undertaken. It
was foolhardy, this lady told her, to travel in Siberia without a
revolver. For good measure she herself invariably carried two.
A little later, a gentleman who turned out to be the Mayor of
Vladivostok urged the same precaution, producing his own
from his pocket and musing that it had once saved his life. If
Miss Meakin had not brought her pistol with her, she should
certainly get one no later than Omsk.

Rumbling along in the mail train behind two wood-burning
locomotives with big conical chimneys, his compartment well
stuffed with humanity if not with cushions, Fraser scrutinized
his fellow-travellers. Shirts, it appeared, were a gauge of status
in the Russia of the time. Among the more genteel they were
of relatively restrained colours – grey, puce, or occasionally
white; and were worn, in European style, inside the trousers.
No such inhibitions marked the shirts of the lower orders.
These were usually of flaming red; and as if to maximize the
impact of this striking hue, hung down outside like a skirt. Fraser
found the curiosity of his scarlet-clad companions a trifle direct
by Western conventions. Repeatedly they asked him where he
came from, where he was going, what was the nature of his
business. To what class did he belong? Was he titled? How
much money had he with him? And was it on his person or in
his baggage? On his way to join the queue outside the toilet
he came upon a stout, cheerful lady standing in the corridor

puffing a cigarette. Politely, he sought to pass – and failed. As
they jammed in the narrow passage, he grunted. 'Ah, you are
an Englishman,' she exclaimed; and they exchanged cards on
the spot.

The train staff was impressive. Miss Meakin noted the good
looks of her conductor; and the courtesy with which, on her
inquiring about hotels in Siberia, he informed her that it was
warmer in Irkutsk than in Moscow. On the mail, the ticket-
collector was a stately, bearded figure in a uniform frock-coat
with white and purple tassels at the shoulder. Attended by two
assistants he came at frequent intervals to inspect Fraser's
ticket, each time examining it with an air of interested surprise
as if he had never seen its like before. Uniforms were everywhere, in the trains, at every stop. The number of officials –
railway officials, police officials, civil officials – was a source of
wonder. All of lower rank saluted all of higher. If a superior
spoke to an inferior, the latter kept his hand to his cap until
the senior turned away. Those of equal rank studiously ignored
each other.

So they trundled eastward, seldom at more than twenty
miles an hour, comparing favourably the smooth, unhurried
riding on the broader Russian gauge with the rush and sway
of Western expresses; until, some twenty-four hours out of
Moscow, the Russian passengers crowded to the windows and
crossed themselves again, and they saw between the slowly
passing girders of a long bridge the broad, muddy waters of the
Volga, with the rafts from Nizhniy Novgorod drifting down,
through the miles and months, towards Astrakhan and the
Caspian Sea; and heard, during a momentary halt, the songs of
the boatmen marking the rhythm of great oars. Then on,
through Samara and Ufa, until another evening came on, and
the climb into the Ural Mountains began. Now the train toiled
up between humped hills, twisting through grey rocks overhung
by beech and oak standing dark against the fading light.
Another curve, and the panting engines would reveal quiet,
long-shadowed meadows dotted with hamlets; would start a
cloud of butterflies, raise a flight of wild duck from a river bank.
An unspectacular range, the Urals, some of the travellers
thought, a little disappointing in itself: but to those sleepless
at midnight the passage of the summit, with the rail-joints

beating faster as the downward speed increased, spelt a moment of meaning. Old Russia was behind. Ahead lay Siberia. Standing at the window in the dawn twilight they might have seen at the lineside, near the lonely station of Urzhumka, a stone pyramid bearing a simple inscription: on one side, EUROPE; on the other, ASIA.

/ Morning brought a large station set in birch groves: Chelyabinsk, the first stop in Siberia. The train pulled in past sallow, slit-eyed Tartars, Bashkirs of bland mien, stolid Kirghiz; past swarthy Cossacks with sheepskin caps set rakishly, cartridge-pockets across the breasts of their long coats, high boots of softest leather. Beyond these faces of another world was a glimpse of tables spread with chickens, hot dumplings, seasoned hash, new loaves, fruit, pails of milk: a buffet-market presided over by the local peasantry. In a trice the train was empty, its passengers surging, unshaved and tangle-haired, across the platform. And though the Westerners among them were familiar with the scrambles for sandwiches at Crewe or Albany, none had seen anything to compare with the fight for food at Chelyabinsk.

Since the eighteenth century the town had been a place of ill omen. Nearly all convicts had passed through it on the hopeless march into the depths of Siberia; and not far off stood the 'Monument of Tears' which marked their last contact with their homeland. Now, every empty space along the platform was occupied by immigrants: heaps of peasant humanity from European Russia, almost indistinguishable from the bundles of possessions on which they sprawled, dirty, cold, hungry, chivvied by authority; yet having made up their own minds, by some primordial upheaval of the spirit, to shake off the usage of the centuries and move into the unknown. And even at this frontier station a difference of attitude was noticeable between the old world and the new. Young Siberian Russians, born and bred east of the Urals, seemed brisker, carried themselves more erect, showed little of the servility of Russia proper.

Three blasts from the engine and they were moving again; past dumps of hides, hillocks of corn, stacks of valuable furs, half protected by tarpaulins or open to the weather, strewn haphazard along the line, awaiting onward transport. Already the Trans-Siberian was overloaded. And then, for hours that became days and nights, the train steamed steadily across a calm ocean of grass, until the eye ached with the flat monotony and sought out for relief the clumps of larch and the roofs of villages that passed like ships hull-down in the distance. In the steppes of western Siberia, in this infinity of grass, nothing seemed to change as time progressed. Horizon succeeded identical horizon; only the rails appeared to move, broadening as they approached from the level rim where grass met sky, rolling beneath the clanging cars, closing in again as they receded into grass and sky behind. Like the melting vista of a planetarium, the sun vanished into the grass; the dome of stars appeared above the grass; a thin moon rode in silence over the darkened grass, suggesting to a watcher from the train the setting of a melancholy dream. And through the night another movement replaced the oncoming of the rails. Far ahead along the track a tiny green light would spring up, grow larger with the seconds until, as it reached the train, the figure of a man was just discernible, standing beside a hut, holding the lamp above his head, turning as the locomotive passed to show it from behind. The light diminished in the distance; and in the night ahead another dot of green appeared. This was the signalling system of the Trans-Siberian: flags by day, lamps by night, held by a chain of men stretching from Moscow to the Orient, many of them good-conduct convicts.

The morning brought relief. Standing on the platform of his car, Stadling saw a great cloud of dust rising from the steppe; and through the cloud, the forms of Kirghiz horsemen riding beside their herds of cattle, sheep and horses. They passed; but a little later more herds appeared, growing in size and number till they were spread about the plain to the limits of sight. Wherever a fold of ground offered a slight vantage-point a mounted shepherd watched, the morning sun striking his tall red boots and belted kaftan. And suddenly the iron horse was challenged. Circling towards the track, booting his pony to a frantic gallop, a Kirghiz boy raced beside the cars. Wild-eyed, he drew ahead of the train's lumbering plod; raised a cheer from its windows; abruptly wheeled; and was gone. There was little now to hold attention till the sun went down again and lights began to multiply around them. They rumbled across 700 yards of bridge spanning the Irtysh river, itself a tributary of the greater Ob, and at long last found themselves in Omsk.

The official *Guide to the Great Siberian Railway*, a lavish production issued in 1900 for the benefit of passengers, was cautious in describing Omsk. It admitted that the monotony of the small wooden buildings, the unpaved streets and the absence of any vegetation due to the saline soil, gave the place 'the aspect of a large Cossack settlement'. But it went on more encouragingly: 'The town includes two gardens, organized by the Society for the Promotion of Elementary Education. A birch wood situated on the northern side of the town is the object of walks by the inhabitants. On the southern side is a sanitary station for those who wish to drink koumiss prepared under the supervision of the railway physicians.'

It was no doubt the prospect of such attractions that caused several of our travellers to break their journey at Omsk. Fraser made a point of sampling koumiss, the fermented mares' milk that was the universal intoxicant of the original steppe peoples; and he assured his hosts that its flavour was delightful. But afterwards he recalled that it took a fortnight to rid his mouth of the taste of the 'vile stuff'. He was not the first Westerner to dislike koumiss: six centuries earlier, a Franciscan friar on a mission to the Mongols had broken into a sweat of shock on taking his first gulp.

Miss Meakin did not record whether she visited a gunsmith; but she and her mother were admitted to the polite society of the town. On several occasions they had heard the sound of wailing, and now inquired what it might portend. On being told that this was the noise of camels, Mrs Meakin exclaimed that these animals should be found in Omsk, and added that she had long wished to mount one. 'Intelligent people,' came the cold reply, 'do not mount camels. They are beasts of burden.'

Local opinion at that time seemed uncertain of the proper attitude to take towards a former inhabitant, who had been known to his friends as *Pokoinik* – 'the Deceased'. The nickname arose from the fact that during his sojourn he had been so ferociously flogged that he was taken down as dead. His real name was Dostoievsky, and according to the *Guide* he had been a man of 'great talent': but a book of his, *The House of the Dead*, had been far from complimentary to Omsk.

Already they were as far east as Delhi: yet, as they left Omsk, nearly a thousand miles still lay ahead before they would reach the centre of Siberia. The train still crawled, a tiny worm, across the steppe horizons. The line stretched on, a foot or so above the flat green table; and in the ditches beside it they could see, for mile on mile, rich black soil lying close beneath the grass.

The black soil of the steppes, and the railway that made it accessible: already, they realized, the combination was beginning to produce a noticeable shift in the very balance of Russia. On either side of the track stood a long succession of black and white posts, stamped with the imperial eagle, marking the boundaries of land reserved for settlement. And into Siberia, to occupy the land, was moving a tide of population, flowing round the travellers from abroad, bearing them on its flood as they journeyed east. At the larger stations they saw, as they had seen at Chelyabinsk, immigrants in their hundreds; peasant families with their corded boxes and shapeless bundles, sitting, staring, sleeping, waiting. It was a movement, they were told, supported by massive government organization. Food was dispensed at cost throughout the journey: for the children and the sick it was free. Chests of medical equipment were available at every station, in the charge of officials trained in first aid. A church car with travelling priests, even with a belfry mounted at one end, was progressing up and down the line, stopping for services where the crowds were thickest. On arrival at his plot of ground each man would receive seed at a nominal price, could obtain tools on credit and, if necessary, a small loan to start him off. For the first ten years on his new land he would pay no taxes.

They passed long trains, packed with immigrants, waiting in the sidings. Some were composed of freight wagons crudely adapted to carry living cargo. Many of the regular trains had immigrant cars attached to them. Seen at close quarters it was a hard journey even for *muzhiks* reared in hardship. Inside, the cars resembled great cupboards whose shelves were stacked with grimy human forms. 'Berths' were bare planks on which the occupants spread whatever rags they had that were not upon their backs. They slept almost continuously, rousing themselves for meals of melons, sour black bread, and tea made from samovars of boiling water kept ready at the stations. As days and

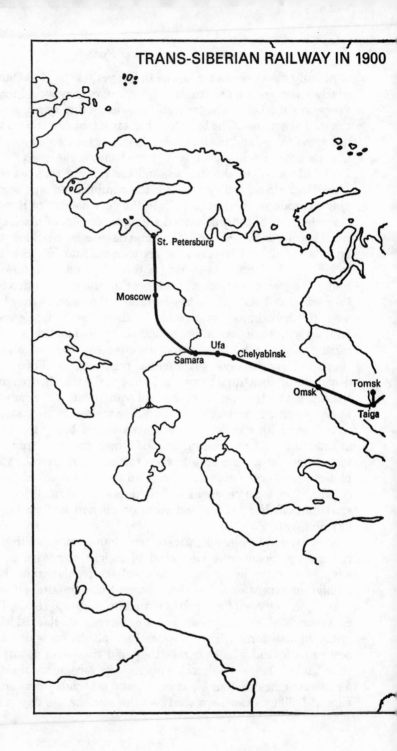

TRANS-SIBERIAN RAILWAY IN 1900

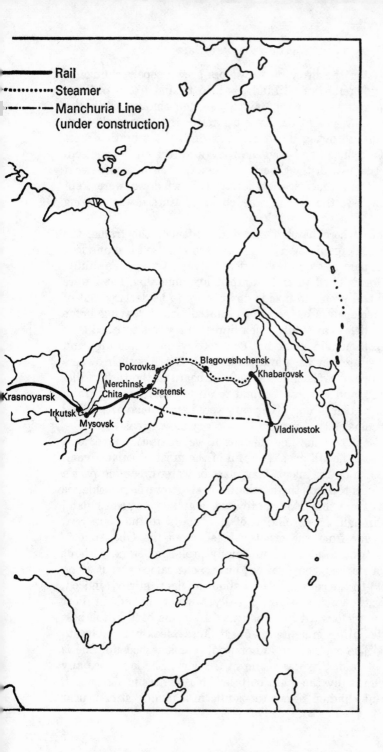

Rail
Steamer
Manchuria Line
(under construction)

Krasnoyarsk
Irkutsk
Mysovsk
Chita
Nerchinsk
Sretensk
Pokrovka
Blagoveshchensk
Khabarovsk
Vladivostok

nights passed the litter on the floors grew deeper: chunks of
bread, rind, refuse of all kinds, swilled to and fro in pools of
tea or worse. When sleep failed the men smoked endlessly,
dragging a few puffs from little cigarettes that were half card-
board tube, throwing down the ends into the vibrating mess
below. To reduce hand baggage they wore their winter sheepskins in the heat of the Siberian summer, lying with the sweat
dripping from their scarlet faces. The windows were kept
tightly closed; the stench was choking. Russia was moving
east.

At stops where batches of immigrants left the trains, the
gulf between organization and reality showed itself in a hundred
anxieties, panics, tragedies – microscopic, poignant. Painfully,
grubby forms filled in and stamped by some alien hand were
unfolded and proffered upside down, only to be declared out of
order. Precious travel permits, granted before leaving home
after long delays and only when bureaucracy was satisfied that
taxes had been paid, could not be traced when hunted high and
low through greasy bags and pockets. Possessions their owners
had no hope of replacing were left on board in the rush of dis-
embarking, and went on beyond recall in the vanishing train.
Savings hoarded through the years were found to have dwindled
to a few coins on the journey. Russia was moving east.

Then, as if to underline this turgid yet majestic movement,
they crossed the Ob, most slothful of the great Siberian rivers;
looked down on the silent, lazy mass of water dreaming past a
myriad lakes towards the northern forests; towards marshlands
larger in extent than France; towards a gulf as long as England
forced through the desolation of the tundra to the Kara Sea.
And not far from the great bridge across the Ob, Annette
Meakin's train came to an unusually prolonged stand without
benefit of station. They waited; but no one came or went along
the track. In the country round about no figure stirred; indeed,
no habitation was in sight. Finally a sailor, bound for Port
Arthur, went forward to investigate. He came back in the best
of spirits, firing enlightenment at Miss Meakin in staccato
English. 'The engine,' he announced, 'has smashed up. She is
sixty years old. She was made in Glasgow. She is no use any
more.' Gradually the train emptied. No one seemed to mind.
Immigrant children began to paddle in a muddy stream near

by. Annette took down her camera and walked to the head of
the train. Eventually her patience was rewarded. She secured
a shot of the 'poor old engine' being towed away by a relief. It
reminded her, she said, of the Fighting Temeraire.

It was usual for travellers to spend a day or two at Tomsk.
Then the capital of Siberia, it enjoyed a lively reputation.
Gold was panned from the sands of the Tom river, and the tea
caravans passed through on their way from China. Millionaires
abounded, as well as former convicts who were sometimes
wealthy men themselves. In Tomsk, it was rumoured, to live
in moral probity was to be suspected of radical notions. But the
maps revealed the odd fact that the main line did not go near
the city. It passed through the town of Taiga, some fifty miles
to the south, from where a branch had been constructed up to
Tomsk. Several times already they had been struck by this
strange tendency for the railway to avoid certain towns logically
along the route. To by-pass an important capital seemed still
more puzzling. Their Russian companions advanced a simple
explanation. It was customary, they said, for surveyors to
inform the townsfolk along proposed lines that technical
difficulties would arise unless it was made worth while to bring
the railway to their doorstep. The response of some towns was
such that the difficulties disappeared: but at stubborn places
like Tomsk they had, unhappily, proved insuperable. So the
passengers bundled into the branch-line train at Taiga and
rattled northward – only to discover that the station at Tomsk
itself had been built, to make the surveyors' vengance doubly
sweet, several inconvenient miles outside the city.

Tomsk came up to expectations. In the dining-room of
Fraser's hotel stood a huge mechanical organ of the latest
type. Set going, it roared out tunes while the figure of a toy
conductor, mounted in front, his arm jerking up and down,
beat time without relation to the frenzy of banging drums and
clashing cymbals. It was the sensation of the city, blaring on
for its crowd of dancing, drinking, shoving, shouting admirers
till four in the morning.

In the centre of the capital, imposing public buildings rose
from a surrounding sea of mud in which pedestrians slipped and
slid about their business. A scruffy old man was pointed out as
a millionaire four times over. Two elegant ladies, splashing by

in their carriage, were identified respectively as a convict's daughter and the fiancée of a convict's son. Another passer-by had an intriguing history. He was a prince, a nephew of the Governor of Moscow. One day he happened to meet a well-to-do Englishman who wished to settle in Russia. The governor had a large, commodious house; and was, conveniently, away. Seizing the moment, the nephew sold his uncle's house as his own for a stiff price. He was exiled to Tomsk, where he was now in flourishing practice as a lawyer.

In the market-place, among heavy, creaking, hooded carts and mud-caked, haggling men, they watched a peasant cutting a friend's hair. First he smoothed down the matted mop, front and back and round the ears. Then he placed a bowl on the head, pressing it firmly down. Finally he lopped off with a pair of shears all the hair outside the bowl. They learnt that in the winter here it was normal to sell provisions in the form of frozen lumps. Not long since, the police had had to intervene when an embattled woman fetched her opponent a crack across the skull with a block of milk.

Some of the travellers were not sorry to leave Tomsk. Its orgiastic squalor was invigorating for a sleepless night or two. But it was hardly *kulturny*.

The landscape changed now, as they journeyed on. The flat grass of the steppes was left behind, and they wound between irregular, broken hills. Gradients steepened; and intermittently the speed became a crawl as they climed on to the plateau of central Siberia. All around was the taiga, the enormous belt of forest that spans the northern regions of Eurasia. On either side of the track rose a wall of spruce and fir and larch, still and sombre. From the left of the train the trees spread northward for a thousand miles to the threshold of the polar wastes. To the right they stretched away to the uplands and summits of the Altai mountains, standing at the north-west marches of China. Moving hour by hour through the green gloom, through the pillared depths of brown and black, past deadwood lying twisted in the scrub as if by torture, the mind seemed to contract into a small, sunless shell, bounded by foreboding; to become shy, suspicious, animal.

Yet Russia had reached into the taiga, moving east. They passed villages clustered round great churches, reminiscent of

Quebec; yellow-painted stations set in clearings, each with its water-tower and stack of logs. They passed eastbound troop trains waiting to let the expresses through, filled with young soldiers whose strange sad songs belied their laughing faces and the bright colours of white tunics, red epaulettes, green trousers. Emerging from the forest they saw Krasnoyarsk nursed in its bosom of hills, with its triple-spired cathedral built by a successful gold prospector. They crossed the tremendous Yenisei river, spattered with shipping, marching purposefully to the Arctic.

Then, for relief from the taiga, there was a spell of pleasant, park-like country; of meadows lying between grassy slopes, misty with forget-me-nots and with ranunculus lit to glowing orange by the afternoon sun. At evening they saw the stock making their own way home from the pastures; mares and foals, cows and calves and goats moving in untended procession down village streets, each group turning in at its own yard. Unscathed among the passing hoofs, dogs and pigs lay sleeping; and here and there among them, equally at peace, the prone form of a dead drunk man.

As darkness fell the forest closed in again, and the night was filled with fire. Periodically the glare from the locomotive shot beams of red into the black arcade of branches. Where the rails and ballast of the hastily laid track were being strengthened, the camp fires of the gangs played here on a bearded face bent over a kettle, there on a pair of legs stretched out in sleep. And in the dry summer night, fires were raging in the forest. The train would enter a drifting cloud, darker than the dark trees, and the acrid smell of burning timber would penetrate the cars. Sometimes the glow and flicker of distant flames could be seen against the sky: at others the train would steam through a zone where the blaze had passed, leaving bare poles and ruined spars standing in a sea of smoke and smoulder. *Nichevo,* the Russians said; it would die out of its own accord, by and by.

Through day and night and day again they rumbled on, over sizeable rivers which were but tributaries of tributaries of the Yenisei; through stations with names intricate on the tongue: Nizhneudinskaya, Sheragul, Golovinskaya, Cheremkovo, Sukhorskaya; until, more than three days from Tomsk and nine from Moscow, they passed a crowd of carts waiting at a level crossing, skirted a big freight yard loud with shunting

engines, and pulled into Irkutsk. Packed with their baggage
into droshkies, bouncing over the floating bridge across the
swift waters of the Angara river, they entered the second city of
Siberia. Directly to the south, now, lay the outer reaches of
the Great Wall of China and, farther down the globe, Hanoi and
Singapore. They were a little more than half-way across Siberia.

With its passion for precision, the *Guide* informed them that
Irkutsk had two cathedrals, fifty-nine churches and chapels,
two synagogues and a mosque, a second-class nunnery, fourteen
charitable institutions, five hospitals and a sanatorium for
animals. The town, it assured them, was 'supplied with tele-
phones'; but it hinted, more ominously, that the streets were
'unpaved and badly lit'.

In fact, like Tomsk, it wore an ostentatious robe of sudden
wealth through which the rags of a pioneer existence still
showed. A colonnaded mansion housed the governor-general;
there were white façaded government departments, solid clubs,
a stately theatre. The stone bastions of the Imperial Geographical Society's museum, built in Muraviev's time, frowned
haughtily across the Angara. But in the streets the spanking
equipages of the newly rich raised clouds of summer dust; and,
blinded by the flying grit, one could easily fall through the rotten
boards of the wooden sidewalks and break a leg. The hotels
harboured armies of unwanted guests, renowned for their
intelligence. A careful English visitor, ringing his bed with a
rampart of insect powder, found himself quickly outwitted;
his attackers merely retreated from the protective circle,
climbed the walls, and dropped on him from the ceiling. More
effective, if more costly, were the defences of an American gold
prospector. Sighting a movement on the wall, his hand flashed
to his pocket. A moment later there was a shattering report, and
as the smoke cleared a hole was seen where the bug had been.

Dirty and expensive, Irkutsk was also the wildest city in
Siberia. It was the practice of prudent householders, on retiring
to bed, to throw open a window and fire a shot or two into the
night – to warn malefactors that they would meet armed resistance. Yet it was conscious that the engines whistling in the
station across the river linked it directly with the refinements
of Europe, and that this new relationship called for the cultivation of decorum. At the doors of restaurants, white shirts and

collars were demanded; notices on their walls implored the clientele, as members of a civilized community, to remain sober.

As at Tomsk, fortunes had been made from gold. But Irkutsk seemed also to have its eye on the longer future; to be concerned, as well, with the more prosaic resources of the new territories. Around the city there were already nearly a hundred factories and depots processing hides and furs, soap and tallow, fish and timber. There were signs, too, that enterprising foreigners were beginning to sense the opportunities Siberia offered to exporting countries. German goods were plentiful; and Fraser heard of no less than eight American salesmen of agricultural machines making regular visits to towns along the railway. The Americans, in particular, he noted, understood the promise of the Russian East. They were opening their own West, and realized instinctively that a similar process was under way here; and they saw, beyond the empty, forbidding landscapes and the wasteful muddle that so often marked their initial settlement, the permanent wealth Siberia could yield. Britain, by contrast, seemed content to purvey rather than promote. True, her steel had been laid effectively and unobtrusively into the Trans-Siberian track; and the travellers were soon to see, on Lake Baikal, evidence of her expertise in engineering teamwork. But the only product of British industry in universal evidence in Irkutsk was – sauce. On the tables of nearly every eating-place stood the familiar bottles of brown and red, with their sturdy British names; ready to enliven bortsch, improve caviar, add savour to a reindeer steak; to flavour the Siberian wilderness with the viscous delights of the London chop-house.

Forty miles east of Irkutsk lies the southern tip of Lake Baikal, stretching like a monstrous banana, four hundred miles long, athwart the route across Eurasia. Roughly the size of Switzerland or Belgium, Baikal is the deepest lake in the world. Its surface lies some five thousand feet above the bottom of a narrow rift running through the tumbled uplands of central Siberia, like a pool of rainwater in a long, thin crevice. More than three thousand streams feed it, but only one river flows out – the Angara, rolling from a gap in its south-western shore to pass Irkutsk and finally to join the Yenisei. Two lakes in Africa and three in North America are larger than Baikal: but none are more frightening or less predictable. It was probably formed by a tremendous seismic upheaval. Tremors still shake its bed and the land round about; and the legends that surround it tell of men engulfed by the malign spirits of earth and elements. Here, towering granite cliffs drop sheer into its waters; there, rounded hummocks line the shore like waste from gigantic mines. White summits, standing as if on tiptoe above forests where conifers cling for life to the rock, peer across the lake down steep, irregular ravines. In summer it can present an aspect of calm beauty, and the movements of strange creatures can be followed for a hundred feet or more into its translucent depths. But in summer also, the warm air lying on its cold surface can give rise to fogs so dense that navigation becomes perilous. In autumn and early winter vicious gales, blowing up with little warning, tear along its length raising waves in which small craft cannot survive, and sending the sound of the surf reverberating through the mountains. In December ice forms, up to six feet thick; but owing to the presence of warm springs below, it cannot always be trusted to bear heavy loads.

The builders of the Trans-Siberian believed it possible, though immensely difficult, to drive their track round the south end of the lake to the settlement of Mysovsk on the eastern shore. But the cost was more than St Petersburg would face. It was therefore decided to order a large ice-breaking train-ferry, capable of providing service across the lake throughout the year. The ship was built inside six months by the British firm of Armstrong's at Newcastle-on-Tyne. The whole vessel was then taken to pieces; and its thousands of parts, numbered for identification, were freighted out along the Trans-Siberian. Until the bridge over the Yenisei was finished, the parts had to be transferred to barges as they arrived at Krasnoyarsk, to complete the remaining thousand miles of their journey by river. At the lakeside village of Listvyanka on Baikal the ship was reassembled under the supervision of Armstrong engineers; and despite the scale and intricacy of the operation, and the distance over which it was performed, not a single part of any importance was mislaid. The *Baikal,* the largest ship of her kind in the Old World, was launched into the lake whose name she bore in July 1899.

To the eastbound passengers, after their short run beside

the Angara from Irkutsk to the lake, the first glimpse of the *Baikal* was awe-inspiring as she lay with her tall white sides reflecting the glinting water, and her four funnels rising black against the timbered hills. She was hardly beautiful; but in those untamed surroundings, and with the triumphant story of her building still fresh, she was certainly impressive. Through her cavernous interior, past the massive bogies of rolling-stock already on board, up echoing companion-ways, they were led to cabins with velvet-covered settees, and windows instead of portholes. In calm water the crossing took four hours: in winter, with the ship battering at the ice, going astern, charging ahead again, it could take a week.[1]

At the landing-stage at Mysovsk a shock awaited Miss Meakin and her mother as they stepped ashore. They had been told in Irkutsk that their journey through Eastern Siberia would be crowded and uncomfortable: on this part of the line there were only fourth-class cars. They had laughed it off at the time; but now, as they searched the waiting train for seats, they saw that it was all too true. Managing to find an empty compartment, they thought themselves secure: but their privacy did not last long. Person after person clambered in, each exuding a more powerful odour than the last. Soon every seat was occupied; but this made no difference to the remorseless influx. Three wooden shelves, one above the other, ran along each side above the seats; and booted, sheepskinned forms, made bulkier by miscellaneous belongings, hoisted themselves up until the compartment was stuffed to the roof. A pair of dirty feet dangling before her face finally drove Annette to action. Her calls for the conductor attracted the attention of a senior railway engineer who happened to be on the platform. Seized of the situation he hurried off, promising assistance. In due course he returned. The train was crammed, he said; but an officer and six soldiers were travelling in the baggage-car, and the ladies, if they did not object, could share it with them. They thankfully accepted; and climbing the high step to the baggage-car, found themselves surrounded with consideration. The engineer had

[1] The *Baikal*'s career proved short-lived. An error had been made in estimating the average depth of the winter ice, with the result that timetables became unworkable. The rail link round the southern end of the lake was completed in 1904.

partitioned off a corner with curtains from his house near by; the officer had lit the stove; the soldiers brought hot water, gave them food from their rations.

From Mysovsk to Sretensk, where passengers on the still incomplete Trans-Siberian transferred to river steamers, was a journey of 600 miles through the broken hills of eastern Siberia, over the Yablonovy Mountains, down winding, precipitous valleys, The building of this section of the railway, through wild, remote country, had taken five years in the face of baffling difficulties; and the track, hurriedly laid, was as yet hardly more than provisional. The leisurely speed at which the train had jogged across the steppes and through the taiga now became more modest still. Four days and three nights would elapse before they reached Sretensk.

Snug in their baggage-car, waited on by the courteous officer and his men, the Meakins suddenly realized why this impromptu guard of honour was travelling on the train. On board the *Baikal* they had noticed a number of family groups, poorly dressed but evidently contented, seated on the deck at their midday meal. They had just been remarking on the good picnic manners of the children when a man among them rose to pour out more tea. His ankles were fettered, and he wore a heavy chain. All the men were convicts. Accompanied voluntarily by their families, they were on their way to the penal settlements of Trans-Baikalia. Their chains clanking, they had been marched off the ship at Mysovsk; and now they were immured in two prison vans next to the baggage-car. The soldiers were the escort; and whenever the train stopped four of them leapt down, to stand with fixed bayonets on either side of the track. At one station a soldier, off duty and stretching his legs, picked a bunch of wild flowers and passed it up. Children's hands, stretching through the bars, received it eagerly.

At little more than a walking pace the train staggered up into the Yablonovy range, one locomotive straining in front, another pounding at the rear, their steam momentarily festooning the dark forests with Christmas-tree tinsel. And always the little green flags, held aloft by motionless men at the lineside, urged it on. To the south, now, beyond the mountains, lay the blue infinities of the Mongolian plateau; and beyond again, the seas of yellow clay and white salt of the Gobi desert.

To the north, across 1,500 miles of mountain, scrub and tundra, much of it still unmapped, the enormous Lena river flowed; looping through huge stands of larch and silver fir, broadening as it received exactly one thousand tributaries, passing pinnacled cathedrals of red sandstone and sheer green walls of porphyry; disgorging, even in the perpetual light of the Arctic summer, its tremendous loads of ice into the Laptev Sea.

At the town of Chita the train stopped for an hour; and the travellers were struck by its well-to-do appearance, so unlike the rough, unkempt settlements typical of the Siberian east. A strange story lay behind its prosperity. A century before, it had been little but a stockaded Cossack outpost, and was said to have been given its name by a party of adventurous Italian gold prospectors. But in 1827, two years after the Decembrist plot had shaken Russia, it was chosen as the place of exile for those who had been involved. The existing prison was a dismal, insanitary hole; and their first task on arrival was to build a new one. This done, their labour was turned to the development of the village. Several of the Decembrists were members of noble families – men of taste and standards; and they saw to it that what they did, even under compulsion, was done well. Moreover their wives, facing the terrible hardships of the journey from Russia, joined them in exile, bringing money and the habit of spending it. Chita had never looked back: it was now a flourishing commercial centre. It was evening when the train arrived, and the town was at its doors and in the streets, taking the air. There were Chinese shopkeepers and coolies, Buriat Mongols with high cheekbones set in round, bronzy faces. But it was the Russians whom the travellers found most interesting. There were the usual peasant sheepskins and long shirts: but there were also homburg hats, neat suits, tan shoes and gloves; there was even a frock-coat and top hat. Nor was the atmosphere one of stilted solemnity: rather, this evening parade in the fastnesses of Asia wore an air of established, natural ease.

Between Chita and Sretensk the speed increased. They were moving downward, now, out of the mountains of the inner continent, towards the lower lands of the littoral. Around them were rivers moving eastward too; Kerulen and Argun, Ingoda, Shilka and Onon, on their way to swell the great reaches of the

Amur. Then, some fifty miles east of Chita, near the village of
Kaidalovo, they noticed what appeared to be an insignificant
branch line leaving the main track to the right of the train, and
disappearing to the south-east. The existence of this branch
explained why there was still a gap of 800 miles in the Trans-
Siberian between Sretensk and Khabarovsk, and why they
were now entering a region charged with international tension.
For it was the jumping-off point of the railway Russia was
building across Manchuria.

Until the seventeenth century, Manchuria had been a kind
of no-man's-land between China proper and the vast sub-Arctic
regions of north-eastern Asia. But with the Manchu conquest
of 1644, Manchuria had become part of China. And a series of
treaties had subsequently established the boundary between
Russian Siberia and Chinese Manchuria along the course of
three rivers: the Argun, the Amur, and the Ussuri. For the
builders of the Trans-Siberian Railway, these arrangements
posed a frustrating problem; for they meant that the eastern
section of the line, if it was to remain entirely on Russian soil,
would have to describe a huge semicircle round the north of
Manchuria to Khabarovsk, and then head due south along the
valley of the Ussuri to Vladivostok. This was the route originally intended: the railway had reached Sretensk from Lake
Baikal in 1900, and by that time the line from Khabarovsk to
Vladivostok was already finished.

Surveys along the north bank of the Amur had revealed,
however, that great difficulty would be encountered in closing
the gap between Sretensk and Khabarovsk. The broken, hilly
terrain would render heavy engineering works unavoidable. It
became clear that a route which left the Trans-Siberian near
Chita and ran directly across Manchuria to Vladivostok would
be not only much shorter, but easier to build. The technical
difficulties were genuine; but they opened up a political possibility. For some time Russian eyes had been on Manchuria. Its
potential in resources and trade were tempting; it promised
access to ice-free ports farther south than Vladivostok; and
China, with the Manchu dynasty on its last legs, was weak. The
adverse survey report offered the Russian expansionists the
chance they had been seeking: a railway through Manchuria
would greatly facilitate its outright annexation.

St Petersburg was not alone in such designs. Japan, approaching the Chinese vacuum from the sea, had already attempted to secure a foothold on the Manchurian coast, and was watching closely; and the Western powers, pursuing acquisitive policies of their own in China, were watching both Russia and Japan. But Russia had moved quickly and subtly; and in 1896 she had signed a secret agreement with China whereby, in return for a promise of protection against Japan, she acquired the right to build a railway across Manchuria. Ostensibly the railway would be Chinese: but the method of its financing ensured that control would be in Russian hands. On the conclusion of this pact, ironically called the Treaty of Integrity, the difficult route along the Amur had been given up for the time being, and the building of the Manchurian line had at once been started instead.

Had our travellers, passing the branch at Kaidalovo at the turn of the century, been able to follow it into Manchuria they would have come upon extraordinary scenes. With one hand Russia, hampered by a terrible outbreak of plague among the huge gangs of coolie labour, was driving the construction forward with the greatest urgency: with the other, she was staving off sabotage organized on the largest scale. For the anti-foreign Boxer Rising was at its height in China; and a force of several thousand Russian soldiers was fighting pitched battles around the railway not only with groups of local bandits, but also with fanatical Boxers and with elements of the Chinese army sympathetic to them. To 'assist' the Chinese Government to restore order, and to keep Japan and the Western powers at bay, Russia was now moving enormous numbers of troops towards Manchuria; and the long eastbound troop trains they had seen farther back along the Trans-Siberian were part of this movement.

But the tension beyond the frontier was not to reach its climax yet. The train skirted round it to the northward, heading for Sretensk down the steep, rocky valley of the Shilka. They passed log cabins standing on rafts in the river, busy with women washing and cooking in the open air. They wound through forbidding mountains into the region round Nerchinsk. This was a district rich in silver; and because free men had always been attracted to the goldfields, the mines had long been worked by convicts. Not many years before, the grim conditions of their life and labour had been described by George Kennan, the American journalist whose revelations of the Siberian penal system had shocked the Western world.[1] And if men were not now chained permanently to their wheelbarrows, going in daily dread of the *knut* and the *plet,* they were still working by the glimmer of candles in the chill dripping galleries deep below the railway.

Beyond Nerchinsk, along the final miles of track, Siberia in spring and summer showed her gentler face. Wild flowers painted the slopes between the hills: orange trollius, purple daisies, scarlet Turk's cap, pale blue wild geraniums, yellow day-lilies, paeonies, speedwell, bluebells. In autumn the turning trees fired the evergreens with flame.

'Sretensk.' The officer was calling to the Meakins through the curtains. Realizing they were asleep he repeated louder, 'Sretensk.' Stiff with their four-day journey from Lake Baikal, they climbed down from the baggage-car. There, just beyond the station, the Trans-Siberian proper ended. But inevitably, the station lay across the river from the town. The officer pointed to the ferry, saluted good-bye, and gave them a soldier to see them to the hotel.

At Sretensk the Russian west and east had hardly met. The railway from Moscow went no farther, and the penetration of Siberia from the Pacific had barely reached it. It was a frontier town of shacks and shanties, peopled largely by Cossacks and their womenfolk. And if the streets of Tomsk were paved with mud and those of Irkutsk with dust, the cows and pigs wandering everywhere about Sretensk gave its trackways a still more interesting surface. By day they slumbered beneath an oriental stupor, broken occasionally by the passing of a Cossack girl, her bright beads rattling as she hopped her way through the slush, or by the sudden yells of mounted Mongols herding a batch of ponies through the town. By night, however, the place came to life. A horde of officials, uniformed according to department and degree, arose on every hand, making for the hotel; there to dine, drink, dance, play cards, and dine again. In the rooms above, the windows were curtainless; the bed-springs twanged beneath the mattresses; the corridors were filled with snores.

[1] See George Kennan, *Siberia and the Exile System.* New York: Century Co. 1891.

Tomorrow the travellers would take to the rivers for the next stage of their journey.

Without regret they watched the hovels of Sretensk receding into the waters of the Shilka. For the first three days of their river voyage, their home was a couple of skeletal cabins on the deck of a barge towed behind an ancient steamer. Around them, a mixed crowd of immigrants, Chinese, local tribesmen and domestic animals slept and shouted, ate and fought. By the time they reached the village of Pokrovka, near the Shilka's junction with the Amur, the veneers of civilized routine were cracking. But at Pokrovka matters improved; for here a stern-wheeler, larger, and boasting a dining-saloon, was waiting to take them on down the Amur to Blagoveschensk. The timetable allowed three more days for this run; but its figures were subject to the hazards of the river. The Amur's shallows were notorious, and the rasping grumble of sand along the flat bottom of the ship recurred too frequently for comfort. At periods of low water it was not uncommon to be fast aground for a week or more. On the left bank of the river, between the water and the hills, little Cossack settlements embedded in stands of birch rolled slowly by like a self-repeating film. On the right the horizons were more featureless, yet more mysterious. For this was Chinese Manchuria, and in the centre of the river they were steaming along the frontier. At Blagoveschenk – the 'New York of Siberia' – the hotel eggs were bad, the bread sour, the butter rancid. But a *Life of Tennyson* caught the eye in a near-by book-store; and Miss Meakin, window-shopping in the fashionable quarter, came upon a hat with a long feather trailing from its crown: it was labelled 'Chapeau Boer'. Rumours were flying of Europeans massacred by the Boxers, over there in China. And they heard, too, of an unpleasant episode that had recently occurred in Blagoveschensk itself. The governor, nervous lest the rising should spread to Russian territory, had ordered every Chinese in the town to cross the Amur into Manchuria within twenty-four hours. There were more than four thousand of them, and no boats were available. But when the time limit expired, the Cossacks had rounded them up in batches and goaded them into the river at bayonet point. Every one was drowned.

Then Blagoveschensk in turn was left behind, and they were moving on down-river, this time in a side-wheeler of stately size and comfort; a vessel, as an American passenger put it, worthy of the Mississippi before the railroads robbed it of its glory. For six days, with the paddles thrashing the Amur's curves, with the helm swinging to the ceaseless twists of the channel, they paced the promenade deck, patronized the bar, strummed on the German piano in the lounge – until Khabarovsk rose out of the river ahead, poised near the confluence of Amur and Ussuri, its streets ridged and ravined to the contours of the hills, its red-brick barracks staring out over an enormous, placid world of sky and water. Siberia stretched farther eastward still; another mountain range stood between Khabarovsk and the sea. But this was as far east as they would go. In the same longitude as Alice Springs in the centre of Australia, they changed back from river to rail and headed south for Vladivostok.

The line along the Ussuri had been roughly laid. For thirty hours they bounced and jarred beneath grey skies and the drifting drizzle of the summer monsoon, past the misty shapes of mountains, through woods where elm and maple, cork and walnut mingled with the firs. To all intents it was a military railway. Officers filled the train; the army was in charge at the stations; soldiers worked in gangs along the track. Steadily, the signs of settlement increased: fenced fields, roads, and whitewashed houses reminiscent of European Russia. And the disciplines reappeared as well. The freer air of the open steppes gave way to the old rules, the formalities, the rigid lines of caste. For the coastal belt of the Russian Far East had been populated, not through the filters of Siberian space and time, but by immigrants brought round by sea directly from Odessa.

Suddenly someone gave a shout: and there, surrounded by the white hulls of warships and the square sails of junks, stood a town, tapering out along a tongue of land into the Sea of Japan and the Pacific Ocean. As they jumped down to the platform for the last time, a big notice-board faced them: VLADIVOSTOK TO ST PETERSBURG, 9,877 VERSTS.

Their journey was done.

They had travelled through nearly a hundred degrees of longitude of continuous dry land. And in crossing Asia from Europe to the Pacific – through regions farther from the sea than anywhere else on earth – they had also traversed another continent within Asia. Most of them had passed this inner, landlocked continent without being aware of its existence. For in the sense of a continent with defined boundaries or recognized political frontiers, it never existed. It never had a generally accepted name. But geography and history separated this interior core from outer Eurasia round about it; and to mark its separateness, it has sometimes been called *the Heartland*.

When these travellers made their journey at the opening of the twentieth century, Russia's grasp on a great part of the Heartland was already firm. Despite her inertia and ineptitude, her cruelty and corruption, they had been astonished by her achievements across its vast vacuum of distance. Yet in historical terms Russia was a newcomer. Little more than three hundred years before the building of the Trans-Siberian began, few Russians had set foot east of the Urals. Before their coming, the Heartland had been the home of ancient peoples, stemming from different roots. Some, tall, blue-eyed, fair-complexioned, resembled Europeans. Others were hirsute and ruddy-bearded. Others again were of Oriental stock; round-headed, with narrow eyes and high cheekbones set in wide, sallow faces. Some, in early times, spoke Indo-European tongues; others, Turkish and Mongol languages. Between some there were sharp differences; between others, subtle shadings of kinship and characteristic. Of their origins and interminglings, much is still obscure. Many of them lived and died in constant movement, few were literate, and the records they left – save those which archaeology is gradually revealing – are sometimes scanty or non-existent. So far, the pattern of their presence through different spans of time, of their passages across the Heartland spaces, has been largely pieced together from outside.

Along the Trans-Siberian line the travellers had seen the descendants of some of these older Heartlanders. As part of the human mosaic of the new Russia-in-Asia they had appeared peaceable enough. But their forerunners had been anything but peaceable. Through much of history they had surged across the great plains to carry war into each other's territories. At times they had massed in combination, generating overwhelming waves of power which rolled to the fringes of the Asian interior and beyond, breaking in savage raiding and in years or

centuries of ferocious alien rule on the civilizations round about.
As a result, the influence of the Heartland on the travellers
who had just crossed it had been greater than they might have
cared to admit. The trousers that their menfolk wore had first
been worn in inner Asia. Some of the qualities they most
admired in each other – guts, the will to stick it out, the urge
to aggressive individual enterprise – were qualities deriving at
least in part from the periodic impact on their ancestors of the
Heartland peoples. The Heartland had been in their history
books at school, though its presence there was often unacknowledged. The fall of the Roman empire and the Germanicizing
of Western Europe; the feudal system; the Crusades; the westward reach of the Renaissance; the serf system that had left
its mark on so many of the Russians along the route of their
journey: in the great crises of the past that had led to all these
movements and events, and in much else that had helped to
make the travellers from Europe and America what they were,
the Heartland had played a vital part.

Through the wildernesses they had crossed in the creaking
comfort of their sleeping-cars, others had moved for millennia
before them: warriors sweeping to conquest; merchants plodding the sandy trails of trade-routes. Both had cross-fertilized
the ancient world outside the steppes and deserts of the interior.
From one end of Asia to the other the conquerors had carried
portable goods – ideas and captive craftsmen; the traders, the
bulkier traffic of novelty and luxury. Europe had sent across its
distances metalwares, glass, furniture, coin; and later, Nestorian
Christianity and the envoys of the Papacy. From India, Buddhism had found its landward way round the Himalaya to the
Far East. Westward over the Heartland tracks had gone countless caravans of silk and tea, ginger, rhubarb, porcelain and
paper; and perhaps more significant, the notion of paper
currency and the pure saltpetre that reached the Arabs as
'Chinese snow' and in European hands became gunpowder.

To the inmost regions of Asia, Russia and her railway were
newcomers. But the story of the Heartland, and of its impact
on the outer world, goes back beyond historic time.

2
Heartland and Littoral

*As Geography without History seemeth a carkasse without
motion, so History without Geography wandreth as a
vagrant without a habitation.*
— JOHN SMITH, *General Historie of Virginia.*

BEFORE the story, the setting.

From the line of the Trans-Siberian Railway, passing
across the map of Asia, let the eye draw back like a receding
movie camera until the whole of the Eurasian continent is in
view. This is the largest mass of land on the globe. It is shaped
roughly like a crescent with its horns pointing to the north. The
inner arc of the crescent follows the Arctic Ocean coastline of
Scandinavia and Siberia. On the outer arc, from west to east,
lie Europe, Asia Minor, Iran, the Indian peninsula, the mainland countries of South East Asia, China and the Pacific
seaboard of Siberia. Adjoining the crescent at various points,
but outside it, lie Arabia and Africa, the Antipodes and the
Americas.

A factor common to the lands lying round the outer arc of
the crescent is their proximity to the surrounding seas. The sea
offers freedom of movement between them, often augmented
by rivers capable of carrying seaborne traffic to and from their
inland districts. Moreover, since rainfall derives from the sea,
most of them possess one of the essential requisites for successful
farming. Thus the littoral lands round the outer arc have tended
since early times to support communities living, in the first
instance, by agriculture and trade. These activities allowed the
accumulation of surpluses and the exchange of ideas; these in
turn permitted diversity; and so a great semicircular belt around
the rim of Eurasia came to form the home of societies evolving
the arts and sciences of civilization as we know them. Most of

the peoples of Eurasia have always been concentrated in this
littoral belt; and as a general rule, the closer to the sea they
have lived the greater their wealth and the more advanced
their attainments.

In the interior of Eurasia, however, lies a great region different
in character. As before, the northern limits of this inner region
are bounded by the coastline of the Arctic Ocean, with almost
its whole length ice-gripped for most of the year; and until
recent times this rendered movement along it, or from it, impossible on any regular basis. Far to the south, stretching from
Afghanistan to Burma, stands another enclosing boundary: the
great massif of the Hindu Kush and the Himalaya, forming the
highest mountain barrier in the world. And between the ice and
the mountains lies an enormous area of land drained by rivers
which do not debouch into navigable seas. The centre of Siberia
is intersected by three giant rivers – the Ob, the Yenisei and
the Lena – all flowing north to the Polar ice. To the west, the
Volga, draining an area almost as large as the United States,
discharges into the Caspian. At the eastern end of the continent
another great river, the Amur, flows into the Sea of Okhotsk and
so, it is true, opens on to the Pacific. But the large seasonal
differences of level found along the Amur, and the sand bar
across its mouth, make it difficult for navigation; and its lower
reaches are icebound for nearly half the year. In the south, the
Syr Darya (Jaxartes) and the Amu Darya (Oxus) discharge
into the Aral Sea. From Mongolia the system of the Selenga
river empties into Lake Baikal; and Lake Balkash receives
the waters of the Ili. Of the many rivers losing themselves
inland the most considerable is the Tarim, flowing through
desert country at the heart of the continent to disappear in the
salt marshes around the lake of Lop Nor. Thus of the major
rivers rising in the interior only the Amur gives access to
navigable seawater, and that intermittently. All the others
flow either northward into the Arctic, or discharge into internal
seas or lakes, or peter out in the deserts.

This huge area can be seen as a second crescent lying inside
the total crescent of Eurasia. Its inner arc, like that of the first
crescent, runs along the north coast of Siberia. Its outer arc,
however, encloses the mountain barriers and the basins of the
inward-flowing river systems. From west to east, it follows a

line running approximately down the centre of European Russia, through the Caucasus and the Elburz mountains of Iran, and along the Hindu Kush and the Himalaya; then taking in the Gobi desert and most of the Mongolian plateau, and finally heading north-east along the Khingan and Kolyma mountains to the East Siberian Sea. Within this inner crescent there were, historically, few of the opportunities for economic progress and exchange with the outer world enjoyed by the coastal regions. And it is this unnamed, landlocked continent-within-Eurasia that has sometimes for convenience been referred to as the Heartland.

In outline, its topography is fairly simple. At its southern centre stands the Roof of the World: the majestic mountain complex around the Pamirs and the Hindu Kush that forms the western anchor of the Himalaya. From the peaks of the Pamirs to the Arctic ice a diagonal line can be drawn from south-west to north-east, passing along the Tien Shan and Altai mountains, through Lake Baikal, and down the Lena river to its mouth. North and west of this line the Heartland consists of four immense plains: the uplands of central Siberia, through which the tributaries of the Lena and the Yenisei have etched the canyons of their courses; the flat, featureless table of western Siberia where the Ob and its system wander across the largest area of low-lying land in the world; and, beyond the Urals, the gentler, more varied landscapes of the Volga basin. South of the Urals, around the salty waters of the Caspian and the Aral, lies a fourth area of lowland plain. East and south of the diagonal dividing line lies higher land: the great plateau of Mongolia and the Gobi, five thousand feet or more above sea-level; and the rugged, almost patternless mountain masses of north-eastern Siberia. The low-lying western plains and the higher eastern plateaus are not, however, cut off from each other. Between the Tien Shan and Altai ranges, through the district known as Dzungaria, runs a passageway connecting them. Because of its historical importance, this has sometimes been referred to as the 'Dry Strait of Dzungaria'.

Other factors besides its natural boundaries of ice and mountain and its in-flowing rivers have tended to unify the Heartland region within itself, and to separate it from outer Eurasia. From north to south, four broad belts of differing plant cover

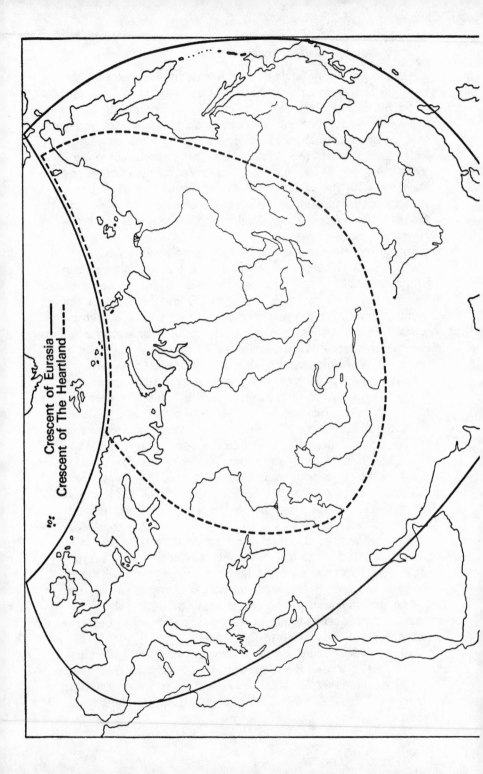

Crescent of Eurasia ———
Crescent of The Heartland -----

extend latitudinally across the region, like the layers of a Neapolitan ice-cream seen in cross-section. Along the far north stretches the tundra, its desolate expanses hidden beneath a white cloth of snow through the long winter night. Under the short summer warmth of the midnight sun it turns to a browny water-logged mass; and a quick spattering of flowers – Arctic poppy and saxifrage – intermingles with the mosses and lichens. Reindeer graze a living from the close-fisted vegetation; and lemming and Arctic fox are fairly common. Birds, migrating in to eat the insects swarming in the marshes, settle on the scrubby, berry-bearing bushes and the few stunted trees along the river banks. Almost everywhere the subsoil is permanently frozen, sometimes down to nearly two thousand feet below ground-level. South of the tundra lies the taiga: the immense dark green belt of coniferous forest stretching from the Baltic to the Pacific, its existence made possible by the moisture held in the topsoil by the frozen ground below. Squirrel, lynx, bear, elk, and fur-bearing animals live among the trees, beaver and pelican by the waters. The land is matted with conifer waste and, like much of the timber, is poor. In both the tundra and the taiga woolly mammoths have been found, one of them so completely preserved in the ice that natives had sold the ivory and fed the flesh to their dogs before the carcass could be properly excavated.

The third belt, this time of brighter green, lies to the southward of the taiga. This is the steppe: a great band of grass, most of it rooted in black, humus-rich soil increased in fertility through the centuries partly by the constant decay of the grass itself, partly by the presence of nutritive constituents from the rocks below. A striking feature of this grassy belt is its tremendous length. Known to its old-time inhabitants as the Earth Girdle, it runs from the foot of the Carpathian mountains in the west through the gateway between the Urals and the Caspian, through the Dzungarian passage, to the Khingan range east of Mongolia. And at either end, beyond the Carpathians in Hungary and beyond the Khingans in Manchuria, lie further plains of grass. Thus the steppe stretches not only across the entire Heartland, but extends into the coastal zones at the extremities of Eurasia. Not all the steppeland is equally lush; and it varies in character. In western Siberia it is low-lying and honeycombed with lakes, some salty, some fresh. East of the Dzungarian gap, on the heights of the Mongolian plateau, its surface resembles an infinite series of shallow intersecting saucers, set between mountain masses and swept by numbing winds. Once, bison and wild horses roved across the steppe: now, its different parts are the home of elk, and horned wild sheep; of ibex, bear and wolf, boar and leopard, hare and fox. Eagles soar in the clear dry air above. As spring spreads and the plains emerge from the winter snow, iris, tulip and dianthus, anemones and wild thyme burst through the grass. In the heat of the continental summer everything withers to a parchment brown.

Towards the southward limit of the steppe the black soil tails off into dun earth, and the vegetation thins and harshens until the fourth and final belt is reached: a series of tawny, tiger-striped deserts curving round the outer rim of the Heartland crescent, straddling the centre of Asia. Around the Aral Sea lie great stretches of hard, arid limestone, of salt crusts and clay hollows, of shifting sand dunes and bare rock split by alternating heat and frost. Some of these deserts – the Kara Kum, the Kyzyl Kum, the Ust-Urt – are among the bleakest and emptiest in the world. Yet the area is not without relief. Round the foothills of the high mountains at its eastern edge lie deep, rich beds of loess; scattered oases and the alluvial deposits of the bigger rivers afford other fertile land; and even in the barrens, scrub and coarse grass, responding vividly to occasional rain, can provide marginal grazing. Farther east, its oval shape almost surrounded by the Tien Shan and Kunlun Shan range, lies another desert: the Takla Makan, with the Tarim river flowing through it. The river, moving through desiccated wastes, holds little attraction; but again, strings of oases round the lower slopes of the encircling mountains offer rewarding sites for cultivation. To the north-east, between the Takla Makan and Manchuria, lies the group of deserts making up the Gobi: a huge expanse of gravel interspersed with plains of gleaming broken salt, with beds of clay wind-chiselled into grotesque sheer-sided tables, with monstrous blocks of black basalt and pinky-yellow hills of sand. Yet even here men and animals can subsist. At rare intervals pools of water dot the desert face, and the clays and gravels yield a little herbiage and tough, woody plants. On the northern fringes of the Gobi, in an

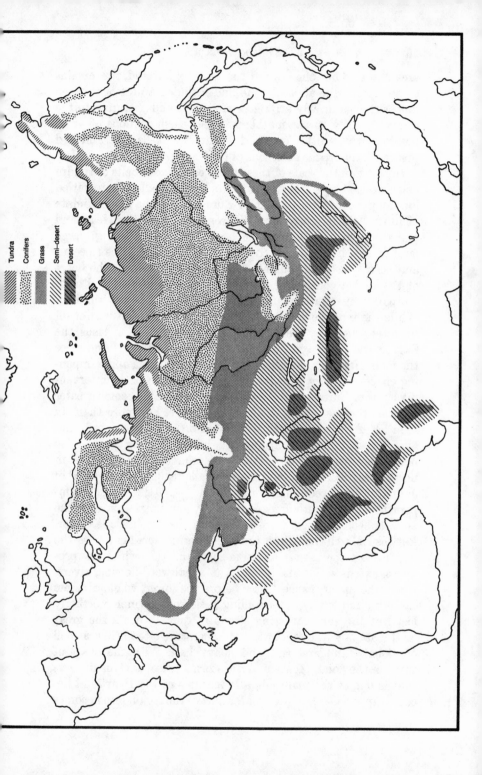

area now arid but once swampy and partly forested, the remains of prehistoric life abound. One find included a nest of thirteen dinosaur eggs, neatly arranged with their ends pointing to the centre, exactly as the mother had left them millions of years before. Two were broken, and within the shells the sand had preserved the fragile skeletons of her young.

Nothing on the scale of these great continuous belts of tundra and forest, steppe and desert exists in the smaller, more varied landscapes of the coastal rim of Eurasia. And the harsh climate of inner Asia reinforces the difference between the Heartland and the milder, sea-influenced lands outside it. Because large land-masses heat up and cool down more rapidly than oceans and their coasts, the climate of the Asian interior – the heart of the largest continent – tends to extremes of heat and cold. Moreover, moderating influences from the outside are minimal. While the inner region lies exposed to the Arctic, it is shut off from the tropics by the chains of mountains – the Caucasus, the Zagros, the Himalaya – around its southern borders. And since the main airstream flows from the west, tempering and dampening effects from the Atlantic are largely lost over the intervening lands of Europe, and the extremes of climate become greater towards the east of the Heartland interior. For more than six months of the year much of the region is snow-covered, and average winter temperatures are below freezing point. The northern areas are colder still; and around the 'Cold Pole' in north-east Siberia the thermometer falls regularly to −60°F in January, and occasionally goes below −100°F. In such temperatures the breath freezes instantly on exhalation and the nostrils become clogged with ice. Only the Antarctic is colder. Between March and June the short spring spreads across the region from south-west to north-east, and the swift thaw produces extensive floods. Along the northward-flowing rivers, where the upper reaches thaw before the lower, whole districts can be inundated by water spilling back from the more northerly ice. But the sun, gathering strength, quickly heats the great land-mass; and the rapid rise in temperature often brings a spell of violent thunderstorms and heavy hail. With the onset of summer the floods recede and the storms cease; and the dryness that is one of the main climatic features of the Heartland becomes apparent. Over the greater part of the region rain becomes

scarce. In the southern deserts it is almost non-existent: day
succeeds day of fierce blue sky and burning salt and sand. Only
a narrow central strip, from the southern Urals to Lake Baikal,
enjoys regular rain; and even in these latitudes it becomes increasingly uncertain towards the eastern zones of the continent.
On the Mongolian plateau, away from the rivers and mountain
lakes, the aridity can become acute. Indeed, much of inner
Asia comes to resemble the brittle, rain-starved interior of
Australia. And moisture, where it does exist, seldom goes
together with warmth. The northern half of the Asian interior,
including the vast areas of marshland which surround the lower
reaches of the Ob, is reasonably wet; but the temperatures are
low. In the southern half, the opposite is true; there is heat,
but most of the land is dry. The combination of moisture and
warmth in which cultivation can flourish is only found in severely
limited sections of the region.

Down the ages of prehistory, profound changes have taken
place in both the landscape and climate of the Heartland.
During the Ice Age, the ice-sheet covering northern Asia created
a wall which dammed the flow of the Ob and Yenisei rivers,
causing huge bodies of water to build up and spread backwards,
and joining the Caspian, Aral and Black Seas together. The
remains of dinosaurs – creatures requiring the buoyancy of
water to support their bulk – in the now dry zones of Mongolia
and the Gobi indicate that this region was far wetter in Creta-
ceous and Upper Jurassic times. Thus in earlier periods much of
the western Heartland was a sea, and large parts of its eastern
area were probably covered with freshwater lakes and marshy
fenland. Since then there has been a gradual process of desicca-
tion, leaving only great 'puddles' like the Caspian and the Aral
in the seafloors of the past. Marked cyclical changes in climate
have also affected inner Asia, as they have other parts of the
world. In prehistory these climatic pulsations were far more
pronounced and violent; but the alternation of prolonged
drought with periods of more plentiful rainfall has continued
into recent times.

The geography of Asia separated the historical peoples of the
Heartland from the coastal regions of the continent. For most
of them the farming and trading, the busy development in

diversity, of the littoral populations represented an alien culture. Along the great interior belts of sedge and forest, grass
and desert, where earth or climate for the most part made the
growing of crops unrewarding, they evolved their own patterns
of life and livelihood.

The northern forests supported peoples clad in skins and furs,
living mostly by hunting and fishing. In scattered settlements
some of them practised a primitive agriculture; but most roamed
the taiga, travelling with reindeer, sled-dogs and a few horses.
Only on the patches of fertile soil along the rivers and in the
desert oases of the southern Heartland, where hot sun could be
combined with irrigation to make the land fruitful, did a number
of settled, wealthy city-states take root, more akin on a small
scale to the farm-based economies of the coastal regions. Between the taiga and the deserts, however, lay the steppeland –
the great strip of grass extending from end to end of inner
Asia; and this afforded a vast natural grazing-ground for
animals. Through much of history, most of the steppe peoples
were pastoralists; and it is around them that the turbulent
story of the Heartland revolves.

Grazing was not always the occupation of the steppes, for
it required long experience and high skill for its successful
practice. It emerged gradually, probably more by a process of
divergence from the settled pursuits of those living closer to the
sea, than as an originally separate calling. The prehistoric steppe
peoples must have had contact with the coastal farmers, for it
was the latter who developed the domestication of animals.
Accepting the keeping of cattle from the farmers, the steppe
men probably first combined it as a part-time occupation with
hunting, fishing, and the gathering of roots and berries. They
may have rejected the farmer's heavy routine work partly
because they were hunters, and partly because the early system
of cultivation practised in the littoral lands of the Middle East
was unsuited to the grasslands farther north. This involved
clearing ground by slashing the bark of trees so that they died;
and then, year by year, burning the branches to provide ash
fertilizer. And even on the cultivable areas of the steppes there
were few trees.

By about 3000 B.C. the distinction between coastal farming
and interior grazing was becoming pronounced; though some

steppe peoples, where land and climate allowed, took permanently to a way of life based on cultivation and others embraced a mixed economy. But among those who adopted pastoralism as their main source of livelihood the divergence produced, at an early stage, the seeds of periodic conflict with the peoples of the coasts. The herdsmen required protection for their animals: protection from each other's depredations, from beasts of prey, and from the natural emergencies frequent in the harsh conditions of the interior. They found this in a cohesive organization subject to the orders of acknowledged chieftains; in a social system inherently more disciplined and warlike than was necessary to relatively peaceful farming communities. Moreover, men with the wind of the steppes in their nostrils came to hold a certain contempt for the plodding life of the farmer on his sheltered, circumscribed acres.

A dominant characteristic of emergent Heartland pastoralism was its mounted nature: it became, essentially, a horse culture. About 2500 B.C. the steppe men began to climb, at first at rare intervals, on to the horses which till then they had kept only for food. But even after the discovery that the horse could be an aid to movement, horsemanship proper took many centuries to evolve. The early domesticated horses may have been too weak to carry a man for long distances: stronger and hardier breeds had to be developed. At the same time, riding demanded the perfection of a whole technology before it could lead to a fully horse-borne life. Horsemen could not control their mounts or ride with ease until bits, bridles and saddlery – at least in a primitive form – had been evolved. Clothes had to be adapted to the new purpose. In pedestrian societies, legs had traditionally been swathed in robes and skirts, and feet in sandals and shoes: trousers and boots – inventions of the steppe – were necessary to would-be horsemen. Possessions of all kinds had to be adapted to what a horse could carry. In all probability mounted life first appeared in the western half of the grasslands; and it was not until about 800 B.C. that the herdsmen north of the Black Sea and the Caspian were firmly in the saddle. But when at length horseback living became an accomplished fact, it effected a revolution among the grassland peoples. It made the supervision of scattered animals quicker and less fatiguing, and enlarged the size of controllable herds. The ridden horse, combined with draft animals hitched to loaded carts, greatly increased the range of regular pastoral movements and, when necessary, made possible total migration over long distances. Like the rise of the aeroplane over the world-scale of modern times, the mastery of the horse along the steppe belt of the Heartland reduced space to more manageable proportions.

As mounted pastoralism spread across the inner Asian grasslands, it resulted in a unique pattern of living, of which many features became common to the peoples of different origins who practised it. They were nomads, but not aimless wanderers. Most of them moved regularly twice a year between accustomed pastures. They would usually spend the summer in the more northerly areas of the grass, camped near rivers or in places of reliable rainfall, taking advantage where possible of higher ground to escape the worst of the heat. The winter would be passed farther south, where there was less snow or none, and where the cold set in later and the spring came earlier. In some areas this pattern might be reversed, the herds wintering in the north and being watered with melted snow, and summering near water in the southern steppe. The spring and autumn were occupied with the movement between the grazing-grounds. This might involve a journey of less than a hundred miles or of nearly a thousand. It was a slow journey, performed at the pace of the animals, with deviations for water and long halts for recuperation.

On these twice-yearly treks the herds were accompanied by every man, woman and child of the encampments with all their possessions. Few of the Heartland graziers had fixed homes, and were often uneasy on the rare occasions when they found themselves between four walls. Their home was the circular felt tent, called by many of them the *yurt*. It might be twenty feet or more in diameter, and was mounted on a wicker frame. Its upper part was conical, with a small round neck projecting from the top to serve as a chimney. The tent might be either black or white, and was often covered with a protective coating of chalk, clay or powdered bone. The chimney and entrance might be decorated with pictures of birds or animals cut and sewn from coloured felts. The *yurt* was perfectly adapted to its purpose. Its shape enabled it to stand up to the highest winds without guy-ropes. Its materials insulated it from summer heat and winter cold. When the time came to break camp, it could be dismantled by the women and children within half an hour.

On the journeys, the larger tents were often mounted on huge wagons, with wheel-tracks of up to twenty feet and with axles as thick as a ship's mast. As many as twenty-two oxen or camels might be harnessed to a wagon, in two lines of eleven abreast. Gear and belongings were packed into chests carried in carts, and a string of twenty or thirty of these might be hitched one behind the other, the whole train being driven by a single girl in the leading cart. So they would set out on another day's march beneath the sun's blinding glare, or against the furious winds of the steppe, or perhaps through clouds of maddening insects; the men riding herd on the animals, the women often mounted like the men, the younger girls and children clustered on the wagons and carts; a great self-contained land-fleet sailing slowly across a green ocean, the dust of its passage drifting to the zenith and away to the farthest steppe horizons.

The composition of the herds varied according to the quality of the grazing-grounds their owners occupied. The lusher zones could support large numbers of cattle, sheep and horses. In the more marginal lands and at the fringes of the deserts, goats and camels would form the staple stock, with fewer sheep and perhaps no cattle. But grazing on natural pastures of any kind was bound to imply an extended system of living. Large concentrations of population were seldom found except during movements or at times of commotion. Normally a camp might be composed of up to ten related families with their tents; but even this number of persons living together – perhaps fifty or sixty all told – would suppose surrounding pastures of good quality for the animals they owned. Several such camps, scattered over neighbouring areas, would form a clan, and several clans a tribe. Loyalty would extend, through the hierarchy of aristocracy and chieftainship, to the tribe; and, at times of purpose or crisis, to the whole people formed by a number of tribes. On occasion it might be stretched to an association of several peoples. But the chain of larger cohesion was subject to the economy at its roots: an economy dispersed in space, never motionless for long, at the mercy of violent natural forces, and demanding a high degree of personal resourcefulness. This made for individual independence, and for ties between smaller units. The perpetual shift of circumstance and interest often frustrated the formation of big groupings, and rendered them transient when formed.

To the Heartland nomad his horses, or more usually, his ponies, were the *sine qua non* of existence. The steppe pony was normally a small animal, standing not more than thirteen hands; coarse, thickset, well-boned, heavy in head and shoulders, Roman-nosed; with a deep, long barrel and full mane and tail. Like the felt tent of his owner, his shaggy coat was proof against most weathers; warm in winter, cool in summer, greasy enough to keep out everything but wet snow driven on a gale. In colour he might be grey, chestnut, bay, blue, black, piebald or skew-bald; but perhaps the most striking were the duns. Theirs was the protective colouring of the steppe: mustard coats, with black mane and tail, black stripe along the back, and often white stockings. Standing motionless in certain lights, they could be invisible 200 hundred yards away. As an individual the steppe pony was seldom handsome, and he sometimes had a nasty temper. But galloping in their herds across the plains, hooves pounding, necks astretch, manes flying, they could be a splendid sight. They lived out, whatever the climate, on the grass of the open steppe, without hay or hard feed. As a result they were extraordinarily tough; they could make do on sparse herbiage and nuzzle through deep snow to reach it. But their endurance, like that of all horses fed solely on grass, was limited: after a long day's work they needed a spell of rest and grazing to recover strength. The more remounts a man had, the better he was equipped to face long treks or periods of emergency. Much of life was spent on horseback. Before they could walk infants were placed on the back of a sheep as a first step to riding. A boy sent on an errand of more than a few yards would not think of running; he would vault on to the nearest pony. Adults ate and drank, held meetings, bought and sold, even slept, in the saddle. The aim of rich and poor was to own as many horses as possible. Great herds of horses were a symbol of status and a measurement of wealth. In nomad legend and ceremony horses played a central part.

The pastoral steppe people could live for long periods almost entirely from their animals. Skins, wool, furs and hides provided

clothing, coverings, boots, armour and containers for liquids. In a region where trees were rare, the usual fuel was dung. From bones and tendons they made tools and weapons. In summer their food came mainly from the milk of different animals, curdled or fermented, or cooked into cakes or cheeses. The seeds of wild cereals were sometimes collected; and here and there millet was grown, to be simmered with milk and eaten as porridge or dried and pounded into flour for keeping. The strong drink was koumiss, made from fermented mares' milk, blueish, biting, potent to the uninitiated. In winter the diet changed to meat, raw or roasted, dried or smoked. But since it was essential, especially among the poorer nomads, not to denude the herds, the game with which the plains abounded formed an important supplementary source of meat. Each autumn, hunts on a massive scale were organized among some of the steppe peoples, in which it was mandatory for every available man to take part; for these provided not only food and sport, but an annual opportunity for military mobilization and manœuvres. When times were bad they would eat almost anything: dogs, cats, rats, mice, marmots, sick or dead animals. A man marooned in snowdrifts and near starvation would open a vein of his horse, drink the blood, and seal up the wound.

Living close to animals, they often behaved like animals. They ate with their hands, using a knife to sever chunks of meat held in their teeth. Greasy hands were wiped on boots to keep them supple. Butter would be slapped into a hairy pocket and carried around till wanted. They might stuff the left-overs from a feast down their trousers, leaving a dripping trail of fat behind them. Personal hygiene was unknown. Babies might be washed daily in the open air for the first few weeks of life to toughen them; but after that they seldom washed again. A garment would be worn continuously, day and night, until it had to be thrown away. Their language, including that of the women, could be foul to a degree. Hardship taught them frugality to the point of meanness: they would suck the marrow from a bone before tossing it to the dogs. To outsiders they could be arrogant, untruthful, ruthless, cruel. As hosts to strangers they were sometimes unbelievably niggardly; even ambassadors to their wealthiest chiefs might go hungry, while being pestered incessantly for gifts.

Yet they had many qualities. To each other they were usually honest, cheerful, respectful. Chests of valuables were seldom protected from thieves. A strayed beast was returned without hesitation. They could be generous in mutual hospitality, even when in need; and though often drunk, quarrels seldom sprang from drink. Their attitude to women, in a society where routine labour was divided between the sexes, was often unprejudiced and liberal. They were usually polygamous: but a man's first wife remained a privileged companion. Fornication was not considered immoral, but adultery was rare. The advice of elder women was freely sought and taken. And their mastery of the steppe was wonderful. In a wilderness devoid of landmarks they could tell where they were by studying a handful of earth, feeling and even smelling it. On journeys, they would check their course across the plains from the flight of birds by day, from the stars by night. Their eyesight, magnified as it were by sensitivity to the light and shapes and movements experienced on the steppes, could seem miraculous: at dawn, when the air was clear, they were said to be able to distinguish animals and men nearly twenty miles away.

But natural disaster was always a possibility, often a reality. And in the hard necessities of guarding against it, of surviving and recuperating, lay countless sources of friction and enmity. Sheltered winter pastures were crucial, for stock exposed to the terrible north winds could perish in the driving, deepening snow; and rancour could arise from the accustomed possession by others of the better winter quarters. Summer pastures might be strictly assigned to different clans or tribes to prevent quarrels resulting from trespass; but the grazing-grounds were not all of equal quality, and confinement to the poorer lands could cause festering jealousies.

Strife was latent, as well, in longer-term factors. The climatic pulsations of inner Asia had a marked effect on the grassland population. Over several decades or centuries certain areas would enjoy a gradually increasing rainfall. As a result herds and people would grow, until that section of steppe would be supporting maximum numbers. This in itself produced pressure to expand into neighbouring territories. Then would come a period of diminishing rain and increasing drought, perhaps at a rate of change too swift for the swollen numbers of people now living on dwindling herds. To get possession of more animals and better lands would then become vital to survival.

There was also a more permanent climatic phenomenon which periodically provoked unrest. In general, the western steppes had more rain than the eastern. In the areas north of the Black Sea and around the southern slopes of the Urals lay the best pastures, and land on which settled farming was possible. The western zones offered a richer and more varied life. Towards the east, as rain became scantier, the conditions of life became progressively harsher until, around Mongolia, they reached their most austere. Down the centuries this lateral gradation of the Heartland tended to draw the ambitions of the steppe peoples towards the west; and since the easterners were hardier, they usually possessed the power to realize them when aroused.

Feuds of mortal bitterness between families, outliving generations. Intrigues between clans for the leadership of tribes. Disputes between tribes over access to grazing-grounds. Envy of one people for the better-found flocks of another. Moves to form alliances of peoples to secure more desirable lands. From all these came a complicated skein of steppe politics which readily exploded into action. Only at times when relative plenty was widespread, or when one group exercised unchallengeable control over a large area, was there anything like peace in the Heartland as a whole. War went hand in hand with pastoralism as an integral part of steppe life; and its objectives were nearly always those of dispossession, displacement, plunder.

Just as peace was spent in the saddle so the warfare of the steppes was mounted warfare, conducted by exclusively cavalry armies of herdsmen turned soldiers for the duration. Once the pressures of necessity or cupidity had induced him to merge his independence in the larger interest, war came easily to the Heartland nomad. A spell of military service meant no great dislocation of his home life; the women and children and the old were quite capable of managing his animals and affairs during his absence. His splendid horsemanship, his hardihood, his understanding of order and method derived from a life spent making and breaking camp, his periods of 'training' in the great annual hunts, and his disdain for the lives of all outside his

own blood, made him a formidable trooper of irregular cavalry:
tough, resourceful, disciplined, ferocious.

In peacetime, each man grazed as many horses as his circumstances allowed. At the onset of war, he chose from among
them as many remounts – sometimes up to ten or fifteen – as
was necessary to the campaign to be undertaken. On the march,
a nomad army might look less like a series of military formations
than a huge herd of horses flanked by fighting men. The numbers
of the horses might be swollen by cattle and sheep; for the
herdsmen-soldiers often took their rations with them, on the
hoof. Provided that it kept to land affording adequate pasture
and water, and marched at a speed consistent with maintaining
its remounts in condition, such an army could campaign over
almost unlimited space and time.

In battle, with the herds far to the rear, the dynamic mobility
of the steppe pony and his rider enabled nomad commanders to
practise methods of combat different in kind from anything
known outside the Heartland. Speed was the essence of attack.
Speed was defensive armour. And manipulated speed, often
highly refined in its timing and control, was the basis of tactics.
Feint was a favourite tactical device. A furious charge might
be followed by a simulated withdrawal over the horizon, marked
by the signs of panic, leading the enemy to believe that the
onslaught had failed and that the attackers had fled for good.
A few hours or several days might elapse, with nothing to dis-
turb the silence of the surrounding country. Then, without
warning, another charge of redoubled violence would suddenly
sweep in, as like as not from the enemy's rear. Variants of these
tactics might be repeated till the opposing force was worn down
to surrender or annihilation. For success they demanded able
generalship, swift and reliable communications, and intelligent
co-operation in the ranks.

A particular pattern characterized the nomadic warfare of
the Heartland, in that an aggression of a purely local nature
could repercuss over enormous distances. One group would
mount what initially might be no more than a large raid on
neighbouring property. If successful, the scale of attack might
be rapidly increased; and the defeated group, driven from their
home lands, would come up against a third. An accommodation
between the latter two might be arranged: but more often the

retreating group would seek to make good their losses by attacking those with whom they had collided. And so, as the result of a single local explosion, a series of impacts – like the cannoning of billiard balls, or the cars of a freight train starting into backward movement – could spread across the Heartland until a large part of the region was in ferment. In these chain reactions it was usually the weaker peoples who were pushed farthest; and their forced migrations, in search of new territory free from pressure, might continue over thousands of miles and many years.

The larger alliances needed for major wars were frequently unstable. For the average nomad trooper, once his taste for slaughter and rape had been assuaged, life after a successful conquest might be more secure; but its basic routines were the same. From conquered peoples living much as he did, there was little startlingly new to be learnt and developed into new forms of permanently increasing wealth. Or if there was, he was incapable of learning it. Plunder was his aim; and once immediate objectives of land or loot had been achieved – or even before – the independence of tribe, clan and family would tend to reassert itself. Great alliances, often difficult to build, were more difficult to hold together. They depended on the personal persuasion or the brute force exerted by those in overall command; and this was bound to be ephemeral. The massive combinations of power which periodically arose in the steppes, making the nomads of inner Asia a scourge to each other, and the Heartland a source of terror to the world beyond its fringes, were usually short-lived. They were less empires – firm, enduring, creative – than temporary confederations, rising swiftly to overwhelming strength, then losing impetus, disintegrating, giving way to others like them.

Though they could live on their own resources when necessary, the Heartland nomads were not self-sufficient in the long run. Agricultural products were always scarce; and nearly everything needed to mark privilege and distinction – personal adornments, good-quality clothing and utensils, horses of special breeds – had to come from the outside world. Moreover, except in the rearing of stock, their economy was one of low productivity. Lack of time and temperament prohibited all but elementary manufactures, and even these were frequently hampered by shortages, in the grasslands, of basic materials like wood and metals. Even such necessities as weapons could often not be made in sufficient quantities on the steppe. A fairly continuous process of contact and exchange was essential with the more varied and productive economies of the coastal peoples.

The cities at the southern verges of the Heartland formed one of the centres through which this trading contact flowed. The markets of Samarkand and Bukhara, for example, displayed a plethora to nomad eyes: fabrics and brocades, plate and goblets, melons and honey, falcons, and silverwork of finest filigree. Not far off, Tashkent specialized in more warlike wares: arms and armour, tents and tack. For their part, the men from the interior offered horses, hides, meat, slaves taken in war, and the spoils of the annual hunts: furs of ermine, marten, sable, beaver. These cities were convenient doorstep trading-posts for the nomads of the central steppes. But for others, exchange was necessary at one time or another with the littoral lands all round the borders of the Heartland: with the farming and industrial wealth of Europe, Iran, India, China. At certain points around this vast semicircle – and especially at the north-western approaches to China – there were, for long periods, no definite lines of demarcation between pastoralist and farmer-manufacturer, but rather fringe zones where the two ways of living intermingled, and trade passed in and out.

The sight of luxurious living to men bred in hardship and accustomed to plundering their neighbours. Their sense that the coastal peoples were effete by comparison with their own wiry war-readiness. The need for expansion brought on by periodic drought and overcrowding on the steppes. The spasmodic rise of ambitious leaders capable, at least for a time, of welding the herdsmen together for an attractive purpose. It is not clear which of these motives and pressures, or what combinations of them, acted as the mainsprings of the successive nomad military eruptions into the littoral lands of Eurasia. But whatever the problems or the states of mind that might focus nomadic attention on the coastal belt, the turning of two-way trade into one-way despoliation could become, for the steppe-dwellers, an irresistible urge.

The Heartland might normally be isolated; but certain factors
in its geography assisted steppe peoples bent on the occupation
and loot of the peripheral regions of the continent. The grass
belt was a potential military highway along which nomadic
armies and their remounts could move clear across the Asian
interior. It formed, as well, an arena wherein the momentum
often necessary for an overpowering lunge into coastal territory
was gradually gathered through a series of successful steppe
conquests. That momentum gained, there were a number of
routes to the seaboard lands open to the mounted armies of the
inner regions. There was little to stop a westward drive. The
grass ran continuously round the north shores of the Black Sea
to the Danube valley; and here, between the Carpathians and
the Austrian Alps, lay the plain of Hungary – an advanced
base and grazing reservoir at the threshold of Europe. Similarly,
at the eastern end of the steppes, northern China lay
dangerously exposed. The only natural obstacle between the
stronghold of nomadic power on the plateau of Mongolia and
the Chinese cities of the Yellow river basin was the northern
tip of the Gobi desert; and this could readily be skirted or, with
good organization, crossed. And like the plain of Hungary, the
prairies of Manchuria offered mounted invaders a forward
grazing base. Farther south, there was another gateway to these
cities and to the wealth of China. This opened from the region of
Dzungaria, through the passage between the Gobi and the
highlands of Tibet, to the Ordos plateau: the huge rectangle of
land, partly bush and scrub and partly cultivated land, enclosed by the great loop of the Yellow river.

Between Europe and China there were other routes from the
steppe to the riches of the coastal lands. The plateau of Iran lay
open to nomad armies moving down between the Caspian and
the Pamirs, grazing their horses on the desert scrub between the
rivers and oases. Nor, despite her great mountain shield, was
India safe: there were two routes from the Heartland round the
western end of the Himalaya into the sub-continent. The first
led over the high, narrow backbone of the Hindu Kush and down
the Kabul river to the Khyber Pass; the second through Herat
and Kandahar to the Bolan Gorge near Quetta. The former was
difficult and the latter roundabout: but both converged on Delhi
and the abundance of the Ganges valley.

To the populations of the littoral lands the invaders from the steppes seemed so hideously outlandish as to be apparitions rather than men. To Jordanes, the historian of the Goths, they were 'unclean spirits, scarcely human and having no language save one which bore but slight resemblance to human speech'. The Greeks called them 'creatures from beyond the North Wind'. A Roman, Ammianus Marcellinus, saw them as 'two-footed beasts, seemingly chained to their horses from which they take their meat and drink, never touching a plough, having no houses; small men afoot, but in the saddle appearing gigantic'. To the Chinese, repelled by the practice of the eastern nomads of coating their bodies with grease to keep out the cold, they were 'the Reekers'. 'They came and they sapped,' wrote a survivor of the sack of Bukhara, 'they fired and they slew, trussed up their loot and were gone.'

Such horror-stricken descriptions were not the accounts of defenceless people. Many of the victims were citizens of the most powerful empire of the time. Yet from almost a thousand years before Christ until the close of the Middle Ages the mounted troopers from the steppes, surging periodically into the strongest states of peripheral Eurasia, killing, occupying, seizing, enslaving, vanishing again into the Heartland spaces, usually proved uncontainable except by the passive process of absorption. This was not because of their numbers. Though European records constantly refer to 'hordes', and Chinese chronicles to hundreds of thousands of invaders, in reality the steppe armies were often absurdly small by comparison with the manpower the littoral countries could mobilize. It was partly that the nomads' concept of warfare was more audacious and their military skills more highly developed; and partly that, as against costly professional armies defending the interests of rulers, they were natural soldiers fighting for their own enrichment with little but their lives to lose. But the steppe superiority was mainly due to the fact that the herdsmen had discovered how to combine their horse-mobility with a weapon against which conventional opposing armies could not stand. With the evolution of this weapon the story of the Heartland opens.

3
Baptism of Fire

*And behold they shall come with speed swiftly: whose
arrows are sharp, and all their bows bent, their horses'
hoofs shall be counted like flint, and their wheels like a
whirlwind.*

– Isaiah, 5, 26–28.

SHORTLY after 1700 B.C. the settled agricultural world
began to be engulfed by a series of shattering invasions
which changed the course of civilizations round much of the
coastal fringe of Eurasia. These invasions stemmed from a new
development in military technology; and this development
took place at the southern borders of the Heartland.

During the previous two thousand years, the original centres
of irrigated farming in the river valleys of the Middle East had
been spreading northward towards the rainwater areas of the
Black Sea and the Caspian, and into Europe. The Indus valley,
with its cities of Mohenjo-daro and Harappa, had been brought
into cultivation. In the Far East, communities had sprung up
along the basin of the Yellow river, growing wheat, barley and
rice. During this period also, the peoples of the Asian interior
were evolving their grazing economy. They had not yet achieved
full domestic mastery of the horses which they had first kept as
part of their food-yielding herds. But they had begun, tentatively, to mount and ride them; and thus to explore the arts
of breaking-in and control.

At the margins of the farmlands and the grasslands there was
much movement to and fro. The pastoralists came to graze their
herds on the stubble, and to exchange their meat and hides for
the products of field and workshop. People from the coastal
belt tended to move inward in search of the metals that their
craftsmen required, and to trade the finished articles – weapons

and ornaments – that were new and tempting to the steppe herdsmen. This contact between the two forms of life was especially marked in the Middle East, and was at its most frequent in the area east of the Caspian where no natural obstacles stand between the plateau of Iran and the dry, inner regions of the Heartland south of the Aral Sea. It was probably in this district, somewhere between the Elburz mountains and the Hindu Kush, that the improving techniques of the farmer-craftsman and of the grazier met to invent a new instrument of warfare.

The wheel, and then the cart, had first been developed in the farming context of the Tigris-Euphrates valley. The early carts had four solid wheels attached to two revolving axles. They were drawn either by oxen or asses, or by small, primitive horse-like animals. The revolving axles made turning difficult, and the draft animals were cumbersome or hard to control. Such carts were only useful for everyday farm work or for ceremonial purposes.

But advancing craftsmanship made possible spoked wheels, turning at the ends of fixed axles; and these ideas were coupled with the elimination of one pair of wheels altogether, by means of harness throwing part of the weight of the vehicle on to the backs of the animals. To this lighter, more manœuvrable two-wheeled conveyance, evolved from a farming background, the steppe men made a decisive contribution. For it seems probable that it was they, with their growing knowledge of horse-management, who first replaced unresponsive draft-animals by the speed and flexibility of the best horses then available. The result of this fusion of skills was the war-chariot.

The chariot might not have been so revolutionary in itself had it not been for the weapon that became part of its equipment. This was the compound bow. An ordinary wooden bow five or six feet long would have been awkward to handle in a small, fast-moving vehicle. Moreover, the 'draw' of fifty pounds or so bringing the arrow to the shooting position would have given an average weapon of this kind an effective range of not much more than a hundred yards. A bow was needed which packed more power into shorter length. This was achieved by combining three materials – wood, horn and sinew – into the structure of the limbs. The triple composition greatly increased

elasticity and 'reflexion', so that, when strung, the new bow
was in high stress even before the arrow was drawn to its head.
And the far greater power so gained made it possible to reduce
length without loss of effectiveness. In strong and practised
hands a well-made compound bow, short and easily manipulable, with a draw of up to a hundred pounds, could be deadly
at 300 yards and might possess an extreme range of more than
four hundred. This redoubtable weapon was not familiar in
the Middle East. Where it came from, and how it appeared on
the northern borders of Iran at the particular time it was needed,
is uncertain. It seems likely, however, that its use for hunting
had long been known in Mongolia. Whatever its origin, it was
the ideal chariot weapon.

The mobility of the chariot combined with the firepower of
the compound bow brought an entirely new and overwhelming
dimension to warfare. At that time cavalry, which might have
countered it, did not exist. On the battlefield, speed was limited
to that of running men weighed down by their equipment. A
formation of chariots charging to the attack would, in itself,
have been a disconcerting sight to opposing foot-soldiers. Much
more daunting were the storms of high-velocity arrows loosed
at them long before they could establish hand-to-hand contact.
Nor was it usually necessary for the charioteers to come to close
quarters at all. Owing to the power and range of their compound
bows, they could change direction while still several hundred
yards away and redouble their arrow-showers as they galloped
along the enemy's front or round his flank. Even if they turned
clear away, they could use their bows with undiminished effect
while retreating. Retaliation against men in swift movement,
armed with weapons of longer reach and partly protected by
the sides of their vehicles, was almost impossible. Repeated
charges from different directions would quickly wear down a
hostile force; and it seems probable that in these chariot
manoeuvres of harrying the enemy from a distance while avoiding close combat lay the origin of the tactics which were later
to characterize much steppe warfare. Chariots could also serve
as troop-carriers, rushing men to where they were most needed
in the heat of battle. Skilled drivers, each accompanied by an
infantryman, would career forward. At the required point the
foot-soldiers would leap down, fight furiously for a short time,

then scramble back into the nearest chariot. In this way lightning attacks could be mounted to relieve pressure or create it.

Nothing like this kind of warfare had been known before; and wherever the terrain was firm and open there was no answer to it. In particular, it greatly increased the power and prestige of the steppe men. They were the breeders and trainers of the horses without which the charioteers could not fight. And their pastoral life endowed them with the martial qualities – toughness, discipline, organization – to exploit the new system.

Soon after this momentous development, powerful invasions began to disrupt the river valleys of the Middle East. These thrusts came in waves, mostly from the north, at a time when the settled regions were ill-prepared to receive them. The Hyksos appeared in Egypt, overthrew the weak regime surviving from the Middle Kingdom, and set up the rule of their Shepherd Kings. The Kassites moved down into Mesopotamia, and after initial reverses swept away the carefully constructed administration left by Hammurabi. The Mitanni established a state on the upper Euphrates. The Hittites pushed into Asia Minor, then farther southward into Syria. These invasions did not come directly from the steppes, but from the mountainous country between the steppes and the cultivated zones. But in all probability the driving force behind them was the great movement of Indo-European-speaking peoples then gathering force in the Heartland and round the Caspian Sea. This was the region where chariots had originated; and the distinguishing mark of these barbarian onslaughts on the ancient littoral world was the part played in them by the new weapons. In return for a share of the spoils, the steppe men are likely to have provided the hill tribes with the skilled commanders, the specialists and the horses that the new warfare required. Troops of freebooting charioteers and bowmen may have attached themselves to the invading armies with the same end in view. A 'cannoning' movement of the kind later to become familiar at times of upheaval in the Heartland was probably taking place, with the peoples on the mountain fringes of the grasslands transmitting to the coastal belt the shocks from the steppes.

The impact of the steppe charioteers on India was more direct. Through the gap between the Caspian and the Pamirs,

the Aryans began their thrusts to the south-east about 1500
B.C. Like the riparian societies of the Middle East, the Indus
civilization had already passed its zenith. But the waves of
Indo-Europeans from the Heartland completed its ruin.
Mohenjo-daro and Harappa were reduced to rubble, and the
surrounding culture of which they were the centres was obliterated. Dispersing resistance, sometimes turning their arms
against each other, the conquerors surged on down the Ganges
valley and into the Deccan. And through the confusion of the
succeeding centuries, vivid glimpses emerge from Indian epic
poetry of a new, warlike aristocracy spreading its code of
chariot-chivalry; of valiant princes, excelling in the skills of
rein and bow, locked in relentless duels:

> A frightful uproar arose among the Panchala host like the
> roar of a mighty lion springing at the leader of a herd of
> elephants. Then that mighty chariot-warrior Arjuna rubbed
> his bow-string to increase the force and velocity of his shafts,
> and rushed at the king of the Panchalas. Quickly cutting
> his enemy's bow in twain, he pierced his antagonist's horses
> and charioteer with five arrows. Then, throwing aside his
> bow, Arjuna took his scimitar and, sending forth a loud
> shout, leaped from his own chariot upon that of his foe . . .[1]

Even distant China seems to have felt the impact of the chariot
outbursts from the steppes. Groups of warriors and wanderers
threaded their way eastward through the mountains and across
the deserts. Using the rivers and oases of the southern Heartland as their staging-points, settling for a time, moving on
again, their journey of three thousand miles or more from the
Caspian region to northern China took several centuries.
Whether their migration had any sense of purpose or destination is unknown. But at Anyang, the site of one of the early
capitals on the Yellow river, equipment similar in every respect
to that used in the invasions of the Middle East has been found:
chariots, and the gear and weapons of their fighting order
including compound bows.

A very different world arose from the subsiding dust of the

[1] *The Mahabharata,* ed. Pratapa Chandra Ray. Bharata Press, Cal-
cutta, 1893, pp. 411–12.

chariot invasions. Three great powers – Egypt, Assyria, and
the short-lived Hittite empire – now straddled the Middle East;
and all had gained their ascendancy largely because they had
mastered the chariot, turned it against its originators, and
retained it in the forefront of their military establishments.
But there were more significant underlying factors. In the
littoral societies of the centuries following the chariot eruptions
– in Mycenaean Greece, in the Middle Eastern empires, in Aryan
India, in the emergent China of the Shang dynasty – a new
outlook is discernible in the exercise of statecraft. Power, and
the techniques of its wielding, have become more important.
So has size. Organized authority has gained in stature. In the
lands all round the rim of Eurasia a tougher strain of rulership
has appeared. The invaders might have been expelled or absorbed: but the waves from the inner continent had imparted
elements of their own character to those they had overrun; a
greater sense of resourceful realism; the habit of command and
its acceptance within the framework of military preparedness.
These qualities had first come to be accepted along with the
invaders, then woven into the fabric of coastal life. As a result,
the lands of the littoral had become rather more similar to each
other. In effect, the Heartland had called into being a ring of
states round itself – states subject to all the disparate fortunes
of history, separated by distance, divergent in manner; but
possessing, in the terms of their governance, the potential of a
common understanding. The chariot had been an instrument
of change as well as of war.

For the steppe peoples, chariot warfare had certain drawbacks.
Any large number of chariots, with their intricate accoutrements, involved a costly upkeep. A wealthy élite was needed
to maintain and command them, having at its disposal a wide
range of specialized workmen as well as drivers and fighting
men. A society dominated by permanent and elaborate orders
of aristocracy was alien to the pastoral scheme of things.
Equally disadvantageous was the fact that though the steppe
herdsmen might be second to none at horsing chariots for
themselves and their allies, they were less capable of building
their own vehicles. Wood and metals were often hard to obtain
in the grasslands. So was the fine craftsmanship of wheelwrights,

leather-workers and smiths. In the meeting of skills which originally produced the chariot, these had been the contributions of the farm-minded communities outside the steppes. And it was just such relatively well-to-do communities that offered a tempting target for despoliation when steppe appetites for plunder were aroused. To be dependent on them for the means of their own conquest would be a fatal weakness. A further development was necessary before the steppe men could realize their full power potential without external help. They required a form of mobility that would be cheaper, and more in harmony with their social system and their need for self-sufficiency.

In due course that development appeared. The principle was simplicity itself: it merely involved transferring the compound bow to the back of a horse. In practice, however, it took many centuries to perfect, for it demanded the acquisition, and dissemination through generations, of a wonderful mastery of equestrian arts. Its evolution can perhaps be sketched by an analogy.

To a novice beginning a course of riding lessons, certain prerequisites are essential. These are, mainly, a well-schooled horse, and the proper tack – that is, a bit and bridle suited to the temperament of the horse and the hands of the rider, and a saddle of a build that places his weight in the right position and affords him maximum use of his legs. These things in themselves have required long experiment and experience to produce, before reaching the point at which the learner can swing himself up for the first time with some hope of remaining mounted. So it must have been on the steppes before riding became widespread. From about 2500 B.C. when the steppe men first gingerly began to mount, some sort of deliberate breeding and schooling of horses, together with the trial-and-error fabrication of tack, presumably went forward. But the advent of the chariot age – an era of driving rather than riding – may suggest that by 1700 B.C. while considerable progress had been made, the integration of man, animal and gear had not yet become sufficiently advanced for cavalry to take the field.

To return to the pupil. Receiving his first riding lessons, he discovers that the lower and upper parts of his body can fulfil different functions. With his legs he ensures a firm seat by grip, and applies to his mount the pressures indicative of the gait he desires, and to some extent the direction in which he wants to move. From the hips down his body, in as rigid a position as possible, is occupied with keeping himself in the saddle and with 'driving' his mount. His upper half is freer. Provided he adjusts the placing of his weight to help his horse over difficult ground or to change gait, his instructor may encourage him, for suppleness, to lean forward on to his horse's neck, or backward till his head is resting on its rump, and to turn from side to side. Similarly, from keeping both hands on the reins at first, he learns to direct and check his mount with one hand, leaving the other free to open gates, for example, or to swing a polo stick; or even, like deft American cowboys, to control a restive horse with one hand while rolling and lighting a cigarette with the other. Sooner or later he learns to put his mount into a canter, to change direction, and to clear modest jumps, without reins at all. Eventually he may be able to emulate the crack army teams who, in the heyday of cavalry, could undo their girths, pull their saddles from between their legs and hold them high over their heads, all at full gallop. He has discovered, in fact, that with long practice he can, for minutes rather than seconds, use the whole of the upper half of his body for purposes not connected with riding.

Something parallel to this separation of functions between the legs and body of a mounted man presumably evolved, very gradually, in the Heartland. Riding skill ultimately reached a stage when the multi-horse chariot could be dispensed with in favour of a single mount; when the rider's legs could replace the charioteer; and when the bowman beside the charioteer could become the body and arms of the horseman, who was now so expert that he could drop his reins and, while keeping his mount at top speed on a precise course, could take his compound bow from its case at his side and fire from it a succession of arrows round an arc of 270 degrees or more.

The achievement was the more astonishing because it was effected without benefit of either saddle or stirrups – the two pieces of equipment which the modern rider takes for granted to ensure his security and comfort when mounted. Only the most primitive of saddles, probably in the form of cloths or blankets, were available to the early steppe riders. The leather saddle, with pommel and cantle to check excessive forward or backward motion, did not appear until much later. And stirrups to rest the feet, to assist the rising trot and control lateral movement of the body, were to remain unknown for many centuries.

For steppe purposes, mounted archery represented a vast advance on the chariot. It increased mobility and saved man-power. It eliminated complex equipment and the difficulty of its maintenance. It was perfectly adapted to the steppe way of life. Its cheapness obviated the need for a special class of society devoted to war-preparedness and its subvention. Every herdsman was now a potential trooper. Moreover, except for increased supplies of weapons when big movements were afoot, it called for no gear that could not be made within the Heart-land. Military accoutrements from the outside became luxuries rather than necessities.

The mounted archer probably came into being in the western grasslands early in the eighth century B.C. For the next two thousand years his terrible dexterity was to remain a dominant force in the story of the Old World.

Unencumbered by chariots and their trappings, bands of horse-men could now move swiftly from the steppes into the culti-vated zones. They could spread panic and scatter local resistance with their volleys of arrows launched at full gallop. They could ransack villages in a few hours, gather up the spoil, vanish before organized defence could be brought to bear. They could operate in hostile territory for almost indefinite periods where-ever there was open country and grass or captured fodder for their horses. If they met with serious opposition they could withdraw and strike elsewhere. Where defence was weak or non-existent they could penetrate deeper, summon larger numbers of their kind, and turn a tip-and-run raid into an expedition in force. In this way probing taps quickly became hammer blows. Before long, the beating hooves and whistling arrows of the mounted archer from the Heartland were making their presence felt all round its south-western fringes. In par-ticular, they became a crucial factor in the affairs of the Middle East.

At this time the steppes around the northern shores of the

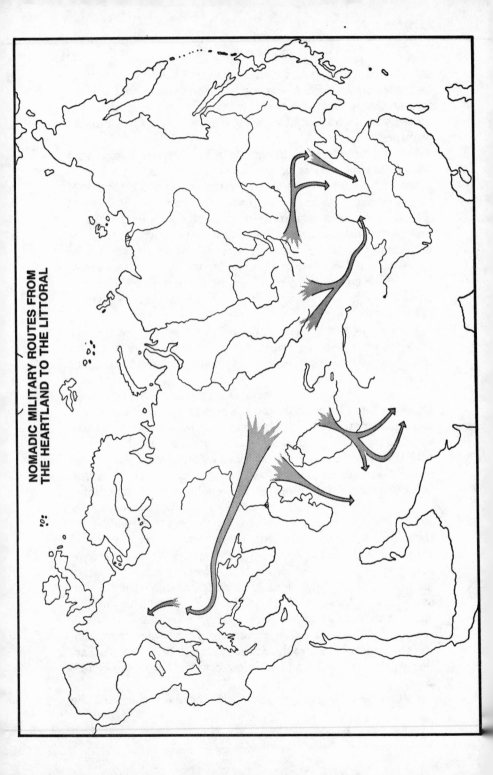

NOMADIC MILITARY ROUTES FROM THE HEARTLAND TO THE LITTORAL

Black Sea had recently been overrun by newcomers from the
east. These were Scythians: members of a large nomadic people
whose homelands lay in the region of the Altai mountains. The
westward movement of some of their tribes may have been due
to pressures exerted by rival nomads, or to a period of drought
which is believed to have set in a few decades previously in the
central Heartland. Whatever the cause of their migration, they
were in firm control of the grasslands of southern Russia by
about 720 B.C.

Though the Scythians were probably of mixed origin, people
of Iranian stock formed the core of their society, and they spoke
a common Indo-European language. A dominant group known
as the Royal Scyths claimed to exercise rulership over all their
tribes. They were big, fully-bearded men, and were said to be
prone to obesity and an exaggerated sense of humour. They
dressed in long coats drawn in round the waist by a belt,
trousers tucked into boots, and tall pointed caps. Perhaps their
most striking feature was the enormous amount of gold they
wore and used. Golden ornaments and belts were common.
Gold plates were sewn to their garments like huge sequins. Gold
gleamed from their weapons. Drinking cups cut from the skulls
of enemy chieftains killed in war were often set in gold mount-
ings. A profusion of golden offerings was customarily deposited
in the great burial-mounds of the Scythian kings in the bend of
the Dnieper river. This gold undoubtedly came from the rich
fields in the Altai district; and its quantities indicate a regular
trade in it between the tribes remaining in that region and those
in the newer western settlements.

In the fertile lands of what is now the western Ukraine, some
of the Scythians put down agricultural roots. Farming communities grew up along the Dniester river, harvesting wheat in
sufficient quantities to yield a surplus for outside trade. But
farther east, around the Sea of Azov, the majority were nomadic
herdsmen, working their cattle and sheep to and fro across the
plains with the changing seasons, spending spring and autumn
on the steppe, passing summer and winter by the rivers for
water and shelter. Among these Scythian tribes the mode of life
that was subsequently to characterize nomadic peoples all
along the grass belt of the Heartland was already recognizable
in outline. They developed the making of felt; and their tents,

though elaborate, were light enough for easy transport on the ox-waggons which followed their flocks. The art with which they decorated their portable possessions, though uniquely their own in its vivid stylized vigour, drew most of its inspiration, as did the art of later steppe peoples, from animal themes. And their small sturdy horses, from which the Cossack ponies of more recent times are said to descend, were their special pride. They ate horseflesh, drank koumiss, passed much of their waking lives mounted. Yet, though they had elaborate bitted bridles, the stirrup was not known to them and they rode on saddle-cloths, relying on grip and balance. Even so, they were formid-able horsemen in battle. They collected the scalps of those they had killed, attached them to their bridles like rosettes at a show, and wore them like medals about their clothing. An outstanding warrior might possess a robe of scalps. They fought with axes, spears and short dagger-like swords. But these were secondary. Their main weapon was the bow, in the hands of the mounted archer.

Separated from the Scythians on the Russian plains by the Black Sea and the Caucasus range lay the empire of Assyria. Following the chariot invasions, the Assyrians had spread their dominion across almost the whole of the Middle East. By a series of remorseless and bloodthirsty conquests they had des-troyed the Mitanni kingdom on the Euphrates, subdued the Kassites, swallowed Babylon and Egypt. Now their huge and powerful realm stretched from the Mediterranean to the Zagros mountains in Iran. It was an ugly empire, ruthlessly ruled in its later period from Nineveh on the Tigris; a rectangular, massively walled, fifteen-gated capital, strategic in location and largely divorced from the life of its surrounding subject peoples. The Assyrian kings, whose names boom like the menace of deep-throated gongs – Tiglath-Pileser, Adadnarari, Sargon, Ashurbanipal – held their territories together by methods similar in many respects to those of modern totalitarian regimes. Provincial governors maintained a ubiquitous system of spies. Terror, in the form of hideous tortures, was a regular instrument of administration. Unrest among the conquered populations was suppressed by mass deportations. Lacking any constructive spirit of their own, the ruling circles showed an exaggerated respect for the culture of ancient Babylon: the royal palace

at Nineveh was a careful copy of Babylonian architecture. But
their real faith was pinned to their army.

This was the largest force of serving and reserve troops that
the littoral world had known. It consisted mainly of foot-
soldiers, among whom were archers, and an engineer corps adept
in the use of siege equipment. Its chariot and cavalry arms – the
former something of a picturesque survival – were regarded as
of minor importance. Essentially, the Assyrian army relied on
massed infantry, meticulous organization and a network of
stone-paved roads to put down insurrection from within and to
repel invaders from outside. But in face of the unrelenting
nature of the despotism which it protected, the army's task
became progressively more difficult. From provinces disparate
in background and interest but united in disaffection, its masters
had taken too much and given too little. Its large auxiliary
units, levied in the outlying possessions for keeping order, became increasingly untrustworthy. By the time the Scythians
were moving west, its reliable core had become ominously over-
extended.

In the course of their migration into the western steppes, the
Scythians had displaced a people known to the Greeks as the
Cimmerians. Originally from eastern Europe, the Cimmerians
had spread into southern Russia and settled there. Wanting
the fine grasslands for themselves, the Scythians had expelled
them, driving them round the Black Sea coast across the
Danube, and through the passes of the Caucasus. Pouring southward, the Cimmerians spread havoc through Asia Minor,
savaging the trading cities which had grown up on the ruins of
the Hittite state. Their incursion created a critical situation
for Assyria. The invaders were at the gates of the empire; and
the Mediterranean provinces took swift advantage of the chaos
to draw together in revolt. Egypt in particular expelled the
Assyrian garrisons from her soil and regained her independence.
Assyria was in no position to retaliate. With her army already
strained, her frontiers began to contract inwards. Falling back
on frightfulness to stifle the rising spirit of rebellion, Ashurbanipal sacked Babylon – an act, for him, amounting to sacrilege
– and destroyed Susa in Iran, near the eastern frontier of the
empire.

Meanwhile, groups of Scythians had been thrusting southward from the steppes in the wake of the Cimmerians. Their initial contacts with the Assyrian empire had often been friendly: but its growing weakness created irresistible opportunities for plunder. Friendship turned to aggressive raiding; and the Scythian raids, probing round the west coast of the Black Sea and through the Caucasus, steadily gained in strength until their momentum suddenly carried the steppe men into the Middle East in an overwhelming surge. The Assyrian infantry, hard pressed from its long series of previous setbacks, could not cope with the fury of the new mounted firepower from the inner grasslands. Seizing the moment, the Babylonians formed an alliance with the Medes from Iran; and the Scythians, hungry for more loot, joined forces with them. This combination scattered the vestiges of Assyrian might. In 612 B.C. Nineveh was so completely gutted that the air traveller of today can only just discern the outline of its ruined walls across the river from the modern city of Mosul. The offensive power of the mounted archer had tipped the balance of the settled world.

Exactly a century later the horse-bowmen of the western Heartland were again to frustrate the calculations of power-politics in the Middle East. As before, their antagonist was the most powerful littoral state of the day. But this time their tactics were defensive.

After the destruction of Nineveh, the Scythians, laden with their spoil, had withdrawn northward to their homelands, leaving the Babylonians and the Medes to divide the former Assyrian empire between them. But within fifty years a new strong man appeared on the Middle Eastern scene. This was Kurush – Cyrus – the semi-civilized head of a little known Persian tribe, who owed allegiance to the king of the Medes. Organizing the Persian aristocracy and their followers around himself, Cyrus first seized the Median state: then, in a few years, gained control of virtually all the territory from the Mediterranean to Iran previously held by Assyria. That done, he turned about and extended Persian rule eastward through what is now Afghanistan. Cyrus was killed campaigning on his eastern frontier. But his son Cambyses carried on his work; and at the latter's death in 521 B.C. the Persian empire, built up in thirty years, stretched from the Nile to the Jaxartes and the Indus.

Darius, the third of the Persian Great Kings, sought to

realize the potential wealth of the empire of which he now
ascended the throne. At its western frontiers lay the Mediterranean world: at its eastern limits, the Arabian Sea and India.
Lying between West and East, the Persian empire straddled
both the sea routes and the land routes between the two most
productive areas of the Eurasian coastal belt. It was in a position
to dominate the movement of goods between them, and so to
become the most important trading entrepot of the time.

Two conditions were necessary if Darius was to make this
vision real. He must secure mastery of the sea; and this meant
wresting from the Greek states their control of the eastern
Mediterranean. And he must protect his northern frontiers from
the horse-archers of the western steppes. For where there was
trade the steppe peoples, and especially the powerful Scythians,
scented plunder; and another incursion comparable to that
which had helped to destroy Assyria would bring Darius's hopes
to ruin. But the strategic problem was a difficult one – even with
the strength of the Persian army, with its splendid core of the
Immortals, at his disposal. Almost within living memory the
Scythians had shown that they could round the Black Sea and
penetrate the Caucasus; and between the Caspian and the Hindu
Kush lay a wider and easier route from the Heartland into the
eastern territory of the Persian empire. It was in this region that
Cyrus himself had met his death, in all probability at steppe
hands.

Darius adopted a plan aimed at securing both his sea and
land frontiers. Between the Scythians and the Greeks a considerable flow of trade existed. The Greeks had come to rely on
imports of grain from the Scythian farming settlements on the
steppes; and this was exchanged against such Greek commodi-
ties as wine and oil. Collection and delivery was effected through
a number of Greek trading posts along the Black Sea coast, from
which the Scythians were not above levying forced tribute
whenever opportunity offered. A successful Persian sweep
around the north shores of the Black Sea towards the east
would break the Scythian power on the steppes, and so remove
the threat from the landward frontiers of Darius's empire. At the
same time it would cut off a valuable supply of food from the
Greek states, and so soften them up for direct action later.

With Darius himself in command, the Persian army crossed

the Bosphorus on a bridge of boats, and began their march across the Danube to the steppes. The Scythians, realizing they were faced with a full-scale invasion, sought the help of other steppe peoples. But no help came. Accordingly, they made their dispositions to contain the Persian power alone, as best they could. Before long their scouts were riding to and fro around the Persian flanks, probing for weaknesses. A poorly defended spot discovered, the scouts would quickly build up into a swarm of mounted skirmishers; and a glancing charge would sweep in, loose off its squall of arrows, and wheel away to safety. Ahead, the main bodies of the Scythian horsemen steadily retreated in three columns. In their wake the advancing Persians found food and fodder burnt, sources of water destroyed. Holding on in pursuit, Darius crossed the Dniester. All around him now were the featureless immensities of the steppe. Columns of smoke marked heaps of slaughtered cattle and, along the rivers, the scorched fields of settlements. Drifts of dust on the horizon hung above the retreating Scythians. Nearer at hand the watching horsemen continued their incessant circling. Bases, with the hope of supplies and reinforcements, lay the best part of a thousand miles behind. In front lay nothing but the open plains, from which rose smoke and dust and intermittent clouds of arrows. To the Persians, accustomed to the grapple and shock of head-on battle, this was warfare with the intangible. Rations began to run low, morale to sag.

Finally, Darius sought to force the issue. He sent a message to the Royal Scyth in command, demanding that he abandon his tactic of withdrawal, and accept either action or parley. If he felt strong enough to overcome the Persians, let him put his belief to the test of battle: if not, let him acknowledge Darius's supremacy by token tribute, and negotiations could follow. The Scythian reply was characteristic of the formal utterances of many later steppe leaders in similar circumstances of challenge. They invariably asserted their confidence in superiority: but they seldom prophesied the outcome in the form of empty threats. 'There is nothing new or strange in what we do,' the Scythian messenger announced to Darius. 'We follow our mode of life in peaceful times. We have neither towns nor cultivated lands in these parts which might induce us, through fear of their being ravaged, to be in any hurry to fight you. But if you must needs come to blows with us speedily, look about you, and behold our fathers' tombs. Attempt to meddle with them, and you shall see whether or not we will fight with you.'

Darius had no alternative but to turn back. All the way to the Danube the Scythians harassed his retreat. He never campaigned northward through Europe again; and his failure in the Russian grasslands in 512 B.C. led by a connected chain of events to the Persian débâcle against Athens at Marathon. As they had a hundred years before, the mobile tactics of the horse-archer, unkempt as the shaggy pony he bestrode, proved a match for the glittering formations of littoral might. And this time they brought to light a dilemma which was henceforth to dog the Persian empire: that of deciding, in the absence of sufficient strength to hold its sea and land frontiers, which was the more vital.

The power of the Scythians was finally broken from the steppe. For some centuries their neighbours to the east had been the Sarmatians, another large nomadic people deriving from the same stock as themselves and sharing a common language with them. The main tribal grouping of the Sarmatians, known to the Greeks as the Massagetae, occupied the partly grassed, partly arid lands to the north and east of the Caspian. Another Sarmatian group, the Sakas, grazed the region between the Aral Sea and Lake Balkash. In their peacetime habit of nomadic life, as in their practice of horse-archery in war, the Scythians and the Sarmatians had much in common. But the Sarmatians were a more bellicose people. The Scythian women never mounted horses, and left warfare to their menfolk. But every Sarmatian girl rode from childhood. Armed and clad like the men, she fought beside them and was forbidden to marry until she had killed an enemy in battle.

When Alexander the Great embarked in 334 B.C. on his tremendous drive through the Persian empire towards the Indus, he pushed north across the Jaxartes river into Sarmatian territory. Here he found himself in savage conflict with the Saka tribesmen. Their baffling fluidity of movement taxed his military inventiveness to the limit, for the Greek concept of tactics was largely based on the momentum of the solid infantry phalanx

against an equally solid target. With the horse-archers riding
round and round his advancing force, there was no solid target;
and Alexander was only able to dispel them by the impromptu
device of throwing out cavalry wings on each side of his phalanx
to break up the menacing, rotating circles of mounted bowmen
by which he was surrounded.

The original Scythian migration from the Altai district into
south Russia in the eighth century B.C. may have been due to
pressure exerted by the Sarmatians. In any case, during the
Scythian occupancy of the Black Sea steppes this pressure from
their rear became increasingly strong. Just as the Scythians
had seized the western grasslands – the best pastures in all the
Heartland – from the Cimmerians, so the Sarmatians, themselves pushed on by nomads farther east, began to dispute
their possession with the Scythians. Eventually the Scythians
were evicted. The native pugnacity of the intruders – no doubt
reinforced by their hard-riding, straight-shooting Amazons –
perhaps gave them an edge in the trial of strength. But more
important was the fact that the Sarmatians had acquired, or
had themselves developed, a new form of horse-warfare.

Hitherto the mounts of the steppe horse-archers had been
small ponies of limited strength. The Sarmatians succeeded
in breeding larger and more powerful horses. This enabled them
to clothe some of their men in comparatively heavy armour, and
to equip them with primitive lances in place of bows. The effectiveness of the early lancers was limited, for owing to the absence
of stirrups they could not put their full weight, let alone the
weight of their horses, behind their thrusts lest they be unhorsed
at the moment of impact; and for this reason they rode at their
enemies clutching their weapons in both hands. Even so, the
length of the lance gave it a decisive advantage in close combat over shorter swords or spears. And the Sarmatian experiments were to prove of great significance, for they meant
that in addition to the lightly mounted, highly mobile
archer, the steppes had given birth to the idea of heavy
cavalry: to shock combat from horseback, as well as missile
attack.

With their new technique of horse-fighting the Sarmatians
scattered the Scythians. But before they disappeared from history the Scythians gave rise to a force that was to become an

important factor in the balance between the steppes and the coastal lands.

Following Alexander's conquest of the Persian empire, the Seleucid dynasty, descended from one of his generals, attempted to restore its fortunes. At this time profound changes were taking place in the littoral world of Europe and the Middle East. Power was finally shifting from the ancient inland cities to larger nation-states along the Mediterranean seaboard, whose principal concern was trade. In seaborne commerce Egypt held a dominant position, for she commanded the all-important sea routes between the Orient and the central Mediterranean, where the star of Rome was rising.

For the Seleucid kings this sharpened the dilemma that Persia had faced under Darius: should they concentrate their efforts on securing the overland trade-routes to the East, or challenge Egypt for mastery of the sea? They first embraced a landward policy: then abandoned it in favour of maritime ambitions. Inevitably this brought them into conflict with Egypt; and by 261 B.C. they had been badly beaten. Worse was to follow: for all the major Mediterranean powers were now aligned in a long and desperate struggle for maritime supremacy. In this general war the Seleucids found themselves allied with Carthage against the combined strength of Egypt and Rome; and the ultimate outcome was their ruin. But while their troubles were at their height, an event occurred in eastern Iran which was to turn Persia's eyes permanently inward towards continental Asia.

On his march to the Indus Alexander had established in that region the province of Bactria, which had afterwards become part of the Seleucid empire. About 255 B.C. the Governor of Bactria, acting independently while his central government was preoccupied at home, embarked on an attempt to expand his territory. He moved north-west towards inner Asia; and his march disturbed a tribe of nomads at the southern fringes of the Heartland. These were the people who were to become known as the Parthians: a group of Scythians who had made their way round the Caspian from the Russian plains and, intermingling with other steppe-dwellers, had occupied part of the semi-desert country between the Caspian and Aral Seas. Now, their pastures threatened by the advance from Bactria, they

shifted their encampments towards the northern borders of
Iran.

Some years later, in 247 B.C. the Parthians moved again.
This time they climbed the Kopet Dagh escarpment to the
Iranian plateau proper. Here they spread out over the cultivated
land, establishing control over the peasant population. Before
long the towns south of the Caspian were in their hands; and
at Hecatompylos, named the City of a Hundred Gates because
of the numerous trade-routes that led to and from it, their king
Arsaces set his capital. Within a few decades, under Mithradates
I, they had conquered most of eastern Iran. Turning west, they
took possession of Seleucia on the Tigris, which had succeeded
Babylon as the trading centre of Mesopotamia.

The Parthian incursion meant that a key sector of the
Eurasian littoral was now held by a warlike people of steppe
origin. Egypt might command the sea: but the new Parthian
domain, stretching from the Syrian desert to the Hindu Kush
and from the Caspian to the Persian Gulf, was a region criss-
crossed by the tracks of landborne commerce. Through it ran
the routes to India from the Mediterranean, Asia Minor and
the Caucasus. It was, moreover, the gateway to central Asia
through which, along the southern borders of the Heartland,
merchants were already feeling their way towards the farther
Orient.

With this region as their new home, the outlook of the Parthians changed. Their interest was no longer the straightforward
steppe pursuit of plunder. They became concerned, rather, to
consolidate their grip on the land trade-routes across northern
Iran and to guard their approaches against all comers. Shaking
off, except in business affairs, the Greek influences stemming
from Alexander's conquest, reviving the old Persian national
religion of Zoroastrianism, they maintained their grasp for
more than four hundred years. At first the Seleucids made
determined attempts to dislodge them, and failed. Later, in
the period of Rome's triumphant expansion into the west,
they utterly frustrated her simultaneous attempt to push her
empire eastward. At the Battle of Carrhae ten thousand Parthians threw seven of the steadiest legions of the Roman
army back across the Euphrates. Their vicious arrows pierced
shields and tunics, transfixed two men at a time. Veering

elusively away from the Roman counter-attacks, they fired rearward over their horses' rumps – so originating the 'Parthian shot' that the Romans neither forgot nor forgave. The result of the disaster was the permanent denial to Rome of physical control of the Asian trade-routes, and the consequent creation for her empire of economic problems that were never solved.

The posture of the Parthians towards the Heartland was equally important; for, in policing the movement through Iran of lucratively taxable trade, they became a bastion against southward eruptions from the steppes. Originally nomadic warriors themselves, they settled down as feudal barons: military aristocrats owning great estates and disposing of the peasantry upon them. But they remained, essentially, horsemen: expert breeders and riders. And their understanding of steppe warfare enabled them to evolve a system of mounted fighting which, later in the story, was successfully to counter the mounted bowmen of the grasslands and play a notable part in the fortunes of the littoral world.

While all these early clashes between Heartland and Littoral were taking place, a movement of great significance was in progress deep within the Asian interior. The arts of the mounted herdsman, from which the skills of the horse-bowman had emerged, had originated in the relatively mild climate and rich pastures of the western steppes. Soon, these peaceful arts and warlike skills began to spread. While the Scythians were making their impact on Assyria and Persia, while Alexander was carrying Hellenism to the foothills of the Himalaya, while the little republic of Rome was transforming Italy into a springboard to imperial power, the practices of mounted nomadism were passing eastward from tribe to tribe across the steppes, into the less temperate regions of inner Asia: across snow-laden table-lands and plains of sun-broiled scrub, through the 'dry strait' between the peaks of Tien Shan and Altai, up into the searing winds of the high Mongolian plateau and beyond. This knowledge of herd and horse and bow took several centuries to cross the Heartland spaces, for it took place against the natural drift of the steppe populations towards the more genial westerly zones. But well before 300 B.C. it had reached the eastern verges of the grasslands. To the more primitive peoples here, some hunters on the prairies, some but recently emerged from the forests of the taiga, all bred to the rigours of the eastern Heartland climate – to such hardened, semi-savage men the methods of the mounted nomadic shepherd and the raiding horse-archer were now available.

With this movement, and its ominous implications for the Pacific coastlands of Eurasia, the scene shifts to China.

4

The Eastern Amphitheatre

They have no fields or ploughlands,
But only wastes where white bones lie
Among yellow sands.

— LI PO, translated by Arthur Waley

So far, the great plains of the western and southern Heartland, stretching from the Black Sea steppes to the Hindu
Kush, have occupied the centre of the stage. Now the setting
becomes the eastern half of the inner Asian continent. Here,
beyond the diagonal line formed by the Tien Shan and Altai
ranges and the waters of Lake Baikal, lie the steppelands of the
Mongolian plateau and central Manchuria; and, to the south
and west of them, the Gobi and the Takla Makan deserts. The
whole region can be seen as a tremendous amphitheatre
of grass and rock and sand curving round the northern
approaches to China; backed, and separated from the western
steppes, by an almost continuous line of mountain and forest
running from the Hindu Kush to the Sea of Okhotsk.

By the third century B.C. this amphitheatre of the eastern
Heartland was inhabited by peoples of differing origin and
occupation. At its centre, most of Mongolia was the domain
of a people known to the Chinese as the Hiung-nu, or Northern
Horse-barbarians. They, as their name implies, had already
acquired the arts of mounted nomadic pastoralism. To the east
of the Hiung-nu, in Manchuria, was another group of mounted
nomads, the Tung-hu or Eastern Horse-Barbarians; and to the
west, beyond the Altai mountains, where Tomsk and Krasnoyarsk now stand, were other tribes of horse-herdsmen. Spread
across the north, in the forest belt of Siberia, were relatively
primitive people, gatherers of wild food from the woods and
waters, some of whom were to emerge from the taiga at various

times and take to a mounted life. Most of those living on the steppes and on the fringelands between steppe and taiga were forerunners of the Turkish and Mongol peoples. The dwellers in the more northerly forests were mainly Tunguses.

The peoples in the south of the region were of quite different background. They stemmed from the great Iranian, Indo-European, movement which had convulsed the westerly zones of the Heartland in earlier times. Part of that tide had flowed east; and when its force was spent it left behind pockets of those who had travelled on it. Thus to the south of the Hiung-nu, between the Gobi desert and the plateau of Tibet, were two important tribes called by the Chinese the Yue-chi and the Wusun. Both were mounted graziers: but both, unlike their nomad neighbours to the north, came from the west and spoke Indo-European languages. Different again were the inhabitants of the Takla Makan – the egg-shaped desert nestling in the mountains of the southern Heartland, with the Tarim river flowing through its parched horizons. These, too, had originated in the west and spoke Indo-European languages. But many of them were abandoning the nomadic life. In the foothills of the mountains surrounding the desert they had found a series of well-watered oases. Here they were settling down, digging irrigation ditches, and taking to the more settled peaceful life of the farmer. Towns were rising at the centres of the oases, each ringed by its irrigated fields, each self-sufficient in food and water, and self-contained in government. Along the southern rim of the desert were Kashgar, Yarkand, Khotan; along its northern edge Kucha, Karashar, Turfan. These and other city-states of the Tarim basin, in the Heartland but not of it, were to become a crucial moment in the centuries ahead.

Of these eastern Heartland peoples poised around the marches of settled littoral China, by far the most dangerous were the Hiung-nu. Their herds were spread across almost the entire area that now comprises both Outer and Inner Mongolia. Some of their tribes occupied the steppes of the northern Mongolian plateau; others possessed the grazings round the southern fringes of the Gobi desert. This position, and the great spread of their lands, gave them command of the two strategic routes from the highlands of continental Asia into Chinese territory. Provided other nomads did not bar their path, they could move

down towards the Chinese lowlands round the northern edges
of the Gobi and through the advanced grazing-base of Manchuria; or, from the southern limits of that desert, they could
advance to the Ordos plateau and the populous basin of the
Yellow river.

There has been much debate as to who the Hiung-nu were.
Some authorities have held that they were ancestors of the
Mongols: round-headed, sallow-skinned, and with little bodily
hair. Others believe that they were ancestral Turks: long-
headed, bushy-bearded men, more similar to Europeans in
feature and complexion. Others again suggest that they derived
from a mingling, possibly of Mongols and Tunguses. But Chinese
chronicles state that they had 'red hair, green eyes and white
faces' and were very hirsute. These records, together with some
archaeological evidence, point to the Hiung-nu as an early
Turkish people; though, by intermarriage with peoples farther
east, including the Chinese, many of them came to acquire
Mongoloid characteristics.

If their ethnic background is still obscure, there is greater
certainty about how they lived. Their life-pattern closely
resembled that of their nomadic predecessors on the western
steppes, and many of its facets were afterwards shared by their
successors in time all across the Heartland grass. They dressed
in long belted coats, with surcoats of leather for protection
against cold and enemy arrows. Their aspect was forbidding.
Above their earrings, the sides of their heads were shaved and
the hair on top was divided into two stumpy plaited pigtails
falling behind the ears. This custom, no doubt practical in the
raging winds of the steppe uplands, gave rise by transmission
through other peoples to the longer pigtails worn much later
by the Chinese. Their homes were the round felt tents already
familiar in the western grasslands: but, as a Chinese historian
remarked, 'their country was the back of a horse'. Their ponies
yielded milk and koumiss, provided the means of working their
herds between the pastures, mounted their galloping archers in
war. In their turbulent predatory society, raiding and under
constant threat of counter-raid, the practice of marksmanship
was mandatory for all able-bodied men; and few were of consequence unless they possessed the skill and physique of the
potential trooper. Toddlers learnt to bestride a sheep or donkey

and to pick off rodents and birds from their backs with toy bows and arrows. As boys they pursued the faster-moving targets offered by hares and foxes. The strength to bend a man's bow was a test of whether a youth had reached military age, with its promise of a share in the spoils of future forays. As their methods of warfare had been acquired from the west, so also had the rituals that marked their successful campaigns, like that of drinking the blood of enemies from bowls carved from their skulls.

Their religion was the Shamanism common among the historic peoples of northern inner Asia. There was a single all-highest god who revealed himself in the spirits, benevolent and hostile, of the natural phenomena round about: fire and water, mountains and caves, storm and wind and thunder. The interaction of these myriad sub-deities made up the good or ill fortunes of life: health or disease in the family, fertility or barrenness in the animals, prosperity or catastrophe in peace and war. They could be persuaded or placated by a caste of supernaturally endowed shamans; and it has been suggested that the wild dances and incantations of these wizard-priests may have been attributable to an acute form of 'Arctic hysteria' – the state of mind, resulting from long periods spent in the vast featureless northern landscape, which can induce compulsive repetition of anything seen or heard in actuality or dream.

But in the nomadic environment, shamanism amounted to more than superstition. It reminded its followers of the need to achieve as favourable a balance as possible between the natural forces by which they were surrounded; between the usage of those which were manipulable, and the acceptance of the uncontrollable. It contributed to awareness of the factors to be reckoned with in the management of the herds, and in the making of warlike dispositions. In the perpetual struggle for survival in the harsh climate and code of the Asian interior, it contained much that was practical precept. Representing an effort to harmonize potentially opposed or disparate influences, it suggested a unity between the living and the dead which must be realized by ancestor-worship. The high god was associated with the sky and the sun; and though the interpretation of his pantheon to humankind at commonplace levels was the business of the shamans, it was the duty of the Shanyu, or

Chief Ruler of the Hiung-nu, to humble himself to the sun each morning as a sign of his renewed preparedness to execute the supreme will on earth.

The China which now lay so perilously exposed to the steppes was still virtually isolated from the western lands of the Eurasian coastal belt. It was a much smaller country than it is today. The farming communities which represented its first steps towards nationhood had taken root in the fertile beds of loess, their fine tilth easy to cultivate with hand tools, lying along the Hwang Ho or Yellow river; and from there they had expanded westward into the valley of its tributary the Wei, where the soil was especially rich. Early China thus lay entirely to the north of the Yangtze Kiang river, which now runs through its centre; and this northward focus meant that any concentration of hostile power in Mongolia or Manchuria was a threat not merely to one section of the country, but to its heart.

At the time when the Hiung-nu were gathering strength, China could already trace her emergence back through more than a thousand years. It had been a millennium both destructive and formative: she had been torn by internal wars of vicious violence; but simultaneously the foundations of her intellectual achievement and commercial importance had been laid. The Shang dynasty – the first line of rulers who were not to some extent legendary – had presided over the agricultural communities of the Yellow and Wei basins during the latter half of the second millennium B.C. Theirs had been a realm of large villages dotted across a landscape often transformed to marsh or lake by uncontrollable flood waters. There were no great cities, and the sea as yet represented the edge of the unknown rather than a route of trade. The Shang feudal pattern was of the small-scale kind later associated in the West with the manorial holding. Peasants were serfs, bound to the soil of local lords: but despite primitive living and cruel customs – human sacrifice was practised – their system afforded balance and stability.

About 1000 B.C. the Shang had been forcibly deposed by a new dynasty bearing the name of Chou. These were rulers of tougher strain, conquerors from the Wei valley; and they brought with them larger, more centralist ideas of government.

It was probably they who introduced the concept, which was to endure until the overthrow of the last imperial dynasty in the twentieth century, that the monarch held office by virtue of the Mandate of Heaven, which only became exhausted when he or his successors, the Sons of Heaven, indicated by their actions that they had ceased to foster the celestial condition among their subjects. On the Shang foundations the Chou imposed a feudalism favouring their own family and followers: but it was a feudalism of bigger units and greater lords, seeking to replace the haphazard local squeezing of peasant serfs by levying taxes and imposing military service on a broader, more regular basis. This larger approach to government resulted in the appearance, under Chou sovereignty, of a number of great domains or dukedoms, roughly corresponding to the economic and geographical regions of Chinese territory.

In 771 B.C. however, disaster had overtaken the Chou regime. Their capital was sacked without warning by barbarians from the west – that is, from the Heartland. Their cohesive, if initially rough, rule disappeared and power passed to the great dukes. For a time these grandees, now virtually kings, sought to keep the peace by relatively enlightened statesmanship. They were men of gallantry; and when fighting broke out between them, as it did, they conducted it according to strict rules of chivalry. René Grousset[1] paints a vivid picture of these princely Chinese hostilities of the seventh century B.C., fought from that stately (though by western standards now old-fashioned) conveyance, the chariot. Drawn by four high-mettled horses, the vehicles bore three men apiece: a driver, with a lancer on his right and an archer on his left. As they advanced to battle the sun flashed on the barbed blades of the lances, on the varnished oxhides of breastplates and the bright paint of shields. Above the rolling formations, before, behind, and at each side, four banners snapping in the breeze portrayed the beasts symbolic of the compass points: Red Bird, Black Tortoise, White Tiger, Green Dragon.

But such restraints did not last. Trials of strength between grandees degenerated into chaotic conflicts between upstart warlords seeking territory and power at each other's expense. By about 350 B.C. this interminable strife between warring

[1] In his *Rise and Splendour of the Chinese Empire*, p. 25.

states had become so savage that the status of its leaders was gauged by the number of heads, hundreds of thousands in a single campaign, that their armies could strike from the dead and from living captives. To relieve the monotony of the mass decapitations, other batches of prisoners were boiled.

But the social balance of the Shang centuries and the princely courts of the earlier Chou monarchy had created the conditions for the emergence of a literate, educated stratum. And as the Chou structure disintegrated, the official, the scholar, and the merchant, clustering originally round the great landed magnates, began to secure a place in Chinese life. Though not yet strong enough to impose order and humanity on the deepening political crisis, reasoned systems of intellect and organization gained stature in the embryo urban centres to compensate for the irrational brutalities in the countryside. Money and markets appeared. Goods began to move along new canals and roads. The influence of the administrator at his desk, the gentleman in his study, began to grow. If anything, the troubles of the times assisted the spread of ideas; for educated men, displaced by the march of armies, sought refuge in the quieter peripheral districts. The teachings of both Lao Tzu and Confucius, traditionally born in 604 B.C. and 551 B.C. respectively, in some degree reflected the miseries of a warlord-ridden country. Taoism, with its emphasis on thought and on simplicity in daily practice as the means of approach to the eternal cosmic energy, offered a mystic release from the surrounding realities. Confucianism, less a religion than a code of honourable behaviour to be followed, in particular, by those charged with government, represented a yearning for a return to the ethical standards set by the first Chou rulers.

During all this time the pressure from the Heartland had been growing. Chinese histories refer, briefly but persistently, to encounters with the barbarians from as early as 1400 B.C. Before they seized the central power, the Chou, as lords of the Wei valley on the western perimeter of China proper, had grappled with raid after raid sweeping in from the fringes of the Gobi. Later, during the long period of internal conflict, one of the warlords, attacked by nomads from the steppes, had realized the ineffectiveness of his lumbering chariots against their fleet mounted archers, and had trained squadrons of Chinese horse-bowmen to counter them. But the raids continued, disrupting sowing and harvesting throughout the border zones; and as their strength and frequency built up, the name of the Hiung-nu became increasingly associated with them. Despite the political fragmentation following the downfall of the Chou, the wealth of China was swelling perceptibly with each decade; and to the Hiung-nu, watching from their bleak highland pastures, this burgeoning was providential. And the civil wars, frequently denuding the Chinese borderlands of defence, made it easy for them to swarm down into the cultivated lands, kill and burn, clutch and capture, and, as swiftly, to vanish back into the Heartland horizons.

But in the latter part of the third century B.C. a forceful autocrat rose to power in China. This was Ch'in Shih-huang-ti, the 'First Supreme Ruler of the House of Ch'in'. Like the Chou, the Ch'in family had originally been marcher lords, owning domains in the western frontier region of the Wei valley; and at one time the fortunes of the two houses had been connected. In 771 B.C., when the Chou had been attacked from the Heartland, the neighbouring Ch'in had come to their aid; and, as a mark of gratitude, the Chou had bequeathed to them most of their family lands along the Wei river on condition that they would undertake the permanent defence of the borders against incursions from the steppes. This the Ch'in had done as best they could, settling on their enlarged estates the hardiest peasants they could find, schooling them in methods of breaking up the smash-and-grab descents of the mounted barbarians. As time passed the state of Ch'in had become a power in the Chinese west, and its rulers notorious for the uncouth, down-to-earth boorishness with which their constant contact with the marauding nomads had imbued them.

In 246 B.C. a boy of thirteen became head of the Ch'in domains. He was described[1] as 'stingy, cringing and graceless'; but as possessing 'the chest of a bird of prey, the voice of a jackal, and the heart of a tiger'. All around him, at the time of his succession, the ambitious youth saw the Chinese states, his own among them, locked in civil war; and in the universal disarray, with his blunt Ch'in realism, he perceived his opportunity.

[1] By the historian Ssu-ma Ch'ien, who died in the first century B.C.

He had at his disposal a following of able, acquisitive advisers, as well as the Ch'in army with its tough tradition of frontier fighting against the steppe tribes. One by one he overthrew or tricked into submission the warlords who for so long had dominated the Chinese scene. By 221 B.C., at the age of thirty-eight, he was master of all China; and in that year he assumed the title of Shih-huang-ti. Thereupon, this first of the true Chinese emperors applied his hard-hewn frontier energies to hammering into a single nation the divided lands and peoples he had conquered. Part military dictator, part orderly administrator, he embarked on a wide programme of unification and expansion. He replaced the lingering system of local exactions by centralized taxation, organized the country into provinces, enlarged its network of communications, and extended its limits southward across the Yangtze river, colonizing parts of the new outlying territories with convicts as Britain first settled Australia. And with the domestic integration of his country under way, he turned his attention to the external menace of the Hiung-nu.

At this time the kernel of the Hiung-nu strength lay at the very door of China, for their headquarters were in the southeastern fringes of the Gobi adjoining the Ordos plateau, and thus close to the great bends of the Yellow river. From here the Shanyu exercised his rule over the tribes grazing their herds across the pastures surrounding the desert and stretching back into the purple distances of Mongolia; and from here he organized their major raiding expeditions into Chinese territory. The name of the reigning Shanyu was Touman; and Chinese pictures of this period, when the Hiung-nu were approaching the height of their power, afford some idea of his appearance. They suggest a tall, deep-chested man of powerful frame mounted on a dimunitive pony of the pure white strain which only the nomad nobility might ride. His long robe falls below the tops of his high boots. He wears a turban-like cap and a full beard; and his features are dark and implacable. His eyes stare upward as if in commune with the supreme god of sky and sun. He holds his loose rein in his left hand, and his bow in his right. From his saddle is slung a quiver filled with arrows. In such a figure the jackal-voiced, tiger-hearted emperor had a redoubtable opponent.

On gaining the central power Shih-huang-ti had appointed as commander-in-chief of his armies Meng T'ien, his ablest general and an outstanding military engineer. A cultivated man of wide interest in the arts, Meng T'ien brought even to his leisure hours the mind of an inventive technologist: he is said to have developed a musical instrument on the principle of the piano and to have perfected an improved kind of writing-brush. Now the emperor made him responsible for expelling the Hiung-nu from their uncomfortably close positions at the north-west approaches to China, and for securing the frontiers against their further depradations. He marched against them with an enormous force, recorded as comprising three hundred thousand men. His campaign was entirely successful: too successful, as subsequent events were to prove. Overwhelmed by the sheer, sudden weight of well-disposed numbers, Touman and his hordes were dislodged from all the lands they had been occupying between the Yellow river and the Gobi, and were forced back helter-skelter beyond the desert into the fastnesses of the Mongolian plateau.

With the immediate threat from the Heartland removed, Meng T'ien and the emperor had time to consider more permanent means of ensuring the safety of the borders and of the rapidly consolidating country within them. The southern perimeter of China might be protected by the icy heights of the Tibetan plateau and the broad reaches of the Yangtze. But the west and north had no such natural defences; and it was from these quarters that the raiders from the Asian interior had always come.

The extraordinary outcome of the collaboration between the two men was due in part to Shih-huang-ti's bold, but in the military context frontier-conscious, thinking; in part to the genius of his general for organizing undertakings on the largest scale; and in part to an innate Chinese liking for walls. From very early times the China of the Yellow and Wei basins had been criss-crossed with walls. They had been erected sometimes to enclose feudal estates, sometimes to mark tribal boundaries, sometimes for the security of the larger towns. During the civil wars the contending warlords had built them along the frontiers of their mutually hostile states, and along sections of the northern and western borderlands which were specially vulnerable to attacks from the steppes. Shih-huang-ti himself, while still head of the Ch'in state, had thrown up a wall to enclose the more exposed confines of his domains. His purpose now was to join together all the previously built north-facing walls into a continuous line of defence. This new wall, partly composed of strengthened existing work and partly of fresh construction, would stretch clear across the northern marches of China for a distance of more than a thousand miles, from Shan-hai-kuan on the Gulf of Po Hai to the edges of the Gobi beyond the Ordos Loop. It would protect settled civilized China from the nomadic barbarian Heartland, and especially from the Hiung-nu, for all time.

Several factors may have dictated the speed at which the emperor urged Meng T'ien forward on this superhuman project. Touman had been temporarily repulsed: but the Hiung-nu or some other steppe horde would almost certainly expand again towards China. Internally, he had on his hands a large surplus of unemployed and potentially troublesome manpower: the armies, now idle, of the states he had overthrown on his way to power; the host of adventurers, malcontents and subversionists thrown up by the years of anarchy. Moreover, he was still a young man of obsessive energy.

Meng T'ien established his headquarters in the Ordos Loop, and from there he directed the vast logistical operations involved in the building. The core of his labour force was the army with which he had thrown Touman back into Mongolia. It was supplemented by countless numbers of less willing hands: prisoners of war, criminals, beggars, misfits, critics of the regime from every class of society. Anyone who could not give a good account of himself at home was liable to be rounded up and sent for service at the wall. Over the most intensive period of construction it is probable that upwards of a million men, drafted in huge gangs to the frontier zones, found themselves at forced labour on the colossal structure rising across the spiky grey hills and the drifting loess dust of the plains. Overworked, under-fed, they were used without mercy. The wall became known as the longest cemetery in the world; for it was said that the exhausted, often still breathing, were flung into the works, partly to appease the spirits of the frontier and partly because the rubble provided a convenient grave.

Legend has it that many thousands were buried beneath the masonry.

Construction methods varied according to the terrain. Along the mountain sections two parallel trenches were hewn from the rock some twenty-five feet apart, and dressed granite blocks, projecting well above ground-level were laid in them. Brick courses were then carried up to a height of twenty or thirty feet, and the cavity between the two walls so formed was filled with rammed-down earth, providing a roadway between the parapets along which several horseman could ride abreast. Farther west, on the flat tablelands, the yellowy spoil was tamped down between timber forms and then faced with stone or wetted loess. At the eastern end, where the wall met the sea, the foundations for the fortress at Shan-hai-kuan were laid by sinking blockships filled with stones on the site. Built into the structure, and jutting forward from its outer face, were squat oblong towers topped by battlemented platforms to serve, like the later Roman mile-castles, as observation-posts and barracks for the garrison troops. Each was separated from its neighbour only by the range of two arrows, the intention being that no spot along the wall should be out of reach of the archers stationed in the towers.

The wall itself, however, was only the principal element in an elaborate system of defence in depth. Its route was planned so as to enclose on the Chinese side the maximum number of watercourses, leaving the outer approaches relatively arid. Outpost towers, which grew in number to some twenty thousand in later times, were spread across the outlying country, so that warning of oncoming enemies could be given and delaying actions fought. On the lands along the defended zones peasants were encouraged to adopt a simple method, long practised in the frontier regions, of slowing and fatiguing the ponies of the steppe bowmen: that of ploughing at a right angle to the expected direction of attack so as to produce uneven ground. An existing palisade of willows, planted in the shape of a gigantic horseshoe round the landward end of the Liaotung peninsula to break up cavalry advancing towards that area, was thickened to form an eastward extension of the wall proper.

Shih-huang-ti did not live to see the fulfilment of his grandiose idea: but the main sectors of the Great Wall, with their ancillary

outworks, were completed within twenty years of his inaugura-
tion of their building. After his time the Wall, and the line it
followed, passed through continuous changes according to the
push and pull exercised by the littoral and continental forces
it was built to separate. Through the centuries and dynasties
parts of it were neglected, then subsequently repaired only to
crumble again; other lengths were strengthened by new construction; long westerly extensions were added; parallel outlying or inner walls were erected and, in turn, fell into desuetude.
Much of the spectacular hilly section commonly seen today by
visitors from Peking is the work of the Ming emperors in the
fifteenth and sixteenth centuries A.D.

These perpetual metamorphoses give a clue to its real nature.
Superlatives have always surrounded so profoundly impressive
a result of human toil. It has been variously described as the
only man-made work visible from space, and as the greatest of
all monuments to the horse. Near the fortress of Kiayukuan,
where the far western stretches, added later, finger out into the
lonely wastes of central Asia, a Chinese inscription reads: 'The
Greatest Barrier of Earth.' Whatever else it may have been, the
Wall was hardly that. It proved impossible to draw an immov-
able line between the two cultures, sedentary and roving,
which, however terrible the clashes between them at periods of
crisis, had much to gain from each other at other times. When
the nomads were quiescent, the Wall might be almost un-
manned save for posts of civil authority; and Chinese peasants
and Heartland shepherds would pursue their callings, intermingled, for many miles on either side. It was never intended as
a substitute for the manpower of defending armies; and it was
seldom a fixed line to be held at any cost. It was rather a base-
in-length from which Chinese armies operating farther north
could be supplied, and on which they could rally during field
warfare. Militarily, its use was limited. It never halted a massive
invasion from the grasslands. But it discouraged smaller raids;
and no steppe conqueror could mount a serious campaign into
China proper without first taking considerable stretches of it
and holding them for the duration of his presence. Equally important, at times of intensifying nomad pressure it kept the
Chinese in, and so reduced the risk of treachery. First erected
by a rising littoral people to counter the simultaneously growing

power of the Heartland horsemen, its role became less that of a barrier than of an approximate boundary through the constantly shifting no-man's-land between them.

Meanwhile, Touman was actively seeking to repair the effects of his original defeat at the hands of Meng T'ien. This vigorous thrust, by forcing the Hiung-nu across the Gobi into farther Mongolia, had not only cut them off from their customary source of trade and loot: it had also deprived them of an important part of their pasturelands. Immense though the Mongolian plateau might be, it could not afford comfortable grazing for the many tribes now crowded upon it. Re-expansion was essential; and if for the present Chinese strength forbade a new eastward advance, an outlet must be sought in other directions. Accordingly, Touman began to form alliances with his steppe neighbours with the immediate aim of seizing land from weaker nomadic peoples, but with the eventual hope of building up sufficient strength to reoccupy the Chinese border regions.

Despite the mauling he had received from Meng T'ien, his power was still unchallengeable among his own kind. His commanding figure suggested the leadership required for great deeds; and if that was not enough to overcome the normal rivalries and dissensions of steppe life, he had behind him the largest army of horse-archers in the eastern Heartland. Demanding total obedience to himself as supreme overlord, he tightened his control first over the tribes and peoples on the outskirts of Mongolia, then over those beyond its fringes. This nascent empire of the Hiung-nu was of a kind to become familiar all across the steppes. Its strengths and weaknesses were those of an association based solely on the promises and threats of a single masterful individual. In the inevitable changes in the personality and policy of its leadership, in the perpetually shifting fortunes of its nomadic component peoples, it contained the seeds of its own eventual dissolution. But in the short term its spread was rapid. Even while the ramparts of the Great Wall were still rising round the Ordos Loop, the Hiung-nu were extending their web of allegiance and influence into the wings of the Heartland amphitheatre facing China.

If the forceful diplomacy of Touman, the first of the great

Shanyus, rallied the Hiung-nu and wove around them a powerful steppe confederacy, the military ability of his eldest son, Maodun, brought their strength to a pitch which was to imperil the very existence of China. A strategist on the great scale, Maodun's ultimate objective, like that of the Shanyus who followed him, was nothing less than the total conquest of the Chinese state that Shih-huang-ti had unified. But he was capable of biding his time, of moving step by step towards his goal. His first concern, as a young prince of the Hiung-nu ruling clan surrounded by intriguing rivals, was to assure his own succession to his father. He did so by an elaborately contrived act of parricide typical of a ruthlessness amounting to genius.

In this affair Touman was not blameless, for he had himself been privy to a plot against Maodun's life. In negotiations he had conducted with the Yue-chi, the Indo-European nomads grazing to the south of the Hiung-nu, the customary question had arisen of the lodgement with them of a hostage; and one of Touman's wives, anxious to obtain the succession for her own son, had prevailed upon him to send Maodun in this capacity. She had then importuned Touman to mount a raid on the Yue-chi, hoping that this would result in the execution of their hostage. But in the confusion of the onslaught Maodun managed to escape. He made his way back to Touman's headquarters, and presented himself before his father. The old Shanyu's heart was touched; and he tried to make amends by placing his eldest son in charge of a picked body of Hiung-nu horse-archers. Maodun, however, was not placated: indeed, he saw in his father's connivance at his attempted murder the excuse he had been seeking to seize power. His attention had been drawn to the invention of an arrow which whistled in flight; and he was now determined to put this novelty to purposeful use. At whatever target his arrow whistled, his entire bodyguard were at once to discharge their own shafts. He drilled his entourage until their response was instant and accurate. Then, to nerve them, he fired first at his most treasured horse, then at his wife. The results of both trials were all that could be desired. It remained only to await the real moment. One day he joined his father on a hunting expedition. As the old man rode slowly past, a whistle cut the air. A moment later Touman was rolling from his horse, his body bristling with arrows. Before the general shock had subsided, Maodun's men had eliminated all possible contenders for the rulership.

His own position as Shanyu established, Maodun set about enlarging and strengthening the Hiung-nu confederacy by a systematic series of military conquests. His eyes were fixed on China: but before advancing on to Chinese soil he judged it prudent to secure his flanks and rear against any possibility of interference from the Heartland interior while his back was turned. First he lunged north-east upon the Tung-hu, his nomadic neighbours in Manchuria, seizing a large proportion of their pastures and forcing them to submit to his demand that they join the confederacy. Then his cavalry turned about and swept west across Mongolia, into the basin of the Selenga river. Here they took control of the territory of outlying tribes scattered from the foothills of the Altai mountains to the shores of Lake Baikal. His rear protected, Maodun headed south and stunned into quiescence his former goalers the Yue-chi and their neighbours the Wusun, settling his personal account with the former by causing an elegant drinking-bowl to be fashioned from their chieftain's skull. At the same time, for double assurance, he penetrated the Tarim basin, demonstrating his strength before its oasis-cities, and exacting from them hostages and tribute as a guarantee of their future attitude.

Every potential military force of any size in the eastern Heartland was now either Maodun's ally or his vassal. From Manchuria to Tibet the empire of the Hiung-nu dominated the great semicircle of the landward approaches to China. The grass channels leading down from Mongolia into the densely populated valley of the Yellow river lay open. Across them, now, stood the forbidding façades of the new Great Wall of Shih-huang-ti. But to the steppe commanders, leading wave on wave of mounted men, walls did not imply the finality with which the Chinese mind had endowed them. They were temporary obstacles to passage, not dissimilar to many raised by nature; and if they did not yield to head-on storm, their cavalry armies could flow round them. Due to Meng T'ien's foresight, there might be little water on the circuitous march round the Wall's end: but troopers and horses alike were hardened to thirst.

Moreover, Shih-huang-ti was dead. And China, reacting against the driving dictatorship he had imposed, was once more in revolt and anarchy. Maodun seized the moment. His mounted archers poured down from Mongolia, reoccupying almost all the Gobi fringelands from which Meng T'ien had chased them only some twenty years before. By the time order was restored in China, the Hiung-nu had crossed the outer bend of the Yellow river. Behind the swarming bowmen, their flocks and herds, tents and wagons, were fanning out across the Ordos plateau. The western stretches of the Wall already lay behind them.

After eight years of chaos following the death of Shih-huang-ti, a peasant's son called Liu Pang gathered the government of China into his hands. He had been, successively, a minor functionary, a policeman, an adventurer on the margins of banditry and a rebel warlord; and it was in the latter capacity that he fought his way to the throne in 202 B.C. A wayward, untutored character with a weakness for drunken reminiscences of his youth, Liu Pang nonetheless founded one of the most illustrious of the Chinese dynasties; for, as the emperor Kao-ti, he was the first ruler of the house of Han. Under the Han, China was to pass through a great era of intellectual and physical expansion; and the long period of their rise and decline, extending over more than four centuries, was to coincide closely with that of their most formidable external enemies, the Hiung-nu.

The methods of Kao-ti were not those of his Han successors who, among their other measures of enlightment, opened the bureaucracy to public examination and so brought into being the dedicated civil service which was to be unparalleled elsewhere till modern times. He suspected principle and intellect alike. A rough and ready authoritarian, he saw that the rigid framework of state erected by his strong-willed predecessor was the key to his own power. But he was shrewd enough to realize that Shih-huang-ti had goaded China too fast and too far. Ruling with a more moderate degree of centralism, he quickly gained sufficient national support to face the menace once more pressing against the north-west frontiers.

The first Han attempt to grapple with the Hiung-nu, led by Kao-ti himself, was far from auspicious. It was based in the first instance on faulty intelligence. Reconnaissance reports of the outlying nomad dispositions suggested that their strength had been greatly over-estimated. Maodun's fighting men, it seemed, were modest in numbers, tattered in appearance, and poorly mounted. Relieved and encouraged by these reports, Kao-ti marched northward with an army of nearly a quarter of a million men. But the new emperor had neither Meng T'ien's tactical ability nor Maodun's cunning. And his army was almost wholly composed of infantry. The open country into which the Chinese slowly advanced was admirably suited to the swift manœuvres of the Hiung-nu horse-archers: but at the same time it was sufficiently undulating to conceal large bodies of them. Maodun had in fact hidden his main forces; and Kao-ti's scouts had failed to detect their presence.

Faced with the Chinese host, Maodun 'fled'. Inexperienced in steppe warfare, Kao-ti believed what he saw. The Hiung-nu were in retreat. Like his father, Maodun had evidently met his match. If harried with determination, he would not stop until he reached Mongolia. The Chinese army moved forward in pursuit; and the emperor himself, eager to come to grips, hurried ahead of it to the frontier town of P'ing Ch'eng, accompanied by little more than a bodyguard. Within a few hours the deserted landscape around the town was alive with hostile troopers. Looking out from the walls, Kao-ti found himself cut off from the main Chinese body by swirling masses of black, white, grey and chestnut horses – the mounts of four distinct Hiung-nu armies. With perfect timing, Maodun had turned about and sprung the trap.

For several days the emperor remained immured and impotent, with no hope of rescue from the outside. At length, however, one of his ministers, who happened to be with him, devised a means of breaking the perilous deadlock. This astute official established contact with Maodun's senior wife, and managed to play on her jealousy. Precisely how he did so is obscure; but it seems possible that he caused a suggestive picture of a Chinese girl to be smuggled into her quarters, along with a number of tempting gifts. The implication that the physical capture of Kao-ti by her husband would result in the latter's moral enslavement was not lost on the lady; and in her anxiety, she exercised her influence. Maodun withdrew his armies, denuding the surrounding country of every head of livestock and every piece of movable property that his men could load on to the backs of their remounts. The way was open for the emperor's escape.

This episode led to a significant re-thinking of Chinese policy towards the Heartland. The Great Wall had proved of little avail. And it was now clear that the Hiung-nu could no longer be thrown back by force. But where military means had failed, an appeal to nomad avarice might succeed. The *status quo* might be purchased with presents; and the stability so secured might be further reinforced by the richest gift of all: that of a Chinese princess. If Kao-ti were to give his daughter to Maodun in marriage, the Shanyu would become the emperor's son-in-law; and since he would undoubtedly make so exalted a personage his chief wife, her descendants, relatives of the Chinese imperial house, would rule the Hiung-nu into the distant future. This theoretically watertight proposal had two inherent drawbacks. The empress refused point-blank to hear of such a fate for her daughter. And in the longer term the Hiung-nu, while quite prepared to claim kinship with the Han when it suited them to do so – as it later did – were most unlikely to accept as their rulers a line of Shanyus so open to pressure from China. In principle, however, the policy of buying peace brought immediate results. Kao-ti made no further attempt to recover the frontier lands; and during Maodun's lifetime the products of the littoral Orient – silks, grain, wines, delicacies, concubines – flowed into the Mongolian grasslands in a steady stream. And with them went a princess: no beauty, but an authentic connection of the imperial family whom the emperor passed off as his daughter. The empress made no protest, and Maodun seemed satisfied. He had good reason. True, he had not evicted the first of the Han from the throne of China: but at his death in 174 B.C. he had achieved virtually all else he had set out to win.

'The Hiung-nu are not more numerous than the population of a single Chinese province. What renders them intractable is that their habits and their diet are entirely different from those of the Han; they have no desire for our things. We have sent them silk costumes; they have worn them to shreds hunting in thickets and then declared that silk was not as good as their hides. We have sent them delicacies to eat; they have found them infinitely inferior to their milk and koumiss.'

This report, submitted by a Chinese mission to the Hiung-nu shortly after Maodun's death, pointed to a perplexing problem. The new policy of keeping the nomads at arm's length by tribute had enjoyed an initial success, not least because of the dazzling novelty of much of the merchandise it had placed before their acquisitive eyes. But now that the first wonder excited by the Chinese products was wearing off, the very width of the gulf between the two societies was raising doubts as to its lasting effectiveness. As if to underline the difficulty, Maodun's successor, in the early years of his rule, abruptly broke the purchased peace in favour of traditional aggressive custom. His troopers breached the Wall in strength and surged down towards the Wei river, at one moment reaching the gates of the capital city of Ch'ang An. This time they gave way before a lively resistance; though once again, in their retreat, they skimmed off all they thought worth while from the rich areas they had overrun.

But the imperial advisers remained convinced that retaliation was no answer. The gulf in military methods between China and the Heartland was even more unbridgeable than that in daily customs. The Hiung-nu archer-cavalry, it was pointed out, could cross the steepest mountains and the swiftest rivers, push their ponies along apparently impassable defiles, survive every extreme of wind and weather; and when attacked they melted into the distance, only to thunder forward again when least expected, behind a hissing cloud of arrows. Rejecting demands for a definitive campaign, the ministers pursued their efforts to find solutions along the less risky lines of statecraft. Contacts with the nomads were used to stimulate their need for the choicest wares that China could offer in tribute and trade. And despite the dangers of the scheme, friendly nomadic tribes, kept liberally supplied, were allocated pastures in the frontier districts to absorb the shock of raids. As a crowning measure the second Han emperor, Wen-ti, achieved a treaty of coexistence with the Hiung-nu. 'All that lies north of the Great Wall,' it asserted, 'is the country of the bowmen, and is subject to the Shanyu. All that lies south of it is the country of hats and girdles, and is subject to the Chinese emperor.'

This agreement reflected the realities of the situation. Between the two great powers of eastern Asia – the riparian and littoral state of the Han, and the continental confederation of the adjoining steppes – deadlock had been reached. The strength of China – agricultural, industrial, intensive – was in almost exact balance with that of the perpetually armed, grass-based, extensive empire of the Hiung-nu. The archer-herdsmen could still raid and run, as had been their habit for nearly as long as China had existed; but the potential of resistance now stemming from her advancing economy and population rendered their ambitions of total conquest unrealizable, at least for the foreseeable future. The Chinese farmer-craftsmen, also for the time being, could buy off their fierce unpredictable neighbours: but they could not hope to destroy them.

But while the Chinese could increase their stature within their existing boundaries, the Hiung-nu could not. To their restless, warlike communities, dependent on far-flung pasturelands, human enlargement meant territorial expansion. And the power they had accumulated had inevitably produced all-round growth. Moreover, while the average tribesman might still have little use for the more exotic articles of civilized life, they had become essential to the nomad aristocracy. For they were marks of distinction, bestowed by the Shanyu and his chieftains to hold the loyalty of their subordinate rulers and generals. Silks and sauces might be unsuited to the austerities of the Mongolian steppe: but their quantitative possession was evidence of favour and standing. With the spread of empire, the demand of its hierarchy for such rewards had become insatiable.

In the east, no more territory was readily to be seized; and the amount of tribute flowing in was limited by Chinese calculation. To the west, however, in the inmost core of the continent, the prospect was different. Here, thanks to the kinder climate, the grass was richer, water more plentiful, life easier. And the farther the westward penetration, the more luxuriant the steppe became. The peoples enjoying these relatively genial zones, mostly mounted nomads like themselves, could be dispossessed and driven out. And with land secured, loot would follow.

At the risk of some repetition it may be well briefly to summarize here the position at this time in the central and western Heartland, and in their adjacent coastal zones.

The nomadic Indo-European neighbours of the Hiung-nu, the Yue-chi and the Wusun, were grazing the country to the south of the Gobi desert. West of them, in the oases scattered round the rim of the Tarim basin, other Indo-Europeans had put down their settled roots. Far to the south, beyond the Himalayan ranges, lay northern India. Here, since the times of the chariot invasions and the warring princedoms which had followed them, progressive creation of wealth had taken place, catalysed by trade with Alexandria and the Mediterranean, and fostered by the evolution of central monarchy. In 321 B.C. the warrior-king Chandragupta had founded the Mauryan empire; and less than a century later Asoka had deepened its material splendour with his great humanitarian code. Its capital Pataliputra, on the site of modern Patna, had become one of the most celebrated diplomatic and intellectual centres of the civilized world. After Asoka's death, however, and partly due to his liberal encouragement of local rule, the empire of the Mauryas had entered a period of strain and decline. Meanwhile, the steppes of the central Heartland were mainly occupied by the Sarmatian peoples, with the Sakas predominating in the pastures around Lake Balkash. Adjoining these nomadic groups lay two large littoral kingdoms: Parthia, and the Greek state of Bactria originally formed by Alexander. Both had recently profited by the misfortunes of their coastal neighbours. The break-up of the Seleucid empire had allowed the Parthians to seize Mesopotamia and to add it to their existing realm in Iran; and the eclipse of the Mauryan dynasty in India had tempted the oriental Greeks to push east and absorb the Indus valley into their domains. In the western Heartland the grass plains of south Russia were still grazed by the Scythians, while across the Black Sea in Asia Minor a number of small littoral states clustered round the crowded mosaic of palaces and markets where Europe and Asia met. In the far west, beyond the Carpathians and the Danube, the peasant manpower of Italy had been absorbed into the legions, the mortal struggle with Carthage was approaching its triumphant climax, and Rome was throwing out the wings of her power to the ends of the Mediterranean.

Such was the Eurasian scene when, about 165 B.C., the Hiung-nu launched a violent attack across the Gobi on the Yue-chi.

This was the triggering explosion which was to send a series of shock-waves to the farthest limits of the steppes, and into the coastal belt beyond them. The Yue-chi, after an initial stand, gave way and retreated towards the central Heartland. They flowed westward round the Tien Shan range, some through the Tarim basin, others through the Dzungaria passage. Beyond the mountains, in the region of Lake Balkash, they came upon the Sakas. Hounded on from behind by the Hiung-nu, the Yue-chi drove the Sakas before them towards the Jaxartes river and began to possess themselves of their pastures.

The Sakas were now in movement. Swarming across the Jaxartes they headed south round the foothills of the Pamirs. Approaching the Hindu Kush, part of the Saka horde turned west and surged against the frontiers of Parthia. The greater part, however, continued southward into Bactria. Disrupting the Greek state, driving many of its inhabitants ahead of them, they climbed the Hindu Kush and emerged through the Khyber pass into the upper Indus valley. Occupying Taxila, its capital, they moved forward again into the Ganges basin. The Mauryan empire, already in decay, was finally fragmented; and the Greek presence in the orient was scattered.

The upheaval in the central Heartland stirred other Sarmatian tribes into westward movement. Driving their herds through the grass gateway between the Urals and the Caspian, they clashed with the Scythians in southern Russia; and the Scythians in their turn, pushed towards the Danubian limits of the steppes, eventually sought admission to the Roman empire. This was refused; and in the west, for the time being, the thrust from inner Asia was contained.

Before the Saka wave had broken into India another explosion within the Heartland set a new tide in motion. The Wusun, originally neighbours of the Yue-chi, began to move west. The two peoples had been on increasingly bad terms; and now that the Yue-chi had been driven from their homelands the Wusun pursued them, with the double purpose of wiping out old grievances in blood and of seizing from them the new pastures on which they had settled. With Hiung-nu assistance, the Wusun attacked the Yue-chi in the territory around the Jaxartes which they had wrested from the Sakas only a few years before. The

Yue-chi were forced into movement again. They streamed southward into Bactria, colliding with the Sakas, mingling with them, driving them on; and the immediate effect of this new upheaval was to throw a second nomadic wave against the north-eastern frontiers of Parthia.

Parthian resistance proved more stubborn than that of Greek Bactria or India. For since their migration into Iran, the Parthians had been developing a weapon to counter the steppe pony and the compound bow. Themselves once horse-archers of the steppe, they had realized that the whirlwind onslaughts of the mounted bowmen could only be broken by a force which could stand against their arrow-storms, and advance with comparable mobility into their masses. Through their contact with the central Heartland they had undoubtedly witnessed the Sarmatian experiments with the breeding of bigger war-horses coupled with the use of primitive lances; and in the crude but revolutionary Sarmatian lancer companies they had perceived the germ of such a force.

From the magnificent Nisaean horses pastured by the old Persian kings in the rolling lands south of the Caspian, the Parthians had bred a strain of 'great horses'; chargers of unprecedented size and strength. Fed on dried alfalfa to keep up their condition the year round, these enormous animals could not only carry a lance-wielding rider encased in armour plate, but could also wear chain-mail themselves. To field this heavily armoured cavalry in significant numbers it was necessary to impose a military form on large sectors of the Parthian economy: to squeeze the towns for metals and smiths, to foster in the countryside great estates where the labour of the peasantry was devoted to breeding and maintaining the great mounts for their lordly riders. It was necessary, as well, to reorganize the Parthian army. The infantry was relegated to garrison duties, and in their place two classes of horsemen rode into battle: the barons, with the sun glinting on their armour, on their gold accoutrements, on the mail slapping the sleek sides of their gigantic horses, moving forward to halt and turn the oncoming archer hordes; and their retainers, gathered around them and equipped like their enemies as mounted bowmen, to counter-attack and pursue. This formidable answer to steppe warfare suffered from only one serious drawback: the Parthian lancer, like his Sarmatian prototype, had no stirrups, and the weight he could put behind the thrust of his lance was thus limited.

But the Parthian great horse not only stopped the momentum from the Heartland launched by the Hiung-nu. It served as a model for the later Byzantine cataphracts; and, by onward transmission, for the knights of western Europe. And as in Iran it had demanded a landed baronage for its maintenance, so in Europe the availability of the mounted knight and his retainers could only be ensured by the king's grant of the estates required for their upkeep. Between the weapon acquired by the Parthians from the steppes and the feudal system of medieval Europe there was a direct link.

Soon after their occupation of Bactria dissensions broke out among the Yue-chi, splitting them apart into a number of quarrelling tribes. Eventually, however, their ruling clan managed to reimpose order. This clan was called by the Chinese the Kwei-shuang. The name was gradually modified to Kushan; and with their unity restored, the Yue-chi as a whole became known as the Kushan. Finding their westward course barred by the Parthians, the Kushan turned east, leaving part of their people to retain their base-lands in Bactria. Crossing the Hindu Kush, they replaced the Saka dominance in the Indus basin by their own rule, then forged down the Ganges to Benares. All northern India was now theirs, as well as the large areas, stretching nearly to the Aral Sea, which they still held in Bactria. Their empire thus straddled the mountains dividing the southern Eurasian littoral from the central Heartland. And their kings, assuming the title of Maharaja, established their capital at Peshawar, whence the vital linking passes through the Hindu Kush could be controlled. One steppe people had replaced another as overlords of India.

This tremendous series of armed migrations took nearly two centuries to gather momentum and to roll, through collisions of people upon people, to the distant edges of the Heartland. As they died down, four great powers became distinguishable round the rim of continental Asia: in the west Rome, as yet virtually untouched by nomadic incursion; in the south Parthia and the new Kushan empire, both littoral states created by former steppe peoples; and in the east, China. By her slow and

painful achievement of balance with the Hiung-nu, China
had indirectly set the first of the great shock-waves in motion. But by the time the waves had reached their height, the
Hiung-nu were no longer impelling them westward from
choice. They themselves were being pushed from behind.
The pendulum of power, so long loaded in their favour, had
begun to swing.

By the middle of the second century B.C. the old China of the
northern river basins had begun to press against its boundaries.
More land was needed to feed its growing population. Economic
activity was expanding. Technical invention and financial
transaction were reaching new levels of sophistication. The
spread of industrial skills and of transport facilities was swelling
the volume of manufacture and traffic. As a result, merchants
with well-stocked warehouses and with risk capital to invest
were casting about for fresh outlets for their goods. But the sea
still could not provide a complete answer to the need for wider
trading horizons. For China, owing to her dependence on the
Yellow river, was not yet a truly littoral power. The great stream
which all along had been the main artery of her development
was subject to constant shifts and floods; and as a springboard
for seaborne commerce it was unreliable. Her growing trade
might need better access to the ocean for its ultimate fulfilment:
but in the meantime it required routes towards the west across
the landward distances of central Asia.

The Emperor Han Wu-ti, ascending the throne in 140 B.C.,
was a man for the times. Energetic, spirited, resplendent,
extravagant, he has been compared to Louis XIV. As forceful
as Shih-huang-ti or Kao-ti, he was less authoritarian than either;
for he had a faculty of choosing well, and using creatively, the
talent around him. He opened public office to examination and
so gathered into his administration educated men, normally
of Confucian background. Yet for all his lofty concern with the
principles of government, his personal interests were unortho-
dox. To the consternation of the court he would disappear to
enjoy the danger of hunting big game without attendants; and
he had a taste, perhaps equally hazardous, for the numerous
weird elixirs which, his alchemists asserted, ensured immortality. Ambitiously expansionist, he became known as the

Martial Emperor. He tried to set the face of China seaward by annexing coastal Korea; and he promoted more definite settlement of the huge living-spaces to the south tentatively opened up by Shih-huang-ti, extending Chinese colonization beyond Canton into what is now Viet-Nam.

Before Wu-ti's accession the Hiung-nu had embarked on their own expansive movement towards the south-west in search of wider and better pastures. They had already dislodged the Yue-chi, and so sparked off the upheaval in the central Heartland. Now, as the turmoil spread, their dominion was reaching into the depths of inner Asia. From their homeland in Mongolia their influence extended over a chain of allies, vassals and occupied enemies from Manchuria nearly to the Aral Sea. This posed a double challenge to the emperor's ambitions. Their presence along the Chinese frontiers was more menacing than ever; and it had been strengthened down the years by Chinese defections on a disturbing scale. These had been caused by a short-sighted article in the Chinese military code which laid down that defeated generals should be executed, and additional reprisals visited on their relatives. As defeat in the countless minor collisions with the nomads had been frequent, an alarming number of senior officers and their families had transferred their persons and allegiance from the Son of Heaven to the Shanyu. At the same time the Hiung-nu confederacy spread a hostile curtain across the Chinese path into the west.

To relieve the borderlands and to clear a path to the west, Wu-ti conceived an original plan. China would ally herself with the nomadic enemies of the Hiung-nu in the Heartland. Beyond the Gobi, the Hiung-nu were driving the Yue-chi towards the south-west. If the latter could be persuaded to turn on their pursuers, the Hiung-nu could be assaulted simultaneously from two directions: from the east by the Chinese, and from the west by the Yue-chi. The collaboration of the Yue-chi would therefore be sought. But it was one thing to propose this plan: quite another to effect it. To establish contact with the Yue-chi meant a journey of two thousand miles or more through rugged, little known territory patrolled by a highly mobile enemy; and a further difficulty was that their whereabouts was not precisely known. Whoever was sent to invite their co-operation would require exceptional resourcefulness in addition to a persuasive tongue. The man chosen was Chang K'ien, an officer of the imperial bodyguard with a high reputation for integrity, courage and athletic prowess. Taking with him a hundred men he left Ch'ang-an in 138 B.C. on his dangerous mission.

The emperor now turned to the equally formidable task of keeping the Hiung-nu at arm's length until Yue-chi collaboration should be forthcoming. As he relied in civil affairs on men of self-proved ability rather than of rank, so he picked his generals from the hard fibre of the working people. Two unusual officers were available. Wei Ching, who was placed in overall command, could scarcely have sprung from humbler origins: he was the illegitimate son of a servant girl. As a young man he had spent some years as a cattle-drover; and he was also a crack shot with a bow. These two qualities gave him a military outlook akin to that of a Hiung-nu commander. As second in command the emperor chose Wei's nephew, Huo Ch'u-ping. At the age of eighteen Huo, an outstanding horseman, had urged the incorporation into the Chinese army of strong bodies of mounted archers. Promoted to senior rank, he set about their formation.

With their forces better equipped for steppe fighting, Wei and Huo based their strategy on the methods of their Heartland enemies. Avoiding the setpiece slogging-matches of the past, they would confine themselves to swift disruptive strikes into Hiung-nu territory. They would begin by out-raiding the raiders; and if that proved effective, the pressure on the raiders' domains would be steadily increased.

Over eight momentous years their strategy succeeded beyond all expectation. Leaving the Chinese borders in 127 B.C. Wei crossed the Gobi, penetrated to the Ongun river deep in Mongolia, and did widespread damage to the Hiung-nu encampments before extricating his army more or less intact. Huo followed this up with a lightning attack on the lands within the Ordos Loop which the Hiung-nu had occupied on and off since Kao-ti's reign. His impetus drove them from the country south of the Great Wall; and heavily armed colonies of farmer-soldiers were at once established in the frontier areas he had recovered.

One day while these campaigns were still in progress, Chang K'ien arrived back from his mission to the Yue-chi. He had an extraordinary tale to tell. Soon after leaving Ch'ang-an he had fallen, as was almost inevitable, into the hands of the Hiung-nu. Accepting his fate with equanimity, he had married a Hiung-nu girl and settled down to rear a family. Only after ten years' captivity had he managed to escape with a few companions and continue his journey. He had eventually located the Yue-chi near the Oxus river, from where they were mounting their invasion of Bactria. The Yue-chi had received him courteously, but had firmly rejected the proposal he unfolded. Their forced migration had brought them to good country; better still might lie ahead; and their experiences of the Hiung-nu had not been such as to invite renewed contact. Still undaunted, Chang K'ien had remained with his nomadic hosts for a year, travelling in the Asian interior and amassing information on its geography and peoples. On his way home he had again been captured by the Hiung-nu; and once more, this time after a relatively short imprisonment, his attempts to escape had succeeded. He had been away thirteen years; and only two men out of the hundred he had taken with him now stood at his side.

He had failed to secure the alliance with the Yue-chi: but his journey had been of incalculable value. Till then, Chinese knowledge of central and western Asia had been largely based on hearsay and even legend. Thanks to Chang K'ien's carefully gathered intelligence the emperor now had an objective picture of much of the Heartland and its human occupants. Moreover, the journey had provided confirmation of the vague belief that beyond lay states and empires comparable to China in their settled, varied endeavour. Tall stories of Parthian Iran, of Asia Minor, even of Rome, began to fit into a more coherent pattern. The traveller brought back tangible evidence of advanced western societies: the alfalfa plant, the vine, and the art of making wine. With such industrious peoples the possibilities of trade might be almost unlimited. Equally important from a military viewpoint, he described with a soldier's eye for horse-flesh a superb breed of horses he had seen in the Ferghana valley, on the western slopes of the Pamirs. These animals, he reported, possessed unique speed and staying power, and their hard hooves were resistant to the roughest ground. These were the horses which were to become known as the Celestial Steeds of Ferghana. They had probably originated, like the 'great horses' of the Parthian chivalry, among the Nisaean herds of Iran, but their more pronounced Arab strain gave them a finer and lighter build. Chang K'ien was specially struck by their inexplicable habit of 'sweating blood' – a tendency now believed to have been due to the presence of a parasite in their skins. These mounts, he emphasized, would be of the greatest value to the emperor's armies.

Finally, the circumstances of Chang K'ien's second escape from the Hiung-nu aroused close interest: he had got away, he said, in the confusion resulting from dissensions among their chieftains. Such cracks in the monolithic façade of the enemy might be exploitable; and it was this that encouraged Wu-ti to strike again at the Hiung-nu without benefit of western allies.

The same two generals, uncle and nephew, now enlarged their objectives. Wei headed again for the heart of Mongolia with larger forces, while Huo set out northward from the Ordos into the borderlands between Mongolia and Manchuria, with the intention of severing contact between the Hiung-nu and their eastern allies. As before, speed and surprise paid off. Huo scattered the hastily assembled armies of the Shanyu's governor in the east, extracting a terrible toll of men and horses. And at Lake Ulan in central Mongolia Wei came upon the Shanyu himself, surrounded by a host of mounted archers stretching to the steppe horizons. Wei had with him a corps of chariots. Knowing they would be useless in the fast-moving pitched battle he could not avoid, he formed them into a defensive ring round his supplies and service troops. Then he flung his cavalry into action. All day charge and counter-charge thundered inconclusively to and fro. At length, as dusk approached, the wind increased; and raised on the wind, a furious sandstorm enveloped the bloodstained steppe, blowing into the eyes of the Hiung-nu. In a last bid for victory Wei ordered the exhausted squadrons on his flanks into an encircling charge. Blinded by clouds of sand and arrows, shot and cut to pieces, even the Hiung-nu could stand no longer. They turned and galloped from the closing trap. This time no rally followed. The rout was genuine. The Shanyu made off in a chariot behind a team of mules.

The Battle of the Sandstorm was the swansong of the chariot. The Chinese had become almost as mobile as their enemies. By adopting their methods they had severely shaken the dominance of their Heartland foes. In a few years the Hiung-nu had lost some ninety thousand fighting men, and the less staunch of their confederates were beginning to fall away. For their part the Chinese, urged on by Wu-ti's prodigality, had not spared their own casualties. Twenty thousand men were dead; and, much more serious, a hundred thousand horses. But though the Hiung-nu were far from broken, they had been cleared for the time being from the Ordos plateau and the adjoining path into the west.

Wu-ti at once sought to place a Chinese foot in the western door. His first moves were aimed at securing the natural passage-way that connects the Ordos plateau with the oases of the Tarim basin. To the north of this passage lies the Gobi and Mongolia; to the south, the Nan Shan range and Tibet. If a friendly people could be settled at the southern rim of the Gobi, they would form a convenient buffer between the Hiung-nu in Mongolia and a Chinese westward drive into the passage. The Wusun had originally grazed this region; but they had now disappeared into the west, and were driving the Yue-chi across the Oxus river. Perhaps they could be induced to return. Again Chang K'ien headed west, this time to treat with the Wusun. He was authorized to tell them that if they would return to their old pastures, the reward would be the hand of a Chinese princess for their chieftain. The Wusun proved crafty negotiators: they obtained the princess, but declined to move back. Once more Wu-ti decided to press on alone; and by 108 B.C. Chinese forces had marched into the passage and occupied Lop Nor and Turfan, the two oases at the mouth of the Tarim basin.

The emperor now lengthened his westward stride. Beyond the Tarim basin, beyond the Pamirs that formed its western boundary, lay Ferghana with its capital at Kokand. Here were the splendid horses which Chang K'ien had discovered on his first journey. The Chinese army urgently needed remounts to make good the losses sustained in the recent campaigns against the Hiung-nu. An alliance with the ruler of Ferghana would not only provide a regular supply of the best horses in the world, but would extend the Chinese presence through the length of the Tarim basin and into the central Heartland. Successive missions from Ch'ang-an approached the ruler, but all met with the same reply: under no circumstances would he part with a single horse. Finally, in an acrimonious exchange, several Chinese were murdered. Wu-ti remained inflexible in his demand. So insistent was he that it seems possible the Ferghana horses had become linked in his mind with his pursuit of immortality: such celestial steeds might ensure a swift ride to Heaven. At all events, force was now the only answer. A first Chinese army, largely composed of deliquent youths with a stiffening of gaolbirds, wound its exhausting way across the deserts and through the mountain passes, only to be quickly routed by the ruler's troops. A second of better quality, sent to replace it, laid siege to Kokand. Eventually the ruler, threatened with a rebellion of his townsfolk, gave in and admitted the Chinese to the stables. They picked out some two dozen of the finest horses, and several thousands of lesser value. As a horse-coping venture the exorbitant cost of the expedition outweighed the reward; for only a few thousand men and a thousand animals survived the long march home. But its political intentions were well fulfilled. All through the Tarim basin word spread that the Chinese had achieved their purpose; and the oases-states, hitherto carefully conciliatory to the Hiung-nu, were deeply impressed.

Meanwhile the passage from China into the Tarim basin was assuming the aspect of a heavily protected military highway. Swarms of forced labourers were extending the Great Wall from the Ordos plateau far out along the arid southern edges of the Gobi; and beyond this new line of defence against the Hiung-nu, a chain of forts was rising in the desert. The Wusun having declined to act as a human stockade, the road to the west was being sealed off from the north by masonry stretching half-way from the Yellow river to Turfan. Into the lonely spaces, wherever there was water, self-sustaining military colonies were moving. For the Chinese it was a daunting land of grey gravel, yellow sand, black basalt, white bones. The boom of the wind stirred the speech of hostile spirits; the shimmer of mirages called forth their dwellings. But behind the sheltering ramparts, between the clustered hutments of the armed settlements, trade began to plod; probing first for markets in central Asia, then reaching for the outskirts of the littoral world beyond. In 105 B.C. a Chinese ambassador was received at the borders of Iran by an imposing body of Parthian cavalry, and conducted to the throne-room of Mithradates II. Gravely, the sovereign accepted the rich silks that were laid before him; and sent back, for the emperor's diversion, an ostrich egg and a troupe of conjurors.

Chinese power was growing, the range of its influence extending. The emperor's strategy of holding back the Heartland, as it were, with his right arm while thrusting into it with his left hand had been triumphantly successful. He now felt strong enough to bring the whole problem of the Hiung-nu to a head; to offer them peace, or destruction. A mission was sent to Mongolia to propose that hostilities should cease and that the Shanyu should acknowledge Chinese sovereignty; incorporation into the empire would bring far greater benefits than could be gained by arms. The proposal was refused. Falling back on the alternative, Wu-ti began a fresh mobilization. But to his surprise and disappointment, the opening phases of the new campaign produced no great results. And then an event occurred which, though minor in itself, was ominous for the future.

A young officer called Li Ling begged permission to lead a striking column against the Hiung-nu while a more massive invasion was prepared. He required only five thousand men, and all would be infantry: he had, he said, no need of cavalry. This was strange, for Li Ling was a knowledgeable soldier; he came of a well-known service family, and was himself a distinguished horseman and archer. It was stranger still that, just when the vital role of the mounted arm in steppe warfare had been fully demonstrated, his request should be granted. He marched north, however, following Wei's route towards the Ongun river. At first things went well enough; he repulsed a force of thirty thousand Hiung-nu horsemen. But soon he was surrounded by more than twice that number. Round and round his column they rode, shooting in their arrows to wear him down. Realizing his predicament, Li Ling turned for home. The harassment steadily continued, always from a tantalizing distance. By ones and twos his men fell to the circling, thudding bows. The climax came when he was but two days' march from the shelter of the Great Wall. As his force passed through a gorge, an avalanche of boulders crashed down upon it from the surrounding hilltops. Four hundred men reached the Wall, and Li Ling was not among them.

Militarily, the episode was unimportant, though it revived sagging morale among the Hiung-nu. More damaging was its political effect in China. Under Wu-ti the influence of the cultivated Confucians had greatly increased. They already filled many of the senior posts in the government; and they tended to disapprove of war in principle. They were quick to point to Li Ling's fate as evidence of the futility of an aggressive policy towards the steppes. In the long run, moreover, the educated bureaucracy Wu-ti initiated was to develop into the permanent mandarinate; and the voice of this powerful caste was usually to be raised against military action. The frontier zones, it was repeatedly argued, were of marginal value for arable farming; it would be better to leave such unrewarding land to the nomad herdsmen. This advice ignored the brutal realities: the endless incursions spreading slaughter and ruin; the captives lashed away to slavery; the very real threat of the total conquest of metropolitan China. None the less, as the titanic struggle with the steppes continued, it was always the reverses that the mandarins recalled in urging peace at almost any price. They were often to recall the Disaster of Li Ling.

For the present, however, the westward momentum was sufficient to overcome pacifist influences. After Wu-ti's death the penetration of the Tarim basin continued. From bases in the Lop Nor district, Karashar, Kucha and Yarkand were occupied by diplomacy, treachery or force. Across the gritty wilderness, past the riven red hills of Turfan, moved supplies and troops, officials and couriers, and, indefatigably, traders. For those stationed in the deserts of the Chinese Far West, in the alternating torrid heat and numbing cold, life was lonely and comfortless. Danger hung over the rocks and dunes standing stark against the harsh light or obliterated behind curtains of whirling sand or snow. In the silent solitudes there was often little to do but mark the passage of travellers and think of home:

Thick, thick the evening snow falls on the camp gate,
The wind tears at the red banners, frozen too stiff to flap.
To the eastern gate we come to see you off
And as you go snow fills the road to the Tien Shan.
A turn of the hill, a bend of the road and you are lost to
  sight;
All that is left is the track on the snow where your horse's
  hoofs trod.[1]

But a few hundred miles to the north the Hiung-nu were
contending with more serious troubles. The delayed effects of
the Chinese offensives against them were becoming apparent.
Their prestige had suffered severely, and the confederacy was
showing increasing signs of strain. The huge losses of men and
mounts had diminished their fighting power. Their herds and
flocks, constantly chivvied and chased by the ranging Chinese
cavalry, had dwindled. And in the stress of adversity the
quarrels among their chiefs, first noted by Chang K'ien and
since fanned at every opportunity by Chinese intrigue, were
becoming more acute. In an attempt to mend their fortunes
they renewed their lunge south-westward from Mongolia,
circling round the Tarim basin towards the pastures of the
Jaxartes. This brought them into collision with the Wusun, who
at once called on the Chinese for help. At last the time had come
for a double-fronted attack, and a hundred thousand men were
dispatched in answer to the appeal. Held in a vast pincer movement between the Wusun and the Chinese, the Hiung-nu fought
savagely. Then, after several years of indecisive warfare, they
sought to break off the campaign. On the homeward march to
Mongolia their main army was caught by terrible blizzards in
the passes of the Altai mountains. In the driving snows and
freezing winds troopers and horses succumbed in masses. Drifts
and crevasses accounted for most of the rest. Only a tenth of the
Hiung-nu strength survived.

This crowning calamity brought to flash-point the strife in
the Hiung-nu leadership. Two rivals, each with a great following, claimed the Shanyu's throne. The hordes of the south, close
to the Gobi and the Ordos Loop, united round their chieftain,

[1] From Ts'en Shen, 'Snow Song', translated by Arthur Waley in 'A
Chinese Poet in Central Asia'. *History Today,* November 1951.

Khujanga. The northern tribes, between the Altai mountains and the Amur river, rallied to his brother Chirche. All Mongolia was on the verge of a civil war of unforseeable outcome. By secret diplomacy China had done her utmost to provoke the split. She now intervened openly. Her paramount interest was to secure stability on her frontiers and along her passage to the west. Peace here could be purchased by supporting Khujanga and the southern faction. China embraced Khujanga's cause.

Soon afterwards the sentries on the Wall looked down on a cloud of dust approaching from the steppes. The dust became a host of horsemen: and in their midst rode Khujanga. He was met with deference, and escorted by the emperor's household cavalry to Ch'ang-an. There he presented himself before Hsuanti, Wu-ti's great grandson. He knelt, prostrated himself, and struck his head against the floor. A Shanyu of the Hiung-nu had kowtowed to the Son of Heaven as a sign of submission. The year was 51 B.C. Five thousand miles away, at the farthest point of the Eurasian littoral, the Roman empire was emerging from the ancient republic. Caesar had invaded Britain, conquered Gaul. Two years later he would cross the Rubicon.

For Chirche, the rival claimant, northern Mongolia was no longer safe. Sooner or later his brother, with the powerful help of his new Chinese overlords, would attack him. He must move away. The old path to the south-west was blocked by the Wusun, and they had already shown their stubborn strength. So Chirche and his hordes sought a more northerly route into the west. Through the Altai range and the Dzungaria gap the massive migration of their herds and horsemen began.

Two great forces were now penetrating into the core of Asia. The Chinese were driving their imperial route westward through the Tarim basin. And farther north the displaced tribes of the Hiung-nu were spreading down from the Mongolian plateau into central Siberia, following the carpet of grass that led across the Ob and the Irtysh, past the Urals and the Caspian, to the Black Sea, and the gates of Europe. Through the oases of the southern Heartland a route of trade was being marked out between the empires of the littoral world: across the broad green belt of its middle latitudes, a military highway for the horsearchers of the steppes.

·   ·   ·   ·   ·

For some two hundred years China had been fighting for her existence against the steppes. Only behind bulwarks of blood and granite, thrown up and maintained at untold cost, had she been able to secure the respite to create her thriving state. By painful trial and error she had managed to reach equilibrium with her Heartland enemies. Then, by a series of herculean efforts, she had begun to push them back. With Khujanga's submission and Chirche's migration to the west, it seemed that at last the end of the struggle was in sight. But all that had been achieved was now to be undone.

In 48 B.C. shortly after receiving Khujanga's homage at Ch'ang-an, the emperor Hsuan-ti died. During the next fifty years the incompetence of three successive emperors brought China to the verge of ruin and the Han dynasty nearly to extinction. The weak-willed Yuan-ti allowed the intrigues of the palace eunuchs to dominate public affairs. His successor, Ch'eng-ti, pored over the books in his study and the girls in the brothels of the capital. The third, Ai-ti, passed his time with boys. Decay at the centre encouraged the growth of arbitrary power outside it. Once more the provincial aristocracy began to flourish. Eager to add to their possessions while the chance offered, owners of great estates embarked on the wholesale eviction of smaller farmers and peasants; and these, deprived of their living, had no choice but to sell themselves into serfdom. Dealers in slaves and cattle struck their bargains side by side. A revolutionary situation of mass poverty against concentrated wealth was in the making; and out of the crisis emerged a nephew of the dowager empress called Wang Mang. Nine years after the birth of Christ in the Roman province of Syria Palestina, this obscure politician had himself proclaimed emperor.

Wang Mang brought to the emergency the views of the doctrinaire political theorist who believes that only total state control can remedy social imbalance. With every humane intention he introduced sweeping reforms which took little account of human reality. He nationalized the land, confined the ownership of slaves to the government, sought to stabilize prices and interest rates. His rigid *dirigisme* quickly led him into deepening difficulties; and growing resentment of his tiresome restrictions was aggravated by bad harvests and by floods along the Yellow river which reduced starving communities to eating human flesh. Within a decade the threat of revolt was greater than ever, this time against the chaos produced by dogma.

Out beyond the north-west borderlands, Khujanga was long since dead; and the respect for China and for things Chinese that he had represented had died with him. Moreover his people, concentrated during his lifetime in the southern half of Mongolia, had expanded northward to fill the vacuum left by Chirche's departure. With the grazing-lands of all Mongolia to wander, they rapidly recovered from the disasters that had led to their subjection to China. And China, by relaxing her watchfulness at the frontiers in her slide to weakness, assisted the resurgence. The advent of Wang Mang helped it further. The host of officials required to enforce his myriad domestic interventions brought the bureaucrats to the forefront; and they, always pacifist in tendency, were glad to leave the nomads to their own devices. At the same time, Wang Mang tried to regulate the supposedly dependent Hiung-nu by measures comparable in their lack of realism to those he was imposing on the Chinese. He attempted to divide their shifting tribal pastures into fixed provinces, and then to replace their Shanyu by a Chinese puppet. Both plans inevitably failed; but, backed as they were by threats of non-existent force, they were enough to infuriate the Hiung-nu. Feeling their renewed strength, their aggressive hostility to China was swiftly rekindled. And with the spread of the old steppe spirit of delight at the prospect of predatory war, their former confederates began to rally to them again.

This had an immediate effect on the Chinese possessions in the Tarim basin. Sensing the proximity of revived nomad power in neighbouring Mongolia as against the distance and decline of China, the oasis-states trimmed their sails to the wind. Karashar broke into revolt; and from there the flame of rebellion spread round the basin. In awe of the Hiung-nu, city after city declared its independence until only Yarkand was left to maintain its ties with China. In a few decades the structure of Chinese hegemony in the eastern Heartland, so laboriously built up, had collapsed. The Hiung-nu were once more a formidable force at the threshold; and the passage to the west had caved in before the sinister reach of their influence.

In China, the rising tide of frustration duly burst its bounds. The peasant insurrection of the Red Eyebrows – so called because its partisans painted their eyebrows vermilion – swept aside such resistance as the government could muster. Their lead was followed by the urban artisans and the business interests; and in the uproar Wang Mang was pursued to the summit of a tower in the grounds of the imperial palace and there dismembered. After further civil strife, in which Ch'ang-an was severly damaged, legitimacy was restored. In A.D. 25 a Han prince, assuming the title Kuang-wu-ti, was proclaimed emperor at Loyang; and that city thereupon became the capital.

Like Charles II at the English restoration, the new Chinese monarch embodied in his magnetic public figure the universal hopes of release from a drab regime. But the problems that beset Kuang-wu-ti on his accession might well have baffled a less able and active ruler. The misrule of seventy years had not only reduced China to internal confusion. It had deprived her, through defections like those that had occurred in the Tarim basin, of nearly all her outlying possessions; and as a result her imperial stature in the Orient had crumbled. The tasks of repair and recovery were such that nearly twenty years of the new regime elapsed before the emperor could come to grips with the situation in the north-west.

By this time the nomads were exerting dangerous pressure on the zones adjacent to the Great Wall. The Hiung-nu revival had continued; and now, when called upon to reaffirm their acknowledgment of Chinese suzerainty, they rejected the demand out of hand. This ominous sign coincided with accumulating evidence that other, independent, warlike hordes were appearing in the region of the Khingan mountains in Manchuria. It looked as though the double threat could only be dispelled by a full-scale preventive war. It happened that the most experienced commander available, Ma Yuan, was in the far south, dealing with a rebellion in Indo-China. He travelled some fifteen hundred miles from Annam to the Wall. Soon, northern China was on a war footing.

At this crucial point Ma Yuan's work was done for him. The eastern Heartland was entering a period of climatic change; and in A.D. 46 a drought of exceptional severity struck the Mongolian plateau. The rivers shrank, smaller water-courses dried up, the grass withered. The desolation was aggravated by swarms of locusts settling on the wilting pastures. Cattle and horses dropped from heat and thirst until the baked brown earth was littered with rotting carcasses. Half of the Hiung-nu herds were wiped out. Hunger followed; and families lay dead around their tents and beside their beasts. In a few months the increase of decades had shrivelled away. But the drought continued for three years; and before it lifted, famine and misery had produced their usual result. Quarrels over the means of survival broke the nomads apart. As before, the split developed between north and south: between the tribes of the better watered pastures of the Altai-Amur belt, and those of the more arid areas near the Gobi. But this time the rift was far more bitter; and internecine civil war, intermittent but unending, set in between the factions. Again the Chinese supported those closest to their frontiers. Accepting the risk involved, they allowed the southern Hiung-nu to settle in the Ordos Loop as guardians of the frontier.

The Hiung-nu farther north were now in danger from two enemies. Their own kind were pressing against them from the south; and behind the southerners stood China, feeding her allies with supplies and subsidies. A third peril soon became apparent. The new nomadic movements in Manchuria became more pronounced. From the Khingan mountains horsemen began to probe their way into northern Mongolia. Gradually the numbers of the intruders increased. Gradually the Hiung-nu of the region, weakened by the long drought, fell back until some of them, filtering through the Altai range, began to debouch into Dzungaria and the steppes round Lake Balkash. The newcomers from the east were ancestors of the Mongols. The Chinese called them Sien-pi. The name was to be modified significantly on different tongues: Sien-pi – Si-pi – Sibir – Siberia. Before their relentless progress the more northerly Hiung-nu were being forced out of Mongolia, in the wake of Chirche's migration.

From the viewpoint of Loyang, these developments appeared satisfactory. The Sien-pi could be judiciously supported in their progress into northern Mongolia, though a wary eye would have to be kept on them lest they should turn south towards China. In the meantime a start could be made with the reopening of the passage to the west. By A.D. 73 the mouth of the Tarim basin was once more in Chinese hands. But beyond lay the chain of oasis-states which had thrown off Chinese rule at the time of Wang Mang. One by one they would have to be reoccupied by conquest or persuasion.

The recovery of the farther west was largely the work of Pan Chao. A man of daring courage with a cool resourceful mind, Pan Chao was one of the more remarkable figures of Chinese history. He came of an intellectual family. His brother and sister were both distinguished scholars, and as a young man he had himself embarked on a career of study. But he found himself irresistibly drawn to the hard military life of the frontiers; and by the time the army was standing at the threshold of the Tarim, he was one of its most adventurous commanders.

Ahead lay Lop Nor, the nearest of the defecting principalities; and Pan Chao was sent forward to persuade the ruler, by peaceful means if possible, to return to the Chinese fold. He was greeted respectfully on arrival; but as negotiations proceeded he noticed that the ruler's forthcoming attitude was changing to one of hesitant reserve. Taking aside the official in charge of his party, Pan Chao abruptly questioned him; and the unguarded reply betrayed the reason. An envoy from the Hiung-nu had unexpectedly appeared, and was now bivouacked on the outskirts of the town with a strong posse of troopers. Pan Chao had only some forty men with him, and he had no authority to resort to arms. But that evening, while a howling wind blew outside, drink flowed in the Chinese quarters. When his soldiers had reached a state of inspiration, Pan Chao led them out. A few, carrying drums, stole round to the back of the Hiung-nu camp. The others, armed with bows, deployed in front of it. Suddenly, above the wind, a frantic yelling and drumming arose, suggesting a surprise attack by a large hostile force. Simultaneously Pan Chao himself ran from tent to tent with a torch, setting fire to their felt sides. As the Hiung-nu stumbled out his bowmen discharged volley after volley into them, then rushed in drawing their swords. The envoy and thirty of his guards were killed on the spot, and most of the rest died in the fire. Next morning, Pan Chao silently showed the envoy's

head to the ruler. Without further ado Lop Nor renewed its
allegiance.

This was typical of Pan Chao's methods. Trusting to sheer
audacity and to his knowledge of local politics, and often with
only a handful of men behind him, he went from state to state
of the Tarim basin restoring Chinese authority. Everywhere
the Hiung-nu presence preceded and followed him, warning
rulers of the consequences of treating with him, striving to
undo his work after he had passed. To and fro he marched and
counter-marched; for several states, having been won over,
revolted again at Hiung-nu prompting, forcing him to return
and deal with the second insurrection. As he penetrated deeper
into the basin, support from home became progressively weaker.
The mandarins, alarmed by the extent of his successes, began
as usual to question the value of so much arid desert territory.
His reports to Loyang dwelt on the wealth of the oases, on
their fertile irrigated fields and lush orchards: references to the
dry wastes in between were minimized.

At length, of all the larger Tarim city-states only Karashar
remained obdurate. Summoning reserves from the nearest
garrisons, Pan Chao arrived before the town and demanded to
see the ruler. In his place the commander of the Karashar
army appeared. Pan Chao looked closely at him – and recognized the features of a Hiung-nu. To send such a man to
him was a calculated insult. In his anger Pan Chao insisted that
the ruler and all his court should attend a banquet in the Chinese
camp. On receiving the peremptory invitation a number of the
court left in haste for the surrounding hills. The rest, including
the ruler, did as they were bid. Over several courses Pan Chao
read the ruler a homily on the discourtesy of those who had
fled. As he finished speaking his men entered, tied up the guests
and took them outside. One by one, on the precise spot where
they had executed a high Chinese official some years before,
their heads were struck off. The town of Karashar was
thoroughly looted; and the district gave no further trouble.

During all this time the trickle of the Sien-pi into Mongolia
was becoming a flood. Soon the northern Hiung-nu found themselves beset on all sides. The invaders were steadily eating into
their domains from the east. Their neighbouring allies and
vassals, seeing that their power and possessions were dwindling,

turned on them to seize what they could for themselves. From the security of their pastures near the Chinese frontier, the southern Hiung-nu attacked them. Renewed drought and hunger reduced their capacity to fight back. In A.D. 87 the Sien-pi mounted a major thrust into their remaining territory. In ferocious hand-to-hand combat they seized their chieftain, carried him off, flayed him, and paraded his skin through their camps in wild celebration of their triumph. Two years later a large Chinese expeditionary force marched north to join in the general onslaught. In ever greater numbers the northern Hiung-nu moved through the Altai mountains to the safety of the plains beyond. Their empire in the eastern Heartland was tottering.

In A.D. 102, with Chinese prospects everywhere bright, Pan Chao asked permission to retire. He had been stationed in the Tarim basin for thirty years with never a sight of home, and had served three successive emperors. With the title of Protector General of the Western Regions, with honours heaped upon him, he returned to Loyang. In the last months of his life the redoubtable old pro-consul, wise in the ways of the west, briefed the younger captains who would follow him. 'Most of our colonial officials,' he told them, 'are dishonest crooks who have turned up on the frontiers because things were getting too hot for them at home. The natives, on the other hand, are like wild animals – they take fright easily, and it is hard to win their confidence. You should bear in mind the proverb that a man who opens his eyes too widely has no friends.'

Before his retirement, however, Pan Chao brought about an event significant of the results of his stewardship in the Chinese Far West. On several occasions during his administration of the Tarim he had exchanged embassies with the Kushans in India and the Parthians in Iran. In A.D. 97 he sent one of his officers, Kan Ying by name, on another visit to Parthia, instructing him to penetrate if possible to Ta-ch'in beyond. Ta-ch'in was the Roman empire; and no Chinese had set foot there. Kan Ying made his way to Iran, fulfilled his mission to the Parthians, and told them of his desire to push on farther west. The Parthians at once made difficulties. The journey, they said, was long and its dangers great. Their discouragement was so firm as to amount to virtual prohibition.

Two considerations lay behind this negative attitude. On the Parthians' western border the might of Rome was uncomfortably close. Across the Euphrates she was deeply entrenched in Syria. And now a powerful China was advancing from the east. A military link-up between them on Parthian soil was to be avoided at all costs; and any contacts which might help to precipitate it were to be prevented. Equally important was the preservation of Parthia's commercial interests. For centuries merchants from the Mediterranean had been crossing her territory to India and probing steadily deeper into central Asia. Chinese ascendancy in the southern Heartland was at length making a great trans-Asian trade route a reality. Trade of enormous value was now flowing east and west across Parthia. And the Parthians, as intermediaries, wanted no direct exchange of business information between China and Rome. Undivulged prices at either end made for bigger profits in the middle.

So Kan Ying never reached Rome. But the Parthian reaction to his plan to do so demonstrated the new stature of China as a central Asian power.

The great trans-Asian trade-route was the Silk Route.

Towards the end of the first century A.D. a general upsurge in the fortunes of the littoral world around the rim of the Heartland was approaching its peak. The empires of the coastal belt were more wealthy, more densely peopled, more powerful than ever before. In particular, two super-states stood at opposite ends of Eurasia. China's westward drive had been part of a wider policy of imperial expansion that accompanied her national growth. Now her thriving urban and commercial society was based on a population of some fifty millions, living under a system of government in which the traditional principle of absolutism had been tempered by a considerable measure of egalitarian practice. At the other end of the landmass lay the world of Rome.

The size of the Roman empire was reaching its zenith. To territories stretching from Britain to the Sahara and from the Atlantic to the Red Sea, Trajan was adding the lands north of the Danube and was thrusting towards the Caucasus and the Persian Gulf. The flood-point was approaching; and under his successor Hadrian, a change would set in. Complimenting the army of Africa after watching its manœuvres, Hadrian would underline his satisfaction with its steadiness rather than its dash: 'If you failed in anything, I would call your attention to it. If you had excelled in anything, I would remark on it. But it was the even level of your performance that pleased me.' Henceforth the emphasis was to be on consolidation and stability. The wall from the North Sea to the Solway Firth, the palisade from the Rhine to the Danube, would rise; and the task of the thirty legions, supported by an equal strength of colonial auxiliaries, would pass from conquest to the holding of the ten thousand miles of outer frontier.

Within this colossal framework lay some of the richest and most commercially energetic countries of the day; among them Asia Minor, Egypt, Gaul. The calm waters of the Mediterranean provided an ideal central arena for the passage of merchant shipping; and when not required for troop movements the great network of roads – over six thousand miles in Britain alone – assured the collection and distribution of trade over most of the surrounding land surface. As a result, a fair proportion of the massive wealth of a society liberally as well as actively minded tended to spread among its eighty million members. The fantastic ostentation of the upper classes had been stimulated by the hedonistic emperors like Caligula and Nero. But purchasing power, and the itch for acquisition, had percolated downward through the middle strata to freed slaves making up for their years of deprivation, and outward to retired soldiers building up a comfortable life in the remote provinces where they had served. Though it was held improper for the equestrian and senatorial orders to engage in trade, many in fact accumulated huge commercial fortunes; and in the great markets sheltering beneath 'the unmeasured majesty of the Roman peace' a swarm of smaller operators feverishly pursued a quick penny from import-export deals. 'I built five ships,' – so Petronius records the breathless tale of his freedman Trimalchio – 'got hold of a cargo of wine and sent it off to Rome. Every one of the ships was wrecked. Do you think I lost heart? I built some more, bigger and better. I got another cargo – wine, bacon, beans, perfumes, slaves. Fortunata did a marvellous thing: she sold all her jewellery and clothes and handed me a hundred gold pieces. That was the leaven of my fortune. I made a clear

ten million. I built a house, bought slaves and cattle. Whatever
I touched grew like a honeycomb.'

In the Roman honeycomb, oriental wares were increasingly
the rage; and to satisfy the demand for them traders looked to
the great manufacturing states of the littoral east: the Kushan
empire, and China. The Kushan empire, embracing the whole
of northern India as well as Bactria, was now one of the most
advanced regions of the world. It was the natural meeting-place
of ideas and influences stemming from Greece and Parthia,
Ceylon and south-east Asia. Its rulers, the former Yue-chi,
had been content to accept the cosmopolitan culture they had
conquered, and had themselves become fervent devotees of the
Buddhism which was the cement of its society. Brilliant and
humanitarian, the Kushan empire was also highly indus-
trialized; and Rome was its best customer. Bound for the west,
a constant stream of ships and caravans left its ports and
market-cities, carrying spices, pearls, dyes, and above all the
cotton goods for which the Indus valley was renowned.

In China, the manufacture of silk was already so old that its
precise origins were no longer remembered. Legend attributed
to the third millennium B.C. the first observation of the cater-
pillar of the mulberry-feeding moth as it ejected from its glands
the continuous thread from which it formed its cocoon; and the
realization that this thread might, with infinite care, be un-
ravelled and woven into a fabric. At first the prerogative of
reigning sovereigns, the wearing of silk had spread down through
princes and dignitaries, generals and gentlemen, to the com-
monalty. In silk special services came to be rewarded, foreign
debts settled, taxes sometimes paid. Silk components appeared
in everyday articles: in bows and musical instruments, fishing
tackle, containers, cups, padding for warm clothing. By Han
times the great silk industry, resting almost entirely on the
delicate-fingered patience of the women, was a measure of the
economic pulse of China. And to rougher foreign hands, caressing
the soft translucent rolls as the merchants' men displayed them
– silks of hues tumbling through the rainbow, silks of warp and
weft distinct in colour, silks vivid with petals and wings,
brocaded and embroidered silks, silks of damask weave – such
multifold beauty, the tangible treasure as it seemed of some
other spotless world, was irresistible.

The annexation of Syria helped to prepare the way for the influx of silk into the Roman empire, for it established a Roman-controlled terminal at the western edge of Asia. A few years later, in their disastrous attempt to push farther east, the Romans had what may have been their first glimpse of silk; for at the critical moment in the battle of Carrhae the Parthians, gaining the upper hand over the gasping legions, suddenly unfurled their great silken banners. Thereafter the demand for the new luxury grew so explosively that in A.D. 14 the Senate felt compelled to limit its social and economic impact by a decree forbidding its use by men: henceforth only women might wear it.

At first the import of silk could only be spasmodic. The tracks and staging-points in the Asian interior were still in nomad hands or within reach of their influence; and the alternative sea route was not yet practicable. But as the great Heartland eruptions of the second and first centuries B.C. settled down, and as the Chinese re-fastened their grip on the Tarim basin, organized trans-continental traffic on a regular basis became possible. True, the tight-fisted attitude of Parthia was a stumbling-block. Among the littoral powers interested in trade across Asia, she alone lacked any liberal spirit. Nationalist, militarist, and – as Kan Ying discovered – eternally suspicious, Parthia sat squarely across the routes between them, taking all she could and giving as little. Efforts were made to find a way round her territory; but her presence had to be accepted, and the protection from the steppes that she afforded in her own interest was welcome to the traders passing to and fro.

The departure-point for westbound traffic on the Silk Route was Ch'ang-an. Here the caravans assembled. Merchants and their agents supervised the loading of the animals; drivers and servants were engaged. Elaborate security measures were taken; for though the major nomad forces had been cleared from the route, attacks by prowling steppe raiders, by savage Tibetan tribesmen and by professional bandits were frequent. The wealthier merchants hired large formations of armed guards; and the smaller traders, placing themselves under the protection of the bigger men, contributed to the cost. Articles of high value like gems were concealed about their owners' clothes or sewn into blankets and the wrappings of bales. Then, slowly, the great bustling congestion would unwind into an orderly-moving procession of anything up to a thousand camels, mules, horses and yaks, with several hundred men riding and walking beside it: an ever-lengthening string extruding itself from the city, crossing the Ordos plateau and the Yellow river, heading out into the vast land-ocean of the Heartland.

For the first four hundred miles they marched in the lee of the massive Chinese defences against the Hiung-nu. On their right, as far as the eye could see, stretched the line of the Great Wall, its parapets patrolled by sentries staring out towards Mongolia and the north. They passed Kiayukuan, the last major fortress in the Wall, with its towers and gates standing between the hills; and a few miles beyond, its masonry abruptly dropping to the summit of a bluff, the end of the Wall itself. China, and her long protective arm reaching into the silence of the interior deserts, was behind them. Now there would be only isolated forts and, still farther west, outposts where little garrisons kept their lonely watch and gambled away the tedious off-duty hours. Steadily they held on towards Lop Nor, as like as not in the teeth of a sandstorm, with the stinging yellow wind driving across the flats of salt and gravel, and clawing at the serried platforms of bare red clay on either side.

At Lop Nor the route bifurcated, allowing the caravans to pass round the northern or southern edges of the Tarim basin as circumstances dictated. The northern road led through the oasis-cities of Karashar and Kucha, at the foothills of the Tien Shan range; the southern through Niya, Khotan and Yarkand. At Kashgar, near the mountain-ringed western end of the Tarim, the tracks converged again; and in this region stood the Stone Tower, marking the halfway point between Ch'ang-an and the Syrian coast. Here, Chinese personnel were exchanged for Afghans and Iranians, and the animals were rested and re-marshalled for the trek through the barrier of towering peaks that now lay ahead.

The transit of the Pamirs was a grim experience. From the Tarim the caravans toiled up, first into the freshening air of mountain meadows, then into the biting cold of the passes. Breath short, pulses pounding, eyes slitted against snowglare, hands and faces wrapped against frostbite, every man was afoot to spare the beasts struggling beneath their loads. On the narrow ledges jutting from the rock walls drivers and animals could lose their foothold and disappear, bounding and screaming, into the gorges below. Above the torrents terrified animals had to be coaxed across rickety bridges or along tree-trunks lashed together; and if these were gone, pushed, kicked and flogged through swirling shallows white with foam and ice. For three hundred miles the nightmare continued until, sick and exhausted, numbers often diminished and cargoes depleted, they stumbled downward from the Roof of the World to the upper reaches of the Oxus and, as it seemed, to another planet: to the Kushan empire, and the great caravan-city of Balkh where the trade from India, coming up through the relatively easy defiles of the Khyber, joined the route.

Moving on towards Merv, they crossed the southern fringes of the vast plains between the Pamirs and the Caspian. This was one of the natural exits from the Heartland, always open to sudden nomad forays. They would pass the tall brick battlements where Kushan fortress-troops scanned the dust-darkened horizons stretching away towards the Aral Sea. Then, climbing to the plateau of Iran, they would see the mansions, with their outlying armouries and stables and their thousands of soldier-serfs, where the barons and their giant horses guarded the steppe frontiers of Parthia. By ancient trackways between the brown bulk of the Elburz mountains and the pink deserts of central Iran, past the snow-splashed dome of Demavend, they threaded through Hecatompylos and Eckbatana, now Shahrud and Hamadan, their loads changing hands beneath the watchful eyes of a monopoly-minded state. Then the road wound down from the Iranian highlands, past Erbil squatting on its sawn-off cone of hillock, into the heats of the Tigris valley and the Syrian desert. On they trudged, often travelling at night for comfort, bells tinkling under the blazing desert stars, a long black line of crunching, grunting shapes shadowing the silvered sand, heading for the Euphrates at Hieropolis, now Menbij, passing at last from an empty burning world into the shaded, busy settlements of Roman Syria. The gates of Ch'ang-an, which they had left a year or more ago, were four thousand miles behind them: ahead, beyond the gleaming curve of the Orontes and the steep-stacked roofs of Antioch, lay the Mediterranean.

All along, the route was fraught with danger and exigency.
In winter, avalanches threatened the high passes; in the spring
snow-melt, flooded rivers would render fords impassable: in
summer, customary watering-places might dry up. Over such
enormous distances political conditions were seldom uniformly
stable: local rebellions, the advent of unfriendly rulers, reports
of unusual nomad movements all added to the problems of the
caravan-masters. To balance these factors and allow for diver-
sions, their time-tables were carefully planned and rigidly
maintained. At certain seasons, and while passing through
unsettled districts, stops during the day's march were forbidden;
and missing men and faltering beasts were often ruthlessly
abandoned. The road was well signposted with bones: its costs
and risks were high. Besides the great bolts of silk and the bales
of Indian cottons, its staple freights were necessarily those that
would yield comparably rich profits: furs and amber, dyes and
delicacies; ivory and indigo, precious stones and works of art;
olive oil and medicines, pearls and perfumes; salt and spices
and slaves. Economically, its trade was heavily weighted in
favour of the east. For despite all her power and wealth, Rome
was largely agricultural. She had relatively little of interest to
offer the sophisticated industrial states of Han China and
Kushan India in return for the imports she took from them;
and the adverse balance could only be made good by metal.
While the plethora of luxuries flowed west to Antioch and
Italy, the Roman monetary reserves, roped on the backs of the
slowly treading camel-trains, drained away through the sands
and snows of central Asia into the Orient. In its reverse direction, the Silk Route was the gold route.

5
Rebound to the West

They cut and felled, and not a man was left;
The sprawling corpses piled up into heaps.
Upon the shafts they hung the heads of men,
And in the carts they loaded up the women.
                    — TS'AI YEN, *Song of Distress*

THE great gulf across the Heartland between Orient and Occident, progressively narrowed by emperors and generals and merchants, was not to be closed.

Early in the second century A.D. cracks began to appear in the Chinese imperial structure. The northern Hiung-nu once more made their presence felt in the Tarim basin; and latent anti-Chinese feeling, fanned by their support, soon produced open rebellion in the oasis-cities that were essential to the Silk Route. In Loyang, prosperity had led to an easy pacifism; and Confucian officialdom, never slow to point to the cost of external adventure, used the prevailing complacency to renew its insistence on a 'Little China' outlook. Pan Chao was dead: but his son Pan Yung, a man of comparable fibre, was appointed Resident in the West to deal with the troublesome city-states. Repeatedly advocating strong measures, he gave an earnest warning of the consequences of indifference to the western possessions. He told the court council that to evacuate the Tarim basin was tantamount to abandoning it to the Hiung-nu. 'The day will soon come,' he went on, 'when the barbarians once again treat our frontiers with contempt and the gates of our cities have to be kept closed in broad daylight.' For the time being Pan Yung managed to shore up the position in the Chinese West. But his prophecy was to prove an understatement of the cataclysm to come.

Compared to their great forebears, the Han emperors of this

period were of poor calibre. Lethargic, and surfeited with affluence, they let the levers of power slip from their hands into those of their entourage. Government became increasingly the preserve of intriguing eunuchs, gold-digging courtesans, and a swarm of their hangers-on; and these in turn came into conflict with the permanent officials who were striving to preserve the fundamentals of the regime. In the absence of competent government, expenditure soared; partly to finance a multiplying roster of public 'services', and partly to pay for the pork-barrel politics of the court. Taxation grew progressively more burdensome, nepotism more widespread, administration more arbitrary or negligent. Within a few decades the native enterprise and industriousness of China was spiralling downwards beneath a stifling blanket of state intervention, inefficient where it was not corrupt. An opposition gathered strength, led by a Taoist sect, and aimed particularly against the degenerate excesses of the court; and in A.D. 184 revolution broke out. The generals, advancing behind the claims of rival pretenders to the throne, trampled on the hopes of the revolutionaries; law and order disappeared; and the country was once more engulfed in chaos.

As usual, the misfortune of China was the opportunity of the steppes. In the huge amphitheatre of the eastern Heartland two movements were in progress, both fraught with implications for the littoral world. The Sien-pi were continuing their westward advance across Mongolia. The basin of the Selenga and its tributaries, with its wooded hills and well-watered pastures, was in their hands. The retreat before them of the northern Hiung-nu had become a mass evacuation. The grass passage of Dzungaria and the passes of the Altai mountains were choked with their cattle and wagons as they streamed away from their homelands to escape the relentless pressure from behind. Some of their tribes, turning south in the search for new areas in which to settle, had tried to occupy the Tarim basin: hence the disturbances there that had led to Pan Yung's warning. But the main body held on into central Siberia, towards Lake Balkash and the grasslands stretching into the farther west. The Sien-pi gave them no respite. By the middle of the second century A.D. they had secured the whole of northern Mongolia, and their fore-riders were pressing through the Altai on the heels of those they had dispossessed. Other tribes could assemble no force capable of stopping them, for the collapse of the Hiung-nu confederacy had fragmented the nomads throughout the region. More immediately ominous, bands of Sien-pi troopers began to launch exploratory probes against the Chinese frontier.

Simultaneously, south of the Gobi desert, another and quite separate nomad movement was taking place in the reverse direction. About a century before, during the divisive civil wars among the Hiung-nu, China had supported the southern faction; and had afterwards permitted them to settle on the Ordos plateau, on the understanding that they would protect her frontiers against their northern relatives. Since that time the southern Hiung-nu had discharged their undertaking in good faith. They had given their great ally little trouble, and had added to the discomfiture of the northern Hiung-nu whenever the chance arose. Now, however, the spectacle of China wasting away her strength was too much for their steppe instincts. They began to plunder the Chinese borderlands. And, encouraged by the lack of resistance, they enlarged their ambitions from loot to land. To the east of the Ordos plateau lies the great rectangle of territory that forms the modern province of Shansi. Crossing the Yellow river from their legitimate pastures in the Ordos, the southern Hiung-nu took possession of this rectangle. This eastward movement more than doubled the size of their lands. Further, it placed a nomad horde, increasingly aggressive in intention, inside the Great Wall and within striking distance of the Chinese capital.

As the southern Hiung-nu had calculated, Chinese reaction to this audacious and alarming stroke was negligible. The warlords and their puppets were too preoccupied with their own machinations to take account of the mortal threat now looming over all of northern China. A general of some political capacity called Ts'ao Ts'ao was in process of seizing control of the Yellow river area, and was striving to extend his dictatorship to the whole country. But this was foiled by the appearance of two other semi-military regimes: one in the far inland districts adjoining Tibet; the other in the still underpopulated regions of the lower Yangtze river. By A.D. 220 the Han dynasty had virtually vanished in the turmoil; and for the next sixty years China was split into three kingdoms based on the north, the west and the south. Internally, the fragile web of industrial life, dependent on the infrastructure maintained by a sensitive administration, disintegrated. Outside, the unchecked nomadic waves now surging on the eastern steppes rendered the land roads into Asia impassable: their dwindling cargoes passed to the sea routes, and remained seaborne for several centuries. In the scrambles for power and the deepening dislocation they produced, warfare, disease and starvation gutted the countryside. Steadily the population fell to less than thirty millions. Eventually the superior weight of the north prevailed; and in A.D. 280 a semblance of unity was reimposed, and a new dynasty inaugurated in Loyang, by one Ssu-ma Yen whose father had been chamberlain to Ts'ao Ts'ao. But the rule of the new regime proved, if anything, worse than that which had led to the upheaval of A.D. 184. The monarchy quickly lost control to a set of even more rapacious subordinates; and while the palace plundered a desperately impoverished people, successive occupants of the throne took to murdering each other for the shadow of power. But this time there was no revolution from within. Instead there was invasion from Shansi.

Since their seizure of Shansi the southern Hiung-nu had watched and waited. Their lands had again been subject to drought, and this increased their appetite for the fleshpots of metropolitan China. They were well aware of her growing weakness: but during the period of the three kingdoms the armed regime of Ts'ao Ts'ao, with its grasp on the resources of the Yellow river basin, was too strong for military challenge. But with the further plunge into decadence under the house of Ssu-ma, they reckoned that the time had come to close in on the tremendous prize. Their first move was not without political adroitness.

In the second century B.C. Kao-ti, the first Han emperor, had presented a princess to Maodun, then Shanyu of the Hiung-nu, in the hope that a marriage between the ruling families would increase Chinese influence over their dangerous nomadic neighbours. Nothing had come of this calculation; but a precedent had been set, and the giving of Han princesses to the Hiung-nu chieftains became an intermittent custom whenever it was thought advisable to buy off their depredations with specially attractive forms of tribute. Chinese poetry of the period makes many references to the stream of tearful royal girls, jolted in crude nomad carts and escorted by uncouth troopers, disappearing one by one into the steppe horizons:

Full in her face, the desert sand; full in her hair, the wind.
Her pencilled brows have lost their black, the rouge has
melted from her cheek.[1]

The ruler of the southern Hiung-nu now sought to turn this former practice to his advantage. The earlier Shanyus were his ancestors. Therefore, he held, owing to their many intermarriages with Chinese princesses, he was a descendant of the Han on the female side. And since the Han had been submerged in the current disorders, he was the rightful heir to the imperial throne. Styling himself Liu Yuan – for Liu was one of the Han family names – he announced his claims from his headquarters in Shansi in A.D. 308. Though his logic may have been inexact, his claim, in the chaotic circumstances of the time, was perhaps not quite as outrageous as it sounded. From their many contacts with China during their period as wardens of the frontier, the chiefs of the southern Hiung-nu had become partly sinicized; and Liu Yuan was no exception. As a young man he had passed some years in China, and was familiar with its history and administrative patterns. Now, drawing on this experience, he proclaimed the birth of a new state in northern China, to be headed by himself, in which Hiung-nu and Chinese would be equal; and as an earnest of his intentions he began to replace his tribal entourage by a hierarchy of ministers and officials. At the same time, true to the steppe aspect of his character, he mobilized from his horde an army of fifty thousand mounted archers to stiffen Chinese support for his new order. Liu Yuan's revolution, however, did not mature, for he died shortly after its promulgation.

His son, Liu Ts'ung, preferred more direct methods. He also had spent his youth in China and had studied the classics; but the unlettered nomad in him had no patience with his father's elaborate political manœuvres. Moreover, he had at his side two formidable henchmen. Liu Yao, a member of the ruling clan, was an albino with the strength of a giant; bending a hundred-pound bow and raising it to his glaring red eye, he was reputed to be able to discharge the arrow through an inch of solid metal.

[1] Po Chu-I, translated by Arthur Waley.

Shih Lo, if less physically powerful, was equally uncompromising in his nomad outlook: as a child he had been kidnapped and sold into slavery in China; growing up, he had managed to steal some horses from the imperial stud, which happened to be close to his place of work; and with these as the backbone of his enterprise, he had set up as a bandit. These two barbarians, now the senior commanders of Liu Ts'ung's army, were avid to be let loose at Loyang. Soon their troopers were ranging southward towards the capital, pillaging the country round it, and cutting off its lines of supply.

At this time Loyang, despite the troubled decades it had passed through, was one of the most splendid cities in the world.[1] As well as the seat of the imperial court, it was the headquarters of the central government and the provincial administrations. Near by stood the tombs of the emperors and the most revered of the national shrines. From the palace buildings the mother-of-pearl blinds, like a battery of heliographs, caught the sunbeams and threw them across the great square outside the gates and down the length of a broad, tree-shaded avenue. Through the city ran a central boulevard, divided into three lanes. Along the outer two, one-way traffic flowed. Along the middle roadway only the emperor and the principal officers of state might drive. In the three markets more than half a million people bargained and jostled. Much of China's past and present was crowded into this stately yet seething complex a few miles south of the Yellow river.

By the spring of A.D. 311 Loyang was short of food. The nomad cavalry was tightening its grip on the market-gardens beyond the walls. Then came shocking news. The Chinese army, hastening forward to intercept Liu Ts'ung's forces, had been pulverized by Shih Lo; and the emperor's prime minister, who had taken personal command of it, had been captured. Worse, the victorious nomad general, hesitating to execute his distinguished prisoner by the common method of beheading, had had him killed by the brutal expedient of demolishing the house in which he was lodged. It was clear that contact with Chinese civilization had not changed the Hiung-nu once their lust for blood and loot had been fired. Panic broke out in the city.

---

[1] See Arthur Waley's vivid description of it in 'Loyang and its Fall', *History Today*, April 1951.

Vehicles became unobtainable. Holes for valuables were frantically dug. Family heirlooms were stuffed wherever concealment offered. It did little good. Out of the north-east four mounted armies appeared, commanded by the white-headed, red-eyed Liu Yao. The southern and eastern gates were quickly forced. Clattering ponies and yelling horsemen burst into the city, bows thudding, arrows darting; and soon the first buildings were ablaze. For two weeks the invaders had to shoot and slash their way through ferocious resistance before they gained the palace; but when they reached it a ghastly climax ensued. The emperor's guard was slaughtered in a bloody shambles, the heir to the throne struck down. The concubines of the harem were raped wherever they were found, and the empress fared little better at the hands of Liu Yao himself. The emperor, trying to escape, was seized and handed over to Liu Ts'ung, who first made him serve as his butler, then put him to death in a sudden rage. By the time the furnace that had been the palace cooled, thirty thousand Chinese were dead. Then the city was combed for plunder; homes were ransacked, government offices turned out, tombs and temples denuded of every treasure that could be carried away. The final blow was struck by Liu Yao; for with the shell of Loyang in their hands, a dispute broke out among the nomad commanders as to where their own new capital should be. Some favoured Loyang itself: others held that it was too exposed to counter-attack from other parts of China. Tiring of the argument, the albino general cut it short by burning the rest of the city to rubble.

The sack of Loyang was only the beginning of China's agony. Two hundred miles away another emperor of the Ssu-ma house was established at Ch'ang-an, the former capital and once the busy terminal of the Silk Route. For a time Ch'ang-an's defences baffled the Hiung-nu bowmen, inexperienced as they were in siegecraft. But finally they starved the city into surrender by riding in an unbroken circle, day and night, round and round its walls – as the Sarmatians had encircled Alexander's phalanx six centuries before. And in the wreckage of the city, a second Chinese emperor was set to work, this time as a scullion, before being murdered in a fit of Hiung-nu fury. Till A.D. 318 Liu Ts'ung ruled on, devoting much of his time to the satisfaction of his gargantuan sexual appetites. His son, even more debauched, was assassinated immediately on his succession: and then came the implacable generals, Liu Yao, Shih Lo and their kind, to drink and fight and kill among the ruins their armies had created. It is recorded of Shih Lo's nephew that he liked to have works of Chinese scholarship read to him, and to honour his guests at ceremonial feasts by causing a concubine to be killed and cooked for their special delight.

Meanwhile northern China was delivered over to total savagery. In the struggle to find food and avoid physical violence, the survivors of the pillaged cities took to every kind of crime and corruption. Cultivators disappeared from the fertile fields of the river valleys; and the Hiung-nu, with no interest in farming, deliberately let them grass over for pasture. Wild beasts stalked where peasants had lovingly raised their crops. Implored to prevent wolves from eating the villagers, a nomad governor merely remarked that they were starving and would desist when they were gorged. Other tribes from beyond the borders, wholly alien to China and her ways, began to push in and settle their herds on the deserted lands. Foremost among them were the Sien-pi, who came flooding down from the north to share the pickings. To defend their property, the Hiung-nu attacked them; and the once-wealthy provinces, already spoiled and stripped, became the scene of continuous chaotic warfare between the two most formidable hordes of the eastern steppes.

Crushed by repeated waves of nomad strife, flight from reality became the dominant urge in the Chinese mind. Many sought relief in the religions of detachment: in Taoism, with its indifference to daily life; and in Buddhism, introduced by travelling monks from India in the heyday of the Silk Route, with its doctrine of personal negation and its emphasis on monastic retreat. But a more practical form of escape, likewise born of the hideous times, was to become of profound significance for Chinese nationhood. As the terror raged on in the north, all who could do so gathered what was left to them and moved away. A stream of migrants headed southward, into the colonies beyond the Yangtze Kiang founded by the expansionist emperors from Shih-huang-ti onwards. The vast lands which had hitherto been inhabited by 'peaceable barbarians' with Chinese settlements scattered through them now became, and were permanently to remain, Chinese. And here, near the mouth of the Yangtze, the 'Long River', readily navigable for the greater part of its tremendous course, its arm reaching to Tibet and its fingers feeling into the deepest interior, a separate capital was established at Nanking in A.D. 318.

So it came about that the mounted archers from the steppes, invading the ancient north, ravaging the banks of the always unruly Yellow river on which it had been based, were responsible for the birth of China as a truly littoral state. She would retain her stance in the north: but henceforth she would look seaward as well, would trade across her coastal waters with the other countries of the Asian periphery, and ultimately imbue many of them with the tireless efficiency of her merchants and artisans. In that respect the Hiung-nu, the Sien-pi, and the nomadic surges that rolled upon her northern frontiers after them, were China's making. In another, they were her undoing. For eventually, when her southerly coastal civilization laid her open to seaborne penetration, she could not find the answer to intrusion from the further oceans. With her thinking attuned to centuries of conflict with the 'horse barbarians' of the steppes, she misjudged the sea-going 'red barbarians' from Europe, and the different nature of the power behind their ships.

But for the millions left along the Yellow river there was little relief for nearly a hundred years after the fall of Loyang. Then at length, from among the steppe factions still quarrelling over the northern lands, one tribe emerged supreme; and from its leading clan came a line of rulers, known as the Toba, who drove out their nomad rivals, patched up the frontier defences, and began restoring order. Men of ability, they effected a working compromise between the grassland and the sown that at least afforded security of life and limb to their shattered Chinese subjects, and allowed the long slow process of intermingling between conquerors and conquered to gather way. The first Toba monarch set up his headquarters near the Great Wall in A.D. 398. Not for two centuries after that were North and South, the old China and the new, to be united beneath a native dynasty.

A few decades after the fall of Loyang a hitherto obscure nomad people, who were an offshoot of the Hiung-nu, suddenly began to expand in the region of the Gobi desert. Among the Chinese,

preoccupied with repairing the ruin around them, their rise was
little noticed; but to the Toba rulers they were well known. The
Toba regarded them as both dangerous and repulsive. They
called them Jouen-Jouen: the writhing ones. As soon as they
were flushed out they slithered away like snakes, only to re-
appear elsewhere. And they were unusually primitive: they
could scarcely count, let alone read. These people were the
Avars; and their meteoric growth was to have profound consequences, first upon their kinsmen in the eastern Heartland
and then, by chain reaction across the steppes, on the coastal
world of Eurasia.

At different times since the second century B.C. groups of
Hiung-nu had been moving out of Mongolia towards the west.
Sometimes this movement had been voluntary; more often it
had been forced. Internal quarrels, climatic changes, pressure
from China and from other nomads had all played their part in
motivating it. As these Hiung-nu groups, mostly from the northern areas of Mongolia, successively migrated westward
beyond the Altai mountains, the record of their subsequent
wanderings becomes a blank. To all intents they vanished into
the interior spaces of the Heartland. But it seems likely that
the upsurge of the Avars about A.D. 350 drove still more Hiung-
nu into the west; and that these, pushing upon the rear of the
previous migrants, gave a final decisive westerly impulse to their
related tribes already in central Siberia.

In the western Heartland, and in Europe beyond, two great
tides of human movement had been flowing prior to the Avar
explosion. On the south Russian steppes the Scythians had been
dispersed by the more aggressive and better mounted Sarmatians. The Sarmatians had moved into eastern Europe, taking
possession of the country north of the Danube, then ensconcing
themselves and their herds in the wide grass plain of Hungary.
And from northern Europe the huge masses of the Germanic
peoples had begun to move south upon the frontiers of the
Roman empire. At first the Roman defences held against them;
and as a consequence large parts of these migrations were deflected eastward. The Gepids, the Suevi and the Vandals spilled
into Hungary and wore down the Sarmatian presence. The
Goths penetrated farther, driving into south Russia and spreading, in the reverse direction, over the lands through which the

Sarmatians had previously advanced. And owing to their contact with the Sarmatians, the Goths absorbed into their farming
culture facets of the nomadic way of life. In the grasslands
around their villages in the Ukraine they took to horse-breeding,
and became equestrians as well as farmers.

Behind the encircling frontiers erected by Hadrian in the
second century A.D. Rome had been passing through an era of
turmoil not unlike that which had led to the splitting of China
into three kingdoms. The relative liberalism of the earlier
empire had rigidified into dictatorship, which in turn had dissolved into bloody civil wars. At length, in the opening decades
of the third century, the controlled corporate economy imposed
by Septimius Severus and Caracalla had made life more secure
and more widely prosperous. But underlying this period of
ease throughout the Mediterranean world there were severe
latent stresses. As a result of comfortable living the birth-rate
began to fall; and the added toll of epidemics brought the decline
to danger-point. The demand for luxuries continued to strain
the gold reserves, and this produced repeated financial per-
plexities. The status of the wealthier provinces increased at the
expense of the central power, diluting the imperial idea with
considerations of local interest. The long dependence on slavery
had sapped energy and will. Then external events began to
buffet the creaking Roman structure. In 227 the Parthian
regime in Iran was overthrown by the Sassanid dynasty of
native origin; and the new monarchy was strongly nationalist
in outlook. In the past there had been intermittent warfare
between Rome and Parthia: now, with Sassanid vigour challeng-
ing Rome in western Asia, the old struggle flared up again more
fiercely and frequently than before. And the need for troops in
the east perilously reduced the strength of the Rhine and
Danube defences just at the time when the Germanic waves
were rolling with increasing force upon them.

It was this situation that brought the strains within the empire to breaking-point. Rome was no longer strong enough to
fight two enemies on two fronts. Where possible, it became
necessary to make terms with the barbarian tribes; to buy them
off with subsidies, and allow them to settle in the frontier districts. But as the political power had tended to move from the
centre to the periphery, so the army had become provincial

in its roots. Many of its officers and men, recruited in the countries where they served, were colonial in origin and outlook; and in the northern provinces they were defending the soil of their birth against rapacious, uncivilized invaders. In 235, resentment against the policy of compromise with the barbarians pursued by Alexander Severus burst into open revolt. The army assassinated him. This act plunged the empire into mob rule by the military. Emperors were appointed at the fancy of the soldiers, and done away with – often in murderous camp revolutions – at the first sign of divergence from the wishes of the ranks. In thirty-three years, twenty-three military dictators rose to the army's cheers, fell to its jeers or its swords. During their moments of power the more forceful among them tried to establish a cohesive plan of defence, shifting their capitals from northern Italy to the Balkans as they strove to stem the changing pattern of Germanic pressure at the borders. Far to the rear, the Roman state sucked from the public every asset that could help to keep the army in the field: taxes mounted; capital vanished; standards fell; civilian life languished.

Towards the end of the anarchic century quarrels among the tribes swarming at the frontiers afforded a temporary respite. A series of more resolute emperors seized it. Aurelian re-secured the lines of the Rhine and the Danube. Diocletian, virtually declaring a state of permanent emergency, fastened upon Roman society an enormous governmental machine with the purpose of directing the entire economy to the survival of the state and its fighting forces. Finally, Constantine accepted the geographical realities that had been overtaking the empire. Its size, and the violence of its internal conflicts, had rendered rule from Rome increasingly difficult. The city had become too distant from the wars with Persia and from the critical zones of barbarian pressure along the Danube. In trade and industry the eastern provinces had been growing in importance as those of the west declined. In 330 the wrenching adjustment was made. The capital was moved to the old Greek town of Byzantium, where the Bosphorus joins the Mediterranean to the Black Sea, and a single mile of calm water separates Europe from Asia. As China, overwhelmed by invasion, had already established a rallying-point at Nanking, so western Rome, beset by comparable enemies, sought from Constantinople to recoup her fortunes with the spirit and resources of the east. Almost impregnable yet powerfully magnetic, dismissed as a decadent rump yet continuingly vital, the great city was to hold the south-eastern approaches to Europe for over eleven hundred years. Almost from the start it felt the impact of the steppes.

One day about the year 374, so the apocryphal story goes, a mounted herdsman from within the Heartland, following a strayed heifer, splashed across the shallows of the Strait of Kerch between the Black Sea and the Sea of Azov. He was surprised to discover land beyond the strait; and still more surprised to find himself gazing upon settled villages, well-tilled fields and plentiful crops. He hurried back to tell his fellow-tribesmen; and before long a host of nomads was moving forward towards this reported paradise. The settlements were those of the easterly Ostrogoths. The nomads were the Huns.

The exact relationship between the Hiung-nu of Mongolia and the Huns who had now appeared at the gates of Europe is uncertain. No doubt they had undergone many changes during the long years and vast distances of their journeys, colliding with other nomadic peoples, raiding some, absorbing others; their own tribes collecting, discarding, interbreeding with, those of the strangers they met as they moved on into the gentler climate and more abundant pastures of the western steppes. They had destroyed the nexus of the Sarmatian group of the Alans, nomads like themselves, but armed with lances as well as bows and mounted on bigger horses; and they were now accompanied by large vassal bands of Alan cavalry. Sustaining themselves from the herds that they drove with them, but forced by numbers and the exigencies of migration to fall back on hunting and root-gathering, they were ravenous for the food and comforts of the littoral world. Soon they were swarming over the Ostrogothic settlements in the Ukraine.

The Goths had never seen such creatures. They believed them to be beasts rather than men, born of union between evil spirits and witches. Their weird features and uncouth clothing, their seeming inseparability from their horses, the waddling stumble of their gait when dismounted, above all their utter disregard of life, plunged the Germanic people into panic. 'Their swarthy aspect was fearful,' wrote Jordanes, recalling popular horror of them. They had a sort of shapeless lump, not a head, with pin-

holes rather than eyes. Short in stature, quick in bodily movement, ready in the use of bow and arrow, they had firm-set
necks which were ever erect in pride.'

The districts first attacked were swiftly overwhelmed and, to
escape extermination, one section of the Gothic population
joined the Hunnish hordes. The greater number of Goths became a river of refugees heading for central Europe, and appeared in the territory of their neighbours, the western Visigoths. Athanaric, chief of the Visigoths, prepared to stand on
the Dniester river; but he was instantly outflanked. Galloping
headlong under the moon, the Hunnish advance guards churned
through a ford a few miles upstream and fell upon his rear with a
hurricane of arrows. Resistance crumpled. Their stunned army
retreating with the crowds of homeless civilians, the Goths
streamed west towards Transylvania and the Danube frontiers of
the Roman empire. Behind them, for the time being, the horizons
remained empty of horsemen. The sheer volume of the loot
that they were already seizing had slowed down the Huns'
progress.

By 376 the north bank of the Danube was seething with
Gothic refugees pleading for permission to cross. From the
frontier, urgent requests for instructions were sent to Constantinople. At length word came that they were to be admitted.
But the Roman handling of their reception was disastrous.
The authorities were still sceptical of the tales of savage hordes
advancing from the east; and instead of regarding the Goths –
whose fighting forces were still largely intact – as allies in a
terrible emergency, the officials on the spot treated them as so
much useless flotsam. The Goths had lost everything, and many
were starving. Their plight was now made worse by Roman
arrogance and by profiteering from the sale of supplies. Their
resentment spread and deepened until a local brawl with some
legionaries sparked off riots. The riots exploded into wholesale
rebellion, and before long the Goths were rampaging through
the Balkan provinces of the empire in an orgy of massacre and
arson.

After two years of unsuccessful attempts to restore order, it
became clear that the Romans were faced with a powerful
nation in arms; and that the Goths numbered among their
supporters not only other Teutonic contingents, but even bodies

of Hun and Alan mercenaries eager for battle and plunder. With every unit he could mobilize, the Emperor Valens marched into the Balkans to destroy the main Gothic camp at Adrianople. On arrival he launched his assault at once, without waiting for reinforcements which were on their way from Italy. The flower of the Gothic army was its cavalry, descendants of the men who had learned the arts of horsemanship from the Sarmatians on the Russian steppes; but when the battle opened they happened to be some miles from the scene. Quickly mustering, they rode hard for the field. Without pausing to regroup, they thundered straight in upon the Roman flank. The impact of their powerful horses flung the wing back upon the centre, and within minutes the whole Roman army was a welter of reeling, struggling men so closely jammed together that they could not raise their weapons. The lances of the Goths, probably assisted by the arrows of their Hunnish mercenaries, did the rest. Eventually the survivors burst out into flight: but the emperor himself and all the senior Roman commanders were already dead.

This catastrophe had consequences that were to prove significant in the coming years. The Roman world had been won by the *gladius* and *pilum*, the short sword and the spear, of the infantry legions: cavalry had played only a minor role. The fate of that world was now in the balance; and it was seen that the mounted archer and the heavily-horsed lancer – the products of the steppes – were in the forefront of its assailants. Theodosius I, reorganizing the shattered army of Valens, faced the implication. Within a few years of Adrianople the greater part of the Roman army was on horseback. The mounted bowman became one of its important components; and its numbers were swelled by many thousands of Germanic lancers, recruited under their own leaders as 'federates'. The mobile weapons and warfare of the Heartland, already adopted by China and by Parthia in their struggles to contain the nomads, were being transmitted to the western littoral.

Their fighting strength temporarily broken, the Romans came to terms with their European enemies. The Visigoths were allotted lands in the Danube area; and the Ostrogoths, after further forays into Greece, were pushed north to join them, their new chief Alaric being handsomely bribed into the service of Constantinople. These arrangements were made not a moment too

soon, for reports were coming in of wild horsemen spreading
terror through the Roman territories south of the Black Sea.
Bodies of Huns had penetrated the Caucasus, and were wheeling
through Armenia into Asia Minor and Syria. Here lay some of
the wealthiest districts of the empire: provinces whose prosperous industries and farms made the arduous ride through the
mountain passes well worth while to the nomad raiding parties.
'They filled the whole earth with slaughter and panic,' wrote
St Jerome, 'as they flitted hither and thither on their swift
horses. They were at hand everywhere before they were expected. By their speed they outstripped rumour, and they took pity
neither upon religion nor rank nor age nor wailing childhood.
Those who had just begun to live found themselves facing death
and, in ignorance of their plight, would smile amid the drawn
swords of the enemy.'
Meanwhile the Hunnish strength on the Russian steppes was
accumulating. Fresh migrants were pushing west along the
grass corridor between the Urals and the Caspian, joining their
kinsmen in the grass expanses north of the Black Sea. Hitherto,
the south Russian plains had been inhabited by Indo-
Europeans: Scythians, Sarmatians, Goths. Now they were
filling up with tribes and clans from the remotest reaches of
north-eastern Asia: with men of Turkic origin, some with Mongol and even Tungus blood. Already they had seized from the
Goths lands that were glutting their stomachs and fattening
their beasts; and they were becoming aware of the far more
fabulous abundance that lay beyond these western marches of
their native Heartland.
About A.D. 400 they began to move forward into the heart of
Europe, driving along the grass passage between the Danube
and the Transylvanian alps. With the Hunnish archers and Alan
lancers went their droves of remounts, and the herds of cattle
from which they drew their living rations. They were heading
for the great pasture-reservoir of the Hungarian plain that was
to serve as their advanced base. In numbers, they were almost
certainly a mere handful compared to the manpower of the
Roman empire and of the barbarian peoples massed along its
northern borders. In many ways their equipment was inferior.
The Hunnish ponies had neither the size nor the stamina of the
stable-fed horses that the Goths possessed and that the Romans

were building into their new armies. The nomads had no siege-engines for reducing the larger cities. Until they reached Hungary they had to keep moving, for the grazings over which they passed were quickly eaten. In spring, after wintering out, the mounts were weak and their riders vulnerable. They could not operate in wooded country, where there was little grass and the trees obstructed their arrows. But their steppe tactics largely compensated for these drawbacks. They operated in small formations which could assemble and disperse at bewildering speed. Free from any desire for prestige or military honour, concerned solely with loot, they would refuse battle except when circumstances were wholly in their favour. They would scatter before powerful opposing forces, waiting until the enemy was off his guard. Then they would swiftly concentrate; launch their furious, oblique, arrow-tipped charges; dissolve into the distance again. For missiles they had javelins as well as bows. In close-quarter fighting they used nets and lariats as well as swords. Perhaps unconsciously, they also wielded psychological and political weapons. Their ferocious looks, coupled with the stories of their atrocities, were terrifying to European soldiers. They could be seen to be fighting to enrich themselves, while their opponents had often already been hounded from their homes or were conscripted semi-slaves. The cool objectivity with which they fired crops and massacred innocent bystanders, so as to leave no military resources in their rear, appeared as frightfulness. In parley, their word seemed worthless; for each tribe fought separately, without regard for the actions and undertakings of another.

The Hunnish drive stabbed into the barbarian peoples spread along the Danube. As the pressure from the Russian steppes increased they began to give way before the successive impacts; and through the opening years of the fifth century a chain reaction of the kind familiar on the steppes submerged the middle latitudes of Europe beneath a westward-moving human mass, staggering back from the Balkan frontiers of Constantinople into the western Roman empire. From their new settlements north of the Danube the Goths were once more uprooted. They recoiled upon the Vandals and the Suevi in Hungary; and these in turn, together with numbers of Alans who had found their way into the region, were harried across the Rhine into Gaul,

bursting through the Franks as they went. West Rome succeeded in deflecting the main stream of the tide away from the
approaches to Italy, forcing it round into Spain. But this served
only to create another threat to the empire; for the Vandals,
pouring through Spain and across the Strait of Gibraltar, circled
back along the African coast towards Carthage, from where
their corsairs could threaten the sea supply-routes throughout
the Mediterranean. In Portugal the Alans settled; and it was
from here that they, the steppe horsemen most adept with
lance and charger, passed on to Europe the finer points of the
war techniques from which western feudalism was later to
emerge. In the wake of these migrations the Franks and the
Burgundi crossed the Rhine as well, flooding into the ordered
Roman countryside of northern Gaul.

Amid such tremendous shocks to the fabric of the western
empire, Alaric's irruption into Rome itself was a relatively
minor episode. He had evacuated Transylvania in good time,
and was probably in search of booty rather than safety. Raiding
into Italy, he would be further from Hunnish attempts to take
from him what he seized. He seems likely to have regarded
Rome primarily as a source of supplies for his men; and he
broke into the city in 410 only after lengthy negotiations had
failed. Food stocks proved disappointingly low; Alaric soon
moved on; and though his Goths carried off much portable
property, they did little large-scale damage. And being Chris-
tians, they left the possessions of the church untouched. Compared to the holocaust at Loyang ninety-nine years before, the
act that came to symbolize a turning-point in the Western record
was a gentlemanly affair.

So far the Huns had had little direct contact with the Roman
empire. Apart from their raids into Asia Minor and their westward passage through the Danube provinces, the blows they
had inflicted on Rome in the Balkans and in Italy had been those
transmitted by the peoples they had displaced. And partly
owing to their disparate tribal system, their intermittent
relations with the Romans had often been friendly. They had
captured a disaffected Roman general and returned his severed
head to Constantinople. They had pursued a Gothic movement
into northern Italy and supported the Romans in breaking it

up. Hunnish mercenaries had become attached to the Roman forces; and some Roman commanders, as well as Gothic chiefs, had acquired Hunnish personal bodyguards. But in 408 came a southward raiding lunge into the province of Thrace, between the Danube and Constantinople. The raiders, probably at no more than tribal strength, were severely mauled: but the episode served renewed warning on the eastern empire that behind the uprooted peoples were relentless steppe invaders intent on the exaction of booty and tribute from whatever source it might be had. Constantinople turned to her defences. The landward walls of the city, facing into Europe, were massively strengthened. Plans were laid to place a river-fleet of two hundred ships on the Danube.

Meanwhile the Hunnish tribes were debouching on to the plain of Hungary, establishing their nucleus between the Theiss and the Danube, spreading out their tents and herds over the great bowl of grass encircled by the uplands of eastern Europe. Here their pastoral way of life began to mingle with the farming pattern of those among the Germanic folk, mainly Ostrogoths and Gepids, who had been content to remain in the region as their subjects. Settling down, but still nomadic in their military mobility, the Huns gradually extended their rule, largely through vassal kings, over the huge arc of northern Europe stretching from the Rhine to the Baltic and the Russian forests that their advent had thrown into turmoil. During these years of consolidation they crossed the Caucasus again and launched an attack on Persia in search of food and loot: but faced with enemies almost as adept as themselves in swiftly-moving horse-warfare, they achieved nothing and withdrew. They mounted another, and more successful, tribute-levying foray into Thrace: but except for this the Roman world of the south, preoccupied with the enormous forces of migration that the Huns had set in motion, saw little of the horse-archers from the Heartland for the best part of a generation.

During this time, however, changes were taking place in the Hunnish leadership. At the period of their first irruption into Europe the Hunnish chieftains had been vaguely identified, half mythical figures. About 420 a more clear-cut line of rulers appears; members of a single family, evidently possessed of a greater capacity to weld the independent tribal spirit about

them into a more cohesive whole. The first, Oktar, was succeeded by his brother Rua; and Rua by his two nephews who,
for a time, ruled jointly. One of these two brothers was Bleda, a
loud, good-humoured oaf. The other was Attila.

According to Roman eyewitnesses, Attila was short in
stature. His head was large, his nose flat, his eyes flecked with
grey, his complexion swarthy, his beard wispy. This suggests a
Mongoloid appearance; and he had the broad, deep chest noted
by the Chinese as common among the eastern nomads. His
posture and manner were arrogant, and he had a habit of
rolling his eyes as if to observe the effect of his presence on those
around him. At the same time he was said to be gracious in
granting favours, and faithful to the many he took under his
protection. He was monstrously vain, frequently drunk, and his
sexual appetite was insatiable. Yet as he sat among henchmen
feasting off looted gold and silver, he himself invariably dined
from plain wooden bowls. Against such a partner the simple,
rambunctious Bleda stood little chance. Eventually his brother
murdered him.

Though Attila's own interest in plunder may not have been
marked, the power that it was his passion to wield depended on
his ability to satisfy the lust for booty of the Hunnish hierarchy.
He was, essentially, a leader of rapacious warriors; and under
his command the Hungarian plain became a springboard for
squeezing the wealth from the European littoral. From 440
onwards he launched his troopers on a series of full-scale raiding
expeditions into the eastern Roman empire.

The first, shrewdly timed to coincide with the distraction
caused to Constantinople by the Vandals' capture of Carthage,
took the form of a softening-up thrust across the Danube. The
defences of Belgrade and its outlying border stations were
wrecked, and thousands of their inhabitants captured as slaves.
The blow had the desired effect: fear spread along the frontier,
and a great gap was torn in the Danube line. Two years later
came a far more powerful incursion. Driving eastward down the
Danube, the Huns destroyed the headquarters of the river
fleet, turned south to Nish where they seized a large supply of
weapons, and then, taking Sofia, headed down the valley of the
Maritsa towards Constantinople itself. One by one the cities
along the route crashed to rubble or, if difficult to invest, were

skirted. The loads of loot grew heavier, the streams of prisoners longer. Outside the capital the east Roman forces, despite their recasting since Adrianople, gave way before the arrow-storms. But on the great semicircle of the newly completed walls the Hunnish bowmen could make no impression; and at the edge of the Sea of Marmora their momentum petered out. Constantinople fell back on its diplomacy and its bullion. The price of withdrawal was agreed at six thousand pounds of gold down, and an annual tribute of two thousand more. In 447, however, Attila struck for the third time; and as he advanced, again towards Constantinople, a succession of earthquakes hit the city, causing widespread destruction and bringing down a long section of the walls. In the emergency every able-bodied man turned to. Within three months the damage had been made good and another line of defences added. But Attila avoided the capital. He was brought to battle by the last remaining troops that east Rome could muster; and though the victory was again his, the Hunnish losses were almost critical. Breaking away, his men fanned out across the lower Danube, once more ransacking the Balkans from the Black Sea to the Aegean.

In less than a decade these three irruptions sucked the life-blood from the eastern empire. Its army was decimated, its treasury depleted, its provinces drained. An understanding with Attila was essential; and in 449 a Roman mission travelled north to negotiate with him. The historian Priscus accompanied this mission; and he left a remarkable account of the Hunnish headquarters. It was a strange mixture of the nomadic and the settled: a huge palisaded village set in the featureless plains, admirably suited to cavalry defence. Among its rough hutments rose the impressive but incongruous outlines of a stone bathhouse, built by a captured Roman architect who was now serving as bath-attendant. He was not the only European in this outpost of the steppes: there were officials, craftsmen, slaves, from all over the Greek and Latin world, not least among them Attila's Italian-born secretary. As the chieftain rode into the camp he was met by groups of girls, singing and plying him with food and wine as they walked beside his horse. Later, a feast was held in the main hall of his quarters. At the centre of the room, in front of a screened dais on which stood his bed, Attila occupied a couch. Before him were two of his sons, their eyes down-

cast in apprehension. At his right sat the senior Hunnish digni-
tary present. The rest of the company took their places along the
walls, the Huns and their Roman guests interspersed. Elaborate
ceremonial toasts were drunk; and these over, the banquet was
brought in. Everything was done in Roman style: the diners
gathered round small tables, helping themselves from the great
silver trays and drinking from the massive gold cups which had,
not long before, been Roman property. Among the boisterous
gobbling throng Attila could be seen taking his simple meal
from his usual wooden bowl. The first banquet finished, the cycle
was repeated: more toasts were drunk, more looted plate
appeared heaped with a second feast. Then singers came to
chant the glories of the Hunnish arms; and in a mist of alcohol and
evocation many were moved to tears. They were cheered up,
however, by the entry of a lunatic whose gibbering filled
the hall with guffaws, and by the antics of a hideous deformed
dwarf who had been Bleda's jester. All night the torches flared;
and through the drinking and the din Attila sat on, expression-
less.

During these hours of revelry Attila may well have been
pondering his next move. The main question facing him was
probably that of where to find still more spoil quickly, and with
the lowest cost in manpower. His troopers were already affluent;
and to preserve the distinctions between them and their leaders
it was necessary to load upon the higher commanders and the
tribal heads an ever-growing quantity of material privilege.
As with the Hiung-nu chieftains before him, his need for a
perpetually increasing volume of tribute was imperative. More
might be wrung from the eastern empire, but its extraction
would be difficult and the returns diminishing. The western
empire was still untouched. He made up his mind: he would
come to terms with Constantinople, and march into the west.
Pretexts were not hard to find. There was a dispute as to the
ownership of some gold vessels from the church at Sirmium,
which Attila claimed to be his; but more important, there was
Honoria. This headstrong west Roman princess, finding herself
on the verge of a forced marriage with a worthy but uninspiring
senator, had sent Attila a secret message imploring his assistance; and had enclosed with it unmistakable tokens of devotion
to the Hun she had never seen. He now made use of this

convenient episode. He demanded Honoria as his wife, with half the west Roman empire as her dowry.

The west Romans temporized. Attila did not. Gaul, rather than Italy, was his objective; for he believed that since this province was now largely occupied by Germanic peoples driven there by the first Hunnish incursions, any resistance it offered would be weak and confused. With all available Hunnish forces, and with mounted formations drawn from the conquered peoples, he advanced through a terror-stricken Europe and crossed the Rhine near Coblentz. Wheeling left-handed in three widely separated columns, his armies fell upon nearly every centre of any size between the Rhine and the Seine. Cologne, Trier, Metz, Cambrai, Arras, Amiens, Rheims, Beauvais, were stripped of their treasure and went up in flames. Then, by-passing the little town of Paris as unrewarding, Attila made for Orleans.

In his calculation that Gaul would fail to unite against him, he was nearly right; for as he lunged south, divisive political forces were coming into play among those rallying to face him. The Visigoths, now settled in southern Gaul, began to move up to meet him under their elderly king Theodoric. And a west Roman army, commanded by Aetius, set out from Italy. Aetius was the product of an older Roman regime whose day was passing. A man of great wealth as well as a senior government servant, he was the owner of immense estates in Gaul. For some years his official task had been that of attempting to prevent the Germanic refugees from fastening too tight a grip on the province; and in discharging it he had come into repeated conflict with the Visigoths, at one point using Hunnish mercenaries against them. Moreover his duties to the state had inevitably become fused with the interests of his class; and in seeking to preserve the latter he had again used Hunnish troops to deal with rebellious serfs and slaves. In the eyes of the Visigoths, Aetius was a thoroughly doubtful ally; and they made it clear that they, and the supporting contingents about to join them, were entirely competent to repulse Attila without his help. But the fate of Orleans was now in the balance; and in the nick of time past quarrels were patched up. The leading Hunnish detachments were actually inside the city when the approach of the Visigothic banners and the Roman eagles was reported. The Huns immediately retired, for the last thing they wanted was a hand-to-hand encounter in the cramped surroundings of the town.

Falling back in search of open ground, Attila turned to face his combined pursuers in the gently contoured country of Champagne. Here, between Troyes and Chalons, at a spot known as the Catalaunian Fields, Heartland and western littoral came to grips. It was a struggle between approximate equals; for the Huns no longer had the exclusive advantage of mobility and weaponry they had once enjoyed. The Visigoths had acquired, by transmission from the Sarmatians, the heavy horse and the lance; and their army was now composed of mounted lancers. Beside them was a contingent of Alans whose central Asian fighting traditions had always been based on similar equipment. The Romans had horse-archers as well as heavy cavalry: Adrianople had impressed on them the superiority of steppe methods of combat. The issue was thus not between nimble nomad cavalry and plodding western infantry, but for the first time between two mounted hosts: between the steppe originators of cavalry warfare, and the West which was learning that warfare from them; between the speed of the mounted bowman and the weight of the horse-lancer. Neither arm had yet achieved the height of its respective powers; for it was just at this time that the stirrup, born in primitive form in India, was coming into common use in China and had not yet spread across Eurasia. The dash of the mounted archer and the thrust of the lancer were still limited by the grip that muscle could exert upon flank. Even so, a battle of furious intensity and terrible carnage raged on through the day. Attila seems to have become obsessed by the loss to the Romans of an area of sloping ground which he deemed vital; and in his determined efforts to retake it the Hunnish flank became exposed. The Visigoths, realizing this, charged the Germanic contingents opposite them, then wheeled and bore down with all the strength of their big horses into the Hunnish ponies. In the charge Theodoric was hit by a flying javelin and fell to death beneath the ponderous hooves of his squadrons. But the Huns, though far from beaten, failed to recover fully from the violence of the impact. The heavy cavalry had gained the edge.

That night Attila retreated into the ring formed by the wagon-train at his rear. He surrounded it with his archers, and prepared for a grandiose gesture in the event of disaster on the following day. At his orders a huge pile of inflammable equipment and booty was heaped up. On top of it he is said to have placed his wives, and to have declared himself ready to join them in immolation if an attempt was made to capture him. But the pyre was never lit. Aetius declined to renew the action. He was a politician first, a general second; and the extinction of the Hunnish presence in western Europe could well result in Gothic supremacy. He retired from the field, persuading his allies to do likewise. Attila's homeward route was deliberately left open.

But the tide, in any case, was ebbing. The waves first set in motion by Wu-ti and his successors had rolled across Eurasia through five thousand miles and six centuries. They had almost reached the English Channel; but now their force was spent. Attila mounted one more raid, this time into Italy. Padua and Verona fell; and Aquileia, the main city of the north-east, was utterly annihilated, its surviving population streaming away to the Adriatic shore, there, as the story goes, to found Venice. The Huns had changed the face of Europe and bled it of its treasure: but the casualties that Europe had exacted in return had sapped away the Hunnish strength. A famine in Italy further weakened Attila's men, and disease followed famine. Negotiations with an embassy led by Pope Leo I gave him the chance he sought. He agreed to withdraw; and from this arose the belief that the unarmed servant of God had saved the West from the Hunnish warlord.

The end came quickly, and with all the melodrama with which Attila had surrounded himself at the Catalaunian Fields. With his empire breaking up around him. and now an old man, he married a young Germanic girl. The following day he was found bathed in his own blood, with his terrified bride prostrate across his body. The bleeding from a burst artery had choked him. The Germanic peoples who had been his vassals soon rose against his quarrelling successors; and by 454 the remnants of the Huns were flowing back through the Carpathians, into the Heartland whence they had come.

Europe was not the only region to be ravaged. While the Huns were pillaging the Roman empire, the southern littoral of

Eurasia was under assault from the Ephthalites, a kindred steppe people.

The Ephthalites' background is uncertain. They probably stemmed from a combination of the Tarim basin peoples and the Yue-chi, with a strong admixture of Hunnish blood. The Byzantine historian Procopius, writing in the sixth century described them as 'the only ones among the Huns who have white bodies and countenances which are not ugly'; and they are sometimes known as the White Huns. Their original pasture-lands lay to the south-west of Mongolia; and just as the rise rise of the Avars may have imparted to the Huns who invaded Europe the impact that finally drove them westward, so it started the Ephthalites into movement in the direction of Persia and India.

The Persians, under their expansionist Sassanid monarchs, had wrested from the Kushan empire large parts of its domains in the region of Afghanistan; and these the Ephthalites overran. But the inner frontiers of Persia proved impenetrable; and a period of stalemate set in, during which the Persians held the Ephthalites at bay as much by duplicity as by force of arms. They promised their assailants a princess in tribute and substituted a serf girl; and after both sides had agreed not to pass a column erected to mark the frontier, the Persians moved it bodily forward, on a huge wagon hauled by elephants, to a position more favourable to themselves. To break the deadlock, one part of the Ephthalite horde turned, and headed towards India.

As in Persia the native dynasty of the Sassanids had expelled the Parthians as foreign usurpers, so in India the Gupta dynasty had risen as a movement of national resurgence against the Kushans who, like the Parthians, had originally been an alien steppe people. The Guptas now reigned in splendour over the Ganges basin, and the Kushan dominions had contracted to a few small states along the Indus. The Ephthalites quickly mopped up these Kushan provinces, then poured on along the Ganges; and by A.D. 500, within fifty years of Attila's death, they had extinguished the Gupta regime. Their conquest was accomplished with extreme ferocity. Almost every city of significance was ruined and the noble capital, Pataliputra, was reduced in population to a village. Eventually the invaders were forced back into Kashmir by a wholesale popular rising against the horrors they had perpetrated. But the lustrous fabric of northern India had been torn beyond repair. Only along the southern shores of the peninsula, distant from the savagery and nourished by seaborne trade, was continuity of life sustained.

Finally, the Ephthalites along the Persian frontier were overcome as well. Temporarily disengaging his armies from their endless wars with Constantinople, King Chosroes allied himself with another steppe people who had appeared from inner Asia. Mercilessly attacked on two sides, the Ephthalites were so completely broken that only small groups of them survived.

Their extermination marked a turning-point in the story of the steppes. The tremendous train of events tracing back to the struggles of China with the Hiung-nu were at an end. Another era was opening. For the allies of Chosroes were Turks. A new power was rising in the Heartland.

6

Blue Sky and Grey Wolf

The Turks go to war as if to a wedding.
— Venetian comment

'WHEN the Blue Sky of heaven and the dark earth beneath it were created, there were created between them the sons of men. Over the sons of men rose the Khaghans who were my ancestors. When they had become masters they governed the Turkish people and handed down their laws. They had enemies in the four corners of the world: but going against them in arms, they subjugated them and brought them peace. They caused those they conquered to bow their heads and bend their knees. They gave us for our inheritance all that lies between the Khingan mountains in the east and the Iron Gates that open towards the Oxus river in the west. All that lies between these bounds was the realm of the Blue Turks.'[1]

This inscription, on the tomb of a Turkish chieftain at Kocho Tsaidam in Mongolia, celebrates the emergence of the people who were to remain a force, first in the Heartland then in the littoral world, from the sixth century A.D. until the present day.

The origin of the Turks is still debated. The Hiung-nu are believed to have been a Turkish people, and Turkish tribes in central Asia were included in the Hiung-nu confederacy under Maodun. Iranian peoples then occupied the western Heartland, and the forebears of the Mongols its more easterly limits; and it has been suggested that the early Turks represented a mixture, differently proportioned according to locality, of Aryan and Mongolic stocks. But it has also been said that the term 'Turks' has no ethnic significance, and that the tie linking them together

[1] From V. Thomsen, 'Inscriptions de l'Orkhon', *Mémoires de la Société finno-ougrienne*, V. Helsingfors, 1896, pp. 97–98.

is confined to that of language. The distribution of the Turks across the Heartland became wide, and the differences in their appearance, as well as in their cultures, pronounced. They were later to be found not only in the steppe zones, but in regions as remote as the north-eastern coasts of Arctic Siberia. Some were fair-haired and blue-eyed, others dark and bronzed. Some were crop-growers, others pastoral nomads, yet others forest hunters. The early Turks with whom the Chinese came in contact became known to them as the Tu-chueh, from a Turkish word meaning 'strong'.

The particular group which set the Turks on the road to power was a clan bearing the name Assena. In the fifth century, finding themselves too close for their liking to the autocratic Toba sovereigns in north China, the Assena sought the protection of the Jouen-Jouen, or Avars, who then dominated Mongolia; and to remove themselves from Toba reach they migrated to the neighbourhood of a mountain in Jouen-Jouen territory. Owing to its shape this mountain was called Durko, a word which in some Turkish dialects still means 'helmet'. Its whereabouts is uncertain. Some have held that it was near the north-west frontiers of China; others that it was part of the Altai range at the western borders of Mongolia.

Under Jouen-Jouen rule these Turks pursued their traditional life-pattern, which was similar to that of the Hiung-nu. They were tent-dwelling graziers – horse nomads and mounted archers. They practised shamanism; and the reference to 'Blue' Turks in the Kocho Tsaidam inscription indicates their claim to being the chosen people of the Supreme Sky. They believed themselves to be descended from a grey wolf; and the staffs of the banners they carried in war were capped by a wolf's head fashioned in gold. From the Jouen-Jouen they adopted the titles 'Khan' and 'Khaghan' for their leaders, the former signifying chieftain or king, and the latter king of kings or emperor; and these styles subsequently came into wide use in the Heartland. The Turks of Mount Durko, however, possessed an asset rare among Heartland peoples: they were expert metal-workers, a skill they may have learnt from the craftsmen of Minusinsk, from whom the Chinese are thought to have acquired the art of working bronze. This may suggest that Durko was probably in the Altai range rather than close to

China; for Minusinsk, on the upper waters of the Yenisei, lies on the Siberian slopes of the Altai, and the region round about is rich in minerals.

As smiths, the Turks of Durko were no doubt useful to the Jouen-Jouen; and the advantages accruing from their special expertise steadily increased their prosperity. Growing strength sharpened their ambition; and about a century after their migration they were powerful enough to challenge their Jouen-Jouen masters in Mongolia. They had lent military aid to the Jouen-Jouen to help them put down rebellions among other vassals, but had been bitterly disappointed with the rewards they had received for their loyalty. Accordingly their Khaghan, who bore the same name, Toumen, as the redoubtable Shanyu of the Hiung-nu in earlier times, came to an understanding with the Toba in China, who had always detested the Jouen-Jouen. As a result the Jouen-Jouen were attacked from two sides at once. So completely were they overwhelmed that almost their entire horde was driven headlong from its pasture-lands. It was the end of the Avars in Mongolia. Their rise had been explosive; and their downfall was correspondingly catastrophic.

The Turks took possession of their territories; and about the year 522 Toumen established his headquarters on the Orkhon river in northern Mongolia. Shortly afterwards he died; and the very large areas of which he had swiftly become master were divided between his two sons. The elder, becoming chieftain of the Turks in Mongolia, took over his father's tent-capital on the Orkhon. The younger moved to the south-west, leading his horde beyond the Altai into the central Heartland, and establishing himself on the Ili river, in a region now in the Kazakh Republic of the U.S.S.R. Thus after Toumen's death the empire of the Turks came to compromise two khanates, an Eastern and a Western, with their nuclei each located not far from a great Heartland lake: for the waters of the Orkhon, joining those of the Selenga, discharge into Lake Baikal; and the Ili flows directly into Lake Balkash.

It was the Western Turks who joined forces with the Persian king Chosroes against the Ephthalites on the north-eastern marches of Iran. With the Ephthalites ground to pieces between the two armies, the victorious allies divided up their lands; and this had the effect of doubling the territories in central Asia controlled by the Western Turks. Their herds moved down from the neighbourhood of Lake Balkash to occupy the huge area of pasture and desert west of the Pamirs, and began to penetrate into the country between the twin rivers of Oxus and Jaxartes known as Transoxiana.

Between them the Eastern and Western Turks now dominated virtually the whole of the eastern half of inner Asia from Manchuria to the Persian borders; and their snowballing prestige attracted into their orbit kindred steppe peoples outside the regions directly under their sway. Well might the unknown author of Kocho Tsaidam commemorate the first swift triumphs of their leaders: within a few decades of overthrowing the Jouen-Jouen they stood at the apex of the largest confederation the Heartland had yet seen.

About 555 a new horde of warlike nomads appeared in southern Russia, between the Caspian and the Sea of Azov. There is some doubt as to whether they were remnants of the Avars or of the Ephthalites. But it seems certain that they were debris hurled across the steppe from the Turkish explosion farther east, and probable that Jouen-Jouen chiefs were among their leaders. In any case they became known in Europe as Avars. A few years after their arrival they established contact with the Emperor Justinian, who was then struggling to rebuild the Roman world after the disasters precipitated by the Huns.

It happened that Justinian had work for the Avars to do. Since he was fully occupied with the problems of reimposing his authority in Europe, the presence of a martial people prepared to act as wardens of his steppe frontiers would save manpower urgently needed elsewhere. And the eastern borders of Byzantium were at that time being threatened by the Bulgars. These were another grassland people, kinsmen of the Huns, who had drifted west in the wake of the Hunnish hordes in the fourth century. Some of them had come to rest in the Russian plains between the Volga and the Don, and had remained there. But others had penetrated into the Balkans and, shortly before, had surrounded the walls of Constantinople. There had been panic in the city; and though the Bulgars had been driven off, they were still hovering uncomfortably close to its approaches. Justinian

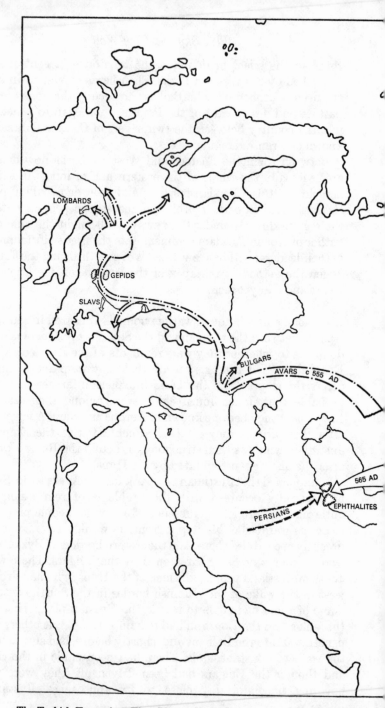

The Turkish Expansion, First Phase: Sixth Century A.D. Rise of Eastern and
Ephthalites: Turkish push into China blocked.

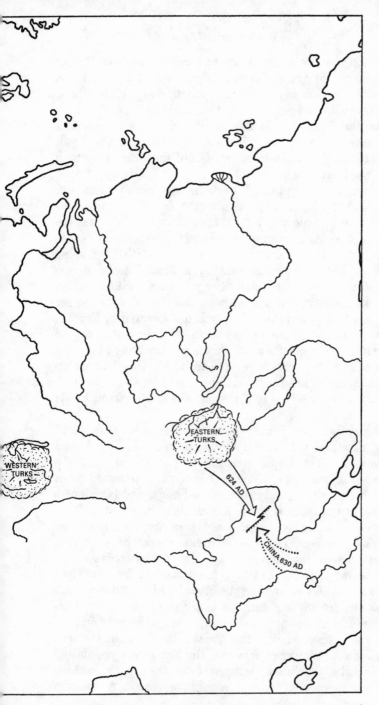

estern Turks in the Heartland: propulsion of Arabs into Europe: destruction of

engaged the services of the Avars to break up the two Bulgar
concentrations. Pursuing the double prospect of Bulgar lands
as well as Byzantine pay, the Avars punctiliously fulfilled their
undertaking. Moving north from the Caucasus foothills, they
subjected the Bulgars in Russia to their rule. Then, sweeping
across the plains to the lower Danube, they fell upon those still
in Europe, slaughtering a large number of them and absorbing
the rest into their own horde.

These operations appeared to fulfil Justinian's intention.
But actually the Avar occupation of the Don-Volga area was
short-lived, and a century later Constantinople was to see the
Bulgars again. And, more immediately, the emperor's encouragement of the Avars produced a deeper crisis. For, as so
often transpired, the recruitment by a littoral state of one
Heartland people to repulse another proved a perilous policy.
Success against the Bulgars whetted the Avars' appetite for
further conquest – and they already had a foothold in Europe.
Moreover, shortly before his death in 565, Justinian ceased
his payments to them. Soon the Avars were moving along the
channel of grass towards the west; and by 568 they had set up
their headquarters not far from the site of Attila's old capital.
The forward pasture-base of Hungary was in Heartland hands
again.

As before, fear spread through Europe. For as they advanced
the Avars collided with two Germanic peoples, the Gepids and
the Lombards. The Gepid strength was shattered; and the
Lombards, sacking and stealing as they went, were forced down
into northern Italy, already reduced to hunger and lawlessness
by the decline of Roman order. 'On all sides we see war,' Pope
Gregory the Great lamented. 'Our cities are destroyed, the
strong places razed. The blows of divine justice have no end.
Some are gone off into slavery, some left limbless, some killed.
What is there left of delight?' And the passage of the Avars had
a second effect. For some time the Slavs had been filtering into
the Balkans from their early homelands north of the Carpathians: but their movement had been confused and to
some extent checked by the great Germanic migrations.
Now, as the Avars forged forward, the Byzantine population
of the Danube provinces scattered from their path, seeking
refuge in the mountains and along the coasts. A vacuum

was created in the Balkans; and into it the Slavic tide began to flow.

While maintaining their grip on southern Russia, the Avars thrust out their tentacles from Hungary to the Alps, the Elbe and the Baltic. But in 582 their khaghan, Bayan, began a series of assaults in the direction of Constantinople. From this point on they found themselves opposed, like the Huns before them, by a defensive resilience as stubborn as their own determination. Asian horse-archers destroyed Belgrade a second time: but five years later were themselves thrown back at Adrianople. They raided into Thrace, only to have their Hungarian bases almost extinguished by a Byzantine counter-attack. They ravaged the outskirts of Constantinople, seizing a quarter of a million captives: but they could make no dent in the towering ramparts of the city. The crux came in 626 when they joined with the Persians, the old enemies of Byzantium, in an all-out attempt. The Persians lined the Asian shore of the Bosphorus: the Avars massed on the European side. Assault followed assault, with the Persians striving to cross the narrows and land in force. But the Byzantine fleet, by preventing a link-up between the besieging armies, saved the day. Crippled by their losses, the Avars crept back to Hungary with their fighting strength permanently impaired.

No longer inspiring terror, they lingered on till 791, when they were scattered for good by Charlemagne and his son Pepin. Even so, three Frankish campaigns were necessary to draw their fangs and recover their loot, and to send their chiefs to Aix-la-Chapelle to be symbolically baptized. They had entered the West as the residual flotsam of a once-powerful steppe empire, put to flight by the sudden boiling up within the Heartland of the still greater Turkish power. Yet for two generations they had been the most redoubtable presence in Europe. Few traces of their occupation have so far been found; but it seems possible that they left the western world an important military legacy.

The saddle, with its raised pommel and cantle preventing excessive forward and backward movement on horseback, and so ensuring a firmer seat for the mounted soldier, was already in use in Europe before the Avars came. But some believe it was they who transmitted from the Orient the idea of the

stirrup. If so, they revealed to the West the final major breakthrough in equestrian technique. Providing the rider with lateral
support and control, the stirrup vastly increased the horse-
archer's agility, making his fire at full gallop more deadly; and
it enabled the lancer to charge with the full weight of his mount
behind the force of his weapon. It was the long-needed device
that brought both arms of cavalry warfare to the pitch of
perfection.[1]

While these events were taking place in Europe, troubles were
besetting the two mighty Turkish khanates which had risen so
swiftly in Mongolia and central Asia. A quarrel of mortal bitterness had broken out between them. It was a weakness to which
the Turkish peoples were even more susceptible than most
steppe-dwellers: time and again fierce internal dissensions were
to frustrate the wielding of their full power. This first of their
many rifts had its roots in a dynastic dispute; but it was aggravated by the Eastern Turks' jealousy of the vast lands acquired
by their Western kinsmen after the latter's rout of the Ephthalites. And in 582 the rupture was made the more final by a
Western Turkish attempt to take over the Eastern khanate. The
two confederations split apart in permanent hostility. The
author of Kocho Tsaidam comments darkly on the parting:
'The younger brothers were not like the elder; and neither
were as their fathers before them. Khaghans without wisdom
mounted the throne; and the empire of the Turks was rent
asunder.'[2]

The Turkish quarrel produced a brief period of quiet in the
eastern Heartland. And this in turn was one of the factors which
made possible an event of supreme importance in the Orient: the
rebirth of China as a unified nation under a native emperor. For
nearly three centuries northern China had lived under Heartland
domination. But her enormous powers of assimilation had been
at work. Steadily she had absorbed her conquerors, opposing to
their aimlessness the purpose of her intelligence and the passive

---

[1] Cf. Réné Grousset, *L'Empire des Steppes,* p. 232; and for an absorb-
ing discussion of the evolution of mounted shock combat see Lynn
White Jnr., *Medieval Technology and Social Change,* Oxford University
Press, 1962, pp. 1–38.

[2] Thomsen, op.cit., pp. 98–9.

presence of her numbers. The cementing bonds of Toba government had finally cracked; and the north had become divided into two kingdoms. In 581 Yang Chien, a resolute Chinese servant of the Toba, managed to reunite them under himself; and a few years later his army brought into his orbit the southern state of Nanking, largely peopled by refugees from the nomad invasions. In 589 China emerged from her long drugged sleep with her spirit revivified, and with the colossal potential of the Yangtze valley and the south added to her stature. Yang Chien became the first of the two Sui emperors, ruling a state of the first magnitude from a restored Ch'ang-an.

With the Turks, and especially the Eastern Turks, on his doorstep in Mongolia the new emperor took no chances. He ordered the Wall to be extensively rebuilt; and his agents, circulating among the dissident clans, did their utmost to widen the existing breach between the Eastern and Western khanates. But it fell to his son, Yang-ti, to come face to face with the khaghan of the Eastern Turks and, in so doing, to realize how impressive – despite the division between Orkhon and Ili – the Turkish power still was. For their part the Mongolian Turks, eager though they might be to repeat the exploits of their Hiung-nu ancestors, had sensed that the new vitality of China demanded caution. Their immediate interests, they decided, would best be served by an act of formal homage. Accordingly, the Chinese Son of Heaven and the Turkish Viceroy of the Supreme Sky met in their respective panoplies at the edge of the open sea of the steppeland grass. The Turkish chieftain duly made obeisance: but the occasion was more in the nature of an eyeball-to-eyeball show of strength. Each sought to overawe the other. Yang-ti, giving full rein to his passion for showmanship, caused the huge circumference of his headquarters to be enclosed by a gigantic canvas curtain on which was depicted the imposing skyline of the Chinese capital. The khaghan brought with him his entire army, deploying it beneath its waving wolf-headed banners as far as sight could reach. And if China's magic could create the illusion of Ch'ang-an in the wilderness, it was equally clear that the Turks were only waiting for a change in Chinese fortunes to strike at the real thing.

The chance came, or seemed to come, when Yang-ti was overthrown in 618. His craving for splendour, added to the cost of his foreign campaigns and his grandiose public works at home, proved too much for his people. Throwing in their lot with an insurrectionary movement, the imperial guard rushed upon the emperor, stabbed his son in his presence, and then strangled him. In the ensuing disorders the Eastern Turks saw the signal they had been awaiting. In the footsteps of the Hiung-nu they swarmed into Shansi, and by 624 were approaching Ch'ang-an.

But the Turks had made a serious miscalculation. In the fourth century, when the Hiung-nu had seized Shansi and sacked Loyang, China had long been weak and decadent. Now, she was in the first flush of renewed vigour. The abrupt ending of the short-lived Sui dynasty marked a change not of national spirit, but merely of government. And the young prince who fought his way to the succession was more than a match for his steppe adversaries. He was T'ai-tsung, the first of the T'ang emperors; and his handling of the emergency at Ch'ang-an in the early years of his reign showed his quality. The unexpected sight of his advancing troops alarmed the invading Turkish forces, and the khaghan gave the order to retire. T'ai-tsung, however, did not immediately give chase. From Shansi himself, he was aware that nomad cavalry, by scattering and reforming, could often turn the tables on their pursuers. Holding on to the Turkish rear, he waited; and towards evening a torrential rainstorm came down upon the armies. Realizing its significance, he closed and charged. In the downpour and darkness the Turkish bows became unusable, and the Chinese sabres quickly turned retreat to rout.

In 626 – when the Avars were vainly battering at Constantinople – the Turks tried again. Investing Ch'ang-an with an immense body of horse-archers, they threatened its destruction unless tribute were forthcoming. T'ai-tsung was at a disadvantage, for there were few troops in the city at the time. Seeing that the issue would hinge on his personal conduct, the young emperor ordered his small garrison to emerge slowly from different gates to give the impression of solid numbers, while he himself rode ahead of them towards the Turkish ranks, alone. Within earshot he drew rein; and in the tense silence, addressing the multitude of hostile nomads in their own language, he proposed single combat. He had gauged their minds correctly. Warriors recognized a warrior. The Turkish leaders dismounted and hailed his courage. Then, as they stood by their horses' heads, and as the sparse Chinese battalions formed behind him, T'ai-tsung lectured them on the theme of honourable coexistence. Peace was concluded, and the Turks withdrew.

Four years later they made a final attempt. But in the meantime the Chinese had been busy fomenting discord among them; and T'ai-tsung now flung his full strength into the heart of their Mongolian lands. The khaghan was delivered to him by a subverted tribe, and submitted on behalf of himself and his people. 'The Turkish lords gave up their native styles and assumed Chinese titles. For fifty years they devoted to the Chinese Emperor their energy in peace and their prowess in war. To him they made over their empire and the foundations on which it stood.'[1]

In other words, the path of the Mongolian Turks from the Heartland to the littoral Orient was blocked. Any outlet for the restless Turkish energy would have to be sought in the west.

The power of the Western Turks, like that of their Eastern neighbours, was initially little diminished in spite of the quarrel between them. From their headquarters near Lake Balkash they held a huge region of central Asia decisively within their grip. Passing through on his way to India in 630, a Chinese Buddhist pilgrim left a vivid description of their khaghan and the military might that surrounded him. The felt walls of the great tent in which he sat were ornamented with shining gold, dazzling to the eye. Over his green robe a silken sash ten feet long was swathed round his body. On each side were ranged his nobles, their plaited hair falling to long coats of rich brocade. Behind them stood the archers of the bodyguard. All round the encampment the khaghan's mounted troopers, their banners moving between herds of horses beyond count, stretched to the horizon. Yet within a few months this commanding figure was dead and his following scattered. The Karlucks, one of his subordinate tribes, rose in rebellion and murdered him. Immediately, the Western Turkish khanate split up into a number of mutually hostile groups.

But if the Turks were repeatedly victims of their own endless rivalries, they were largely compensated by their extraordinary

[1] Thomsen, op.cit., p. 99.

capacity for self-perpetuation. Their fire extinguished here, it flared forth again elsewhere. Their strength reduced by inter-tribal strife in one part of the steppes, it reappeared in the expansion of kindred tribes in another. And as the power of the Western Turkish khanate succumbed to fragmentation, so corresponding Turkish power began to grow in the form of lesser, but still impressive, concentrations on the south Russian plains.

The most significant of these offshoot confederations were those of the Khazars and the Bulgars, both peoples of Turkish origin. For some centuries the Khazars had occupied lands in the region of Russia to the north of the Caucasus. Here, on the direct line of march of westward-moving hordes, they had been tossed about on the waves stirred up by the passage first of the Huns, then of the Avars. But as these waves died down, quieter conditions on the Black Sea steppes gave them a chance to flourish; and at the time when the Western khanate was breaking up round Lake Balkash the Khazars were expanding northward towards the line where the grasslands merge into the forests of central European Russia.

This northward movement brought them into contact with their distant kinsmen the Bulgars, who had been conquered by the Avars at Justinian's instigation. But the Avar power in Europe was now declining, and the Bulgars were regaining their independence. About 640, as a result of the Khazar expansion, the two peoples came together in the district where Volgograd (Stalingrad) now stands between the converging courses of the Volga and the Don. And the numbers and momentum of the Khazars had the effect of driving a wedge between the Bulgar tribes, like a ship forging into ice.

One section of the displaced Bulgar horde migrated westward and crossed the Danube. Again, Bulgars stood at the approaches to Constantinople. Their arrival happened to coincide with the prostration of the emperor, Constantine IV, by an attack of gout. It was an unhappy seizure; for his son, Justinian II, officially admitted them to the empire, and for more than three centuries, in combination with the Balkan Slavs, they intermittently harried the Byzantine capital, at one point killing the emperor, Nicephorus I, in battle and working up his skull into a drinking-bowl. Eventually, Slavicized and converted to Christianity, they were absorbed into the community of Europe. The remainder of the Bulgars, giving ground to the Khazars, moved eastward to the Volga, there to found the khanate of Great Bulgary. With a longevity rare among steppe states, it survived until the thirteenth century.

With the Bulgars divided and pushed aside, the Khazars settled down to occupy a major part of southern Russia. They had already endeared themselves to Constantinople by lending forty thousand men for the incessant Byzantine wars with Persia. Their relationship with Byzantium became firm and faithful; and this in turn progressively civilized them. Making the most of their advantageous position on the routes of water-borne trade, they became middlemen in the lucrative commerce between Europe and northern Asia. Close contact with Jewish merchants caused their leading clans, originally worshippers of the Sky, to adopt the Jewish religion. Yet relatively enlightened and advanced though the Khazars became, their realm was to prove less durable than that of their Bulgar neighbours.

The Chinese had effectively halted the drive of the Eastern Turks into their territory. But they were not now content to rest on their laurels. The long nightmare of the nomad occupation had not been without its stimulative effects. In absorbing her steppe occupiers China had drawn from them something of their own aggressiveness, hardihood, persistence. These qualities were now superimposed on her own traditional virtues, and not least on the innate sense of order which permitted the imposition of reasonable taxes for the public purpose. Moreover, from 618 onwards the old strengths and the new lay in the hands of a determined warrior-emperor. T'ai-tsung's compelling personality had greatly gained in popular esteem as a result of his bold demeanour before Ch'ang-an; and since that emergency he had built up under his command a first-rate army. In addition to an élite corps, mainly of mounted archers, always held in readiness at the capital, the Chinese forces now comprised more than six hundred thousand regulars and reservists whose liability for training and service passed from father to son. From this enormous pool of manpower the emperor could mobilize at any time a field army approaching a quarter of a million. His decision to use this instrument to carry the war into the Turkish camp well accorded with the new mood of national resurgence.

In Mongolia the Eastern Turks presented no problem. T'ai-tsung had already shown them his teeth, and they were bound to good behaviour by treaty. The reduction of the more distant Turks of the Ili-Balkash region, the successor-factions of the former Western Turkish khanate, was now his objective. As the Chinese forces moved out into the Heartland from the Ordos Loop and the shelter of the Wall,

> Waggon wheels rumbling, horses neighing shrill,
> Every man with bow and arrows carried at the waist,[1]

they seemed as if inspired again by the spirit of Wu-ti. For in the district of the Dzungarian Gap they came upon one of the dissident Turkish hordes, and the result of the encounter was less a victory than a massacre. News of the Chinese triumph spread among the other Turkish tribes in central Asia; and its effect was the same as that produced by T'ai-tsung's offer of personal combat at Ch'ang-an. Undefeated, but deeply respectful of war-like will, many of them accepted the penetration of the Chinese commanders and the demands they brought of subservience to the emperor.

There remained the crucial strategic zone of the Tarim basin, lying between China proper and her newly pacified nomad sub-jects on the Balkash steppes. Since the collapse of Chinese sov-ereignty in the fourth century, and despite more recent exposure to Turkish raids, the oasis-cities had regained much of their for-mer prosperity. Their caravan trade had brought them a meas-ure of the wealth of Byzantium and of the refinement of Sassanid Persia. They now stood at the height of their culture; a vestigial, almost nostalgic island of ancient Iranian origin, settled, polished, elegant, in a Turkish ocean. But their rulers were bound to be susceptible to the surrounding nomad pressure, and their dependability was vital to China's military lifelines and to her renascent economy. One by one Kashgar, Yarkand, Khotan, Kucha, opened their gates to T'ai-tsung as they had done to Pan Chao. In the event, this reimposition of Chinese rule in the Tarim marked the end of any independent Iranian presence in the Heartland.

By 648 the power of China seemed unchallengeable. She had already disrupted the Turks of Mongolia. She now dominated

[1] Tu Fu, 'Song of the War Chariots'.

inner Asia from the Yellow river to the Pamirs. Beyond that, her indirect rule of the vassal Turkish tribes farther west gave her control of the steppes and deserts stretching from the Ferghana valley towards the Aral Sea. In effect a gigantic arrowhead of Chinese authority, its converging sides bounded in the north by the Altai mountains and in the south by the Tibetan plateau, had been driven into the Heartland and was pointing at Persia and the Caspian. Even outside this vast triangle Chinese influence extended into Afghanistan and Kashmir.

But while T'ai-tsung's might was still moving west, a new power was on the march from the southern fringes of Eurasia. And this power, whose sudden expansive ardour was already transforming the littoral scene, was to rekindle the Turkish flame in central Asia.

So far, the seventh century A.D. had been China's century. In the arts of peace and war alike the scale and splendour of her rebirth had dwarfed the remainder of the world. No other Eurasian state, littoral or continental, could compare with her new size and energy. The greater part of India still lay beneath the ruins of the Ephthalite conquest. In the European west, though many still clutched at the straws of Roman institutions, the reality of Roman power had long been dead, submerged beneath the great Germanic migrations and the successive steppe invasions. Princes and popes were preparing for the struggle to possess its residue. Confusion and danger were magnetizing lesser men to the hope of security held out by the land and its owners: the feudal order was taking shape. Poverty and stagnation were entering their darkest phase. In many respects, certain of the nomadic peoples of the Asian interior were better off. On the western steppes the Khazar and Bulgar confederations were more than mere polarizations of primitive hordes. Under relatively stable governments they were living by peaceful trade as well as by tribute and plunder. Even the restless, acquisitive Turks of central Asia were in touch with the material benefits of both Chinese and Persian civilization. Probably at no previous time had the Heartland been in closer contact with the littoral peoples; and if this contact had sharpened its awareness of littoral weaknesses, it had also brought to many steppe-dwellers a higher standard of life.

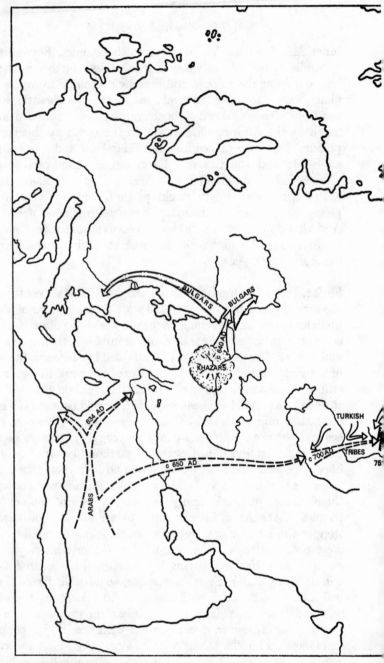

The Turkish Expansion, Second Phase: Seventh Century A.D. Expansion of Khazars
Central Asia.

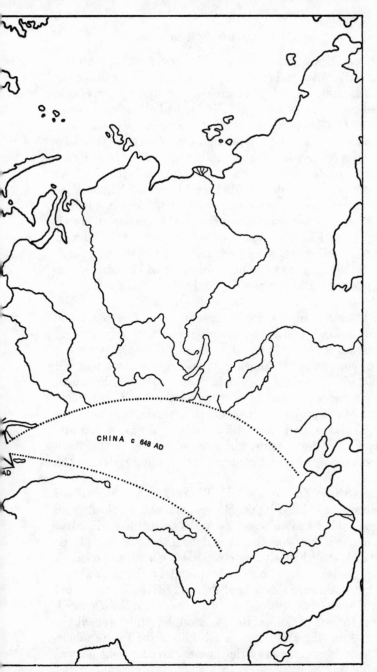

CHINA c 648 AD

opulsion of Bulgars into Europe: expanding Chinese and Arab empires meet in

In the coastal world no rivalry was more damaging than the incessant strife between Persia and Byzantium. This continuing conflict had drained their resources, preoccupied their effort, frustrated much of their economic life. It had also spread recurrent tension and destruction through the area of the Levant and Mesopotamia that formed the no-man's-land between them. In 627 the emperor, Heraclius, had finally resolved the issue by an overwhelming defeat of the Persian army on the Tigris river. At last the deadly wars between Mediterranean and Middle East were at an end. But scarcely had the two armies buried their dead than the Byzantine emperor and the Persian monarch each received an identical message. To both, in the triumph and disaster of the moment, it seemed trivial and irrelevant; for it was written in the scrawl of a little-known desert language, and it called upon them to recognize the only true God. The message was in Arabic, and its sender was Mohammed.

As with some of the great outbursts from the Heartland, the propellant behind the Arab explosion was probably that of increasing aridity in the Arabian peninsula coupled with the growth of population. Its driving forces were as much political and economic as religious; for the faith evolved by Mohammed, originally home-orientated in its social context, quickly became an instrument of imperial expansion in the hands of the bigger merchants of the Red Sea cities. As they surged across the borders of their homelands, the first objective of the Arab armies was the seizure and control of the trading system of the Levant.

This was the region over which Byzantium and Persia had been fighting for so long. Its people were thoroughly disaffected. Many were inclined to welcome the Arabs as liberators. Nor had the two empires the strength left to defend these outlying territories, which they had alternately possessed and despoiled. A few years earlier Byzantium had ultimately triumphed over Persia: but both were exhausted. Painfully Heraclius collected an army, only to see it pulverized in a blizzard on the Yarmouk river, near the Sea of Galilee, in 634. Soon the Arabs were at the frontier of Asia Minor, probing the foothills of the Taurus mountains. Almost simultaneously they were wheeling right-handed towards Persia.

At first the Persians put up a stubborn defence. In view of the losses inflicted on them by the Byzantines their commander-in-chief, Rustam, advocated delaying tactics. But a new king, the youthful Yezdegird, had recently ascended the throne; and he, filled with zest for a glorious Persian victory, overruled his cautious old marshal. At Kadasiya, near the Euphrates, Rustam's army made a spectacular stand against the Arabs behind a massed front of elephants. For three days and nights the Persians held the invaders: but then, after a furious Arab night attack, they were routed on the fourth morning and Rustam was killed. Within a few years the Arabs had forced the Zagros mountains; and a second Persian defeat at Nehavend, near Hamadan, opened the whole Iranian plateau to their victorious drive. In 651 they were at Herat, in the foothills of the Hindu Kush; and Yezdegird, the last of the Sassanid monarchs, hounded from refuge to refuge across the kingdom, was assassinated in the spreading disorder. The Arabs occupied the caravanserais of Balkh; and soon afterwards their advance parties were securing the ferry-points along the left bank of the Oxus. From here, as they stood among the willows and tamarisks lining the great river flowing quietly to the Aral Sea, they could look across into Transoxiana. They had arrived at the southern gateway to the Heartland. And the two most powerful nations of the day, the Arabs and the Chinese, were on a collision course – with the Turks of central Asia between them.

Meanwhile, the core of the mushrooming Arab empire was shifting northward from the Red Sea deserts into Syria. Disputes between the groups surrounding Mohammed's sons-in-law Ali and Othman, between the purely spiritual conception of Islam and its more imperialist expression, had finally been resolved in favour of the latter. To the expansionists, the conquered territories were now more important than Arabia; and on Ali's assassination in 661, Muawiya, the Governor of Syria, became the first of the Ummayad caliphs. The reins of power passed from Mecca to Muawiya's capital, the great trading city of Damascus.

The triumph of the party supporting an outward Arab policy was soon followed by renewed military action. Egypt had first been invaded in 639, and Alexandria captured three years later. Now the drive began through the Byzantine possessions of the North African coast towards the Straits of Gibraltar and Spain. At the same time an Arab fleet was building, to challenge the seapower of Constantinople in the eastern Mediterranean. By 673 it was in the Sea of Marmora; and until 677 the city was under annual attack from Arab vessels in the Bosphorus. But in that year came a check; for in the recent Syrian invention of Greek fire the Byzantine fleet had a new and terrifying weapon. Pots of crude oil, mixed with saltpetre to produce spontaneous combustion on impact, rained on the Arab ships. Their rigging dissolving in liquid flame, their crews hideously burnt, the Arabs withdrew.

This setback to their central spearhead, aimed at Byzantium, had the effect of reinforcing the pressure of the Arabs westward into Spain and eastward through Iran towards the Heartland. Some fifty thousand Arab families had already been settled in the huge area of Khorasan, in north-eastern Iran; and from there, in the early years of the eighth century, Arab troops mounted a new drive across the Oxus. Bukhara opened its gates to them; and soon they were penetrating through Samarkand and into the region of Tashkent. They were now beyond the Jaxartes, and in direct contact with central Asian Turkish tribes under the protection of China. Resisting the invasion of their pastures, the Turks fought back. Simultaneously they appealed to their Chinese overlords for military aid.

By this time the Chinese were once more deeply embroiled with the eastern Heartland. The Turks of Mongolia, subdued by T'ai-tsung in 630, had gathered their strength again. By the end of the seventh century they were ravaging through Shansi into the Yellow river basin; and in 706, under their ferocious leader Khapaghan, they annihilated a Chinese army on the Gobi frontier. The spirited T'ai-tsung was dead, and the succession had passed to weaker hands. Raid after raid surged down from Mongolia, staggered back beneath the weight of looted T'ang prosperity. 'Slaves became slave-owners, serfs the masters of serfs', runs the Kocho Tsaidam inscription. 'We, the Turks, had laid our plans and brought them to fruition.'[1] Taking vengeance on the Chinese, forcing outlying Turkish tribes into his imperium, spasmodically helping his compatriots to fend off the Arabs, Khapaghan nearly succeeded in reimposing unity on the Turkish peoples. But his methods were too savage even for his own harsh kind: in 716 he was ambushed by a hostile Tur-

[1] Thomsen, op.cit., p. 105.

kish band and killed. All over the Turkish Heartland chaos
followed his death; and in the rush of revolt against his domin-
eering Eastern Turks, the tribe of the Uighurs took possession
of their lands and leadership, establishing their nucleus near
Karakorum on the Orkhon river, not far from the original
Eastern Turkish capital. It was a place later to become known
and feared throughout Eurasia in other nomad hands.

While it lasted, the hegemony of the Uighurs was to prove
fortunate for China; for they were the most intelligent and
peaceable of the Turkish peoples in the eastern Heartland. But
their rule on the Orkhon was not established till 744; and in the
meantime, fully occupied with the rise and fall of Khapaghan,
the Chinese had done their best to avoid a confrontation with
the Arabs advancing into central Asia. Instead, they encouraged
the resistance of their vassal Turkish tribesmen on the spot.

None the less the clash came. It took the form of a relatively
minor brush precipitated by a piece of discreditable Chinese conduct towards the Turks. But its results were out of all proportion to its importance. The Chinese viceroy in central Asia was
Kao Hsien-chih, a general of some renown who had helped to
carry the T'ang occupation of the Far West to its farthest limits.
At the time, the district of Tashkent formed a frontier bulwark
against the Arabs, and was held by a Turkish tribe loyal to the
Chinese. Kao Hsien-chih suddenly accused the khan of Tashkent
of negligence in his military duties. The charge was made for
personal motives, and was without foundation. In spite of the
khan's vigorous denials Kao marched to Tashkent with a Chinese force, executed him, and purloined the contents of his treasury. Not unnaturally, this caused a furore among the neighbouring Turks. The murdered khan's family called upon them to
avenge the injustice, and at the same time appealed to the nearest Arab commander. Both responded. Turkish companies came
down from the north, and Arab garrisons set out from Bukhara
and Samarkand. The climax of the affair came in 751 in the
valley of the Talas, a small river in the heart of central Asia half-
way between Lake Balkash and the Jaxartes. Caught between
the Turkish and Arab forces, Kao ordered a retreat by night:
but in the darkness his troops lost touch with each other, and the
Chinese retreat became a flight. From Kao's stragglers, and from
Chinese settlers in the district, the Arabs rounded up a batch of

prisoners, among them a number of silk and paper workers. The capture of these men proved of great importance; for the subsequent presence in Persia of the silk craftsmen, with their up-to-date knowledge of sericultural methods, enabled that country to draw ahead in the trade with Europe; while the papermakers passed on their secrets just at the time when improved writing materials were vital to the spread of Arab culture.

But the economic consequences of the Talas skirmish were nothing compared to its political effects. It happened that this was only one of three military reverses sustained by China within a few months. Simultaneously, her frontiers were under barbarian attack both in Yunnan and along the Liao river in the north; and the failure of her attempts to contain these pressures, together with her undignified scuffle with the Arabs, provoked a revulsion of public feeling against colonial adventure. The fervour of resurgence under the Sui and the early Tang had worn off. Now there seemed little in sight for the average man but taxation and forced service to maintain the vast imperial perimeters.

> Over the desert I saw the sun rise,
> Under the desert I saw the sun sink:
> And to get here I travelled ten thousand leagues.
> What is fame, that we buy it with marches like this?[1]

The old cycle of contraction following expansion was at work In 755 rebellion broke out. All the domains in central Asia, acquired with such exertion by T'ai-tsung, were evacuated. At home the T'ang regime was shored up less by its friends within China than by – of all people – the Uighur Turks of Mongolia. Foreseeing the debt his support in the crisis would create, their khaghan brought a host of his horse-archers down to Ch'ang-an. For nearly a hundred years, until their own homelands were taken over by rival Turkish hordes, the Uighurs maintained the Tang in power.

Although they were ultimately unable to stem the slide of China into another period of disintegration, the Uighurs benefited greatly from their timely intervention. Chinese princesses and material gifts of every kind were showered upon them. And their khaghan's presence in Ch'ang-an also had a strange

[1] Ts'en Shen, translated by Arthur Waley.

religious outcome. While in the city he met a missionary of the Manichaean faith – the curious blend of Mazdaism and Christianity which had arisen in Persia some five centuries earlier. The khaghan adopted this faith, and on his return to Mongolia made it the official religion of his people. Among its tenets was a ban on the consumption of butter and milk, two of the staple foods of pastoral nomads. Accordingly, a fair number of Uighurs turned from grazing to crop-growing. A more settled life heightened their native intelligence. Literacy followed: and the Uighurs became the scribes, clerks and teachers of the Heartland, the founders of Turkish literature and the confidential advisers of steppe governments.

After Talas the Arabs' penetration of central Asia lost its impetus. On all fronts their military effort was passing its zenith. In 717 they had made another, and more determined, attempt to capture Constantinople; and once more they were frustrated, this time by the resolute defence organized by Leo III the Isaurian, the greatest of Byzantine soldier-emperors. And in 733 their westerly spearhead, feeling its way through the Pyrenees into France, was blunted at Tours by Charles Martel. Their conception of a huge trading empire, knitting the sea routes of the Mediterranean and the land routes of Asia into a single system, was dimming. But if the Mediterranean was proving stubborn, they would at least secure firm control of Asian commerce by consolidating their position in Persia. This shift of emphasis towards the east was reflected in another change in the Arab leadership, and in the location of its headquarters. At about the time of Talas, the Ummayad regime was overthrown. The caliphate passed to a new dynasty, that of the Abbasids; and the capital was moved from Damascus to Baghdad. Baghdad lay close to Persia, and the Abbasids themselves had close connections with its wealthy eastern region of Khorasan. The effect of these events was to magnetize the military and political, as well as the cultural, thinking of the Arabs in the direction of the Iranian plateau. In pursuit of their landward economic goals they now pushed their commercial settlements up to the Black Sea and the Caucasus. Already, under the Ummayads, they had entrenched themselves beyond the Oxus: during the reign of the Abbasid Haroun al-Rashid, 786–804, they reached out to Kabul and Peshawar and advanced in greater strength through Transoxiana to the Jaxartes. Soon their existing garrisons at the door of the Turkish Heartland were reinforced by more permanent trading communities.

At this time, under the stately Persianized sophistication of the Abbasid court at Baghdad, the Arabs reached the summit of their intellectual achievement. But at the far-off frontiers of their empire the process of recession was inexorably at work. The consolidation in the east only served to undermine further their hold on the west. With an undefeated Constantinople on the northern flank, their maritime colonies of the Mediterranean could not be adequately controlled from continental Baghdad. One by one Spain, North Africa, Egypt, fell away. Then the symptoms of weakness appeared in Persia itself. In the northeast, on the verges of the Heartland, the powerful local family of the Samenids took over the city of Bukhara in 875; and, while carefully maintaining a respectful posture towards Baghdad, claimed sovereignty over the whole region between the Caspian and the Jaxartes – much of it grazed by Turkish tribes. Then another Persian family, that of the Bouids, seized control of western Iran. While retaining its attachment to the Moslem faith the Arab conquerors had brought, the Iranian plateau was re-asserting its independence from the conquerors themselves. Hitherto the caliph at Baghdad had been both head of Islam and ruler of the Arab empire. Now he was physically hemmed in by the Bouid regime; and although his spiritual powers supposedly remained intact, his secular orders henceforth carried little weight beyond the immediate neighbourhood of his capital. All along the northern frontiers, from the Black Sea to the Pamirs, the temporal writ of Baghdad was losing effective meaning. The Arab power was fading. The ground was loosening for a westward Turkish avalanche.

The first tremors of the approaching eruption were felt in the western Heartland, where for more than two centuries the Khazars had occupied the region from the lower Volga to the Caucasus.

During their initial outburst the Arabs had invaded the territory of the Khazars and destroyed their capital, at that time located near the Terek river west of the Caspian. But in alliance with the Byzantines, the Khazars had thrust the Arabs back and had held them beyond the Caucasus. Thereafter Khazar-Arab relations had alternated between friendship and hostility. Both were trading peoples; and during periods of peace the commerce between them had contributed almost as much to the Khazars' prosperity as had their traditional good relations with Constantinople. By the early ninth century, when the empire of Baghdad was at its short-lived height, they had become the dominant power on the western steppes.

The military decline of Baghdad created a vacuum in the Black Sea–Caspian area; and the Khazars, though often peaceably inclined, could not resist attempting to fill it. Raiding parties wound their way through the Caucasus passes into Armenia, and larger forces gathered into the Khazar confederation still wider sectors of the Russian steppelands. But these expansive adventures soon had to be abandoned; for over the eastern horizons a threat to the Khazar state itself was appearing.

Movements of unusual size in Turkish central Asia were just then becoming perceptible. Nomadic populations were growing, outstripping the capacity of arid grazings to maintain increasing tribes and herds. To the coastal regions these movements might not at other times have presented a significant menace, for they did not originate as a deliberate descent upon the littoral communities. As with the onset of previous Heartland tides, they were at first more in the nature of folk-wanderings, given direction by the sense that farther south and west lay 'climes of bliss' warmer, softer, more rewarding lands. But the incipient Turkish drift coincided with a period when the chain of fortresses and guard-posts that formed the containing ring against the steppes was thinly held. China had collapsed. Persia was intent on shaking off the Arab power. Baghdad was reduced to military impotence. All round the southern Heartland, littoral attention was focused on internal change and disturbance.

The Karlucks, who had played a leading part in breaking up the old Western Turkish confederation, were among the first to strike their tents. Moving west from the Balkash steppes they pushed ahead of them the Petchenegs, another tribe who had once been subjects of the West Turkish khaghan. In their turn the Petchenegs collided with the Ghuzz, a powerful group of tribes grazing around the Aral Sea; and the Ghuzz, after giving the unwelcome arrivals further impetus towards the west, fol-

lowed in their wake. Soon the dustclouds rising from the Petcheneg migration were rounding the northern shores of the
Caspian, crossing the Volga into Khazar territory. Collecting
their strength and combining with the Ghuzz, the Khazars
swarmed upon the Petchenegs and chased them from the Volga
district on to the Black Sea plains. And here, to the north of the
Sea of Azov, the far-tossed Petchenegs came upon the Magyars.

The Magyars were subordinate members of the Khazar confederation, but were relative newcomers to the region. They
were a branch of the Finnish group of tribes which, although of
Turkish stock, inhabited the more northerly forest zones; and
they had migrated to the western steppes from their original
homelands near the Ural mountains. Formerly, living in the
borderlands between the wooded marshy taiga of north-west
Siberia and the steppes proper, they had subsisted partly by
hunting and fishing, and partly by cattle-raising: but on the grass
of the south Russian prairies they had, in contrast to most of
their Finnish kinsmen, become warlike horse-nomads. Now,
however, they found themselves up against one of the most
fiercely aggressive Turkish tribes of central Asia. Bending, then
breaking, before the Petcheneg pressure, they headed west. By
890, under their Khazar-nominated Turkish khan Arpad, the
Magyars were streaming across the Danube.

Circumstances combined to propel them farther into Europe.
Once more the Byzantines employed a steppe people to suppress
their like: they set the Magyars upon those Bulgar tribes which,
admitted to the Balkans by Justinian II, had periodically made
trouble for Constantinople ever since. Savagely attacked, the
Bulgars appealed to the Petchenegs for help; and they, from
their new pastures near the Black Sea, drove the Magyars on into
the Transylvanian mountains. Here the Magyars found another
patron in the German king Arnulf, who was at the time embroiled with the Slavs; and the momentum of their onslaught on
the Slavs launched them into that haven of westward-moving
Heartland hordes, the Hungarian plain. For Europe, the terrible
years of Attila the Hun and Bayan the Avar had come again.

The early decades of the tenth century saw the Magyars raiding Italy, advancing across southern Germany. Here, in 933,
they were severely checked: but the setback only had the effect
of diverting their search for loot elsewhere. In 934, and again in

942, they were bought off by tribute from beneath the walls of Constantinople. Then, moving in a great arc from the coasts of Marmora, through the valleys of the Danube system and around the Alps, they threw their full might into western Europe. They ravaged Lorraine, devastated Burgundy and Champagne. But they had overreached their strength; and in 955, meeting the Germans under Otto I near Augsburg, they were overwhelmed at the Battle of the Lechfeld.

But the great grass basin at the heart of Danubian Europe became the Magyars' permanent home. They had had much contact, peaceable as well as warlike, with a branch of the Bulgars known as the Onoghurs; and from that association Hungary took its name. For a time they remained the 'ogres' of subsequent nursery threats: but within fifty years of the Lechfeld they were accepting Christianity. One of their chieftains, baptized, and later canonized as St Stephen, set them on the road to westernization; and henceforth the Hungarians, like other Heartland peoples who settled at the edges of the littoral world, became a bulwark against the steppes.

So far, the rising pressure from the Turkish Heartland upon the weakening frontiers of the Baghdad empire had been felt in the steppelands to the west of the Caspian. The series of collisions which had brought the Petchenegs into south Russia and sent the Magyars reeling before them into Europe had been in the nature of a preliminary tremor. But meanwhile, to the east of the Caspian, where the heart of central Asia adjoins the Iranian plateau, the scene was being set for a major earthquake.

It was in this region that the Arabs, penetrating beyond the Oxus river across the threshold of the Heartland at the height of their expansive phase, had first come face to face with Turks. In its initial phases, the confrontation had been hostile: but as the decades passed and contacts became more frequent, the Turks found much that was sympathetic in the Arab nature. The two peoples shared a common background. Both were nomads, horsemen, warriors. The concept of the Holy War, Christian in origin but adopted into the Arab ethos, was entirely comprehensible to the Turkish outlook. Moreover, in the Arab custom of employing slave-soldiers the Turks perceived a source

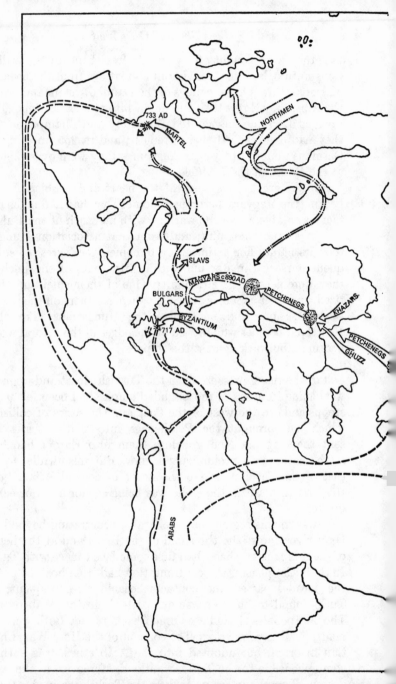

The Turkish Expansion, Third Phase: Eighth and Ninth Centuries A.D. Chinese Turkish push propels Magyars into Europe: Northmen expand from Scandinavia

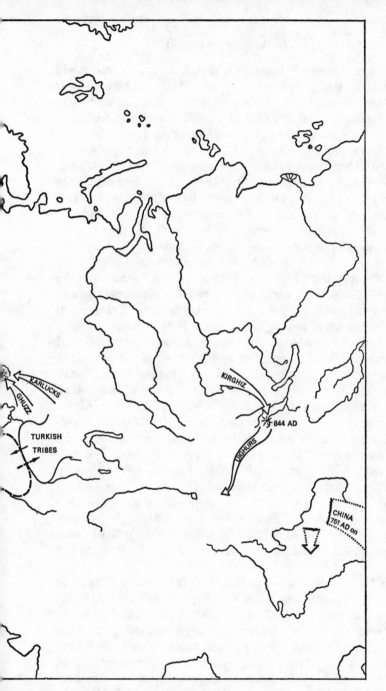

empire collapses: Arabs, checked in north and west, concentrate eastward: westward

of commerce: prisoners taken in inter-tribal Turkish wars could
be profitably traded to Arab governors. And as it became clear
that slave-soldiers in the Arab service often rose to positions of
eminence and power, the idea of accepting such service themselves became attractive to Turks of standing. Frustrated individuals, ambitious chieftains, whole bands of eager freebooters,
began to filter across into the Arab world in search of military fortune. And since the Arab cavalryman, though skilled with lance
and sabre, was unversed in the deadly arts of mounted archery,
Turkish horse-bowmen found themselves in high demand.

Secular affinities were cemented by bonds of religion. Like
many other steppe peoples the Turks, though traditionally worshippers of the Sky, were seldom religious fanatics. Independent
by nature, they were often open to missionary influence from the
outside – though their very independence sometimes led them to
embrace unexpected beliefs, as the Judaism of the Khazars and
the Manichaeism of the Uighurs showed. In the Iranian gateway
to the Heartland the Arabs, as their settlements developed, had
built mosques for the benefit of their own communities; and in
this way the wandering Turks of the region became familiar with
the external facets of the Moslem faith. Moreover, under Arab
rule Persia had accepted Islam; and when, in the ninth century,
the Samenids of Bukhara claimed their native Persian sovereignty over the lands south of the Aral Sea, they embarked on
active conversion of the Turkish tribes grazing there. This produced in growing numbers of Turks a sense of spiritual unity
with Persia; and, through Persia, with the great Islamic world
beyond. And on the lower level of steppe acquisitiveness, religious contact sharpened Turkish awareness of the lush wealth of
Mesopotamia and the eastern Mediterranean. If the nomad Turks
belonged to Islam, Islamic wealth should surely belong to the
Turks.

Thus the flow of the Arab tide across the Iranian plateau to
the verges of central Asia in the seventh century, followed by its
ebb in the ninth, had an effect like that of a magnet thrust into
a scattered mass of iron filings and then withdrawn. The Arab
presence on their Heartland threshold had attracted the Turks:
and now, as the power of Baghdad waned and retreated, this
attraction – military, religious, economic – began to draw them
out in its wake. Other factors assisted the process. Partly as a

result of Talas, the Turks of the region had shaken off the steady-
ing governance of China. The heavily mounted Persian barons
of the Parthian tradition, with their retinues of peasant-archers,
had ceased to form an effective deterrent against the steppes:
some had left their estates for the comforts of the trading towns
in Khorasan and Transoxiana; others were engaged in feudal
strife with the ruling Samenids. At the same time the Samenids
were wasting their own strength in an armed quarrel with the
Bouids of western Iran. The barriers were down. From the Caspian to the Pamirs the routes from the interior to the littoral
were open.

About 955 a disturbing incident took place at the court of the
reigning Samenid monarch. Alp-tegin, a Turkish Moslem soldier
who was in Persian service as commander of the royal guard,
attempted a *coup d'état*. Gathering family and followers around
him, he suddenly declared himself Governor of Khorasan. To
this impudence the Persian king reacted vigorously. Alp-tegin
was flushed out and hotly pursued through Balkh towards the
southern fringes of the Samenid realm. He and his adventurers
came to rest in the town of Ghazna in the Afghan hills not far
from Kabul; and here they established their headquarters – a
tumour on the Samenid skin, feeding on the caravans passing
through central Asia. But it was an active tumour; for the
bandit-lair of the Ghaznavid Turks took root and grew. A Turkish state had gained a footing on Iranian soil.

Not long afterwards came a more ominous development. A
junta of Persian barons, pursuing their own struggle for power
against the Samenid rule, called in the aid of a Turkish horde –
the Kara-khanids – from the Balkash steppes. Realizing their
chance, the Kara-khanids began to move through Transoxiana
in the direction of Bukhara. In despair for the city of their origin, the Samenid family swallowed their pride and sent an
urgent plea for help to the Ghaznavids. The result of these ill-
fated Persian moves was that a Turkish pincer closed on eastern
Iran. The Kara-khanids swarmed in from the north-east, and
the Ghaznavids swept up from the south to 'protect' Khorasan.
Then the jaws of the pincer snapped shut. The Ghaznavids occupied Khorasan; and the Kara-khanids overran Transoxiana,
capturing the last of the Samenid kings as they advanced. By
999 the whole of eastern Iran was in Turkish hands.

By this time the Turks from Ghazna were no longer a small exiled faction. They were swollen by their conquest of Khorasan. And in the redoubtable figure of Mahmud they now had an ambitious and ruthless chieftain.[1] Determined to use his rising strength as a springboard to further aggrandizement, Mahmud pushed down into India, seizing the Punjab in 1004, penetrating to the Arabian Sea, and forcibly spreading Islam wherever his troopers marched. From this time dates the hold of the Moslem faith over north-west India. But the southward outburst of the Ghaznavids exposed their possessions in Khorasan to the eyes of the Kara-khanids in neighbouring Transoxiana. It was not in the Turkish nature to leave so large and tempting an area unmastered. The Kara-khanids invaded Khorasan. Mahmud hurried north to drive them out; and a prolonged and bitter contest set in between the leading clans of the two hordes for the dominance of eastern Iran. The prize went to neither: for there now appeared a far more formidable Turkish host which was to sweep both rivals from the stage. The newcomers were the Seljuks.

The Seljuks were a branch of the Ghuzz group of tribes. Originally, their home pastures had been the grassy plains of central Siberia that lie in the region of the upper Ob and its tributary the Irtysh. Their founder, according to their part-factual and part-legendary tradition, had been one Tukuk, surnamed Timuryalik or 'Iron Bow', whose active years had been spent as a trooper in the Khazar army. In this service Tukuk had risen to high rank; and during it he had had a son who was named Seljuk. The father's prowess had attracted the notice of the Khazar khan, and under this powerful protection Seljuk had grown up. In manhood the son rejoined his kinsmen on the central steppes; and under him they and their followers began a southward movement which brought them to the banks of the Jaxartes river, at the northern border of Transoxiana. Here, like other Turks in touch with Arab-Persian influence, they gave up their shamanist religion and became staunch Moslems.

Hitherto the Seljuks had been a clan rather than a tribe – a

[1] For him, says Gibbon in his famous Chapter LVII, the title of *sultan* was invented by the ambassador of the caliph of Baghdad, 'who employed an Arabian or Chaldaic word that signifies *lord* and *master*'. Mahmud was thus the first Turkish Sultan.

minor offshoot of the innumerable Ghuzz. But Seljuk's grand-sons, Toghrul and Chagri, were to prove themselves nomad warriors of magnetic character. It was their ability, and that of their immediate relatives, to attract and command fighting men from the restless growing tribes around them that transformed a small group of chieftains into a number of large, aggressive hordes, sometimes mutually jealous, but capable of acting in concert when their leaders shared common purposes. Thus in their early days the Seljuk Turks were less a separate entity than a focusing of disparate Turkish strength under a single family.

The extinction of the Samenid realm was the signal for the Seljuks to make another southward move, this time from the Jaxartes to the neighbourhood of Bukhara and Samarkand, in the core of Transoxiana. This brought them into the storm-centre of the struggle between the Ghaznavids and the Kara-khanids for eastern Iran. Unable as yet to challenge the snow-balling power of Mahmud of Ghazna, they accepted him as their overlord. But their intentions were thinly veiled; for when Mahmud inquired how many men they could provide for service under his banner, the alarming reply indicated that no less than two hundred thousand could be summoned. Whereupon the idea was canvassed of severing the thumbs from all Seljuks of mili-tary age – so as to render them unable to draw a bow – before it was too late.

But the time for preventive measures was past. Drawn by the calibre of the leaders and the prospects of reward, recruits to the Seljuk ranks were swelling in numbers. Land was needed for their herds; and the Ghaznavids were asked to make available part of the great area of Khorasan which they had recently re-taken from the Kara-khanids. The request was refused. The Seljuks mobilized to take by force what the Ghaznavids would not give; and soon Turk was once more fighting Turk for the rich territory of Khorasan. Then Mahmud died; and with his relent-less will no longer rallying them, his armies began to fail. In 1040 they were smashed to pieces at Dandarkan near Merv. The power of the Ghaznavids in central Asia was annihilated, and the survivors fled southward to their possessions in India.

After this overwhelming victory Toghrul – 'the Falcon' – was confirmed as supreme leader of the Seljuks. He is said to have been appointed by the time-honoured method of causing a child to draw an arrow from a bundle of shafts each marked with the name of a candidate. But he was the logical choice: he was Seljuk's elder grandson, and he had held together through a long and successful steppe war a family of proud princes, prone like all Turkish chieftains to disputes of mortal intensity.

After Dandarkan the prospects before him could scarcely have been brighter. In effect, the Seljuks had driven a spearhead down from the central Asian steppes, through their fellow Turks quarrelling over the Samenid corpse, into the heart of the Iranian plateau. All Khorasan was now theirs; and through Khorasan lay the almost undefended route round the southern end of the Caspian to the Islamic Middle East and the Christian Mediterranean. True, the troops of the Bouids still held western Iran: but beyond them there was little to check a westward drive until it came upon the great network of fortresses and roads protecting the Byzantine provinces of Asia Minor and the approaches to Constantinople itself.

Bands of Turkish freebooters, mostly from Ghuzz tribes, were already heading through Iran towards the west. But before the main Seljuk armies followed in their wake, they strengthened their home base by a further conquest along the Oxus. Centering round the delta through which the Oxus flows into the Aral Sea lay the district then known as Khwaresm. In 1042 Seljuk forces seized this district. The occupation was effected by Chagri on his own account, probably without reference to his brother Toghrul. But it had the effect of securing the Seljuk rear for the time being by blocking the passage from the steppes to eastern Iran. A Turkish slave-soldier, Balka-tegin by name, was appointed to hold the region; and he thus became the first of the rulers afterwards known as the Khwaresm-shahs. These rulers and their territory were later to play a crucial part in the Heartland story.

The Seljuk surge across Iran under Toghrul began as a raid on the largest scale, with the wealth of the settled world as its objective. But as the nomad troopers passed on, with their herds of remounts, between the green-fringed torrents of the Elburz range and the simmering pink vistas of the Dasht-i-Kavir desert, the expedition assumed a rather different character. The Seljku aristocracy were harsh and hardened steppe commanders. But all their lives they had been subject to the moderating play of

Arab-Persian example at the Heartland frontiers; and now, in the actual presence of a culture and a polity of which they had, however remotely, felt themselves a part, they gradually responded to their new environment. Except for a sudden outburst of brutality during the capture of Rey, near the modern Teheran, the wanton savagery that had marked previous steppe invasions of the littoral was largely held in check.

Toghrul's own stature was nowhere more evident than in the all-important field of religious politics. He and his armies were advancing towards Mesopotamia. There, amid the fading Arab magnificence of Baghdad, was the seat of the spiritual head of Islam, the Abbasid caliph Al Ka'im, who was now virtually a puppet in the hands of the Persian Bouid regime. The Bouid state represented a temporal enemy, possibly of considerable strength, in Toghrul's path: the caliph, though physically powerless, a potential ally holding the keys to an infinitely vaster world. Like most Moslem rulers of the time, the Bouid family belonged to the dissident Sh'ia sect: the caliphs, in common with the majority of ordinary Moslems throughout the Arab sphere, had always been orthodox Sunnis. In the past Turkish chiefs, on their conversion to Islam, had usually become Sunnis – partly to assert their independence from other princes, and partly to associate themselves with the great days of the Arabs. Toghrul, a Sunni himself, had all along sought good relations with the caliphate: when he first embarked on his struggle with the Ghaznavids he had written to Baghdad explaining his cause and asking a blessing on his arms. Now, moving into western Iran, he took full advantage of his previous care. He proclaimed himself Protector of the caliph. By this single step he refurbished the caliphal authority; undermined all those – including the Bouids – who had sought to diminish its standing; and, more widely, suggested to Sunni Moslems everywhere that the Seljuk power would be used to revive and restore the Arab glory.

Toghrul's political adroitness stood him in good stead, for in the Bouid-controlled territory of western Iran the Seljuk drive was temporarily checked. A familiar difficulty arose. In a region of cities, the nomad armies faltered for lack of siege equipment; arrows became impotent against encircling walls. Isfahan in particular held out against the horse-archers for a year, and only capitulated when not a scrap of food was left. Here, in the dusty heat tempered by the glittering swirl of the Zaindeh river, Toghrul established his advanced headquarters and took stock of his position. Baghdad had already shown response to his overtures: in the official prayer pronounced weekly in the Great Mosque, his name now took precedence over that of the Bouid sovereign. Moreover, Persian lords from the surrounding districts were appearing with their retinues to offer him allegiance. The signs were favourable: meanwhile he would probe further west. He dispatched Chagri towards the Tigris, and his cousin, Ibrahim Inal, to Hamadan and the hill country of north-west Iran.

From 1045 on, as a result of Ibrahim's advance, Seljuk troopers made their first cautious contact with the outer ramparts of the Byzantine empire. The frontier state of Armenia was the first to feel their mobile, fingering infiltration. Moving up past Lake Urmia, they launched a series of carefully organized raids into the region to the west of Mount Ararat, splitting up into swift flying columns, scouring the country, regrouping, and as swiftly retiring. They pillaged the towns of Kars, Ani, Erzurum, and Melitene in eastern Asia Minor, reached the Black Sea coast at Trebizond, and made a momentary lunge to Sebastea deep in imperial territory. No permanent occupation was effected or intended: but the quick successive stabs were sufficient to suggest weaknesses in the Byzantine defences. They were also enough to bring Toghrul himself into the area for a brief campaign – partly out of jealousy of Ibrahim. He scorched the country round Lake Van, but met with a vexing setback at the fortress-town of Manzikert near by. He had captured an enormous Byzantine siege-engine, and some four hundred of his men had hauled it into position to batter the walls. At this point a Frankish mercenary in the pay of the Governor of Manzikert volunteered to deal with the menace. Emerging from the town with a document tied to his lance, he turned aside and rode casually towards the engine as if to take a cursory look at it. The Seljuks, assuming him to be a lone dispatch-rider, took little notice. Suddenly he pulled three containers of Greek fire from beneath his tunic, hurled them at the machine and galloped full tilt back into the town. The siege-engine exploded into flame. Toghrul, without other means of assault, had to withdraw; and for the time being Manzikert remained an imperial stronghold.

But it mattered little, for Toghrul was not primarily concerned
with Byzantium. Another empire was falling into his hands.
In 1055 the Seljuk build-up in western Iran precipitated a
crisis at Baghdad. For some time Al Ka'im had seen in Toghrul
a potential deliverer from the constraints of the Bouid regime.
But his hopes had hitherto been frustrated by a Turkish officer
called Bashasiri, who, though employed as commander of his
bodyguard, was in fact the agent of the Bouid ruler at the caliphal court. Realizing the probable outcome between the Seljuks
and the Bouids, Bashasiri now changed sides, indicating to the
caliph that he, too, believed the time had come to shake off the
Bouid grip. Accordingly, they jointly summoned Toghrul to
Baghdad to assist in reasserting the caliph's independence.

In response to this climactic call Toghrul appeared before
Baghdad in strength. There was little opposition to his entry;
and one of his first acts in the city was to declare the Bouid ruler
deposed. The military reaction was negligible. The Bouid family
was no longer vigorous; and faced with the massive threat of the
Seljuk archers it vanished into obscurity. Far more significant
was the division of powers which then took place between Al
Ka'im and Toghrul – with the same archers within easy call. The
caliph was reaffirmed as the supreme spiritual arbiter of Islam:
the Seljuk leader from the steppes became his vicar temporal,
invested with all the secular powers the caliphs had once wielded
as rulers of the Arab empire.

Gibbon[1] vividly describes the 'solemn comedy' staged in
Baghdad to seal this momentous pact. 'The Turkish sultan embarked on the Tigris, landed at the gate of Racca, and made his
public entry on horseback. At the palace gate he respectfully dismounted and walked on foot, preceded by his emirs without
arms. The caliph was seated behind his black veil: the black garment of the Abbasids was cast over his shoulders, and he held in
his hand the staff of the apostle of God. The conqueror of the
East kissed the ground, stood some time in a modest posture, and
was led towards the throne by the vizier and interpreter. He was
successively invested with seven robes of honour, and presented
with seven slaves, the natives of the seven climates of the Arabian empire. His mystic veil was perfumed with musk; two

[1] In *Decline and Fall of the Roman Empire,* Vol. X of the 1825 edition
pp. 346–7.

crowns were placed on his head; two scymeters were girded to his side, as the symbols of a double reign over the East and West.'

Within a few weeks the effect of this stately show was somewhat marred by a typically Turkish episode. Ibrahim Inal found himself unable to stomach the affront to his pride caused by his cousin's success. Returning from Armenia, he launched an insurrection against Toghrul. And Bashasiri at Baghdad, overcome by second thoughts, supported the rebellion. Assembling a scratch force he seized the city, declared himself a Sh'ia, and locked up Al Ka'im as too pro-Turkish to hold the caliph's office. Coolly and remorselessly Toghrul first scattered Ibrahim's men near Rey and killed him; then turned and struck down Bashasiri. That done, the reverent farce was re-enacted: the Lord of East and West freed his spiritual colleague from the Baghdad gaol, and personally led the mule on which he rode back to his palace. This time, to make doubly sure, political union was consummated by a family tie. Al Ka'im married Toghrul's niece; and after prevaricating for some months to emphasize his independence, agreed to give his daughter to the Seljuk sultan. The second wedding was about to take place when Toghrul died of a haemorrhage in 1063.

He had begun as a member of an obscure clan of central Asian nomads. Shooting his way through kindred Turks fighting at the Heartland verges, he had burst across Iran to Baghdad and beyond. He had scarcely drawn a bow on Iranian soil. Yet he had ended, acclaimed in every land professing orthodox Islam, as the sole inheritor of all the earthly Arab legacy.

Baghdad had sought the protection of the steppes. As a result, the high civilization for which it had stood was handed over to the steppes. Toghrul's bargain with the hapless Al Ka'im had consequences of the profoundest kind. On the fabric woven by the Arab intellect from the Indus to the Atlantic it loosed the ferocious, lawless code of the Heartland; for the pioneering surge of the Seljuks drove a channel from the steppes for more primitive and barbarous Turkish hordes. By them the searching, synthesizing, tolerant Arab mind was distracted beyond recovery, and the vast sector of the Eurasian littoral which it had illuminated was turned into a zone of plunder. Yet the advent of the Turks was not without subsequent advantage to the Moslem

world. It brought to that world the virility, as well as the
anarchy, of the inner Asian grasslands; and by systematically
stiffening the Moslem cause with the arm of Holy War – the
merciless weapon to which the Arabs had only occasionally resorted – it injected a new ardour, however crude, into the promulgation of Mohammed's faith. Moreover, the Turkish-Moslem
association had its geographical effect: it tended to divert the
more intensive Turkish hunts for loot away from Islamic ground
towards the coastal lands to west and east, where infidels could
be honourably despoiled. And in the end it was a Moslem characteristic, as much as any other factor, that was to prove fatal to
Turkish hegemony: for the passive, conservative element in the
Islamic outlook, which referred the ordering of human affairs to
the will of God, was finally to sap the vigour of the Turks and
render them incapable of military and political flexibility.

All this lay in future time. At Toghrul's death the Seljuks of
central Asia, having pocketed the Arab patrimony, stood at the
Byzantine borders of Asia Minor.

The Seljuks were not the only threat growing upon Byzantium.
For some two hundred years before Toghrul's drive into Iran,
the wider upheaval among the Turks had been spreading commotion across the Asian interior. As early as 844 the Kirghiz
from central Siberia had invaded Mongolia, chased the Uighurs
from their lands along the Orkhon river and forced them south
to the Turfan district, where they gave a final *coup de grâce* to
the old Iranian civilization in the oases of the Tarim basin.
Fifty years later, at the other end of the Heartland, the Magyars
had been pushed into Europe as a result of the westerly surge
through Khazar territory of the Petchenegs and the Ghuzz.

From those times on the eruption had gathered strength until
much of inner Asia was in turmoil. Of the pattern of local explo-
sions that helped to set if off, and of the consequent chain reactions of tribe upon tribe that gave it continuing momentum,
little is yet known. No doubt some of the Turkish waves broke
and died away, unrecorded, before they reached the Heartland's
edges. But some were deeper currents of predatory migration,
mainly flowing towards the promise of the west. The Seljuk outburst was one of these; and it moved west by the path to the
southward of the Caspian Sea. But before the Seljuks left central

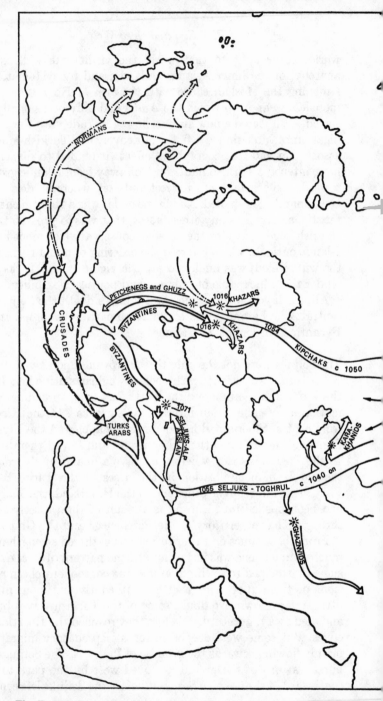

The Turkish Expansion, Fourth Phase: Eleventh Century A.D. Turkish pincers
through Italy: Seljuk defeat of Byzantines at Manzikert and Turkish advance to

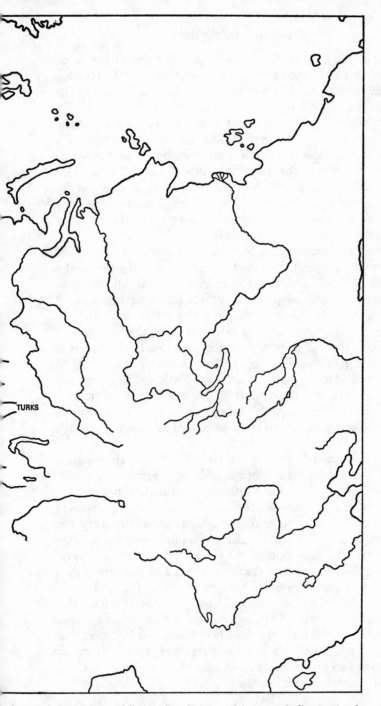

TURKS

ush towards Byzantium and Caspian Sea: Normans drive towards Constantinople
Mediterranean provoke Crusades.

Asia other Turkish hordes were already heading in the same
direction by a different route, pressing west towards the Russian
plains along the broad belt of grass between the Urals and the
north shóres of the Caspian.

While this efflux of horse-borne Turks was pouring across the
steppes towards the western littoral, another movement of a
different kind – less massive but more deliberate in aim – was
growing in intensity from the northern latitudes of Europe. This
was the ship-borne outsurge of the Northmen. In the first instance it was a movement of sea pirates, sweeping from the
fiords and flats of the Scandinavian coasts into the rivers of
Europe and around its ocean shores.

In the ninth century the Northmen felt their way down the
Russian rivers in their shallow-draught vessels and discovered a
water route from the Baltic to the Black Sea. Gradually these
Scandinavians, who came to be known as Rus, abandoned piracy
in favour of trade and were soon in active commerce with Constantinople. To protect their growing interests, their chiefs, half
sea-soldiers and half merchant-princes, organized the defences of
the river region they had occupied; and from this blending of
northern leadership with Slavic population there emerged
the Kiev-Novgorod principalities: the association of riparian
trading cities that was the embryo Russian state, enormous
in extent, and with its south-eastern borders merging into the
steppes.

Meanwhile, oars flashing beneath the black and yellow shields
ranged along the sides of their longships, dragon bows forging
through flying spray, other Northmen were striking out into the
Atlantic and across the North Sea. They secured a permanent
foothold in Alfred's England, and later the whole country was
temporarily absorbed into the Danish empire of Canute. Another
wave established the Duchy of Normandy in northern France;
and from this base, adding French methods and manners to their
turbulent native energy, the Normans expanded again by land
and sea. They devoted much of their national effort to their
invasion and occupation of England; but before William's cross-
Channel enterprise had been launched, Norman freebooters were
leading expeditions into the Mediterranean world. Here, by
1071, they had taken over a large part of the western provinces
of the Byzantine empire in Italy.

These two movements – the Turkish onrush from the Heartland and the Nordic outburst from north-west Europe – had in effect been advancing towards each other, with Constantinople and Byzantium between them. Byzantine military attention was already focused on the menace from the steppes. By the beginning of the eleventh century, while the Normans were still consolidating their hold on the French Channel coast, the drift of the Turkish tribes on to the Black Sea plains had reached threatening proportions. It was bearing heavily on the Kiev-Novgorod state which had been created by previous Nordic expansion. The Byzantines went to the aid of their Kiev-Novgorod neighbours; and in 1016 the two allies jointly attacked the Khazars. Their object was to convert the Khazar lands into an outer bastion against the general Turkish pressure.

In the emergency, to damage the Khazars was a paramount blunder. It arose from the fact that there had long been intermittent hostility, mainly due to trade rivalry, between the Khazars and the Kiev-Novgorod princes. These conflicts had weakened the Khazars; and their power had been further reduced by the overrunning of part of their lands by the Petchenegs and the Ghuzz. But their friendship with Byzantium had been enduring; they were still the most stable and civilized presence on the western steppes; and it was in their interest to help to stem the chaos that was engulfing the region. The new assault on them virtually destroyed their fighting strength. As a result, they could no longer hold up the advance of Turkish hordes far more primitive than themselves.

About 1050 the powerful Kipchak Turks left their homelands round the Irtysh river in central Siberia and joined the westward flow. Emerging through the Ural-Caspian gate, they uprooted the Ghuzz from their pastures on former Khazar ground near the lower Volga. The Ghuzz retreated before the tide, and in 1054 seized part of the Russian steppes from the Petchenegs. The Petchenegs in their turn gave way, burst across the Danube, and reached the walls of Constantinople. Maintaining their inexorable pressure, the Kipchaks now appeared on the Black Sea steppes, rolled back the Ghuzz into the Balkans on the heels of the Petchenegs, and took possession of most of the south Russian grasslands for themselves. Byzantines, Bulgars and Petchenegs turned on the Ghuzz; and by 1065, with great difficulty, had them under partial control. This violent chain reaction, largely made possible by the ill-judged onslaught on the Khazars, projected the seething upheaval in the Heartland into Byzantine territory. Large bodies of the most savage of the Turks were now in the Balkans, looting and killing whenever they could.

Thus about the time that William was landing at Pevensey, three separate threats were looming at Byzantium from different quarters. Turkish tribes, milling forward round the north shores of the Black Sea, had penetrated the imperial frontiers. Land-hungry adventurers from Normandy, already in virtual possession of Byzantine Italy, were preparing to mount an offensive across the Adriatic to the Balkans. And the Seljuks, who by this time had thrust across Iran, were at the threshold of Asia Minor. In all its tormented history Constantinople had seldom been so menacingly beset.

Toghrul had bequeathed the Seljuk leadership to Alp Arslan, his favourite nephew. Like his uncle, Alp Arslan, the 'Valiant Lion', was more than a grim tyrant of steppe descent swept to eminence by the ferocity of his horse-archers. His physical figure was impressive. Tall and commanding, he added to his stature by his custom of wearing headgear of unusual height. A deadly marksman even by Seljuk standards, his moustaches were of such size and length that he would tie them behind his head before raising his bow. But though possessed of a temper at times ungovernable, he was simple in habit, open-handed and often open-minded as a ruler, fearless and honourable as a warrior. Like other Seljuk aristocrats of his generation, he fell at an early age under the spell of Persia; and this deepened his natural intelligence and strength of character. He modelled his code of behaviour on that of the old Persian champions, whose knightly deeds he loved to hear recited. And in the Nizam al Mulk, his able and cultivated Persian vizier, he found a teacher whose sensitivity he sought to absorb into his own rougher outlook.

The domains under Seljuk occupation were now immense. They stretched from Afghanistan to Mesopotamia and from the Caspian to the Gulf of Oman. The new sultan took rapid steps to reaffirm his authority along his eastern borders: but in the west, beyond the Euphrates, the position was less secure. At the north-eastern end of the Mediterranean stood Byzantium, increasingly assailed but still the most formidable littoral empire of the day. And farther south lay the Egypt of the Fatimids. This Arab dynasty, partisans of the Sh'ia sect, held themselves to be the rightful sovereigns of all Islam, basing their claim on their supposed descent from the Prophet's daughter Fatima and her husband Ali. They had all along been rivals of the Abbasid caliphate of Baghdad, and had been alarmed and aroused by the handing over of the Sunni secular destiny to Toghrul. At the time, the rule of the Fatimids extended northward from Egypt into Syria; and it was the possibility of an anti-Seljuk alliance between them and Byzantium that fixed Alp Arslan's strategic attention on his western frontiers. In his view, the more dangerous potential enemy was Egypt. But before launching a major offensive towards Cairo he felt it necessary to guard against interference from Constantinople. Toghrul and Ibrahim had already raided into the eastern provinces of Byzantium. He would now mount against them a more solid demonstration of Seljuk strength. In the event, what was intended as a limited cautionary campaign paved the way for a cataclysm that shaped the modern history of eastern Europe.

The great rectangular plateau-peninsula of Asia Minor is naturally protected on three sides by the sea, and its north-eastern corner by the rampart of the Caucasus range. Its south-eastern borders are vulnerable to overland attack from the Tigris-Euphrates region and from north-west Iran: but in the eleventh century an enemy advancing from these directions was confronted by a redoubtable Byzantine system of defence in depth. A succession of walled, garrisoned fortress-towns was dotted through the valleys between the mountains of the plateau; and these were linked with the hub of the empire at Constantinople by a chain of splendid highways along which reinforcements could be quickly drafted into any threatened zone.

The weakness in the system was at the north-eastern end of the rectangle, where the small state of Armenia lay tucked into the tumbled hilly country between the Caucasus and Lake Van. Until 1022 Armenia had been independent, though its rulers' relations with their great neighbour to the west had never been friendly owing to religious tensions. In that year Byzantium had begun a gradual occupation of Armenia which had proceeded, piece by piece, until almost the entire state had been annexed. The ostensible reasons were the growing Turkish pressure from the Heartland, and the easy access into Asia Minor offered by the Armenian valleys. But the country was rich, and the belief arose that the Byzantines had more material motives. In any case the Armenians acutely resented the occupation; and a policy intended to bolster a questionable sector of the Byzantine outer defences only succeeded in aggravating its unreliability.

It was against Armenia that Alp Arslan moved. In the political circumstances, he reckoned, it should not be difficult to seize; and by its occupation Constantinople would be warned against meddling in his Egyptian plans. In 1064 he attacked and destroyed the Armenian capital; and its ruler was suitably compensated for his lack of resistance. This opened the valley routes to the more easterly of the fortress-towns on Byzantine soil proper. Those which proved too tough to crack were by-passed: but at Melitene and Sebastea – where they had already heard the whistle of Ibrahim's arrows and the terrifying war-shrieks of his troopers – Byzantine forces were scattered. Then, in 1067, Caesarea was assaulted.

By these lightning strikes, spread over three years, Armenia was completely sealed off by the Seljuks. More, the onslaught on Caesarea had carried them to the exact centre of the Asia Minor rectangle. Gratified by his success, Alp Arslan let his archers press on. In 1069 they were swarming round the walls of Konya. Next year they probed their way almost to within bowshot of the Aegean Sea.

These latter thrusts were plunder-gathering raids rather than expeditions of conquest. They left intact the framework of the imperial defences in western Asia Minor. And the sultan himself, satisfied that he had achieved his purpose, now withdrew to the south with his main army to open his campaign against Egypt. He left much of eastern Asia Minor, however, as well as Armenia beyond, in Seljuk hands; and Turkish bands were everywhere at large, disrupting communications and causing fearful loss of life and property. Among the towns they had captured was Manzikert – where, a few years before, Toghrul's besieging horde had been frustrated by the courage of a Frankish mercenary.

Despite Alp Arslan's partial withdrawal, the situation as seen from Constantinople was critical. The provinces of Asia Minor were vital to the empire. They formed its strategic shield against the east. Their crops and meat fed the capital. Above all, they had always been the principal source of manpower for the Byzantine army. It was essential to drive out the Seljuks and reassert the imperial authority throughout the region. That authority, however, was not being challenged only in Asia Minor. It was in an advanced state of decay in the metropolis itself.

While the threats from the Heartland and from Italy had been growing, the empire had been enduring some fifty years of continuous misrule. Under the emperor Basil II it had attained unprecedented heights of prestige and prosperity: but at his death in 1025 the rot had set in. Since then Constantinople had seen a succession of feeble or intriguing rulers, male and female, passing swiftly to and from the throne, assisted in their shady progress by a crowd of eunuchs, courtesans, sharks and, occasionally, poisoners. It was the period of 'the noiseless dissolution of the Roman system'.[1] As the external perils loomed larger, the shows and spectacles staged by the court for the public diversion grew in extravagance and cost as if to wish away the approach to the abyss. At length Constantine X, ascending the throne in 1059, tried to reverse the downward slide by a series of rigid economies. Unhappily his most dramatic retrenchments fell on the armed forces. At his death in 1067 – when Alp Arslan was already half-way across Asia Minor – his mother, the Empress Eudoxia, married again; partly because she was in love, and partly because the situation was held too grave for the succession to pass to the adolescent heir. Her new husband was Romanus Diogenes, a general of distinction and a member of a well-known family from Cappadocia – one of the provinces which the Seljuks were at that moment ravaging. Romanus was a brave soldier and, as his subsequent conduct proved, a man of honour; and his feelings for the plight of the empire were strong. He was, however, far from being the exceptional figure required by the dimensions of the crisis. He was not free from involvement in the intrigues of the court. He was disliked by the army.

[1] Bussèll, *The Roman Empire from A.D. 81 to A.D. 1081*. Vol. I p. 340.

And as a strategist he was impetuous to the point of carelessness. In the early months of 1071 he decided to take the field with the largest army he could mobilize.

Over Romanus' march to his fateful encounter with the Seljuks hung the aura of inevitability of Greek tragedy. Fifty years earlier the issue could scarcely have been in doubt. For until then the Byzantine army had been the most efficient military establishment in the world. The position of the empire at the flash-point between Europe and Asia had compelled Constantinople to evolve a fighting machine far ahead of the time. It was a machine that relied not on the courage of the individual soldier or the brilliance of an outstanding general, but on a settled, logically determined doctrine of war. It was essentially a defensive doctrine, for the Byzantines at root preferred diplomacy to trials of strength: but within that function it produced victories with almost automatic regularity. Everything was harnessed to the basic aim of bringing superior force to bear on an invader wherever he might violate the frontiers. To that end the combat units of light and heavy infantry and cavalry, and of missile-hurling artillery, were highly trained and carefully proportioned; and their effectiveness was maximized by ample numbers of supporting fortress-troops, engineers, supply and medical specialists. The pride of the army was its heavy cavalry: the *cataphracti*, which had derived from the Parthian pattern. 'The commander,' one emperor asserted,[1] 'who has six thousand of our heavy cavalry and God's help needs nothing more.' As the pressure from the steppes had grown, the role of this branch had become increasingly important. In campaigns against Heartland invaders the mail-shirted cataphracts, wielding sword and dagger, bow and lance from the backs of their big weight-carrying mounts, had become the main striking force, with the infantry, if not left behind altogether, playing a secondary part. Their use, like that of every arm, was explicitly codified: facing a steppe enemy they should close at once, and ride him down before his arrow-clouds could tell and before he could resort to his usual tactic of simulated flight. Against just such a foe as Alp Arslan the Byzantine army had been as perfectly organized, equipped, instructed, as foresight and planning could devise. Advice was even laid down for operating in the specific

[1] Nicephorus II Phocas.

topography and weather conditions of the different regions of the empire, including Asia Minor.

Romanus was advancing with some sixty thousand men, mainly cavalry, against the forty thousand mounted bowmen that the Seljuks and their auxiliary tribesmen could muster. The Byzantine system was still, theoretically, as sound and viable as ever. But the preceding half century of maladministration and cutback had eaten away its quality. It was a skeleton without flesh or spirit. Many of the crack regiments had been disbanded; others were far below strength. The depleted ranks had been filled by alien mercenaries of doubtful loyalty: by Norman and Frankish heavy horse, unruly, and with no experience of Heartland warfare; by Slavs and Bulgarians; and by large contingents of highly undependable Turks – Petchenegs, Ghuzz and Kipchaks, only attracted by the scent of blood and loot. Probably no more than thirty thousand men were native Byzantines. Support and service, formerly so superbly organized, were equally shaky: garrison towns were short of men, depots were undervictualled, arsenals sketchily stocked. But among all the problems perplexing Romanus as he moved on along the great imperial highway to the east, the most incalculable was perhaps the man riding by his side. This was Andronicus Ducas, a nephew of Constantine X. The Ducas family detested Romanus; for his marriage to the empress-mother, and his subsequent elevation to the imperial purple, had displaced them. Andronicus shared his family's bitter feelings, and Romanus had felt obliged to bring him lest he should plot behind his back in Constantinople. The commander-in-chief was uncomfortably aware that the senior general serving under him was his implacable personal enemy.

Romanus' intention was to push right across Asia Minor, clearing the Seljuks from the country along his route. He would then enter Armenia, seize the Turkish-held fortresses there, and re-establish Byzantine authority while Alp Arslan was engaged elsewhere. Despite his many difficulties, his operations in central Asia Minor met with considerable success. He restored control of the Sebastea district, and then moved on east towards the sources of the Euphrates.

Two rivers, rising in the mountains of Armenia, running parallel and then converging, form the headwaters of the Euphrates. On the map their courses resemble the prongs and neck of a tuning-fork. Both these rivers afforded natural military routes from Armenia into Asia Minor; and for this reason possession of the fortresses on their upper reaches was important. On the northern stream lay Erzurum, which Romanus secured. He then turned, and headed for the southern stream. The fortress here was Manzikert.

Manzikert – sometimes known as Malaskird or Minazkird or Minazjird – was a smallish town, built of black stone and set about with gardens. It was dominated by the walls and works of its fortifications, now paced by Seljuk sentries. It lay about thirty miles north of Lake Van; and on the shores of that lake stood another fortress, Akhlat, also held by the Seljuks. Romanus' aim was to recapture both Manzikert and Akhlat. This would make doubly sure of the southern branch of the Euphrates. And it would also open another possibility. He believed that Alp Arslan, with the main Seljuk army, was in Iran; and if the entire Manzikert-Akhlat zone were in Byzantine hands, it could serve as a springboard for an attack into Iran after Armenia had been cleared.

Romanus' information was wrong. Alp Arslan and his army were not in Iran at all, but near Aleppo in Syria. And, in contrast to the faulty Byzantine intelligence, his messengers were keeping him accurately abreast of his opponent's progress. Realizing that a threat to his whole position in the north was developing, the sultan took decisive action. Handing over command in Syria to a subordinate, he detached as many men as he dared and set out with them for Asia Minor.

Approaching the fortresses which were his objectives, Romanus divided his army into two separate task-forces. He sent his Frankish cavalry under their captain Roussel de Bailleul, together with a supporting contingent of Kipchak Turks, to take Akhlat. Then he himself, with the balance of the Byzantine strength, invested Manzikert. Here, again, he achieved his purpose: after a short siege he captured the river-fortress and dispersed its Seljuk garrison. That done, and since no word reached him to suggest that Alp Arslan was reacting, he dispatched some of his best heavy infantry to assist Roussel at Akhlat.

Alp Arslan was in fact approaching as fast as he could push his troopers. He crossed the Euphrates near Menbij and skirted the Syrian desert to Mosul on the Tigris. Here he collected the local garrison and some groups of Turks ejected from Asia Minor by Romanus, including the survivors from Manzikert. Not yet satisfied with his strength he sent to Iran for reinforcements, ordering them to meet him at Khoi, about a hundred miles east of Lake Van.

Romanus was still at Manzikert, and still ignorant of the sultan's movements. While waiting to hear from Roussel at Akhlat he was looking into his supply situation. His stores were running low, and the country round was barren. He therefore took advantage of the lull to send out large parties, accounting for a significant part of his remaining numbers, on a long-distance search for rations and fodder.

Meanwhile the Franks had laid siege to the lake-fortress at Akhlat. Suddenly, Roussel received reports that an immense host was advancing upon his lines. It was Alp Arslan, with the flower of the Seljuk army. Reaching Khoi, he had apprised himself in detail of the dangerously divided position in which the Byzantine army now lay. The moment his reinforcements arrived he had swept forward to Lake Van and circled its southern shore to Akhlat. Utterly surprised, the Franks abandoned the siege and started to withdraw. And it was then that the tensions latent in the Byzantine army began to surface and take control. Instead of retreating towards Romanus at Manzikert, they fell back towards the west – out of the area of operations altogether.

Already Alp Arslan had disposed, by his mere appearance, of an important part of Romanus' forces. Without delay he relieved his Seljuk garrison at Akhlat and pushed north towards Manzikert. The endurance of his troopers had been astonishing. Most of them had ridden five hundred miles or more in a few weeks, through desert heat and mountain cold: yet their commanders now showed no hesitation in leading them forward to what, in all probability, would be a crucial battle.

At this belated point Romanus learnt that the sultan himself was in the region. The news was disconcerting, but not necessarily disastrous: his fortunes had held until now, and provided he could reunite his own army with Roussel's he stood an excellent chance of further success. He left Manzikert at once, heading for Akhlat, and sending a message ahead to Roussel to meet him on the way. He did not know that this message, on which everything turned, could not be delivered. For Roussel, whether from forgetfulness or spite, had failed to inform him of the Frankish defection. Nor does he seem to have been aware that Alp Arslan was so close. As the Byzantine regiments clattered and swung along the Manzikert–Akhlat road, no scouts were thrown out to reconnoitre ahead. Romanus was advancing unprepared and unprotected.

The surprise was as complete as that which had overtaken Roussel. Without warning the leading Byzantine echelons found themselves confronted by the dense masses of the Turkish horse-archers. Before they could deploy the air was filled with arrows hissing towards them. They fell back in disorder on the main body, and in their confusion nearly caused a general rout. For Romanus, the hazy assumptions of the preceding weeks focused in a moment to reveal the stark reality. Alp Arslan was upon him. He had split his army; then split it further to reinforce the Franks; then split it a third time by sending out valuable troops to forage. The Franks, wherever they might be, were not where they were needed. And the foraging squadrons were far beyond emergency recall.

Even in the mouth of peril Romanus concealed his anxieties behind a bearing of confident dignity. Across the gap between the armies a posse of Seljuks cantered forward. The sultan was sending to propose negotiations, for his men still had a healthy respect for their Byzantine enemies. The emperor replied that he would only consider peace in return for an immediate evacuation of imperial territory and an undertaking never to invade it again. Such terms were an affront to Turkish pride. Once more the issue between steppe and littoral had come to climax. The supreme figures of the two worlds were face to face.

The Battle of Manzikert was fought on 19 August 1071. At first light Alp Arslan, rising from his prayers, put on a plain white robe, perfumed himself with musk, and had his horse's tail carefully plaited. He is said to have armed himself with a scimitar instead of his usual bow. He watched his marshal, a eunuch called Taraug, ranging the Seljuk army into a huge loose crescent, its horned wings extending far to each side of the relatively compact Byzantine array.

At his centre, and under his own command, Romanus drew

up the cataphracts, supported by the remaining heavy infantry whose long bows were capable of lifting an arrow-barrage over the heads of the armoured cavalry in front of them. These magnificent units, combining shock and missile strength, formed his main counter to the sultan's lightly mounted archers. And being all Byzantines, they were his most trustworthy troops. To right and left, to guard against Seljuk outflanking movements, he placed his swarms of Turkish light horse. At his rear, in accordance with the tried Byzantine precept that he who can mount the last charge wins, he stationed a large reserve of mercenary heavy cavalry chiefly composed of Normans and Germans. In command of this powerful force, potentially of crucial importance, was Andronicus Ducas.

As the Seljuks began their advance an ominous event occurred. First one, then another of Romanus' Turkish contingents broke their ranks and moved forward to meet them. Soon almost the whole Turkish component of the Byzantine army had deserted to the enemy. It was not wholly unexpected; their allegiance was known to be lukewarm. But it meant that as the battle opened Romanus had only two formations left: his own centre, and Andronicus' reserve.

Maintaining their crescent disposition, the Seljuks now pressed forward in their loosely ordered masses. Sweeping at full gallop into range they discharged their arrow-storms, then quickly turned and made off. Repeatedly the cataphracts attacked through the murderous downpour, striving to make contact. As each Byzantine assault lost its impetus the Seljuk waves surged back, sharp-shooting as they came. As the cataphracts regrouped, the infantry behind launched their own protective streams of arrows until the sky was roofed with flying shafts. Again and again blood-stained horses and sweating men charged, rallied, charged once more. Every time the Seljuks wheeled and gave, whipping round in their saddles to fire a final volley as they sped away. Hour after hour the tantalizing, exasperating attempts to get to grips continued; and at each attempt the Byzantine losses grew.

By afternoon Romanus' cavalry were flagging. Determined to force a decision before sundown, he ordered his entire command to advance. At first their solid weight drove the Seljuks back. The tide seemed to be turning. But the manœuvre was leading

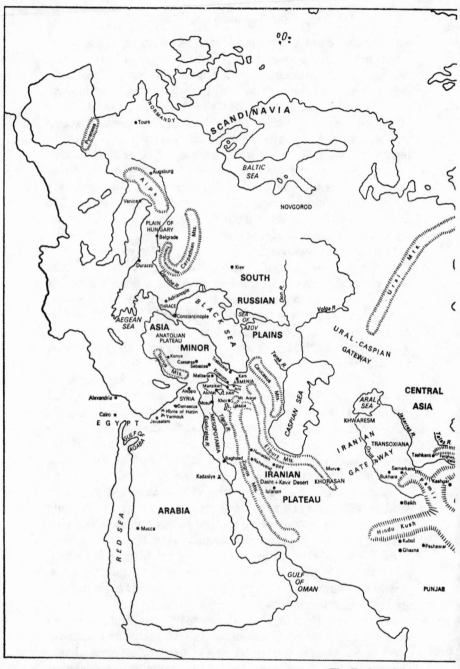

The Turkish Orbit

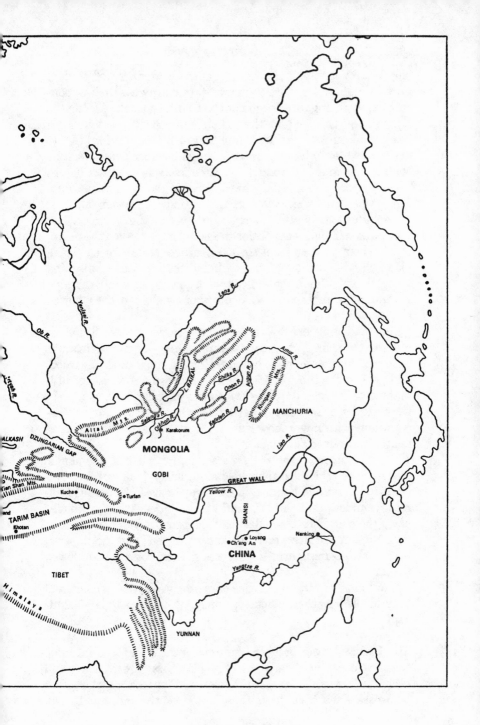

only to a repetition, in slower time, of the frustrations of the day. Farther and farther the Seljuks retreated, drawing their opponents on, watching for the moment to counter-attack. Among the Byzantines, the heat of the long August day was telling on heavily accoutred men and mounts nearing exhaustion. Before nightfall water in large quantities would be essential. But in the country ahead every well and watercourse was in Seljuk hands. The only certain supply lay to the rear, in the Byzantine camp. There was no alternative: Romanus ordered a retirement.

Cool and steady still, his regiments began their retreat. But there was still light enough for the Seljuks to observe the movement. Their great crescent stopped, turned, and followed. Then, black clouds swirling in the twilight, they gathered way and charged. This time they did not wheel away. As the Byzantine rearguard swung round to fight, their yelling droves hurled themselves upon it.

All now hung on the reserves of heavy cavalry. Romanus ordered them in. But no forward movement among their ranks answered his command. They remained immobile: then turned, and headed for the westward hills. It was the moment of ultimate treachery. Andronicus Ducas was exacting his revenge. In the field, he believed, the battle was already lost: but in Constantinople he might now win a throne. The vital squadrons melted away into the dusk.

As the centre of the Seljuk crescent lunged into Romanus' rear its horns encircled the whole of his army, locking it in a pincer grip. A terrible hand-to-hand affray ensued. Romanus himself, wounded, and with his horse sinking beneath him, fought on to the end. But as the darkness deepened panic flared out at last. Broken and desperate, the survivors fled; and the imperial bodyguard, leaping over the corpses of their comrades, followed them.

Next morning the Byzantine emperor, weak, dishevelled, and only identified with difficulty, appeared before Alp Arslan his captor.

The Turkish power had now endured in the Heartland for more than five centuries. The cycles of its play – its growth, decay and rebirth, through time and across the spaces of the great landmass – had been discontinuous and vastly complex. But an overall pattern, already familiar in broad outline, had governed its impact on the littoral fringes of the continent. Foiled in their attempt to gain a lasting foothold in China, the Turks had turned about and sought outlets in the west and south: across the Russian steppes and through Iran. And at the borders of Iran they had, as it were, been sucked out of inner Asia by the undertow from the breaking of the Arab wave.

At Manzikert they forced ajar the door to the Mediterranean and Europe. The Seljuks had acted as the battering-ram; and within two years of the battle their occupation of Asia Minor began in earnest. Even so, their own interest in the region was still limited. It was rather their kindred Turks, more uncouth and undisciplined than they, to whom the eastern provinces of Byzantium appeared as a paradise, first for plunderers, then for herdsmen. Auxiliaries and camp-followers from other clans and tribes fanned out in the wake of the conquerors, slaying and seizing wherever they went. And behind the looting bands came the slower, larger migrations, trekking in with their wagons and tents, womenfolk and flocks. As the Hungarian plain had served previous hordes as an extension of the steppes, so the Anatolian plateau offered to the Turkish nomads an extension of the central uplands. Its altitude and plant cover were not dissimilar to those of their former home: but the climate was less rigorous and water a little more abundant. Compared with the semi-desert zones they had left behind it was a promised land. The Seljuk princes struggled to impose order as the inflowing migrants forced out the Byzantine peasantry; and to provide, through economic and even welfare measures, the foundations of an organized state – which later emerged as the Sultanate of Rum, or Rome.

But in the meantime the Turkish flood poured southward over the Levant, its leaders quarrelling over the division of territory and spoil. Over each town, sometimes over the country round each village, a different warlord arose to assert his individual authority. Twice a Turkish vassal-chief attacked Jerusalem; and having finally wrested the city from the Fatimids, was himself displaced and murdered by a Turkish rival. Bandits multiplied wherever trade and travellers moved: along the sea coast, beneath the snows of Hermon, out on the camel-tracks of the Syrian desert. Eventually, farther east, the ancient irrigation

system of Mesopotamia began to disintegrate under the disputes
of the invaders; and many of its intricate works, maintained and
renewed down the centuries, vanished in salt and swamp until
the advent of present-day engineering.

Manzikert brought Constantinople still closer to the precipice.
A single battle could hardly have proved so significant if other
factors had not already undermined the whole Byzantine imperium. Of the continuing viciousness at the centre, Romanus'
end was symptomatic. Magnanimously freed by Alp Arslan he
returned to the capital; and there, at the instigation of Andronicus and his faction, his eyes were put out so atrociously that he
died of his wounds. The Norman stab through Durazzo towards
the Bosphorus was held, and finally petered out: but Byzantium
in Italy was irretrievably lost. The Petchenegs seized on the
general distraction to rise again and sack their way down
through the Balkans to Adrianople. In Asia Minor there was
almost inextricable confusion as Turks, refugees, and remnants
of the army – including Roussel himself – marched and migrated
to and fro in pursuit of their own ends. It was only the resourceful reign of Alexius Comnenus, opening in 1081, that preserved
the inner core of the empire from immediate dissolution.

Europe had been pushed north by the Arabs. It was now
about to be pushed west by the Turks. And to this younger,
emergent Europe it seemed that Byzantium was no longer capable of defending Christendom. Intervention was necessary; and
the New World of the north and west, crude and schismatic in
Byzantine eyes, called itself in to redress the balance of the Old.
Twenty-four years after Manzikert the First Crusade was
launched; and much of its effective fighting force was Norman.
So the two great movements originating from sea and land, from
west and east, each wielding weapons pioneered on the steppes,
met in the Levant in head-on collision of shock and missile warfare.
Mounted on their great steeds, 'armed at all points exactly, cap-
à-pie', the Christian descendants of the Northmen stormed into
Jerusalem through streets, it is said, knee-deep in Moslem blood.
But at the Horns of Hattin Saladin's horse-archers halted the
western onset; and behind the walls and parapets of the great
Crusader castles, motionless stone monsters squatting from the
Taurus to the Gulf of Aqaba, the Frankish East settled down to
its weary decades of attrition. The long Crusading effort, with

its strange mixture of high faith and squalid treachery, did nothing to relieve the Byzantines. They had wanted mercenaries to help them recover the vital defences of Asia Minor. Instead they found themselves at first unwilling allies in a strategy closely linked to the Levantine trading interests of the new Italian city-states; and then the outright victims of Western greed. The devastation of Constantinople by the Fourth Crusade, egged on by the itching palm of Venice, brought the empire to the point of no return. After that, only one more assault was needed to bring down for ever the great bastion that had stood for so long against Asia and the steppes.

After Manzikert nearly four centuries were to elapse before the final assault came. It was to be delivered by Turks, but not by the Seljuks. They had seen Byzantium as a potential threat; and they had embarked on their operations in Asia Minor merely to prevent its use as an offensive base against them. Of all the territories the Seljuks overran, Persia was the land they loved. Here they dismounted from their horses and put down their roots. From Persia, and largely through Persian administrators, Alp Arslan's son Malik Shah presided over an empire that straddled the Eurasian littoral from the Mediterranean to Tibet. But the Seljuks were Turks: the inevitable succession quarrels followed Malik's death, and by 1100 his huge dominions were being sliced up into independent fiefs.

Moreover the Seljuks were borne down by a problem that they could not solve. To admit themselves to Persia in the first instance, they had necessarily opened the gates from central Asia to the Iranian plateau. They had been unable to close them securely in their rear – although they had conquered Khwaresm for that very purpose before setting out for the west. Now, despite repeated attempts to beat them back, other hordes were striving to gain admittance. Even during the brief period of the Seljuk grandeur, the gates were giving before the pressure of new forces building up within the Heartland.

7
Manchurian Interlude

But the majestic River floated on,
Out of the mist and hum of that low land,
Into the frosty starlight, and there mov'd,
Rejoicing, through the hush'd Chorasmian waste,
Under the solitary moon.
— MATTHEW ARNOLD, *Sohrab and Rustam*

ALONE among the major states lying round the periphery of the Eurasian land-mass, China had been left virtually unscathed by the Turkish outsurge of the tenth and eleventh centuries. She had, in effect, put forth her giant strength to roll back the more aggressive of the Turks from her doorstep and into the west. And from that effort she had sunk back exhausted.

The year 751 had marked a sudden turning-point in the fortunes of the great central Asian empire built up by the early T'ang emperors. In that year China, still expanding westward, had been repulsed by the Arabs on the Talas river; and almost simultaneously her armies had suffered reverses at two other points along her frontiers. As a result, wearying of her imperial burdens, she had evacuated almost overnight her huge dominions in the Heartland and had withdrawn into a multiplying web of domestic discord. In 755 an insurrection had broken out. The Uighur Turks, crossing the border to Ch'ang-an, had propped up the Tang regime; but neither the policing Uighur troopers nor the efforts of their Tang employers had managed to stem the growth of civil chaos. Through the following decades the cycle of misery had cut steadily deeper into Chinese life. The rebellion had destroyed wealth, emptied the imperial treasury. To finance the maintenance of a precarious order, crushing taxation had been imposed. Trade had dwindled. Peasants had abandoned their holdings by the thousand. The population had fallen by some twenty millions.

In 874 another revolution broke out. Even more destructive of life and property, this second upheaval spread from the Yellow river districts into the provinces of southern China. Once more the T'ang, now at their last gasp, sought help from outside; and this time a Turkish tribe known as the Horde of the Sand Dunes sent an army from the Gobi desert to support them. But the tumult had gone too far to restore the situation. The warlords intervened and deposed the last T'ang emperor, a boy in his teens. The familiar pattern of national disintegration followed. In the south, provincial viceroys and army commanders set up autonomous governments in their own localities. Around the Yellow river the Turks of the Sand Dunes, faithful in spirit to the extinguished T'ang dynasty, established a kind of caretaker regime. But in 936 a Chinese general, determined to drive them out and seize power for himself, was tempted to call in aid from the Heartland yet again. Twice the T'ang had obtained loyal help from the Turks of Mongolia and the Gobi. The ambitious general decided to look elsewhere. He turned northward, to Manchuria.

Here, beyond the Great Wall, between the Liao river and the southerly stretches of the Khingan mountains, lived a people called the Khitans. Their territory corresponded roughly to the present-day province of Jehol, to the north-east of Peking. They were a grassland people of horse culture, living by herding and raiding. For many centuries they had figured intermittently in Chinese chronicles, sometimes penetrating the defences of the Wall and looting the towns of the northern Chinese border. It was their cavalry which had inflicted one of the defeats of 751 that had caused the collapse of the T'ang empire. Since then their ruling clan, the Yeliu, had produced a chieftain of exceptional stature; and. under his leadership the Khitans had expanded both west and east. They had invaded Mongolia, driven the Kirghiz Turks back to Siberia, and taken the unusual step of inviting the Uighurs to move back to the lands along the Orkhon river which the Kirghiz had taken from them; though the Uighurs, having settled in the Turfan area, declined the offer. To the east, the Khitans had overrun the kingdom of North Korea and extended their domains from central Manchuria to the coast of the Sea of Japan where Vladivostok now stands. During this conquest they had reduced to servitude a people called the Jurchets who, though still backward and isolated, were to become more formidable than their conquerors.

Thus in the early decades of the tenth century the Khitans were an energetic and acquisitive people: thoroughly dangerous allies for an insecure Chinese adventurer to embrace. A measure of the result of his rashness is afforded by the fact that from the word *Khitai*, the Turkish form of Khitan, stems *Cathay* – China. But the Khitans themselves were not Turks. They were descendants of the Sien-pi, and of Mongol extraction. And with their appearance the Mongol name, like the growl of distant thunder on the steppes, begins to sound across the medieval Heartland.

In answer to the general's appeal fifty thousand Khitan horsemen, excellently organized into divisions and squadrons, swarmed down from Manchuria through the Wall, fanned out across north China, and drove out the Turks of the Sand Dunes. They rewarded their Chinese ally by setting him up as a puppet-emperor, but instantly demanded from him the price of their own services. That price was most of the region of north China they had occupied, including a frontier town till then of little consequence called Yen Ching. Their helpless client could only comply; and though the Khitans were harassed for some years by guerrilla resistance and by rival warlords, the firm establishment of their rule over the Chinese north was only a matter of time.

While the Khitans were securing their position in the region of Yen Ching, events of significance were taking place farther south. The Chinese army, tired of the disruptions which had torn the country for so long, appointed a new emperor. The choice was a fortunate one; for Chao K'uang-yin, the first emperor of the Sung dynasty, proved not only a strong, but a far-sighted and humane sovereign. Patiently, and as much by persuasion as by force, he pieced together his broken realm into renewed nationhood, until by the end of his fifteen-year reign most of central China was again united.

To his successors, ruling a people who were now regaining their self-confidence, the Khitan presence in the north came to be seen as an affront rather than a menace. They took military action to recover the lost territories. It was a hazardous move;

for the Khitans, although they were rapidly adopting the Chinese way of life, retained all the martial prowess of their grassland origin. The Chinese columns were put to flight. And the Khitans, roused to retaliation, chased them southward to the banks of the Yellow river opposite the city of Kaifeng, which was serving as the Sung capital. There the pursuers were stopped by an act of courage reminiscent of T'ai-tsung's intrepid conduct in the face of the Eastern Turks before Ch'ang-an. Against the advice of his officers, the third Sung emperor refused to abandon the Kaifeng garrison to its fate, and personally headed a force marching to relieve an outlying town. By this staunch gesture the Khitans, like the Turks before them, were deeply impressed. Mollified, they withdrew to their possessions around Yen Ching, and began the long transformation of the one-horse town into the seething compound of Chinese and nomad, settled and transient, that was eventually to become Peking. The attempt to push them back into Manchuria had failed: but by 1004 fighting had ceased, and a treaty recognizing their hold on northern China had been concluded.

During the struggle with the Khitans, however, another blow had fallen along the Chinese frontier with the Heartland. This was dealt by the Tanguts, a people of Tibetan background. Originally, the Tanguts lived in the district round the Kokonor lake, on the north-eastern fringes of Tibet. But in the seventh century they had been driven by hostile tribes to seek admission to China. This had been granted; and they had been allotted lands in the southern part of the Ordos Loop, the area within China closest to the homelands from which they had fled. Here the Tanguts had settled down to a mixed economy of grazing and commerce, deriving much of their livelihood from contact with the trade passing from China into the Asian interior. China had saved them from probable extinction: they repaid her by throwing off their allegiance at the moment when the Sung were heavily embroiled with the Khitans. Declaring themselves independent, they took over the whole of the Ordos plateau and much of the land to the west of it that forms the modern province of Kansu. Their new realm was named Hsi-Hsia. To the Sung, this coup was doubly alarming: it meant not only that another large slice of China was now in alien hands, but also that the critical region of the Ordos, vital all through history for defence against the nomads of the interior, had passed from their control. Beset by their troubles in the north, however, they could not prevent the new state from taking root.

For the weakness which allowed the Khitans and the Tanguts to ensconce themselves within her boundaries, China was to pay dearly. Till now, Heartland intruders had come upon her across the Gobi from the Mongolian plateau. The Khitan descent opened a new route for invading horse-archers: that from the Manchurian prairies. And athwart the old route of steppe conquest from the Gobi and the north-west there now stood the none too friendly Tangut kingdom of Hsi-Hsia.

The new balance of danger, however, was not to alter for a hundred years. Through the eleventh century, the unoccupied provinces of China enjoyed a period of respite from further Heartland threat. There was time to turn again to art and scholarship. To engage, on the foundations of relative stability, in the luxury of political debate. To argue the merits of conservatism and reform as roads to the good society. It was a century of experiment and ideas, presided over by a succession of Sung emperors themselves intellectually inclined.

Then, in 1100, Sung Hui-tsung came to the throne. Philosopher, theologian, painter, in many respects he was an outstanding member of a dynasty distinguished for its patronage of culture. But in the field of statecraft, the old sore of the Khitan occupation of the north dominated his mind. Though this question had long been virtually dormant, he reopened it. Under the Khitans, Yen Ching had developed into a sizeable city: with passionate conviction he urged that the time had come to encompass its return to China. The more pacifist of his advisers were lukewarm; and in his obsession the emperor cast about for other help. With forthright enthusiasm but little prescience he determined to enlist the Jurchets.

These were the people whom, among others, the Khitans had subjugated during their initial expansive phase. They were a Tungus people of the farther Manchurian north. Their country was the region of grassland and timbered taiga that lies between the Sungari and Ussuri rivers as they flow northward to their junctions with the Amur. Some were stockmen, others hunters in the woods. Watched by their chieftains seated on skins, they danced frantic corroborees reflecting their feats of arms and reproducing the play of lightning with flashing mirrors. To the Chinese they were unspeakably barbarous, more savage than the wolves howling round their camps. But they had acquired much of the military skill of the steppes proper; and this, together with their growing numbers, had brought them to the threshold of aggressive adventures of their own. They were spoiling to launch a full-scale onslaught on their Khitan overlords.

With the Jurchets Hui-tsung made a gentleman's agreement. If they attacked the Khitans from behind, overran the occupied lands of northern China and captured Yen Ching, his troops would not oppose them. In return they were to hand the city itself and its adjoining districts back to China. It was the proposal of an unbalanced amateur. The Jurchets, at that stage of their evolution, were far from gentlemen. And the Khitans, now peaceable and largely sinicized, had in effect become a buffer against just such wild invaders.

Aguda, the Jurchet khaghan, speedily fulfilled the first half of the bargain. In 1114 he entered north China with a host whose battle order – leather-armoured lancers in front, horse-archers in support behind – was not unlike that of the Byzantine formations. He tore apart the Khitan state, dispersed its forces and seized its capital. He was less easily persuaded to live up to the second part of the agreement; but after some delay he grudgingly yielded Yen Ching. The Chinese, however, emboldened by this success, proceeded to make further demands; and it became clear to Aguda that they were not only working towards a recovery of all the territory south of the Great Wall, but were helping their cause along by secretly stirring up the dispossessed Khitans to guerrilla warfare.

This exercise in brinkmanship provided the Jurchets with the pretext for an explosive reaction. Reoccupying Yen Ching, they lunged down to Kaifeng. Here, no such scruples troubled them as those which had turned the Khitans back from the city: they stormed into the streets, got hold of Hui-tsung and deported him bag and baggage to their Manchurian fastnesses, where the refined imperial aesthete died amid the cold dark forests. Then, having tightened their grip on the north, their armies headed for central China. Firing and killing, grabbing at the vast wealth that met their eyes on every hand, they raced down to the

Yangtze river and beyond. Here at length their advance was slowed, less by the woefully inadequate Sung militia than by the unfamiliar topography now around them. In the criss-cross of the countless streams and canals the Jurchet units lost touch with each other. Their horses bogged down in the rice paddies. Remounts ran short. The peasant population, bewildering in its teeming numbers, harried them. Their momentum exhausted, they turned; and with difficulty made good their retreat to the Yellow river.

Hui-tsung's son, thankful to see the end of the fury loosed by his father's folly, let them go. But the effect of the terrible Jurchet raid was similar to that of the Hiung-nu irruption of the fourth century: another great wave of Chinese energy was forced southward. Henceforth the Sung capital, the hub of China and the heart of its affections, was the beautiful city of Hangchow – more safely sited on the great bulge of coast below Shanghai, and naturally defended by mountains, waterways and sea. Everything north of the Huai river – half-way between the Yangtze and the Yellow – was abandoned to the Jurchets.

Having burnt their fingers in central China, the Jurchets remained content with their northern domains. In 1153, like the Khitans they had displaced, they made Yen Ching their capital, renamed it Chung Tu, and set about increasing its size and stature. From it, borrowing Chinese methods of administration, they organized a powerful state stretching from their frontier with the Sung to the Amur river and the verges of the Mongolian plateau. To their khaghans who ruled this empire of northeastern Asia they gave the dynastic name of Kin, meaning Gold – the Golden Kings.

Northern China had exchanged one Manchurian invader for another.

The upsurge of the Jurchets repercussed right across the Asian interior into the central Heartland, and thence to the farthest edges of the Iranian plateau.

Shortly after their arrival in north China, and while they were engaged in breaking up the Khitan regime, the Jurchets had seized a number of distinguished prisoners. Among them was a certain Yeliu Tu-shih, a member of the Khitan royal family. This prince escaped from his Jurchet captors; and realizing that the Khitan cause was lost, he gathered friends and followers about him and set off into the west to seek his fortune elsewhere. As he passed through Mongolia bands of herdsmen-archers, always ready for a possibly lucrative adventure, joined his standard. Before long he had moved through the Dzungarian gap and, with a very respectable force at his disposal, was encamped in the neighbourhood of Lake Balkash.

Here he involved himself in the politics of the Turkish tribes of the region. They were, as usual, quarrelling. Yeliu Tu-shih played them off against each other; and soon, with the aid of his superior wits and his willing army, he managed to extend his sway over most of the Turks from the Altai mountains to the Jaxartes. To this large realm, deep in continental Asia, his Turkish subjects gave the name of Kara (Black) Khitai; and Yeliu Tu-shih bestowed upon himself the imposing title of Gur-Khan – Lord of All.

The Kara-Khitan empire was more than the evanescent creation of an audacious group of exiles. The Gur-Khan was an able, sophisticated man, a product of Chinese education; and his state reflected his capabilities. He reinforced his army from among his warlike Turkish vassals; and his enlightened government, conducted along Chinese lines, granted to the component tribes – which included the literate Uighurs in the Tarim basin – a considerable degree of autonomy. From the outset, however, there was a difficulty. The Khitans were of Mongol origin; and many of them, through their previous contacts with China, had a Buddhist background. There was thus both a racial and a religious gulf between rulers and ruled, for most of the Turks of central Asia were fervent Moslems. Though the Kara-Khitans sought to assuage their subjects' feelings by encouraging freedom for all religions, these differences were ultimately to rebound against them.

In 1137 – at about the time when the Jurchets were evacuating the Yangtze region – the Kara-Khitans decided to venture still farther west, across the Jaxartes. Their forces scattered the local Turks at the approaches to the river, and followed up their victory by crossing it into Transoxiana. Here they confronted an adversary of far greater calibre; for they were now advancing on the easterly outposts of the Seljuk empire.

By this time the Seljuks had passed the peak of their power.

The kernel of their empire, based on Iran, was being dismembered by its mutually jealous rulers. But at its zenith, both Alp Arslan and his successor Malik Shah had been aware of the vital need to keep strong forces east of the Caspian, lest other hordes from the steppes should break in upon it. Indeed in 1072, shortly after Manzikert, Alp Arslan himself had been killed on the steppe frontier while holding back the pressure of Turkish tribesmen envious of the Seljuk possessions. And at Malik's death twenty years later, a soldier of marked ability and courage had been charged with the task of ensuring the continued security of the steppe gateway. This was the renowned and romantic Sultan Sanjar, Malik's youngest son. He was a figure comparable to Saladin. Among friends and enemies alike he was celebrated for his valour, chivalry and good faith. And as Saladin later stood for the defence of Islam against the Crusaders in the Levant, Sanjar, as the guardian of the Heartland borders, represented the defence of the Persian civilization inherited by the Seljuks.

When the Kara-Khitans crossed the Jaxartes, Sanjar was Governor of Khorasan. From his headquarters at Merv he exercised vice-regal powers over all the Seljuk territories in the region of eastern Iran. Among these territories was Khwaresm, the district in northern Transoxiana, at the mouths of the Oxus, which the Seljuks had seized before they set out to conquer Iran. Since that time the Khwaresm-shahs had been Seljuk appointees. They had remained loyal enough during the empire's heyday: but with the onset of its decline they began to entertain ambitions of independence. Sanjar had already been compelled forcefully to remind the Khwaresm-shah Atsiz of where his allegiance lay.

On hearing of the Kara-Khitan incursion into Transoxiana, Sanjar mobilized and advanced to meet them. He was used to alarms of this kind. On many previous occasions he had thrown back raids from the steppes. But this time the defender of the frontiers met his match. Colliding with the Kara-Khitans near Samarkand in 1141, his army was so roughly handled that he had to fall back into Khorasan. Quick to take advantage of his discomfiture, the Kara-Khitans spread out over Transoxiana. Soon they were overrunning Khwaresm and demanding the submission of Atsiz. No realistic alternative was open to the Khwaresm-shah; and he perceived that by accepting the inevitable he might further his aim of independence from the Seljuks. More or less willingly, he recognized the suzerainty of the Kara-Khitans.

The defection of Khwaresm gravely weakened Sanjar's position: but he was not now strong enough to attempt its recovery. And with Seljuk Iran in discord and division behind him, his chances of reinforcement were slender. He therefore played for time. But time was against him, for a few years later another blow fell. The Kara-Khitan invasion of Transoxiana had uprooted a horde of Ghuzz Turks who had been grazing in the region; and this large body of nomads had crossed the Oxus and sought shelter in Khorasan – that is, in the heart of the territory for which Sanjar was responsible. The Sultan well knew how ferocious these unwelcome refugees could be: they were kinsmen of his own Seljuk people. But since he had not the means to repulse them he had allowed them to settle in the neighbourhood of Balkh, sternly binding them to good behaviour and levying from them an annual tax of twenty-four thousand sheep. About 1150 Sanjar's agent, making his yearly visit to collect the tribute, saw fit to complain of the poor quality of the flocks offered. Incensed, the Ghuzz murdered him. And they then chased away a punitive expedition sent by the Governor of Balkh.

Sanjar could not overlook so dangerous an insult to his authority. He took the field against the Ghuzz himself, at the head of every man he could muster. The outcome was a catastrophe. The nomads routed his entire force, seized Sanjar himself, and made a dash for his headquarters at Merv. At the sight of the stately palaces and the Persian standards of wealth that met their eyes there, they went berserk. Tradition has it that they looted Merv so thoroughly that each day of the sack was devoted to the removal of different categories of goods – precious stones and metals, *objets d'art*, furnishings, and so on; and that when they could find nothing else of value they tortured the citizens until what had been buried was revealed. Sanjar, escaping after four years' captivity, and seeing in the wreckage of Merv the undoing of his life's work, died a broken man. And in the meantime the Ghuzz, fired by success and lusting for more plunder, marched on farther into Iran.

The Kara-Khitans, by pushing the Ghuzz across the Oxus, had unwittingly set a primitive steppe horde moving upon the tottering but still magnificent Seljuk empire. They were now,

again inadvertently, to loose a greater barbarian flood through
the dykes thus breached. This came about as a result of events
in their little vassal state of Khwaresm. In 1156 Atsiz died, and
another Khwaresm-shah took his place with Kara-Khitan approval. But in 1172 the throne again fell vacant; and this time
a vicious dispute broke out between two rival claimants. The
Kara-Khitans, as overlords, became involved; and after hesitating between the two, they lent the contender of their final
choice an army with which to enforce his claim. This enterprising man, having secured his own position in Khwaresm, found
a second use for his Kara-Khitan force: he employed it to conquer Khorasan, and so to enlarge his domain at the expense of
the Seljuks. He then died; and his former rival, succeeding him,
not only consolidated his grasp on Khorasan, but launched his
own army into the heart of Seljuk Iran beyond. Under this leap-
frogging assault from Khwaresm, conceived in treachery and
executed with the utmost ruthlessness, the Seljuk regime finally
crumpled. The resistance put up by the last Seljuk sultan,
Toghrul III, was smashed near Rey in 1194. Alp Arslan's death,
Malik's precautions, Sanjar's gallantry, had all been in vain.
Through the steppe gateway the tribal Turks poured in from
central Asia, submerging alike the Seljuks and the Persian civilization which to a great extent had settled and tempered them.
Only the Sultanate of Rum, in Asia Minor, was left in Seljuk
hands. The obscure outpost-colony of Khwaresm had not only
achieved its independence: it had supplanted its masters as the
dominant power from the Aral Sea to Mesopotamia.

Of the headlong expansion of the Khwaresmian Turks the
Kara-Khitans had been the involuntary catalysts. They now
contributed to its further inflation – and to their own undoing.
In the year 1200 Ala ed-Din Mohammed, son of one of the rivals
who had overrun the Seljuks, was established as Khwaresm-
shah. Not content with his swollen realm, Mohammed set about
enlarging it southward by an attempted conquest of Afghanistan. His campaign failed: the Afghans drove him back and began
to mount pillaging raids across his borders in revenge. In his
predicament Mohammed turned to the Kara-Khitans, who still
retained their position as overlords of Khwaresm. Unwilling to
see their subordinate worsted, they sent a strong force to his aid.
With this help Mohammed quickly reversed his fortunes. He

drove the Afghans out of Khwaresm and pursued them into their own country. Within a few years the whole of Afghanistan, like the Seljuk domains in Iran, had been engulfed into the Khwaresmian empire.

Mohammed's manner of rewarding his rescuers was typical of his predecessor's methods. For some time the Kara-Khitans had been at loggerheads with their subject peoples: the old religious ill-feeling between the Moslem Turks on the steppes and their Buddhist masters was flaring up. All along, the Turks of Khwaresm had shared this latent hostility. With their sudden acquisition of power and possessions, their position as dependants of infidels seemed a disgrace; and their indebtedness to the Kara-Khitans only aggravated the affront. With the dual aim of conducting a holy war, and of simultaneously expelling the Kara-Khitans from Transoxiana, Mohammed advanced into the core of their territory between the Jaxartes and Lake Balkash. There he inflicted a damaging defeat on those to whom he owed far more than allegiance, capturing their marshal and setting their central Heartland state on the road to dissolution. And in 1217, with Transoxiana, Afghanistan and Iran at his feet, the Khwaresm-shah Mohammed, at the height of his dubiously acquired glory, made a triumphal progress through his domains, receiving the homage of his sultans and atabegs, their vassals and their vassals' vassals.

Here it might be well to recapitulate; for in effect the events just described were setting the stage for the climactic act in the drama of the nomadic Heartland.

In the tenth century the Khitans, a people of Mongol extraction from Manchuria, invaded northern China. The new Sung dynasty proved unable to throw them out; and the Tanguts from the Tibetan borderlands took advantage of the crisis to establish an independent state in the Chinese north-west.

Then the Jurchets, another horde from Manchuria, seized north China from the Khitans. This second impact pushed the Chinese boundary farther south, and confirmed the division of the country. It also caused a remnant of the Khitans to migrate to central Asia, where they gained ascendancy over Turkish tribes of the region and formed the state of Kara-Khitai.

As the Kara-Khitans expanded they achieved control of the

district of Khwaresm, a Turkish outpost of the Seljuk empire at
the Iranian gateway to the Heartland. Their intervention in
Khwaresm greatly increased the power of the local rulers, and
enabled them to revolt against the Seljuks.

The sudden rise of Khwaresm released a flood of primitive
Turks from the central Asian steppes into the lands of the southern Eurasian littoral. The Seljuk empire, except for its possessions in Asia Minor, was overwhelmed; so also were Afghanistan
and the territories of the Kara-Khitans in Transoxiana.

So at the opening of the thirteenth century, and largely as a
result of the incursions from Manchuria, five states were ranged
around the easterly perimeter of inner Asia. In the north-east
was the realm of the Kin or Golden Kings, where the Jurchets,
partly sinicized but still partly herdsmen-hunters from the wilds,
lived cheek by jowl with their subject Khitans and the original
Chinese population. To the south, contracted into the basin of
the Yangtze, stood what was now China proper under the Sung
emperors. Occupying the frontier region of the Ordos plateau
and the gateway to the Mongolian steppes was the Tangut state
of Hsi-Hsia, with its capital on the upper inland reaches of the
Yellow river near the present city of Ninghsia. In the heart of
central Asia was Kara-Khitai, reduced by internal revolt and
external attack. And from the Jaxartes almost to the Euphrates
stretched the new Khwaresmian empire: an ill-digested, ill-
organized stamping-ground of nomadic Turks from the interior,
drifting on the wave of their good fortune through the graceful
Persian-Seljuk city culture they had overrun.

None of these states was to endure. For the growl of the distant thunder on the steppes was growing louder. From the inner
Heartland a tempest of unprecedented fury, to be felt in nearly
every quarter of the known world, was about to break.

8

The Wind of God's Omnipotence

*The great bird mounts on the wind. Looking down from
up there, are these horses he sees, galloping? Is it primordial matter flying in a dust of atoms? Is the blue the sky
itself, or but the colour of infinite distance?*

— The Book of Chuang-tzu

THE high landlocked plateau that lies between Siberia and
Tibet had already been the storm-centre from which
successive nomad waves – the Hiung-nu, the Huns, the Turks –
had swept across the Heartland to the settled verges of Eurasia.
In the early years of the thirteenth century yet another people
burst from this plateau, and from origins of impoverished obscurity possessed themselves in a few decades of the largest
territorial empire that has ever existed. Theirs was the most
terrible, but in many respects the most significant, of the
great nomadic eruptions. From Indo-China to Austria they destroyed with a deliberate, universal thoroughness never before
recorded. But in the extraordinary degree of control they came
to exercise over the vast spaces that they conquered, they revealed to the small-scale thought of the western Middle Ages
the potentials latent in singleness and size. And though their
monolithic state, like those of their steppe predecessors, swiftly
disintegrated, the vision they left did much to clear the way
for the modern concept of the world. These people were the
Mongols.

Like the Heartland of which it forms an inner core, the immense tableland now known as Mongolia is crescent-shaped. At
its western edge the peaks of the Altai mountains guard the

descent to the plains that stretch away to the Urals. Fifteen hundred miles to the east, the Khingan range separates it from Manchuria and the Pacific littoral. To the south, the region is bounded by a great curve formed by the Tien Shan mountains and the Gobi desert. Massed between the northerly horns of the crescent, and separating Mongolia from the uplands of central Siberia, are further chains of mountains – the Sayan, the Kentey, the Yablonovy – holding in their jumbled grip the long finger of Lake Baikal, with its grim cliffs rising from treacherous, fathomless depths. In these chains three of the great river systems of inner Asia have their birth. From the eastern mountains, the Kerulen, the Khailar and the Kan flow down into the Argun; the Onon and the Ingoda join the Shilka; and Argun and Shilka in turn swell the huge reaches of the Amur wandering to the far-off sea of Okhotsk. From the central heights, Tula, Orkhon and Eder discharge into the Selenga as it winds north to Baikal. And in the western ranges rise the streams that feed the mighty Arctic-bound Siberian rivers, Yenisei, Ob and Irtysh.

The dark robe of the taiga wraps these northern mountains. They stand beneath forests of fir and larch, birch and aspen, through which summits of bare flat granite shoulder up. The deep woods were the home of hunting tribes, pursuing their food across carpets of moss and lichen, sheltering in crude cabins of boughs and bark from the icy blizzards driving down from the tundra and howling in the treetops overhead. Around the mountains' feet meadowlands emerge from the timbered gloom, their rounded humps and dipping bowls fresh, in the year's brief moment of gentleness, with buttercup, thyme and iris. Southward, the landscape changes. Meadows merge into the level distances of the steppe, heavy with snow through the long winter months, burnt by midsummer into browning seas of grass tormented by the rage of sudden noonday storms. Here again the wild forces of the climate only reach a kindly balance in the fleeting weeks of spring; and a nomad of the Mongolian prairies, asked his age, would often reply by telling the number of times the steppe had flowered since he was born. Then, still farther south, the grass gives way to desert: to hardened expanses of clay and gravel broken by rock outcrops and by the flanks of dunes smoking in the winds – searing, dust-filled winds, slitting the eyes and bending the heads of drovers and caravan-masters as they fought their way to the pools and wispy grazings that thread the ochre wastes of the Gobi.

Of this tremendous but merciless landscape the people who were to become known as the Mongols occupied, before their rise to power, only a fraction. While northern China lay under the rule of the Khitans from Manchuria, the Mongols proper were of little account in Mongolia and of none at all outside it. The plateau was then inhabited by many tribes of Turkish and Tungus, as well as Mongol, background. The most considerable of these were the Naimans on the slopes of the Altai mountains in the west, the Kereits in the central districts, and the Tatars in the foothills of the Khingan range in the east. Farther north, and closer to Lake Baikal, dwelt another large community, the Merkits. The most civilized – if the word can be applied to peoples living in a perpetual state of armed rivalry – were the Naimans and the Kereits. Many of them were Nestorians: adherents of the doctrine of the human nature of Christ's birth which had infiltrated the steppes from its inception in Syria. At the same time the Kereits and the Tatars, from their proximity to China, enjoyed a measure of contact with the great world beyond the Gobi.

Sandwiched between the larger tribes lived less important groups; and of these the Mongols were one. Their homelands centred in the relatively small stretch of country between the Onon and Kerulen rivers, in the eastern part of Mongolia. Here, a minor cluster of clans and tribes, they lived surrounded by three neighbours – Kereits, Tatars and Merkits – all more powerful than themselves. They spoke differing dialects of the same language: but they felt no sense of a common identity, and shared no common purpose. They did not yet possess their name; and it was a matter of contemptuous remark that they had no single ruling khan wielding overall powers. They told, however, a vivid legendary story of their beginnings. In the northern forests there roamed a great blue-grey wolf. By the shores of Baikal he took as his consort a tawny doe; and the pair, wandering south together, settled near the Kentey range where the Onon rises, at the foot of a mountain called Burkan-kaldun. From their union the Mongols sprang: the people of the Blue, or heavenly, Wolf, as the Turks before them had been the people of the Grey Wolf and the Blue Sky. The site of Burkan-kaldun

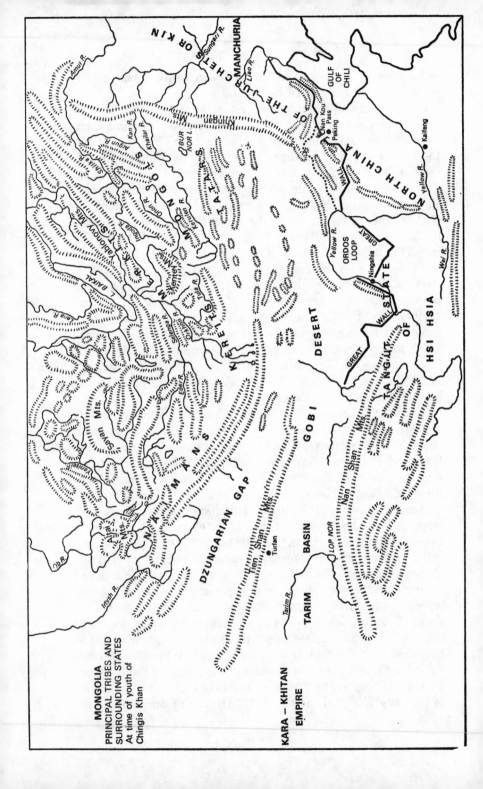

MONGOLIA
PRINCIPAL TRIBES AND
SURROUNDING STATES
At time of youth of
Chingis Khan

KARA – KHITAN
EMPIRE

TARIM
BASIN

LOP NOR

Tarim R.

Turfan

Tien Shan Mts.

DZUNGARIAN GAP

N A I M A N S

Irtysh R.

Ob R.

Altai Mts.

Sayan Mts.

L. BAIKAL

Selenga R.

MERKITS

Kobdo R.

Edel R.

Uvs

Tula R.

Orkhon R.

Selenga R.

Kerulen R.

Onon R.

KEREITS

Khangai Mts.

Tannu Ula Mts.

Yablonovy Mts.

Amur R.

MONGOLS

ONGGIRATS

Khailar R.

Kan R.

BUR
NOR L.

Khingan Mts.

T A T A R S

GOBI DESERT

Nan Shan Mts.

TANGUT

HSI HSIA

STATE

WALL

GREAT

WALL

Ningshia

Yellow R.

ORDOS
LOOP

GREAT

Wei R.

Yellow R.

Kaifeng

Peking

Nan Kou
Pass

GULF
OF
CHILI

NORTH CHINA

OF THE JUCHETS OR KIN

MANCHURIA

Liao R.

Sungari R.

is now lost; but the story suggests that its tellers were originally people of the taiga who gradually emerged from the forests on to the open plains. In the early days of their known history they were, in fact, still in a 'half-way' state, relatively primitive, semi-savage, and deriving their livelihood partly from the forests and partly from the steppes. While some were still woodland hunters, most were already herdsmen-archers of the meadows and prairies, mounted, fully mobile, and entertaining, as rangers of the free grassy spaces, a certain disdain for their tree-bound kinsmen.

At this time the competition among the steppe tribes for increased power and possessions was exceptionally fierce. Dominant pastoral clans would seek by intrigue and alliance to enlarge their hold over kith and kin, or to seize the better grazing-grounds of neighbours by out-and-out annihilation or enslavement. In the bitter struggle for survival, the people of the Onon-Kerulen district had little chance of improving their lot through the unified command of force which alone spelt respect. Poor even by steppe standards, the hazards of the cruel climate aggravated their poverty; and the univeral anarchy reigning among their own tents, as well as among the larger tribes around them, kept them divided. No man could tell when the sudden drum of hooves and whistle of arrows might herald a raid which would leave him minutes later – if he was still alive – destitute of women, horses and cattle. In such vicious kaleidoscopic turmoil, loyalty went wherever momentary advantage might suggest. Submission was a commodity to be bartered according to the peril of the day. There was little room for consistent, single-minded allegiance.

To some extent, however, their fortunes took a turn for the better as a result of the military policy of the Khitan regime in north China. For the Khitans, in securing the territories they had conquered against incursions from the steppes, did not put their faith in the static defences of the Great Wall. Instead they systematically patrolled the Mongolian tableland, mounting preventive campaigns there when necessary so as to keep threatening concentrations of tribal power well away from their frontiers. For this purpose they augmented their own forces with nomad auxiliaries; and the herdsmen-archers of the Onon-Kerulen area, being conveniently available close to the Chinese borders, were among those frequently enlisted. To these needy troopers Khitan pay was welcome: but more valuable was the chance thus afforded them to infiltrate the more prosperous tribes of central and western Mongolia, and even, under the Khitan banner, to take over sections of their pastures.

The second invasion of north China from Manchuria – that of the Jurchets in the early twelfth century – gave, at first, another forward push to the emergence of the Mongols. For as they drove southward to displace the Khitans, the Jurchets collided with a number of lesser nomadic hordes grazing on the eastern fringes of Mongolia; and one of these, fleeing for safety, crossed the Kerulen and attacked the encampments of the Mongols beyond it. One of the clans among the latter had for some time been striving to 'bind the arrows into a bundle'; that is, to unite all the Mongols into an unbreakable entity under their own rule. This was an ambitious group called the Borjigin, who claimed direct descent from the Wolf and the Doe of the ancient myth. The emergency gave them their opportunity. After savage fighting a Borjigin chief rallied his warriors' failing strength and threw the intruders back. His heroism, coupled with renewed awareness of his clan's mystic origin, acted as a magnet. Soon the Borjigin were welding a hitherto impotent and disparate people into a cohesive, disciplined whole. By the time the Jurchets had expelled the Khitans and settled down to rule north China in their place, the Mongols, in their valleys and plains beyond the Gobi, had already acknowledged a succession of tough, determined Borjigin khans. They had also acquired their name: for one of these khans called to mind another of the immemorial legends of the tableland. It was the saga of a mighty horde of ancient time whose deeds had been handed down in epic poetry, and whose name had derived from the word *mong*, meaning brave. To inspire his newly unified people, he called them 'The Brave' after their long-vanished forebears.

It was in 1129 that the Jurchets, from their strongholds around the embryo Peking, launched their devastating expedition towards the Yangtze basin in central China. Since this adventure required a heavy commitment of his armies, the Golden King wanted no trouble from the steppes while it was in progress. But reports persistently reached him of the growing strength of the Mongols; and eventually, to assess their intentions, he decided to invite their chieftain to his court. Grousset[1] graphically describes the meeting between Kabul, the uncouth Mongol khan, and the monarch whose hastily acquired Chinese manners scarcely concealed his own barbaric origin. The Mongol ate with an appetite that astonished even the Jurchets, retiring at frequent intervals from the royal presence to be sick. At length reassured by this process that the strange, subtly flavoured dishes set before him were not poisoned, Kabul allowed himself to relax into more leisurely enjoyment; and finally, in a sudden access of camaraderie, he committed the appalling solecism of leaning forward and giving a sharp tug to his host's beard. A deathly tension followed, broken at last by a laugh as the Jurchet sovereign passed off the hideous episode. But the encounter left the King of Gold uneasy. The new horde in Mongolia was an uncomfortable presence on his denuded flank. For the time being they could be bought off with gifts: but later they must be reduced to size by some means requiring a minimum of Jurchet troops.

Unhappily for the Mongols, they themselves provided the means. For a few years afterwards they became involved in a bitter quarrel, leading to outright war, with the Tatars. The name of the Tatars has been misleadingly used. To the Chinese, *ta-ta* signified simply 'nomads'; and for Europeans, *Tartarus* suggested the Infernal Regions. For such reasons the Tatars came to be equated with the nomads of the eastern Heartland as a whole – including the Mongols. The Tatars were, in fact, the Mongols' eastern neighbours: a tribe of Turkish background powerful enough to attract into their orbit lesser adjacent groups who had assumed their name for prestige purposes. For the Jurchets, the feud between the two hordes was timely. In their eyes, the Mongols were becoming the more dangerous, and they therefore threw their full support behind the Tatars. As the strife increased in scale the Tatars captured the Mongol khan Ambakhai, Kabul's successor, and handed him over to the Jurchets. At the orders of the Golden King Ambakhai suffered an agonizing death by impalement on the knife-backed effigy of a donkey. As he died, he swore vengeance on his enemies; and his warriors, enraged by the ignominy of his end, strove to exact it. They redoubled their

[1] René Grousset, *Conqueror of the World*, pp. 15–16.

onslaughts on the Tatars, and even mounted raids into Jurchet territory in north China. But their devotion was in vain; and in 1161, near the Bur Nor lake between the Kerulen and the Khingans, their horse-archers were caught and decimated by the combined armies of the Tatars and the Jurchets. So total was the defeat that much of the long unifying work of the Borjigin clan was undone. Smashed and pillaged by their implacable foes, the Mongols virtually relapsed into their former state of lawless fragmentation. And because they had tasted the promise of power and plenty, their renewed anarchy was the more embittered. Robbery, murder, rape and treachery once again prevailed among them.

Yet they did not give up. Doggedly they pursued their feud with the Tatars, harrying their camps and rustling their cattle whenever chance offered. In one of these tip-and-run raids, the leader of a Mongol band had a stroke of luck: he captured two Tatar notables, minor chiefs like himself. The Mongol's name was Yesugei. He was a person of some standing; he belonged to a branch of the Borjigin clan, and the blood of former khans flowed in his veins. Considering the afflictions then besetting his people, he was reasonably well-to-do: he had pastures, followers, slaves, and a young wife, Oyelun, a Merkit woman whom he had kidnapped shortly after her marriage to another man. Returning to his tents by the Onon river, Yesugei was met with the news that a son had been born to Oyelun during his absence. A male child was often called by the name of a distinguished enemy taken in war; and Yesugei's infant was accordingly called Temujin, after the elder of his two Tatar prisoners. The name stemmed from a word meaning 'iron'; it could be interpreted as Metal-worker, Blacksmith, or even, by a stretch, Man of Iron. And it was said that the baby left the womb 'grasping in his right hand a clot of blood in the shape of a knuckle-bone'.[1]

Thirty-nine years after the birth of Temujin a great assembly of the Mongol people took place on the banks of the Onon river. The year was 1206. In northern China the Golden Monarchs were omnipotent. In India, the descendants of the old Ghaznavids, pushed ever farther into the sub-continent by the Turkish tide flowing from central Asia, were fastening their hold on

[1] *Secret History of the Mongols.* Translated by Arthur Waley, p. 223.

Delhi and inaugurating the dynasty of the Moslem 'Slave Sultans'. Farther west, in Afghanistan and Iran, the same tide was flooding into the new Khwaresmian Empire of Mohammed. But as yet the Mongols had no eyes for these further worlds. Recent changes in their own world were wonderful enough to claim their whole attention.

Not long before, overwhelmed by their enemies, they had been a scattered, dejected handful of tribes. In less than a generation their prospects had been utterly transformed. Swiftly, suddenly, they had become the most powerful presence in the eastern Heartland. At what had seemed the nadir of their fortunes a new khan had arisen among them who had dispelled their bitterness, bound them together more closely than ever, and led them to the conquest of the entire Mongolian plateau. Now, at his command, they were assembling in the district of his birth to confirm him as their overlord, to celebrate his triumphs in feast and drink and dance. Along the stretches of the Onon men and herds, tents and wagons, multiplied and spread. Huge cauldrons, mounted on carts, were filled with horse-meat and set a-boil. Mares' milk, churned into koumiss, foamed into batteries of skins and pitchers. A long line of stately tents, arranged with strict care for precedence, marked the quarters of the khan's relatives, of his nobles and officers and of their wives, each household surrounded by its separate retinue of serving men and women. At the centre of this ordered metropolis of felt towered a gigantic white marquee, and at its entrance stood the emblem of the new Mongol power: a great white falcon-crowned standard from which floated the tails of nine bay horses, enshrining the deeds and persons of the nine chief marshals of the khan's armies. So potent were the unseen forces emanating from this standard that birds were believed to fall dead from the air as they passed above it.

The ceremonies began in the broad grassy space before the central marquee. Here, attended by the chief shaman, stood the figure the encircling thousands of his warriors had come to honour: the man who had set the Mongols over all the tribes of forest and meadow and steppe. Solemnly the high priest pronounced him Khan by the will of the Everlasting Sky; and the name which he had already received during the years of his growing power was reaffirmed. This name was *Chingis*; and its approximate meaning was 'all that is encompassed by the world-girdling ocean'. Seizing the supreme moment, Chingis Khan turned to his assembled subjects. He demanded, as a condition of accepting office, their unfaltering obedience – even to the infliction of instant death on any he should name. He stepped on to a square of black tent-felt spread upon the ground. The corners were reverently lifted; and, acclaimed by burst on burst of tumultuous shouts, he was borne shoulder-high past the throngs falling to their knees, past the waving tails of the standard, into the great tent.

Within, he took his seat on a throne of skins taken from the pure white horses that were sacred to the Mongols as to other peoples of the steppes. At his side was Borte, the first and always the most respected of his wives. Around him the massive supporting timbers of the tent, gold-adorned, and the heavy brocades upon its walls, soared up into the dim half-light. Before him, gleaming from the shadows, lay a vast pile of the goods dearest to the nomad heart: treasures of precious metals, pelts of rare quality, ornamented weapons, robes and rolls of silk. One by one, group by group, those whose loyalty had earned his gratitude entered and stood before him. They listened to the long citations of their brave deeds; heard his unstinted thanks; took into their hands their sumptuous rewards. Some had been his close companions from boyhood. Others, though they had fought in his ranks from end to end of Mongolia, had perhaps never been face to face with him before. They beheld a man in the prime of life, rising forty, stalwart of build, impressively tall. His forehead was broad, and his beard of unusual length for a Mongol. It seemed to them that a peculiar glow emanated from his face, and that in his eyes was the shine of fire. The colour of these riveting eyes was never recorded; but several who looked into them said they were reminded of the unblinking inscrutable stare of a cat.

This man, now Chingis Khan, Lord of the Land-mass of the World, had once been the child Temujin, born to Yesugei and his stolen wife Oyelun in the time of the Mongols' despair.

The tale of the young Temujin's rise to supremacy over all the tribes of Mongolia is unforgettably told in the *Secret History of the Mongols* – a magnificently poetic account written down some

years after his death and intended only for circulation among
the Mongols themselves. Its narrative is heroic rather than historical. But even when stripped of its more imaginative qualities
and set beside the known facts, a story of almost fantastic adventure emerges: of whirlwind onslaughts by day and night across
the rivers and through the gorges of the huge tableland; of
thunderous pursuits through snows and sands; of enslavement
and cold-blooded extirpation: but also of high devotion on the
part of men who subsequently figured among the greatest of the
Mongol generals. A bare outline of the story must suffice here.

Temujin had been born into a noble family: but it was a family reduced in circumstances and surrounded by perils. At the
age of ten he became a victim of the continuing feud between the
Mongols and the Tatars; for his father, unguardedly taking a
meal by the wayside with a band of Tatars to whom he believed
himself unknown, was recognized and poisoned. Thereupon
Yesugei's followers deserted the camp of Oyelun his widow; and
seeing in her son a threat to their own ambitions, did their best
to murder him. Hounded into hiding, several times escaping
death by a hair's breadth, Temujin survived only by eating
mice clawed from their holes and drinking water pressed from
mud. Eventually he made his way home; the veil of danger
lifted a little, and food became more plentiful. But by now, for
the humiliated aristocratic youth, property had become an obsession. One day, out hunting, his half-brother took more than
his fair share of the game. While he was busy with his knife,
Temujin shot him dead from behind. For this, probably his first
killing, he was scolded by his mother.

Yet for all his self-assertive jealousy, he could exert an extraordinary degree of personal magnetism. In the early years of his
adolescence a number of horses, his family's most treasured possession, were seized by raiders in a sudden attack. Only one
animal remained, and on this Temujin set out in pursuit. Riding
past an encampment of strangers, he stopped to ask a young
man of his own age if he had seen the thieves. This youth,
Bogurchi by name, then and there saddled a horse; and though
he had never set eyes on Temujin before, joined him in his quest.
After a breathless affray with the robbers the stolen horses were
recovered; and between the two companions a lifelong comrade-
ship was formed. The incident was significant: for it marked the

start of Temujin's realization that at this time, when lawless chaos reigned across the steppes and men's shifting allegiances were largely governed by their fears, there could be stronger bonds than the fragile traditional loyalties engendered by the tribal system.

Before his death at Tatar hands, and while Temujin was still a child, his father had arranged his betrothal to Borte, daughter of the chieftain of another tribe grazing in eastern Mongolia. At the age of about eighteen Temujin claimed his bride and so married his first wife. He was now a young chief of high connections, albeit reaching manhood with few resources in a pitiless environment. But he was discovering that if this environment bred terror and death, it could also be made to yield to daring, wits, and faithfulness to proven friends. On these qualities he was beginning to build a following. Not yet twenty, he could assemble warriors about him: men attracted by his personality, and by the promise he seemed to hold out of being able to form around himself a nucleus of protective and even aggressive strength. So far he had been preoccupied with the problems of survival. With his marriage came the expansion of his ambitions into the wider field of steppe politics. One of his wedding presents, the gift of Borte's family, was a robe of superb black sables. Riding off with this princely gift, Temujin laid it at the feet of the khan of the neighbouring Kereits, reminding him of certain services done him by Yesugei, and declaring himself his vassal. It was a move of far-sighted shrewdness, the first of very many; for the Kereits, dominating central Mongolia, were among the most powerful peoples of the plateau.

Almost immediately his astuteness was repaid. As a young man Yesugei had abducted his bride Oyelun from the Merkits. The episode had rankled, and the Merkits now sent a raiding party to carry off Borte in revenge. The raiders swooped down in strength at a moment when only a few men and horses were available around Temujin's tents. Instant flight was imperative. He leapt to his saddle and escaped with his escort, leaving Borte without a mount. There seems little doubt that his desertion of his wife at this critical juncture was calculated and deliberate. An attempt to defend her would have meant certain death for himself and his men. But the Merkits, he knew, would preserve Borte alive as a valued prize. And thanks to the sable robe, help could be obtained to recover her. No love was lost between the

Kereits and the Merkits; and the Kereit khan, with his vassal
Temujin, rode against Borte's captors with a combined force of
some forty thousand horsemen. The Merkit herds and homelands were savagely mauled, and Borte was rescued. The campaign was the making of Temujin among his own people. For the
Mongol nobility, perceiving in him a leader of true Borjigin
calibre, elected him their khan and bestowed on him the name
of Chingis. It was a foretaste of the power to come: the power
he was learning to understand and manipulate.

So, while still in his mid-twenties, Temujin became Chingis,
Khan of the Mongols. But among the mighty constellations of
the eastern Heartland he was as yet a minor star. His further
rise was now, however, unwittingly assisted by the Jurchets in
northern China. Hitherto the Golden Monarch had kept Mongolia in balance by favouring the Tatars; but they, in their pastures close to his north-western frontiers, were becoming too
strong for his comfort. Accordingly, in 1194, he changed his
policy, transferring his support to the Kereits. To Chingis, the
Tatars were the root of all evil. It was they who had handed over
his forebear Ambakhai to the Jurchets, and had thus been responsible for his horrible end: it was they who had done his father
to a lingering death by poison. At Jurchet prompting the khan
of the Kereits now led an expedition against them. Chingis
joined it with every horse-archer he could summon. The result
was decisive, but not final. The Tatar khan was slain and his
treasure appropriated. But the Tatars, to Chingis's chagrin, continued to exist. Moreover they now contributed a force to an
army being mobilized by other tribes who had become alarmed
by his successes. In two furious battles near the Kerulen river –
in one of which Chingis nearly lost his life from an arrow wound
in the neck – the Mongols managed to break up this dangerous
coalition. The effect of the victories was to put the Tatars, at
long last, at Chingis's mercy. And he now felt strong enough to
administer the *coup de grâce* alone, without the help of his Kereit
allies. In 1202 he advanced into the country of the Tatars, overwhelmed their army, rounded up their people in droves, and
caused every male among them taller than the hub of a wagon-
wheel to be slaughtered. By this act he rid himself of the long-
standing hostility of their adult population, but preserved their
future manpower for his own service.

The Merkits had already been severely weakened. The Tatars were now silenced for years to come. All eastern Mongolia was in Chingis's power. Of the great steppe communities, there remained the Kereits in the central region of the plateau, and the Naimans in the Altaic west.

Despite the close bonds between them, the physical proximity of the Mongols and the lone hand Chingis had played in his destruction of the Tatars inevitably aroused the suspicions of the Kereit khan as to his intentions. The break came within a year. The Kereits struck first; and the short war which followed, though it opened in an atmosphere of regrets for past ties, was fought with fearful violence and with the issue far from certain. It culminated, however, in a surprise attack launched by Chingis's entire army after he had misled his enemy into believing that peace was in sight. For three days a critical battle raged. Then the exhausted Kereits surrendered; and Chingis, though his method of achieving victory had been tinged with treachery, acted magnanimously towards a vanquished people to whom he was deeply indebted. No massacre followed the defeat of the Kereits. They were accepted as vassals and incorporated into the Mongol tribes.

The subduing of the Naimans of the west proved an easier task. They were a proud Turkish people, holding the Mongols in contempt as malodorous barbarians. Nevertheless, recognizing the peril in which they now stood, they sent their bowmen streaming eastward from the Altai foothills to meet Chingis before he could invade and plunder their pastures. This move committed them to a campaign in unfamiliar country. Moreover their khan was an elderly man whose resolution had been undermined by the insecurity of his throne. The two hosts converged in the mountains of central Mongolia. As he watched the Mongol myriads advancing, it seemed to the Naiman khan that their generals, surrounded by the panoply of bodyguards and banners, resembled ferocious dogs with 'foreheads of bronze and fangs like chisels. Their tongues are awls and their hearts are of iron. They use their swords as horsewhips. They drink the dew and ride on the wind, but in war they eat human flesh.'[1] He ordered his men into defensive positions at the foot of a mountain. But as Chingis's grim formations continued their approach the

[1] *Secret History*. Arthur Waley translation, p. 278.

Naimans edged steadily back, up to the refuge of the higher slopes. There, during the night before the now unavoidable battle, they turned and ran. In the unknown terrain their horses missed their footing, dashed their riders against hidden rocks, plunged with them into the black mouths of the chasms. Next morning the Mongol attack completed the shambles. At the centre of a last knot of resistance the Naiman khan fell mortally wounded; and his son, one Kuchluk, fled to the south-west to take shelter among the Kara-Khitans on the Balkash steppes. Even there, as later events proved, he was to find himself unable to shake off Mongol pursuit.

For Chingis, the rest was mopping up. By the spring of 1205, save for a few pockets of resistance, the whole of the Mongolian tableland was his.

The assembly of 1206 held to celebrate these triumphs marked the emergence of another great confederation in the eastern Heartland, comparable to those which had been formed by Maodun in the second century B.C. and by Toumen in the sixth century A.D. In the fury of its forging nearly every tribe had suffered; some had lost half or more of their numbers. The living balance – Merkits, Kereits, Naimans, surviving Tatars – were now merged with their conquerors into a single community of 'all the dwellers in tents', to be known henceforth as that of the Blue Mongols. From the Mongols themselves, the ruling core of the new realm, the years of annihilation and absorption had demanded a sustained military effort of an intensity they would seldom be called on to repeat. Though warriors by nature, and though in the decades ahead, with their new vassal-allies, they would overwhelm states far vaster in extent and resources, they would rarely have to fight so desperately again. They called themselves 'the Brave': but from end to end of the plateau they had subdued, valour was as universal as life was cheap.

The Borjigin ancestors of Chingis Khan had attempted to impose unity upon the Mongol tribes. Their descendant had imposed it on all Mongolia. Certainly, his success had been due in part to his steely character. But many others among his followers and foes possessed his attributes of courage, cunning and will. His exceptional quality was insight: his ability to divine political truth in personal experience, and his capacity to turn perception to account. He appeared at the right time, in the right combination of circumstances; and there was thus perhaps an element of the inevitable in his rise. The steppes were ripe for a new confederation: but of a different kind to those of earlier times, with their uncertain ties, now hardening now crumbling, of tribal association. In the twelfth century the tribal system itself was breaking down. Anarchy had reached a point where it could no longer assure a measure of common welfare or of protection for the weak. Chingis alone discerned this underlying reality, and succeeded in injecting a substitute for tribalism into the deeply conservative society of the nomads.

His own background notably assisted this process. In childhood the tribal order had cheated him of his expectations. And all through his years of struggle he had been plagued by a rival: a chief of his own age called Jamuka with whom, in youth, he had been sworn to alliance by tribal custom. The supposed bond, as often happened, had only aggravated their conflicting ambitions. Jamuka had repeatedly lent his aid to Chingis's enemies; and it was not until after the conquest of the Naimans that Chingis had succeeded in liquidating him. By contrast, his link with Bogurchi had been real and heartfelt from the day the two had joined forces to pursue the horse-thieves; and this natural affinity between comrades in armed adventure became the pattern on which he built up first his entourage, then the leadership of his army and his regime. All along he had been careful not to challenge aspects of the tribal system too strong for immediate dissolution: but bit by bit as his fame grew, he had drawn men, and even whole tribal groups, from its failing hold and had inspired them instead with a new and eager loyalty to himself. In this context he was a revolutionary. He led inner Asia from tribalism to organized feudalism, creating from the ceaseless merge and melt of the eastern steppes something more like an imperial Mongolian nation.

In the bitter warfare necessary to effect this transformation, he had shown himself more long-sighted than his opponents. True, his campaigns across Mongolia had proved him a matchless leader of light cavalry in the field: in them, he had brought the dash and mobility of the mounted archer to a new pitch of effectiveness. But the chain of his victories had emerged less from his tactical brilliance than from the caution of his strategic

planning. He had chosen allies and enemies only after cons.
appraisal of the consequences. And he had never tackled `
than one major antagonist at a time. Each of his success
steppe wars had been fought with limited objectives; an `
always, so far as calculation could assure it, within a framework
of the possible. He had brought to the Heartland the qualities of
a true commander-in-chief; something which, for all its long
martial history, it had usually lacked.

As the festivities beside the Onon river continued, the structure that the new Mongol empire would assume became evident
in the gifts which Chingis bestowed on those who had helped him
to create it. He was moulding it in his own aristocratic image. He
recognized an obligation to his people as a whole. 'My bowmen
loom like a thick forest; their wives and maidens shine like red
flames. My task is to sweeten their mouths with gifts of sugar, to
swathe their breasts, backs and shoulders with garments of brocade, to seat them on good geldings, to give them to drink from
pure rivers, to provide their beasts with abundant pastures.'[1]
But such blessings were to descend through a firmly ordered
hierarchy. The new imperium was to be 'democratic' only in the
sense that rank and honours were open to any man of merit; and
an essential component of merit was proved fidelity to the Khan
himself. Many of those now immediately around him, and especially the marshals of his army, had risen in this way. Some
among them were Mongols; others came from tribes now subordinate. There was Bogurchi. There was Jebei, 'the Arrow', a
former enemy who had shot down Chingis's favourite charger in
battle, and, giving himself up after defeat, had had the courage
to admit it. There was Mukali, who had been presented to
Chingis as a boy in token of his father's admiration and had
since become a soldier of dynamic mettle. There was Jelme, a
member of a forest tribe, who had spent a lonely night of peril
on the battlefield sucking the blood from Chingis's neck wound
lest it had been inflicted by a poisoned shaft. And, dour and
silent among these now resplendent figures, stood an inscrutable
general called Subotei. Throughout his steppe campaigns Chingis had valued his opinion above all others: later, at the head of
expeditions launched half-way across the world, Subotei was to

[1] From the *Bilik*, or sayings, of Chingis Khan. H. Desmond Martin,
Chingis Khan and His Conquest of North China, p. 98.

prove himself a strategist of comparable calibre to his master.
On such men, whose names were already commemorated in the
horse-tails of the standard, their Khan heaped goods and honours in return for their devotion to his cause and person.

But his generosity, though open-handed, knew definite
bounds. The greatest prizes were reserved for his own family.
His mother Oyelun was still alive. He had four sons: Juchi,
Chagatai, Ogedei and Tului; and a full brother, Juchi Khassar,
who deserved recompense. These he rewarded with the human
fruits of his campaigns, dividing among them according to their
standing the families of the conquered peoples, together with
their herds and grazing-grounds. Oyelun was handed ten thousand 'tents'; then each son received a lesser number; and lastly
four thousand were given to his brother. At the same time he
made provision for his own household; for besides Borte he now
had several wives, some of them noblewomen from the incorporated tribes. Each was endowed with a 'horde' – a living establishment – suited to her rank. He himself would remain arbiter
of the Mongol destiny, supreme commander, law-giver. But his
realm would be ruled by princes of his own house, each responsible for the order, and for the contribution to war, of his appanage. The real-estate of the empire was to belong to his relatives,
and to no one beyond them; and as it subsequently grew, this
was to be the basis of its fabric.

As the great assembly drew to its end there was still much to
do; for it seems clear that by this time Chingis was regarding
Mongolia as a springboard for further expansion. He now gave
orders which implied that the nomad economy throughout his
domains was to be placed on a permanent war footing. Senior
army officers were to travel the pastures taking a census of the
population by tents, counting men of military age. They were to
satisfy themselves that large concentrations of non-Mongols of
doubtful reliability had been diluted by relocation. They were to
see that weapons were well maintained, that the remount herds
were adequate. They were to concert mobilization arrangements,
and to insist that all able-bodied men should regularly leave
their domestic tasks to join in the massive periodic drives for
game which were the equivalent of peace-time manoeuvres.
'They shall teach their sons to hunt wild animals so that they
may acquire strength, and the power to endure fatigue, and be

able to meet their enemies as they meet the savage beasts in combat.'[1] The women were to be exhorted to take pride in their husbands' repute and readiness; they were to keep their men accoutred and victualled, and be prepared to take their places among the herds. They were to do what they could to help restrain the immemorial nomad weakness for drink. No good Mongol, Chingis laid down, should get drunk more than three times a month. The perfect man would remain perpetually sober. But that, he admitted, knowing his men, could hardly be expected.

As he had set a family aristocracy over the people, so he set a military aristocracy at the kernel of the army. Hitherto his personal security had been ensured by a small bodyguard of one hundred and fifty men. He now enlarged it to an élite division of ten thousand young archers. In theory its ranks were open to all of sufficient skill and spirit: in practice they were largely filled by the sons of chiefs and trusted officers. Its privates, subjected to the harshest discipline, enjoyed unprecedented privileges in return: they were exempt from the orders of the regular army, and held a status equal to that of a regimental commander. Never taking the field except when the Khan himself did so, the Guard was to serve both as a school for senior officers and as a crack last-ditch reserve against emergencies in battle. Simultaneously, and evidently with campaigns far afield in mind, he formed from the army a special service of 'Arrow' dispatch-riders. Unlettered like the generals who were to use them – and like the supreme commander himself – these men carried their missives, often long and detailed, in their heads, usually in the form of jingling verse for easy remembrance. Wrapped in leather bandages to firm their bodies against the headlong motion of their steeds, they were to gallop day and night, eating and even sleeping as they went. None might delay them; and if their horses expired beneath them, the best remounts available were to be supplied.

Where were these preparations leading? A down-to-earth realist, Chingis was well aware that the effect of the many gifts he had bestowed would soon wear off. However handsome the recent distribution, he knew that loyalty required reward by

[1] From the *Yasa* or laws, of Chingis Khan. Vernadsky, *The Mongols and Russia*, p. 104.

regular instalments; and that, to keep it constant, the instalments had to become larger and larger. This problem had beset his predecessors on the tribally supported thrones of the steppes. But in his case it was especially acute; for in the more tightly knit feudal empire he was constructing, he himself was the fulcrum of all power and therefore of all responsibility. Everyone beneath his sway, from the ruling princes of his house to the lowliest among the dependent peoples, would look to him as the provider; as the source not only of 'gifts of sugar', but of food for lean years, and of all the necessities – weapons, tack, utensils – in which the nomadic communities were not in the long run self-sufficient. The resources of Mongolia could not fulfil these growing expectations. They would have to be supplemented, by trade or force, from the wealthier, more diversely productive reservoirs of the outer world. The settled periphery of Eurasia would have to become part of his thinking, and part of Mongol contact.

But Chingis was a Heartland nomad through and through. From merchants and ambassadors he had learnt a good deal about China, the littoral state closest to his borders; and most of what he heard he suspected. The idea of a society based on the yield of permanent farms, of a minutely compartmented, eternally grubbed-over landscape dotted with colossal human ant-hills, was alien and distasteful. From his dealings with nomad tribes along the Chinese frontiers he had no doubt observed what he regarded as the debilitating effects on their native hardihood of its milling, scheming plethora. The prospect of the Blue Mongols, the Chosen of the Steppe Sky, becoming tainted was not only repulsive: contamination could lead to absorption, and absorption to extinction. His instinct was thus to preserve the natural gulf between the inner grasslands and the outer peripheral. His empire should remain in and of the steppes. Tribute should flow in, trade should pass in and out; and his armies, their disciplined purity strengthened by the rewards of their efforts, would open the sources of both and guard the routes along which they moved to the centre. Here, removed from contagion, the pastures, the herds and the women would ensure the self-perpetuating vigour of his peoples as a whole.

It was necessary to tap the wealth of the outside; and desirable to do so by limited, controlled contact. But how, in the first instance, should this contact be made: by invasion and seizure, or by attempts to establish peaceful trade? In the event it was resolved to make the first move by conquest; and from that step a tremendous and terrifying chapter of world history steadily unfolded. But the decision may not have been as inevitable as has sometimes been assumed. As late as 1218, long after the Mongol armies had been committed to their first foreign campaigns, there is evidence that Chingis was as interested in commerce as in plunder; and there seems no reason why he should not all along have been well aware of its advantages. He had, it is true, some old scores to settle outside Mongolia; but that he determined upon force as the initial means of enriching his empire may have been due more to the prevailing situation in north-eastern Asia than to an innate lust for blood and battle.

At the time of his affirmation as Supreme Khan in 1206, the prospects for peaceable trade with the states beyond his steppe domains were far from favourable. To the east, China was divided. All its northern half was occupied by the Jurchets, whose barbarous origins still showed through the coating of civilization they had acquired from their Chinese subjects; and their past attitude to the Mongols hardly suggested that they would respond enthusiastically to proposals for a cordial relationship based on the exchange of goods. The China proper of the Sung regime, now confined to the Yangtze basin farther south, might in more normal times have offered better prospects: but its economy had been disrupted by the depredations of the Jurchets, and its external commerce had been severely reduced. Moreover such trade as continued to move in and out of China passed through the three states lying to the south and west of Chingis's Mongolia: the Tangut kingdom of Hsi Hsia, the dwindling realm of the Kara-Khitans, and the mushrooming empire of Khwaresm. All these states had a vested interest in preserving their control of the caravan routes that traversed their territories; and it was quite possible that the ambitious Khwaresmshah Mohammed, as he moved from strength to strength, might attempt to monopolize all commerce between the Orient and his rich domain of Iran. Not only was it unlikely that a trading relationship could be developed with the surrounding states: it was probable that the stronger among them would sooner or later challenge the new steppe power in Mongolia. In these circumstances a successful pre-emptive strike would ensure the inward flow of wealth in tribute, and would simultaneously neutralize the potential threat.

In which direction should Chingis deliver the first blow? The Jurchets in the east, for all their might, did not specially alarm him. In the past they had usually adopted a defensive posture, pinning their faith to bricks and mortar, and to weakening the tribes of Mongolia by setting them against each other. Few steppe conquerors had ever seen the Great Wall as impenetrable; and all the tribes were now united under the Mongol banner. The west, however, was a different matter. Kara-Khitai was virtually a Turkish-populated state. Mohammed's Khwaresmian empire had resulted from a Turkish inundation, and was now held down by Turks. Large areas of the central Heartland and most of its far western regions, right through to the Black Sea steppes, were in Turkish hands. And the Turks, in terms of steppe warfare, were formidable. They were the only power capable of facing Chingis with armies of mounted bowmen as mobile in strategy, as skilful and wily in tactic, as his own. In his view they were far more threatening than anything the sedentary states, with their static ramparts and often ill-captained hosts, could bring against him. The Turks in the west were the real menace: it was against them that his major effort should be concentrated.

But precautions were necessary. If he marched westward to attack the Turks, he laid his Mongolian base open to the Jurchets. For the cost of an expedition to the plateau while his armies were absent, they would be able to scorch his homelands at their leisure to the point of further military uselessness. Within living memory they had been sufficiently apprehensive of the Mongols – then a relatively small steppe power – to enlist Tatar help to break them: so perfect a chance to rid themselves of any threat from the now infinitely stronger Mongol empire might well prove irresistible. Let there, then, be a preliminary campaign against the King of Gold in north China. Its object would not necessarily be total conquest and occupation, but rather the crippling of Jurchet offensive capacity. And it would bring other benefits. It would provide a quick initial harvest of plunder and tribute. It would exact revenge for the old grudge of the Jurchet alliance with the Tatars, and especially for the murder of Ambakhai. It would destroy the aura of might which surrounded the Golden Monarch. All this would increase Chingis's standing with the Borjigin clan, with his army, and with the newly absorbed peoples of his empire. And with his rear secured, he would be free to turn upon the Turks.

With considerations of this kind in mind, Chingis came to his fateful decision. It happened that just then an embassy arrived from the Jurchet court to inform him of the death of the ruling Golden King. On inquiring who was the successor he was told that Wei-shao, a prince of the Kin house, had ascended the throne. To the ambassador's amazement Chingis abruptly dropped the mask of courtesy and exclaimed that the man was an idiot. And to underline his meaning, he spat in the direction of north China.

Chingis Khan, however, did not rush at once into war with the Jurchets. With his native caution he decided to move first against Hsi Hsia, the kingdom which the Tangut people had wrested from China in the tenth century. Since this kingdom adjoined the western Jurchet frontier its conquest would expose and soften up the Jurchet flank. Furthermore, its military arrangements were Chinese in character: they resembled those of the Jurchets, but on a smaller scale. The armies of Hsi Hsia were numerically superior to those of the Mongols; and across its semi-desert landscape, like knots in the threads of the trans-Asian trade-routes, lay a series of fortified cities. The sight of massive enemy forces manoeuvring round frowning walls would test the steadiness of the Mongol archers accustomed only to opponents as dashing as themselves. The attack on Hsi Hsia would prepare them for the similar, but far more daunting, task they would face in north China.

In 1207 a relatively small Mongol expedition led by Chingis himself set out to probe the Tangut defences. They crossed the Gobi without difficulty, digging for water as they went, and were soon encamped before the bastions of Volohai, the first fortified town along their march into Hsi Hsia. Chingis ordered his men to settle down for an organized siege. But to the Mongol troopers, agog for booty and eager to show their mettle, the long waiting proved unendurable. First one unit then another stormed forward, attempting to scale the ramparts. Each assault was repulsed with savage losses. With difficulty Chingis reimposed discipline: but as day succeeded tedious day murmur and questioning grew. Morale was sagging; and the quick capture of Volohai became vital to its restoration. With no siege-engines at his command, Chingis fell back on his wits. He conveyed to the town commander that the siege would be ended if a thousand cats and ten thousand swallows were lowered over the walls into the Mongol camp. Collecting up every cat and swallow he could lay hands on, the baffled officer complied with the demand. Under cover of their tents the Mongols tied a wad of inflammable material to the tail of each animal and bird; and at a given signal these torches were lighted and their bearers let loose. The terrified creatures fled back into and over the town, starting a multitude of fires. In the ensuing distraction the Mongols carried the walls and seized Volohai.

Alarmed by such ingenuity, the Tangut king sought to gain time to overhaul his country's defences. He offered terms; and Chingis, in return for the promise of tribute, withdrew. Their first venture on to alien soil had taught his soldiers a lesson; and a period of further training, in the shelter of their Mongolian base, was needed to drive it home. The tribute, however, failed to arrive; and in 1209, with his troops reorganized and reinspired, he invaded Hsi Hsia again – this time in force. Stubbornly disputing ground, the Tangut armies nevertheless fell back before the Mongol arrow-storms towards the city of Ningshia. Here the invaders, still without missile-hurling artillery, were faced with the same problem as at Volohai, but in a more acute form. For Ningshia was the Tangut capital. Sited on the banks of the Yellow river as it flows northward on its journey round the Ordos Loop, it was a large and populous centre enclosed by forbidding walls crowded with defenders. And Chingis was now pressed for time: his second onslaught on Hsi Hsia had undoubtedly confirmed his intentions to the watching Jurchets, and their reaction must be expected. Another *tour de force* to get possession of Ningshia was imperative.

Chingis knew that Chinese military engineers sometimes reduced invested cities by diverting the rivers on which they depended for water. He determined to imitate them by diverting the Yellow away from Ningshia. Slowly a giant dam began to rise across the great stream, the summit of its bulk crawling with the ant-figures of Tangut prisoners corralled for slave labour. But as the Mongol generals at this stage of their campaigning had no siege-trains, so their taskmasters were ignorant of engineering principles. Half completed, the dam burst. The river, loosed from all control, inundated the plains around the city. Their ponies struggling in the rising waters, the besiegers had to beat a hasty retreat to higher and more distant ground. It was fortunate for them that the defenders of Ningshia had no heart for further fight; fortunate also that detached Mongol columns, ranging through the desert countryside, had already cut the caravan routes. With their economic life approaching paralysis, the Tanguts sued for lasting peace. The conditions were harsh but realistic. They were to hand over an abundance of the cloth, falcons, and fine white camels for which Hsi Hsia was famous. Henceforth they were to provide troops on demand for the Khan's forces. And, since the Tangut women were comely in Mongol eyes, their king's daughter was to become one of his wives.

So Chingis completed his first foreign conquest. It had ended in success, though humiliation had more than once been only narrowly averted. But the campaign had served its purpose in steeling his men for Jurchet China. And to his strike against the Jurchets he was now irrevocably committed. To re-marshal his armies for the momentous crunch ahead, he ordered their swift return to Mongolia. There was not a day to lose.

The northern China of the Kin or Golden dynasty was one of the most puissant states of the Eurasian littoral. Its masters, the Jurchets, were conquerors of conquerors. The Khitans had seized control of the country from the Chinese, and the Jurchets had ousted the Khitan rulers. All three peoples now lived within its frontiers, and each contributed to its strength. Million upon million of Chinese, toiling on countless peasant holdings, labouring in workshops huddled in the streets of swarming cities, provided the economic foundations of its power. At the same time the grasslands and forests of Manchuria, whence both the Khitans and the Jurchets had come, yielded other primary materials and the warlike tribal manpower that supplemented the Kin military establishment. The capital of this mighty realm was Chung-tu, the city that is now Peking; and its central core was the great plain that stretches southward some three hundred miles from Peking to the Yellow river and beyond. To insulate this fertile, industrious hub from the turbulent nomadic Heartland the Jurchets had immensely strengthened the defences constructed by former Chinese dynasties. They had rebuilt the Great Wall, reinforced it at dangerous points with secondary lines, hedged it about with a series of heavily garrisoned fortress-cities; until a great arc of stone, facing out on to the Mongolian steppes, protected Peking and its wealth-creating hinterland from just such ambitious predators as Chingis Khan.

For all this, there were cracks in the monolithic Jurchet façade. Between the component peoples of their empire, there were undercurrents of mutual hostility. The Chinese had little sympathy for either of their successive conquerors; and the subjected Khitans felt towards the Jurchets the bitterness of a displaced ruling caste. Nor was the country as prosperous as it had once been: for the inrush of the Jurchets had sent a wave of Chinese refugees fleeing to the south, and their departure had drained the north of much of its enterprise and talent. And in 1194 the Yellow river had caused a catastrophe of national proportions. It had burst its banks, flooded vast areas of cultivated land and, amid fearful loss of life and crops, had settled into a new course between Kaifeng and the sea – a course it was to follow until 1853. By the beginning of the thirteenth century, as a result of these internal stresses, the Kin had passed their zenith. But the Kings of Gold still disposed of an enormous standing army. Its close-packed ranks of three hundred and fifty thousand infantry were supported by specialists in fortress-warfare; by ponderous engines throwing rocks, flaming naphtha and primitive bombs charged with gunpowder; and by up to one hundred and fifty thousand horse-archers from the Manchurian tribes. Even though its power was waning, the empire of the Kin and their Jurchet warriors was one of the most formidable in the world.

Chingis Khan attacked it in the spring of 1211. He had concentrated his entire military strength, probably about one hundred thousand troopers, along the Kerulen river in eastern Mongolia. As his preparations neared completion, he left the clamour of camp and council and withdrew, apart, to a spot close to the sacred mountain of Burkan-kaldun. Removing his cap and belt as a sign of humility towards the Everlasting Sky, he prayed for the help of the spirits and for the success of the Blue Mongols. Then, accompanied by his four sons and by every one of his most seasoned marshals, he set out once more across the Gobi, this time into the south-east.

Choking in the dust kicked up by their herds of remounts, the columns of bowmen split up into two armies in the hope of dividing the Kin defence. Each pursued a separate route across the desert, carefully marked out in advance by parties of pioneers. On the march, one of the columns apparently met with a disturbing experience. Suddenly, so the story went, every unsecured metal object – weapons, helmets, spare armour and tack – leaped from its place and careered, bouncing and clanging over the ground, towards a near-by hill. The Mongols afterwards told the tale as an uproarious joke; and later opinion has suggested that their equipment might have been affected as they passed a 'magnetic mountain'. But at the time, to superstitious men facing a crucial trial of strength, it was anything but funny. Occult forces were at work; and their rigid discipline is said to have dissolved in momentary panic.

The Kin reaction to the Mongols' approach was instant and massive. Corps after corps streamed out into the open borderlands to meet them before they reached the main lines of fortified defence. But these formations, leaving their bases at different times, appeared in the field one by one. Against such uncoordinated counter-attacks the galloping, charging, swerving Mongol archers were in their element. Lungeing first at one host then at another, covering the distances between them at a speed which bewildered the Kin generals, they inflicted three crushing defeats in quick succession. The frontier zones were cleared of significant resistance. Before them now was the curtain of masonry, its battlemented platforms alive with troops, that the Kings of Gold had drawn around their inner realm.

Scouting units reconnoitred the ramparts of the fortress-cities forming the outlying bastions of the Great Wall – powerful islands of enemy strength that the invaders dared not leave unreduced in their rear. They reported that between the great gates sealed with iron they could find no chink. As weeks of probing became months, Chingis sought to turn the enforced pause to profit. He captured the royal stud-farms, thus depriving the Jurchets of the source of their best horses. He learned that his presence had set afoot a number of peasant risings within north China; and, more important, that the Khitans in south Manchuria, remembering their Mongol ancestry, had revolted against their Jurchet overlords. He enlarged these divisions in the enemy camp as best he could. But the months of waiting lengthened into years. The great ring of the Kin defences still held, and no breakthrough came.

It was Jebei, 'the Arrow', the general whose shaft had once pierced Chingis's favourite horse, who finally broke the deadlock. Chingis himself prepared the way. In the summer of 1213, more than two years after leaving Mongolia, he managed by a supreme effort to storm one of the outer fortresses. Immediately Jebei plunged ahead, fighting his way through to the Wall itself. Here, at the Nan-kou Pass, in the hills to the north of Peking, he found the weak spot for which the Mongols had been searching for so long. The pass itself is a dark forbidding ravine, several miles in length. The Wall crowned the hills about it, and its steep sides were heavily bulwarked. At its southern end the enemy were waiting. The place could have been a death-trap; but Jebei was a master of feint. His men advanced into the ravine; then paused; and, as if in fear, retreated in disorder. The Kin troops, believing what they saw, rushed forward in pursuit. At the farther end Jebei turned, re-formed, and fell on them. Behind him came Chingis with all his strength. Filling the gorge with arrow-clouds, their horses stumbling over the bodies of the dead, they smashed their way through the pass – and out into open country. The Wall was behind them. Ahead lay the spreading, smiling plains that formed the heart of the Kin empire. Less than twenty miles away they could see the roofs of Peking.

The Jurchets considered the defences of Peking virtually impregnable. But as the dire implications of the Mongol penetration of the Wall became clear, a palace coup took place in the city. The Kin monarch Wei-shao – whose accession Chingis had greeted by spitting with contempt – was assassinated by an army faction, and another prince of his house was installed in his place. This act heightened the general alarm outside the capital, and decided Chingis's next move. He, too, thought the capture of Peking beyond the Mongols' capacity, at least for the time being. He would therefore by-pass it, and take advantage of the panic rising in the countryside. Two other Mongol corps were hastening in to join him: one through Jehol in the north, the other from the west. As they arrived, he regrouped and ordered a general advance southward.

He himself led an army down into what is now the coastal province of Shantung. Another, under his eldest son Juchi, moved along a parallel route farther inland. For both it was a march of wonder through one of the richest regions of the settled world. The Mongols could scarcely believe that such wealth was real, let alone within their grasp. Like children they gazed at the horizons of rice and maize and millet; at bales and bolts and chests stacked to the roofs of warehouses; at weavers' looms, smiths' forges, potters' wheels. Skirting the bigger fortified towns as they had skirted Peking, they pillaged their way across the ancient, ordered landscapes of the Chinese north. All through the meticulous profusion of the plains they carved their tracks of ruin, until they reached the Yellow river. Then, piling their loot on horse and camel, cart and wagon, they retraced their steps northward to the Wall. Meanwhile a third army under Chingis's brother was penetrating into Manchuria, joining up with the rebellious Khitans and subjugating the Jurchet tribes. Neither Hiung-nu nor Turk had ever gouged so deeply or methodically into China.

Nothing could now restrain the elated troopers from an all-out attack on Peking. Chingis's opinion was unchanged: he believed its taking impracticable. It would be bow and sword against three lines of moat, and then a looming mass of battlemented brick forty feet high by thirty thick, its eighteen-mile circumference capped by hundreds of jutting towers. And before carrying the first moat it would be essential to secure four satellite fort-towns, each a square mile in extent, their barracks and armouries linked to the city by a network of underground passages. But such was the euphoria around him that he consented to an attempt. Behind a hissing hurricane of arrows, in a tumult of battle-yells, the Mongols delivered two assaults. They forced their way into one of the outlying towns, and were driven out with terrible losses. In fury they turned upon the city itself. The four towns spewed out their garrisons into the attackers' rear.

In the aftermath of failure, Chingis reasserted his authority. Once more his realism extricated his armies from the impasse.

into which the valour of their ignorance had led them. Except for Peking and a few other large cities, the Kin had been ground down – at least for the moment. Their fighting power, though far from annihilated, had been grievously battered. Within a few months the Mongol tentacles had reached out through the twelve hundred miles between the Yellow and the Amur, leaving a pauperized countryside behind them. As a result the political infirmities of the empire were showing on every hand: not only Khitans and Chinese but even high-ranking Jurchets were going over to the invaders. Chingis extracted the utmost from the moment. He informed the Kin sovereign that he would evacuate north China if suitable compensation were forthcoming. He must retain all that his men had collected from the territories they had ravaged. He must have a princess for his personal use, with a retinue of a thousand youths and maidens. He must have three thousand of the finest horses, and numbers of artisans to practise crafts unknown in Mongolia. And, it went almost without saying, these necessities must be supplemented by a fitting quantity of treasure in the usual form of silks and precious metals. The King of Gold accepted.

Through the Wall, its scarps and parapets now silent and deserted, the chains of human booty and the beasts with their bulging cargoes passed on the homeward trek. Chingis watched their progress narrowly. All was his. None, from the humblest archer to the most elevated marshal, might grasp the wrist of a single slave or touch an ounce of silver without the Khan's approval. Reward was his prerogative, to be exercised with careful judgement. But as he distributed the spoil, an arrow-messenger sped in from Peking. The Golden Monarch, his recital ran, had left the city with a numerous escort. Most of his guards, disgusted with what seemed to them cowardice on the king's part, had deserted him and joined the Mongols. But the king himself had got through to Kaifeng, where he was now establishing his court.

The news was ominous. It suggested a journey into greater safety inspired by mistrust. But it might also imply a change in the whole strategic position in the east. Kaifeng lay on the south side of the Yellow river, beyond the areas that Chingis and Juchi had overrun. They had halted at the river for the simple reason that it presented an almost impassable barrier to armies without technical resources. Behind it the Kin could recover their damaged strength, bide their time, and indefinitely prolong the war. It was the first intimation to the Mongols of China's dogged capacity to fight back; of the timeless, engulfing will to resist which had always, in the end, freed her from the hordes of inner Asia.

Chingis would have to send his armies back; and if the Kin sovereign's departure from the capital had indeed undermined its morale, their first objective should be Peking. He did not go himself: his thoughts were beginning to turn elsewhere. Instead he sent Mukali, the servant-boy who had become one of his most colourful commanders. Jebei, with his detailed knowledge of the terrain, re-secured the Wall and its adjoining works. Mukali, striking across south Manchuria, blocked the path of reinforcements from the north. Once more the twelve gates of Peking closed. From without, its aspect was as awe-inspiring as ever: but of the spirit within, little was left. Its commanding general killed himself. His successor escaped to Kaifeng. Around the city's huge perimeter an immense host of Mongols, Khitans, Chinese, defecting Jurchets, moved up to form an unbroken blockading cordon: Chingis's flair for merging the disaffected into his own ranks was paying handsome dividends. Their food exhausted, their arteries of supply severed, the trapped population secretly devoured human flesh. Then a Kin officer appeared in the besiegers' lines; and as the defenders laid down their arms, he led them in.

Peking fell to the Mongols in May 1215. Almost at the same moment, some 5,000 miles away on the island of Runnymede, King John and his barons were facing each other with Magna Carta between them.

The city had surrendered: but its gutting was comparable to the sack of Loyang by the Hiung-nu in 311. The fires in the palaces burned for weeks. The streets were slippery with human fat. Corpses piled outside the walls festered into hillocks of bones. The treasuries of the Kings of Gold yielded their prodigious booty. But perhaps the most noteworthy prize the Mongols carried off was one of the prisoners they had taken.

This prisoner's name was Yeliu Ch'u ts'ai. He was a highly educated member of the Khitan royal house who had thrown in his lot with the Jurchets. Although only twenty-five when Peking fell, he was already a responsible Kin official. Quiet and

dignified, imposing in stature, he was brought before the Mongol
Khan. Chingis pointed out that he had avenged the Khitans, and
that his captive should be grateful. Yeliu Ch'u ts'ai replied that
he had accepted the Golden Kings as his masters: to rejoice in
their misfortunes would be unseemly. To a feudal aristocrat holding loyalty a primary virtue, the answer was pleasing both in
courage and quality; and from that moment the Khitan's place
at Chingis's side was assured. He became the Khan's chief astrol-
oger, then his principal civil minister. He made the most of
Chingis's confidence: but not for purposes of self-aggrandize-
ment. At the hub of the Mongol empire he was an intellectual
humanist among illiterate barbarians; and he devoted the rest
of his life to mitigating the impact of their savagery upon the
peoples they overwhelmed. Of primitive ancestry himself, he
understood the motivations of the nomads when confronted
with the settled world: the engrained memories of deprivation
that made the clutching of its property almost automatic; the
innate fear that sought to reduce its cities and their populations
to the empty, comforting horizons of the steppe. He knew that
Chingis could not change these things even if he wished; he was
a captive of his brutal background. But he saw that his reason-
ing mind in some measure distinguished him from his time and
kind. 'The Mongol empire,' Yeliu Ch'u ts'ai afterwards said, 'has
been conquered from the saddle. But it cannot be ruled from the
saddle.' Unwearyingly he counselled moderation, urging that the
resources of the conquered countries, human and material,
should be spared. To scorch and slay was inefficient. Taxation,
not plunder, should be the watchword: take the income, but
preserve the capital. Wherever the Mongols subsequently stayed
their hand, it was largely due to the arguments of this one man.
When the generals conceived a plan to eliminate China by wholesale genocide, he frustrated it. When Chingis was considering an
invasion of India, he averted it. His enemies made constant
attempts to discredit him by alleging that he used his position to
line his pockets. But when he died he left only a few books, some
musical instruments, and a store of medicinal drugs he had used
to relieve the sufferings of the subjugated.

With Peking his, Chingis's interest in the east evaporated.
His objectives were achieved. He had removed the sting from
the Kin and filled his coffers from their wealth. Not for many

years, if ever, would they be capable of mounting an invasion of Mongolia. He could not, however, entirely free his hands from northern China. For in pushing the Kin down to the Yellow river he had been sucked into the Chinese sponge. His troops were too few and too inexperienced to occupy effectively the great areas they had overrun; and whenever they turned from one district to suppress trouble in another, the Kin showed an irritating tendency to seep back in their wake. Such retaliation by re-infiltration could gradually rob the Mongols of all that they had won: but to stamp it out called for methods of warfare for which the Khan himself had neither the taste nor the patience. Besides, the campaign had already occupied five years and he had other plans in mind. Accordingly Chingis withdrew as many men as he dared, and appointed Mukali his Viceroy in the east.

Mukali's orders were to destroy the remainder of the Kin power. Accompanied by his eight concubines, and by the all-girl Chinese orchestra to whose music he liked to dine, he campaigned up and down the basin of the Yellow river until, after nearly twenty years of continuous effort, he died of exhaustion at his post.

All along, Chingis Khan had seen the Turks as the greatest potential danger to the empire he had created. It was to secure his rear for operations against the Turks that he had attacked the Tanguts and the Jurchets. Now, leaving to Mukali the long task of mopping up in the east, he turned his full attention to the enormous Turkish world in the west.

Close to the south-western borders of Mongolia lay the steppe state of Kara-Khitai, where the Turkish tribes of the Lake Balkash region were ruled by the descendants of the Khitan exiles known as the Gur-Khans. For some time Kara-Khitai had been in decline. When already torn by internal religious dissensions it had been invaded by the Khwaresm-shah Mohammed and robbed of a large part of its territory. Then a train of events had occurred which not only further weakened it, but made Mongol intervention in its affairs inevitable.

It will be remembered that, during his rise to power, Chingis had subdued the Naiman people of western Mongolia. In the battle which broke their army, the Naiman king had been killed; and his son, Kuchluk, had fled from the field to seek refuge in

Kara-Khitai. Here, the ruling Gur-Khan had received him kindly; and in his generosity had given his daughter, a Buddhist woman, to the exile as a wife. Kuchluk, however, saw the troubles besetting the Gur-Khan's realm as his own opportunity. In 1211, when the Mongols were launching their invasion of China, he led a revolt against the ruler who had befriended him, and seized his throne. He then added blunder to treachery. A shamanist himself, and married to a Buddhist, he began a systematic persecution of the Moslem Turks who formed the majority of the Kara-Khitan population. Several of the Turkish chieftains were admirers of Chingis Khan, and were in friendly contact with him. But Kuchluk's hatred of the Mongols was undying: they had overwhelmed his people and killed his father. Accordingly, he singled out these chiefs for specially savage treatment. And on his return from China, Chingis found messengers from his Kara-Khitan friends awaiting him, with urgent pleas for his aid.

To relieve Kara-Khitai of Kuchluk was an inescapable duty. It was also a convenient pretext for placing a foot in the Turkish door. The task required a marshal who would act with speed, but also with political finesse. Chingis chose Jebei, who was then supporting Mukali in the east. In 1218 Jebei raced from the Korean border to central Asia – some 2,500 miles – with twenty thousand Mongols. Entering Kara-Khitai, he declared that he had come to restore religious freedom. He ordered his men to refrain from looting, and enlisted into their ranks local tribesmen who offered to help him deal with Kuchluk's troops. In consequence he was everywhere welcomed as a liberator, and within a few weeks he had extended the power of Chingis Khan over most of Kara-Khitai. Kuchluk himself, relentlessly hunted across steppe and desert by a Mongol posse, was finally caught and executed in the lonely heights of the Pamir ranges.

After his almost bloodless invasion, conducted with faultless discipline, Jebei allowed himself one lapse into pillage. He had never forgotten that in former days, when they were enemies in Mongolia, he had killed Chingis's charger – a splendid bay with a white blaze on its forehead. The episode had weighed on his conscience ever since. Now, as the price of ridding the Kara-Khitans of their oppressor, he rounded up from their herds a thousand bay horses with white foreheads and sent them, as a token of atonement, to his supreme commander. The gesture relieved his mind.

The fateful effect of the Mongol acquisition of Kara-Khitai was to bring Chingis Khan face to face with Mohammed, lord of all the lands dominated by the Khwaresmian Turks.

Mohammed was now Chingis' most powerful rival in Asia. While the Mongol Khan had been building up his imperium in the eastern Heartland, the Khwaresm-shah had been extending his rule over the west. He had inherited Iran, with all its wealth, from his predecessors; and to it he had added Afghanistan almost to the Indus. Not content with that he had lunged northward, driving the Kara-Khitans out of Transoxiana and pushing them back across the Jaxartes into the steppes – into the arms, as it were, of Jebei. And along the line of the great Jaxartes, flowing quietly through the heart of central Asia to the Aral Sea, the empires of east and west, the Mongol and the Khwaresmian, now confronted each other.

Chingis Khan made a practice of welcoming itinerant merchants and questioning them about the countries beyond his borders; and from them he had pieced together an accurate picture of Mohammed's empire. He knew that in size and resources it was far larger and richer than his own. Moreover, his informants stressed, the Khwaresm-shah could mobilize armies of at least two hundred thousand brave and well-equipped men. Other factors suggested circumspection. The Mongols had been campaigning on foreign soil for more than a decade. In particular, Mukali was still embroiled in China and might at any time require more men. It seems probable that at this point Chingis genuinely wanted a peaceful relationship with his mighty neighbour – at least for a time. He set out to woo him with friendly overtures. He arranged an official exchange of caravans, so that the products available for trade between the two empires could be displayed. Then, carefully choosing envoys from among Khwaresmian notables living in his domains, he dispatched a high-level mission to Mohammed. Laying before him the finest gifts Mongolia could offer, the ambassadors emphasized the Khan's wish for his goodwill. Their master, they hinted, was not without martial achievements: but he had no desire for further conquests. He was prepared to regard the Jaxartes as the natural boundary between east and west; and for his part he would look on the lord of the west as his son. It was the word 'son' that undid the whole approach; for in diplomatic usage 'son' suggested 'vassal'. The Khwaresm-shah was enraged.

Apparently unaware of the mortal offence he had given, Chingis prepared another caravan. This time he would surpass himself. He combed Mongolia for articles of rare value, adding to them samples of the fabulous treasures he had impounded from the Kin palaces. To underline his readiness for two-way trade he collected from his entourage a fund of specie for the purchase of Khwaresmian goods. As the hundreds of camels were loaded he selected a distinguished Mongol called Ukuna to take charge of them, placing at his side, as before, a number of Khwaresmian Moslems whose speech and religion he believed would find favour with Mohammed.

None of these men, none of the precious cargoes in their care, reached Mohammed. The caravan entered Khwaresmia at the frontier town of Otrar, on the Jaxartes. The governor of the town, one Inalchik, arrested it, confiscated the animals and their loads, and executed Ukuna, his Khwaresmian aides and all their attendant personnel as spies.

It is said that when Chingis heard the news the tears ran down his face. But it was possible that the Shah himself was not behind the outrage: Inalchik, known for his suspicion of the Mongols, might have acted without authority. He would apply a final test. Another mission, this time led by a Khwaresmian and two Mongol officials, crossed central Asia to remonstrate with Mohammed and to request the extradition of the governor. Mohammed put the Khwaresmian to death and sent the Mongols back with their heads shaved – an insult beyond reparation.

It was hardly a far-sighted act. For beneath the imposing surface of the Khwaresmian empire lay depths of conflicting crosscurrents. It was young, energetic, ambitious, immense. But its boundaries were inflated beyond its strength; and within them dwelt an incompatible mixture of peoples, civilized and barbarous, settled and nomadic. All were subjected to the ignorant, arbitrary rule of Turkish tyrants of tribal origin, promoted – like Inalchik – to posts of responsibility. Nor was Mohammed's own position sufficiently secure to justify his high-handed methods. The arrogance he had shown to Chingis was but a reflection of his attitude to all. Within his own gates he had alienated the senior officers of his army, the leaders of Islam, and most of the ordinary folk with whom he had come in contact.

The Mongol declaration of war took a form that was now becoming familiar. It was all the more ominous for the calm words in which it was invariably couched. 'You have chosen war,' Chingis announced. 'The Blue Sky alone knows how the issue between us will be resolved.'

Towards the middle of 1219 the Mongol forces began to concentrate in the southern foothills of the Altai, among the streams that form the headwaters of the Irtysh river. From all over Mongolia and beyond contingent after contingent arrived, to spend the summer months working up their physique by hunting while their remounts gathered strength on the surrounding grass. In the autumn their southward movement started. Their route lay through what had been Kara-Khitai: across the rivers debouching into Lake Balkash; through the gap between the Akkum desert and the Ala-tau range at the western end of the Tien Shan chain; and thence to the Jaxartes. They had 1,000 miles to travel before drawing a bow upon the enemy.

At the time of the Khwaresmian campaign the Mongol army numbered about one hundred and fifty thousand men, not counting the troops left in China. Later, under the princes of Chingis's family who succeeded him, it could muster some four hundred thousand effectives whose ranks could be further augmented by auxiliaries from the countries progressively conquered. Though modest in size by comparison with the hosts of the littoral world it faced, it is generally acknowledged to have been one of the finest fighting instruments that have ever been assembled.

Its basic strength lay in its simplicity. It consisted almost wholly of a single arm: cavalry. It was thus far easier to train, equip and supply than the more complex multi-arm establishments of its opponents. True, when it marched upon Khwaresmia the former impotence of its cavalry against walled defences had been largely overcome. Its mounted men were already supported by a corps of Chinese engineers; and as each subsequent campaign yielded its further quota of artisans, this corps steadily grew. Eventually the Mongols could call forward at any moment technicians skilled in constructing earthworks, building pontoon bridges, driving saps, and in working powerful batter-ing-rams and catapults hurling naphtha bombs. Whether their artillerists used explosives is still disputed: but gunpowder cer-tainly appeared in Europe soon after the Mongol conquests. The Mongols also came to possess sources of intelligence so wide-spread as to amount to an organized secret service. But these arms were essentially secondary: the core of the army, and its main offensive power, lay in its horsed units.

The units were built up on multiples of ten. Ten men made up a troop, ten troops a squadron, ten squadrons a regiment of a thousand. The largest unit was the *touman*, or division, of ten thousand. The cavalry comprising these units was of two types. There were heavy shock troops encased in burnished armour of iron scales, their horses' heads and chests protected with leather. These were armed with lances and swords. And there were greater numbers of horse-archers, the traditional missile-shoot-ing light cavalry of the steppes, some swathed in hide jerkins made pliable by boiling, others unprotected. Besides personal kit the archers often carried two bows in oiled waterproof cases at their saddles, and two quivers. One quiver contained the light sharp-pointed shafts used to fill the air with the long-range arrow-clouds for which the Mongols became dreaded: the other, heavier armour-piercing arrows for close-quarter fighting. In addition, the bowmen carried javelins, or a curved sabre slung across their backs with the hilt protruding above the left shoulder for swift drawing.

Two, or sometimes three, toumans made up a striking force; and in Chingis's lifetime these forces were often under the nomi-nal command of one of his sons. But beside the princes he always placed advisers in the shape of his tried generals, and the real authority lay in their hands. These professional officers were all chosen by the Khan himself; and unswerving devotion to him remained the first requisite for promotion to their num-ber. But he looked for other qualities as well. 'Only a man who feels hunger and thirst,' he insisted, 'and by this estimates the feelings of others, is fit to be a commander. The campaign and its hardships must be in proportion to the strength of the weakest warriors.'[1]

The striking forces were handled with superlative skill. Their

[1] From the *Bilik*. Martin, op.cit., p. 43.

target countries were usually invaded by several columns simultaneously or in carefully timed succession; and though the advancing formations were often separated by wide distances or mountain ranges, the arrow-messengers kept them in close and constant touch. The movement of each column was planned so that it could support its neighbours. When necessary they could converge, fight, and diverge again with a speed bewildering to defending armies.

At the outset of a battle, for which open ground was chosen whenever possible, the toumans were normally formed into five ranks stretching across a broad front. The first and second ranks were composed of squadrons of armoured lancers, gaps being left between each squadron. Behind them came three ranks of archers, similarly disposed. As soon as the range closed the leading rank of archers galloped through the gaps between the lancers, loosing salvo after salvo of arrows at the enemy's front. If at the first attempt they failed to dent his line they wheeled and retreated, shooting backwards over their horses' rumps; and the next rank of bowmen moved forward into their place. Though this arrow-attack could be repeated a third time it was seldom necessary, for the effect of the Mongol archery was terrible: one account spoke of men falling before it like leaves in an autumn gale. While the frontal attack was developing, other squadrons would be working round the enemy's flanks, wearing them down with blizzards of shafts. At the critical moment the lancers charged, the terror they inspired and the weight of their impact usually turning confusion into chaotic rout. Orders carried by aides were kept to a minimum to prevent verbal errors. Signallers were attached to each commander, using flags by day, lanterns by night, whistling and flaming arrows. All through the battle a strong force would be held in reserve; if Chingis himself was present it would be the crack corps of the Guard.

By their large approach to strategy, by their firm control of tactics rigid in principle but highly variable in operation, the Mongol generals brought the old shock and missile warfare of the steppes to a point of combined perfection previously unknown. They were also resourceful in their employment of ruse. They would seemingly multiply their numbers by setting dummies astride their remounts. They would conceal their movements behind clouds of dust or the smoke of dry grass set afire. Sometimes for days on end they would feign disorganized retreat until they had lured an opponent on to more favourable terrain. In action, they seldom allowed the wing squadrons to encircle the foe completely; a tempting avenue for flight was usually left open. For the Mongol pursuits were prolonged and remorseless. More casualties were often inflicted in the chase after an engagement than during it.

The 'article', as Wellington might have called him, at the base of the military pyramid was the private trooper – a man much execrated in the literature of outer Eurasia. The Persian poet Amir Khuzru, catching sight of a group of Mongol soldiers, thus described them:

> Their eyes were so narrow and piercing that they might have bored a hole in a brazen vessel, and their stench was more horrible than their colour. Their heads were set on their bodies as if they had no necks, and their cheeks resembled leathern bottles full of wrinkles and knots. Their noses extended from cheekbone to cheekbone. Their nostrils resembled rotting graves, and from them the hair descended as far as the lips. Their chests were covered with lice which looked like sesame growing in bad soil.[1]

The Persian, his people having suffered from the Mongols' attention, was *parti pris*. Undoubtedly the Mongol trooper was scruffy and unkempt; and since he wore his clothes continuously till they fell from his body – lest their washing should offend the spirits of the water – his proximity must indeed have been noticeable. But if he bore any resemblance to the Mongolians of today his physical appearance cannot have been wholly unattractive.

He was usually of middle height, thick-set but seldom stout, broad of shoulder, deep of chest. Above the prominent cheekbones of his wheaten face his eyes were often inflamed from the glare of sun and snow. His raven-black hair, tonsured like that of a monk, fell to his eyebrows in front, and at the back of his head was plaited into pigtails sometimes knotted together. His legs were curved from the perpetual grip exerted on horseback; and since his compound bow required a pull of nearly 170 pounds

[1] *Cambridge History of India*, Vol. III, p. 84.

– more than that of the later English long-bow – the muscles of his arms were like steel hawsers.

Several who observed him in the leisure of camp life remarked on his cheerful placidity; on the dazzlingly white teeth which his ready smile revealed; on his instant obedience to authority. Towards his comrades, they noted, he was generous in hospitality, sharing without stint whatever food he had – and it was often little enough. Although he drank himself silly in the company of friends whenever he got the chance, he was rarely abusive in his cups. But all this, they emphasized, vanished when he was confronted with strangers to the life of the steppe. His attitude to foreigners was ugly in the extreme: he became arrogant, surly, niggardly, devious and grasping, and he would beg with whining tenacity. In war he seldom deliberately tortured those who fell into his hands: but at the least resistance to his search for their valuables he killed without compunction – and sometimes horribly. The same sudden changes marked much of his daily being. At one moment his mouth would be filled with the simple poetry of the illiterate; with images drawn from the flora and fauna, the spaces and elements, of his homeland. At the next, it would utter a stream of unbridled filth. He would sink from happy laughter into fits of morose depression that no coaxing could relieve.

Liable for military service between the ages of fourteen and sixty, his two great assets as a soldier were his toughness and his feral courage. Almost completely weatherproof, he was indifferent to hardships that more ordinary mortals could not survive. He could go for weeks on a little dried milk or flesh. He served without pay, his morale sustained by the hope of loot. He never surrendered unless ordered to do so; rather, he would put himself to death with the same pitiless dispassion he showed to his victims. He was an unknown warrior, for his deeds of valour were performed in the name of his Khan and went unacknowledged. Perhaps it is the very anonymity of this hungry, smelly, lion-hearted athlete, now childlike, now bestial in his veering moods, that places him among the most fascinating of the figures who have fashioned history.

The setting of the coming clash between the rivals of east and west was the great gap between the Caspian and the Roof of the

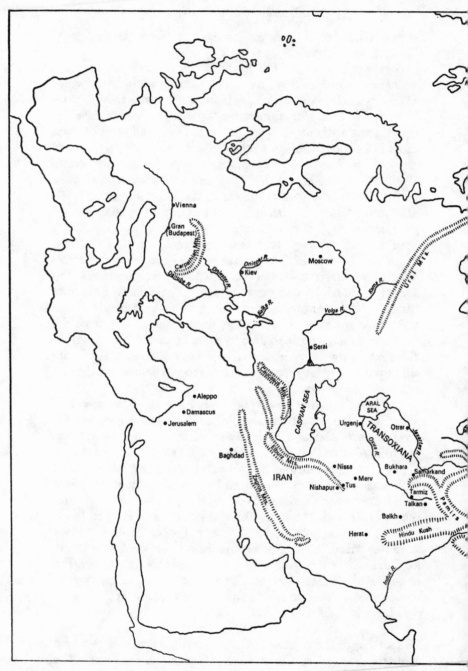

The Mongol Orbit

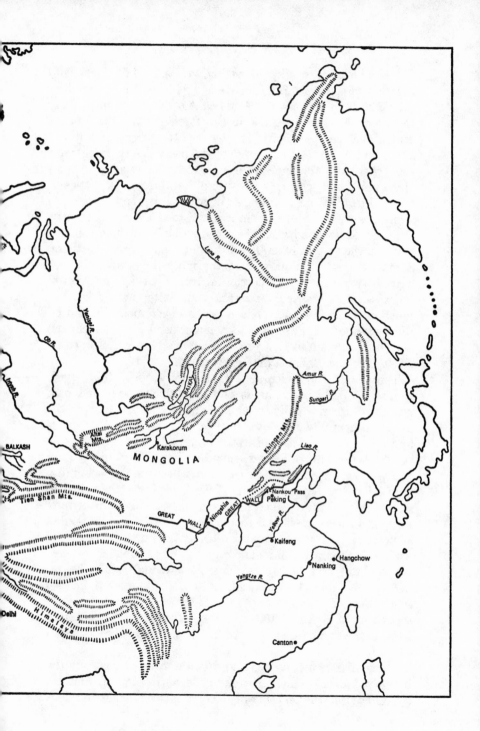

World which had so often served as the channel for Heartland invasion of southern Eurasia. Here, its four sides bounded by the Oxus and Jaxartes, the Aral Sea and the Pamir massif, lay the rectangle of Transoxiana, jutting forward from Iran into the central Asian steppes, with the wastes of the Kyzyl-Kum desert at its centre. To the north-west of the desert, at the mouths of the Oxus, was the nucleus from which the huge empire of Mohammed had grown: the district of Khwaresm, with its capital at Urgenj not far from the Aral. At the other end of the rectangle, near the foothills of the Pamirs, stood a group of affluent cities whose prosperity had been partly built on the commerce between the settled littoral and the nomadic interior. Of these, Samarkand and Bukhara were the most important. Farther west, between the Oxus and central Iran, lay the larger area of Khorasan, like Transoxiana an arid zone dotted with cities. But much of the landscape of Khorasan had been made fruitful by the warp and weft of scrupulously maintained irrigation canals; and its metropolitan centres – Nishapur and Merv, Herat and Nissa, Tus and Balkh – were even richer.

Throughout the region as a whole, two ways of life merged. Across it, Turkish shepherds and their flocks wandered past islands of urban sophistication standing at the junctions of the intercontinental trade-routes. The great cities, with their domes and minarets, citadels and caravanserais, formed an economic pivot of the entire Khwaresmian empire. They enjoyed an almost legendary renown. Samarkand, where the Chinese craftsmen taken by the Arabs at the Talas river in 751 had settled, was celebrated for its silk and paper, its satins and copperware, its plump aubergines and the sweet scent of its melons packed in snow; and, oddly, for the ample beards and moustaches of its women. Bukhara was famous for its carpets; Herat for its turning windmills and the twelve thousand shops in its souks. Learning and religion, history and culture, had flowered on the foundation of markets and manufactures. The mosques and seminaries of Bukhara attracted the faithful of all Islam. Merv boasted the tomb of Sanjar. At Nishapur Omar Khayyam had died in 1123.

Chingis Khan's Khwaresmian expedition was essentially the brainchild of two men of military genius: himself, and his closest adviser, Subotei. It was the first of two Mongol invasions that were undoubtedly the most perfectly planned and executed campaigns ever launched from nomadic Asia. Though it was to be rivalled in ability by Subotei's triumphant march through eastern Europe twenty years later, the assault on Khwaresmia perhaps revealed more fully the astonishing offensive powers of the Heartland herdsmen-archers at their height.

The prelude gave a foretaste of the lightning war to come. In the late summer of 1219 Mongol horsemen appeared on the lower Jaxartes. They seized all the food and cattle they could find, and set fire to every town and village within reach. In a short time they had scorched a considerable area of the frontier zone to ruin. Then, at the first sign of Khwaresmian reaction, they withdrew to the north whence they had come behind a smoke-screen of burning grass. The purpose of their raid was to prevent an attack on their main army as it moved down towards the river.

Mohammed was clear that the first major onslaught must come somewhere along the Jaxartes. But being without more precise intelligence, he disposed his defending forces along the length of the river line, at the same time augmenting the garrisons of Samarkand and Bukhara, the two large cities lying at some distance to the rear of the right-hand end of the line. The result of these preparations was that Khwaresmian troops were extended along some five hundred miles of front, but were nowhere concentrated in sufficient strength to contain an all-out offensive.

In the event the first attack did not fall on the Jaxartes at all, but at a point where Mohammed least expected it. While the main Mongol body was moving southward towards the river, Jebei, with two toumans behind him, was approaching Khwaresmia from the east – through the Tarim basin. Beyond the Tarim lay Samarkand and Bukhara, the city strongpoints behind the river front; and Jebei was in fact striking directly towards them. But across his path lay the mighty ranges of the Pamirs; and by now winter had set in. It made no difference. 'The Arrow' found his way through the snow-blocked passes at some 13,000 feet. It was a feat of extraordinary endurance. Men and horses died by the score, surviving troopers ekeing out the failing rations from the carcasses of their frozen comrades' mounts. Early in 1220, weary and tattered but still a resolute fighting force, they were riding down the Ferghana valley, turning Mohammed's right flank and heading for Samarkand.

The movement took Mohammed completely by surprise. He had not suspected that an enemy could be so foolhardy as to attempt to descend upon him from the Pamirs. Hastily sending forward one of his best generals to grapple with Jebei, he prepared Samarkand for a possible siege. Even as he did so alarming reports began to reach him from the other end of his front, far down the Jaxartes. Enormous numbers of Mongols were approaching the river at the very point where their preliminary raid had utterly destroyed the surrounding country. Again the Shah was caught unawares: he had deemed that this sector of his front, at least, would be safe. It did not seem credible that something like one hundred thousand men, with their trains of baggage-wagons and their swarms of remounts, should be able to traverse a burnt-out landscape, living on nothing but what they carried with them. But it was, indeed, the bulk of the Mongol army under Juchi, advancing to the Jaxartes, reducing its lower reaches, then wheeling leftward and working up the river towards its source. At no point were the Khwaresmian forces, strung out along the bank, strong enough to repulse them. They were rolled back from fort to fort, from stand to stand, by the onrushing Mongol tide. A gigantic pincer was forming, with Juchi and Jebei moving towards Samarkand from opposite directions.

Striving to concentrate his armies, Mohammed sent urgently to Iran for reinforcements. Then came staggering news. Bukhara, far to the rear of the fighting, and closer to the Oxus than the Jaxartes, was suddenly invested by fresh clouds of Mongol horse. It seemed utterly improbable that yet another Mongol force should be in the field: impossible that it should have penetrated without warning to a city protected by the almost uncrossable barrier of the Kyzyl-Kum desert. The news, however, was true. The investor of Bukhara was Chingis Khan himself.

Chingis had waited until Juchi had launched his offensive along the Jaxartes. Then he too, with his other sons, had crossed the devastated area, reaching the Jaxartes at Otrar. There was good reason for him to make for Otrar: it was here that the governor, Inalchik, had seized his goodwill caravan and murdered his envoys. Inalchik at Otrar had been the immediate cause of the war; moreover, he was still in the town. Leaving Chagatai and Ogedei to exact revenge, and taking his youngest son Tului with him, Chingis had moved on into Khwaresmia – and vanished.

The defence of Otrar was long and desperate, for Inalchik well knew what he might expect. When the town fell he retreated into the citadel. When the arrows of the garrison gave out he caused the women to tear bricks from the walls as missiles. It was in vain. The Mongols rushed the keep and grasped their man. His death befitted his love of treasure: his ears and nostrils were filled with molten silver.

While the battle for Otrar was at its height, Chingis had performed the seemingly impossible. With the aid of a captured Turkish guide he had crossed the supposedly impassable barrens of the Kyzyl-Kum, a march of nearly three hundred miles through one of the most fearsome deserts in the world. Now, at the head of a third Mongol army which included the Guard, and with Subotei at his side, he was at the gates of Bukhara.

As Juchi and Jebei converged towards Samarkand, Chingis laid siege to the Shah's only other major stronghold in Transoxiana. To hasten its surrender he employed the simple ruse of leaving one of the city's gates unguarded. Marvelling at their luck, the Turkish garrison poured out through it, apparently to freedom. But as soon as they reached open country Mongol squadrons thundered in pursuit, flushing them out like game, hunting them down almost to a man. Within a month Bukhara had capitulated. Chingis ordered that every civilian should betake himself outside the walls, with no possessions but the clothes he was wearing. Then the empty city was given over to his troopers for ransack. Clattering still mounted into one of the great mosques, their horses' hooves tore the leaves of the sacred books to shreds. A helpless imam exclaimed at the desecration. 'Be silent,' another answered. 'It is the wind of God's omnipotence that bloweth.'

Still Chingis did not stop. Juchi and Jebei were closing on Samarkand, and he hastened on from Bukhara to join them. Their mission at Otrar completed, Chagatai and Ogedei also appeared, with huge droves of prisoners they had seized on their way up the Jaxartes. Nearly the entire Mongol strength was concentrating outside the city: the timing of its component columns, their movements hitherto separated by mountains, deserts, rivers, had been faultless.

Driving their captives before them, the combined forces launched a mass attack through the suburbs. To their surprise a large body of the citizens, mistrusting the mercenary garrison, came streaming out to defend their town. But their impromptu weapons were no match for Mongol arrows, and a wholesale slaughter ensued. Seeing this, the garrison emerged from the gates without their arms. They, like the defenders of Bukhara, were Turks; and as one steppe people to another they sought a friendly accommodation with the attackers. Thrusting them aside, their 'compatriots' stormed into the city. A final knot of resistance in the central mosque was quickly struck down and the building razed to the ground. Within five days of the first assault Samarkand was in Mongol hands. Chingis's attitude to those within it reflected the code of the feudal magnate. The civilians had earned their lives by their loyalty to the Shah: all were spared, though the artisans among them were singled out and drafted to Mongolia. But in his eyes the defecting garrison, thirty thousand strong, had acted as traitors. Every one of them was killed.

At Samarkand the Khan received word that Mohammed had fled from the fighting zone in the direction of central Iran. It was not altogether welcome news. The Shah's armies in Trans-oxiana had been pulverized: but it was possible that with the resources of Iran still at his command he might assemble new forces and return to the scene of his defeats. Chingis sent for the two marshals whose sagacity and speed of action he most respected: Subotei and Jebei. He instructed them to pursue the Shah and put him to death; to break up any reinforcements he had mobilized; but when possible to leave civilians unmolested. He allotted them two toumans for the task. As they and their twenty thousand archers moved off into the west, they probably foresaw little but an enjoyable chase after the rigours they had recently sustained. As it turned out, their ride was to prove far more than that. It was to discover to the Mongols not only Iran, but vast areas beyond its farthest limits.

In the space of five months the Mongols had torn the military heart from the greatly superior Khwaresmian empire, overrun most of its forward region of Transoxiana, and reduced its emperor to an abject fugitive with Subotei and Jebei hot on his heels. In the summer of 1220 Chingis rested his armies in the neighbourhood of Samarkand. Then, dispatching another task force towards the Aral Sea to capture the Khwaresmian capital of Urgenj, he moved on southward into the great bight of land formed by the curving arc of the Pamirs and the Hindu Kush. Here he set about reducing the cities – Balkh, Tarmiz, Talkan – of the upper Oxus region.

At this point his anxieties began. Urgenj proved a tough nut to crack. Its garrison included some of Mohammed's staunchest troops, and they fought off their attackers with frantic devotion. As the siege dragged on the Mongols' difficulties were increased by a blazing row between Juchi and Chagatai, the two senior princes of the Khan's house, who were in command of the expedition. They had always disliked each other; and it was the final gulf which now opened between them that eventually caused Chingis to confirm his third son, Ogedei, as his successor. But the general advising the princes before Urgenj was Bogurchi; and he, companion as well as servant of Chingis, was not the man to let a quarrel affect the Khan's business. He summoned every available technical aid. His artillerists bombarded the town with naphtha, felled the mulberry trees about it for catapult ammunition. His engineers breached the dykes of the Oxus to flood the streets. By the time Urgenj was ready to give in, Mongol tempers were short all round. Its offer of surrender was refused. Its population was divided into three categories: artisans, slaves and useless. The artisans and slaves were herded off to Mongolia. The useless were massacred. It is said that each trooper killed more than twenty captives.

More immediately pressing for Chingis was the situation in the south-eastern corner of Khwaresmia. For in the region of the Hindu Kush an uprising against him was afoot. It was led by Jelal ad-Din, Mohammed's son and heir. Jelal's character was very different from that of his father. He was spirited, adventurous, young, personable; and he was determined to recoup the collapsing fortunes of his house. He had been driven south to Ghazna by the inexorable Mongol advance: but here he turned at bay, proclaiming a holy war against the invaders and rallying the faithful to his banner. The response was immediate.

Chingis was now in an embarrassing position. He himself, with the greater part of the Mongol army, was in the neighbourhood of Balkh – deep in hostile territory. The area under Jelal's control lay to the south of him: but the rebellion might easily spread behind his back into Khorasan, so far untouched by the war save for the swift passage of Subotei and Jebei in their pursuit of Mohammed. If Khorasan rose, Chingis's troops in Transoxiana might be counter-attacked, and his own homeward route to the steppes cut off. The degree of danger called for corresponding risk. Detaching a large force under Tului, he sent it westward into Khorasan, giving the simple order to his son to 'exterminate'. And he himself, with the balance of his army, moved farther south towards Jelal.

Here Chingis received a further setback. He sent forward some three toumans to reconnoitre under a young general called Shigi Kutuku, a protégé whom he regarded with special affection. At this awkward juncture his protégé failed him. Clashing with Jelal's main force not far from Kabul, Shigi Kutuku was roundly defeated. Moreover, grim stories of the aftermath reached the Khan's ears: Jelal's men, frenzied by their unexpected triumph, had been seen driving nails into their captives' heads. But despite his fury, Chingis behaved with calm reason towards his heart-broken commander. He rode over the battlefield with him, pointing out that the ground had been badly chosen. The reverse, he said, would teach him to be less precipitate.

In Khorasan, however, Tului fulfilled his instructions to the letter. Through the winter of 1220 and the following spring, the cities of the Persian east suffered one of the most hideous campaigns of terror ever recorded. It was perhaps during these merciless months that the Mongols first acquired the reputation for ruthless blood-lust of which they have never been acquitted. City after city fell before Tului's catapults and mangonels, his barrages of naphtha bombs and huge arrows mechanically discharged; before the thousands of sacks of earth with which he systematically filled their moats, and the herds of prisoners his assaulting troopers drove in front of them; before the storming-ladders with which they scaled the riven battlements.

Methodical ferocity followed each capitulation. At Nissa, seventy thousand captives were forced to tie themselves together and were then cut down with axes, sabres and arrows. At Merv the besiegers diverted the Murghab river into the city, wrecked every building till only Sanjar's tomb remained, beheaded every man of the Turkish garrison, slaughtered upwards of a million citizens. They rode away from Herat having killed, as they thought, the entire population: but on returning to the town, found three thousand still alive. After they had left for the second time, it is said that about forty human beings, naked, starved, demented, crept from the ruins. At Nishapur, method was fanned by rage; for in the attack upon the walls one of Chingis's sons-in-law was killed. Tului brought every available piece of artillery to bear upon the city; and when it fell he arranged for the widow to enter it in a chariot, at the head of the touman detailed for its occupation. Remorselessly she watched her escort put to death every living thing they met: men, women, babies, dogs, cats, rats. To make doubly sure, the head was struck from each human corpse and tossed on to a growing mound of skulls.

From city to city, despite resistance desperate in its courage, the horror marched. Only those possessed of skills or fit for servitude were set aside. The rest were wiped out; and Tului, the youthful exterminator, seated on a gilded throne, witnessed the obliteration of Khorasan. All that can be said in his defence is that he was acting within the military custom of the Asian city-societies of the time; and that, the youngest son of a father quite capable of executing him for disobedience, he was obeying orders. And though Chingis was sometimes more moderate, it is doubtful whether he would have curtailed the holocaust had he been on the spot himself. The Mongols seem always to have been aware of the paucity of their numbers against the massive populations of outer Eurasia; and when isolated in a sea of suspected guerrilla enemies – as they felt themselves just then – they would stop at nothing to reduce the odds.

Four hundred miles to the east, Chingis was closing upon Jelal. Urging his toumans on, never giving his enemy pause to rest or time to stand, he harried him on through the Afghan hills, across the Sulaiman range, down into the Indus valley. Reaching the river at night, Jelal sought to get his force across before daybreak. It was too late. First light revealed a semicircle of Mongol horsemen tightening around him. He turned his back to the Indus, and fought. He expected a tempest of arrows, but it did

not come. Instead, the horns of the semicircle advanced to close
quarters, drawing their sabres, hacking down the troops on his
flanks. At the centre, where Jelal himself stood surrounded by
several hundred well-mounted men, the Mongols halted. It was
clear that Chingis's aim was to seize Mohammed's son alive, for
that would end all further resistance in Khwaresmia. Jelal determined to thwart him. Scrambling on to a fresh horse, he
charged the Mongol centre with all the remaining strength of his
devoted band. Their impact was sufficient to dent the Mongol
ranks. Chingis took no further chance. The Guard, as usual, was
waiting in reserve. He ordered it in. Its pounding hooves and
vicious volleys quickly overwhelmed the gallant stand Jelal was
making. With a handful of survivors he galloped for the river,
rode at full speed to the summit of a cliff overhanging the water,
and leapt.

Watching him struggling across, still in the saddle, still holding his banner aloft as the Mongol arrows whipped the water
round him, Chingis turned to those around him. There, he observed, was a man they should emulate.

The war was virtually over. The cities of Khorasan were re-
ravaged lest any embers of resistance should still be glowing
among them. A Mongol column chased Jelal and his remaining
followers farther out of harm's way into the Punjab; and
Chingis toyed with the idea of following it himself, with greater
strength, into India. But the chroniclers record that the Khan,
out riding one day, met a strange green creature with one horn.
The animal addressed him, entreating him to return home. Perplexed, Chingis consulted Yeliu Ch'u ts'ai. The Khitan minister
identified the apparition as a unicorn, and gravely asserted that
since it was doubtless sent by the Sky to prevent unnecessary
slaughter, it would be wise to accept its plea as a warning. By
coincidence disease broke out in the Mongol camps.

There were other reasons for calling a halt. The harvest of
invasion had been well-nigh unassessable; to get the captives
and the spoils back to Mongolia would be a major operation in
itself. And there was disquieting news from Hsi Hsia. Like other
vassals, the Tanguts had been required to contribute a contingent to the Khwaresmian war. They had refused in insulting
terms; and they were now in open revolt, plundering the traffic

on the caravan routes. At any time they might join forces with the equally troublesome Kin who were still defying Mukali from their citadel at Kaifeng. Order would have to be restored in the east.

Furthermore, the price of his arrogance had been exacted from Mohammed. Subotei himself, bandaged like an arrow-messenger, had ridden hotfoot from the west to report that he and Jebei had hounded the shah across Iran almost to the Tigris. Losing the scent, finding it again, they had at length run him to earth on the shore of the Caspian where he had died, shattered in mind and body, on the island of Abeskun. The mission fulfilled, Subotei now proposed an extended probe into the west. Let him and Jebei, with the two toumans under their command, ride round the inland sea to explore and gather information. Chingis agreed, setting a limit of three years to the expedition.

He himself made his way home by easy stages, hunting and hawking, summoning sages and notables from China and Persia, listening attentively to what they told him of the religions and affairs of the world he had conquered. He reached the Irtysh in 1224, there to be welcomed by two fine grandsons, Tului's children. He arranged their first hunt, himself performing the preliminary ritual, which custom demanded, of rubbing their middle fingers with fat. One of the boys was Hulagu, who was subsequently to conquer Iran. The other would one day be the Great Khan Kubilai.

'The joy of man,' Chingis Khan is said to have exclaimed, 'lies in treading down the enemy, tearing him up by the root, taking from him all that he has; in making his servants wail so that the tears flow from eyes and nose; in riding pleasantly on his well-fed geldings; in making one's bed upon the belly and navel of his wives, in kissing and sucking their scarlet lips.'[1] Wherever his men had passed in Khwaresmia, they had done little less. They left behind, in Transoxiana and Khorasan, corpses estimated to number some fifteen million. And they left a desert place. Though the region stitched its being together again fairly rapidly, its ancient glories were gone and its burgeoning economy was shrivelled. Only now, with the aid of Soviet and Iranian technology, is it surmounting the centuries of paralysis that the Mongols inflicted on it.

[1] Fox, *Genghis Khan*, p. 88.

But for Chingis the rewards of war were portentous. In a campaign sometimes held to be the most brilliant in all strategic history he broke the Turkish power to his immediate west and south, as he had all along intended. By effecting a mass transfer of property from Turkish to Mongol hands, he gave the core of his empire a second injection of the wealth that he saw as the condition of his rule and that of his line. Such periodic inflows he had also planned from the start – though they had not been gained without a dash of the pollution he had sought to avoid. 'I return to simplicity,' he caused to be recorded on quitting Khwaresmia, 'I turn again to purity.'[1] A Mongol to the marrow, it was true of himself: but after first north China and then Khwaresmia, with their successive hauls of alien faces and strange skills, a tinge of cosmopolitanism began to colour the Mongolian scene.

Lastly, as a by-product of the Khwaresmian campaign he penetrated the farther Heartland west, and laid it open to the later roll of the Mongol juggernaut. For Subotei and Jebei more than fulfilled the instructions they had requested to ride round the Caspian. In 1222 the queen of the small state of Georgia, between Iran and the Caucasus, addressed an urgent letter to the Pope. 'A savage people,' she wrote, 'hellish of aspect, as voracious as wolves and as brave as lions, have invaded my country. The brave knighthood of Georgia has hunted them out – '[2] but even so, she begged for help. The two toumans had in fact shot the Georgian chivalry to shreds. And that done, they and their intrepid leaders vanished among the mountain crags. Jebei had already crossed the Pamirs; the passage of the Caucasus presented few new problems. Exhausted but in good heart the twenty thousand emerged on the northern side of the range, to see before them the infinite horizons of the Black Sea steppes.

Here, Subotei and Jebei came upon the Kipchak Turks; and beyond the Kipchaks lay the Russian principalities. In contrast to the numbers that the region could muster against them, their own force was puny. But the wide plains were cut out for the type of operations at which their men excelled. They continued their advance into the unknown. The Kipchaks rallied their

---

[1] From a stele in Afghanistan. See Grousset, *The World Conqueror*, p. 259.

[2] Prawdin, *The Mongol Empire*, p. 212.

vassals, and a formidable horde gathered against the intruders. By gifts from the booty he had taken in Iran, and by appealing to their common steppe background, Subotei gently tapped in a wedge between the Turks and their allies. Then, having isolated them, he loosed the full strength of his toumans upon them; and before Mongol discipline and fire-power the Kipchaks broke. Alarm spread across the western grasslands. Whole tribes began moving towards the Danube as if before a major migration. Constantinople, stricken by the Crusaders' depradations, prepared for yet another onslaught from the steppes. Unmoved by the tumult they were causing the two generals rode on westward, round the shores of the Sea of Azov, and across the Dnieper. They drew rein at last on the banks of the Dniester; and there, at the doorstep of Europe, they settled down to amass every scrap of information their agents could collect.

Meanwhile the defeated Kipchaks sought Russian support, harping on the possibility that the invaders might next turn north into Slavic territory. Three Russian princes sent help. Out of the northern forests their armies appeared; their warcraft began to prowl the rivers. The Mongols, now on their homeward journey, reached the Dnieper with ninety thousand Russians on their tail. Again Subotei resorted to diplomacy. He sent messengers to suggest that since the Mongols and the Russians both worshipped one god, they should combine to make an end of the infidel Kipchaks. This time his gambit failed: the messengers were put to death. With supreme effrontery Subotei declared war on his ninety thousand enemies; and immediately began a withdrawal towards the east. For nine consecutive days he retreated, apparently in haste to get away. On the tenth, at the Kalka river near the Azov, he found the favourable ground he was seeking. The Mongols stopped and turned. Certain that they had them on the run, the pursuing Russian columns had become separated. The toumans swooped upon them one by one, tearing between them at their usual headlong speed, decimating them. The Prince of Galich took to his heels. The Prince of Kiev fell into Subotei's hands. He had been responsible for the killing of the messengers; and since it was improper to spill the blood of princes, he was pressed to death.

Only one misfortune marred the journey back to Mongolia. During it, Jebei died. Swift and undeviating, 'the Arrow' had

earned his name; and Chingis was deeply moved by his loss. But
he listened absorbed to Subotei's report. His men had ridden the
best part of 6,000 miles; and as a result he had been able to piece
together the geography of eastern Europe. He knew the extent
of Russia, the positions of Poland and Byzantium. He knew of
the existence of the great bowl of Hungary. As to the politics of
the region, the Venetians had been specially helpful. He had
come across their outposts on the Black Sea coast; and in return
for his aid in annihilating a Genoese trading-station near by, they
had produced a mine of information. It was clear that most
Europeans were divided by just such rifts and rivalries. On his
way home he had identified the steppe tribes in the Ural-
Caspian region, and had forced them to accept vassalhood to the
Mongol empire.

Chingis did not live to turn Subotei's discoveries to practical
account. But the impassive marshal never forgot what he had
found out.

In 1226, once more at the head of his armies, Chingis Khan set
out to punish the Tanguts of Hsi Hsia. Though brief, it was one
of the most violent of the Mongol campaigns. During its early
stages he had a serious accident, falling from his horse while
hunting and sustaining internal injuries. Through a winter of
terrible battles fought on the ice of the upper Yellow river he
continued in command: but the effects of his fall, coupled with
the fatigues of a life spent unremittingly in camp and saddle,
began to tell. In August 1227, just as the Tanguts crumpled, he
died at the age of sixty in the Ordos Loop – where the nomadic
and settled worlds, the steppes and the littoral, had clashed in
conflict since the mounted bowman had first appeared. He spent
his last hours outlining to Tului a strategic plan for the final
extermination of the Kin monarchy and the seizure of its stronghold of Kaifeng.

His body was borne back to Mongolia in majesty, and every
stranger along the way who looked upon the bier was slain. They
buried him at a spot now unknown on the sacred mountain of
Burkan-kaldun, close to the headwaters of Onon and Kerulen
where his Mongols had first struggled into cohesive being. At the
mound where he lay, the Guard mounted watch over a Lord of
the Ocean-Encircled lands who had never learned to read or

write, had never assumed the imperial title of Khaghan, had never succumbed to the delights of the civilizations he had conquered, and had never seen the sea. 'I have committed many cruelties,' he is reputed to have said, 'and killed an incalculable number of men without knowing whether it was right. But as to what is thought of me, I am indifferent.'[1] In his indifference he had moulded the Nation of the Archers to his will, and set them on the road to world dominion.

'He was possessed,' wrote Juvaini, the Persian historian who attained high office in the Mongol service, 'of great energy, discernment, genius and understanding. He was an overthrower of enemies, intrepid, sanguinary, cruel. A just, resolute butcher.'[2]

[1] Barckhausen, *L'Empire jaune de Genghis-Khan*, p. 172.
[2] Ata-Malik Juvaini, *The History of the World Conqueror*. Translated by John Andrew Boyle.

9

Pax Mongolica

In Xanadu did Kubla Khan
A stately pleasure dome decree:
Where Alph, the sacred river, ran
Through caverns measureless to man
Down to a sunless sea.
— SAMUEL COLERIDGE, Kubla Khan

WITH the death of Chingis Khan, what can be seen as the first phase of the Mongol empire ended. He had forged its central core in Mongolia. Then, with his Heartland base unified and secure, he had embarked on a tremendous outsurge first into the Chinese east, then into the Turkish west. But his foreign conquests were left unfinished. When he died in 1227, Mukali was still struggling to contain the repeated attempts of the Golden Monarchs, from their fortress-capital of Kaifeng, to recover the territories they had lost in northern China. Though Transoxiana, Khorasan and Afghanistan were in Mongol hands, central Iran had been but passingly subdued and Mesopotamia was untouched. And the penetration of the Russian steppes by Subotei and Jebei had been less an invasion than a grand tour of reconnaissance.

With the advent of Chingis's successors, the second phase of the Mongol imperium opened. Its outset was marked by a series of even more massive military thrusts into China, Europe and the Middle East. Completing Chingis's work, these irresistible drives extended the Mongol grasp to almost every territory of the Old World that could be seized and held by nomad armies operating from the Heartland grass. They were followed by a few decades of relative calm – the period known as the Mongol Peace – when a single steppe people dictated the fortunes of the

land-world from the Canton river to the marches of Poland.
Then came swift disintegration.

Explosive rise, all-embracing power, rapid fall: in outline, the
pattern of the Mongol destiny was not unlike that of previous
empires of the steppes. But where earlier nomad tides, ebbing
into extinction, had usually left only vestiges of flotsam around
the Heartland's fringes, the impact of the Mongols was to leave
a legacy of deep and permanent significance. The scale of their
thought and action; the a-tribal, professional spirit of their
armies; their conscious pursuit of organization and stability:
these ensured that, while it lasted, their empire would be of a
different order. During the years of the great conquests it was,
essentially, a one-way order of ruthless outward expansion. But
as the geographical limits of the steppe pony's performance were
reached, it was gradually to become a two-way order, admitting
trade and travel into the Heartland from the Eurasian littoral,
telescoping the unthinkable distances of inner Asia, joining East
with West. By the time its decline had set in, the Mongol order
had irrevocably altered the balance of continents and unleashed
between them forces that are still at work today.

As Chingis laid down, his third son Ogedei took his place on
the throne of white horse-skins at the apex of the empire. During
the Khwaresmian campaign Chingis had decided that the bad
blood between his two elder sons, Juchi and Chagatai, made it
impossible for either of them to succeed him. In the event, Juchi
had died a few months before his father: but even so the Khan
had refused to reconsider his second son's claim. For Chagatai
was an ultra-traditionalist, brutal and narrow in outlook, and
without talent for practical politics. Ogedei's character was the
reverse. He made up for his lack of principles by an amiable good
humour, by a taste for convivial drinking, and by a capacity for
human judgement resembling Chingis's supreme shrewdness in
the handling of men.

The momentum imparted to the nascent Mongol power by
Chingis's force of will had inevitably set the empire on the road
to further expansion. Ogedei, affable and permissive, was not
the man to question the underlying strengths or weaknesses of
its structure, or the implications of its might. No new political
or strategic concept marked his accession. He simply took up
where his father had left off. And the first major action of the

new Khaghan – for the full imperial title now came into use –
was to implement the plan for the final destruction of the Golden
Kings which Chingis had dictated to Tului on his deathbed.

Two armies swept down from the Mongolian plateau. Their
target was Kaifeng, the city that had all along been the nucleus
of Kin resistance to the Mongol occupation of northern China.
The larger force, under Ogedei himself with Subotei as his effective commander, advanced upon the city from the direction of
Peking. The other, with Tului at its head, wheeled through the
Ordos Loop, then worked its way towards Kaifeng along the
south bank of the Yellow river. Realizing that the full Mongol
strength was now upon them, the Kin took the desperate step of
ordering the breaching of the river dykes. But Subotei got wind
of it. Pushing his advance guard forward, he found gangs of
coolies assembling with their tools on the river bank; and before
the Kin troops could interfere, he annihilated them.

Robbed of its natural protection, Kaifeng fell back on its
numbers and its walls. The defence was long and grim, each side
drawing on all the technical resources at its command. From a
tall tower erected by their engineers the Mongols kept up a rain
of stone and naphtha, supplemented by fire-arrows and by
pigeons trailing burning straw from their legs. The Kin are said
to have replied with rockets. So completely was the country
round laid waste that attackers and besiegers alike were reduced
to cannibalism. Then an epidemic broke out within the city,
killing half its population, denuding its battlements of men. In
May 1233 the great gates creaked open in surrender; and
Subotei ordered that all the surviving inhabitants – upwards of
a million souls – should be cut down. Once more Yeliu ch'u ts'ai
intervened. To Ogedei's accusation of sentimentality he retorted
that the artisans of Kaifeng formed the largest pool of industrial
ability remaining in the Chinese north. Was the Khaghan prepared to sacrifice the wealth they could create, year in year out,
for the momentary satisfaction of revenge ? The Minister had his
way.

Meanwhile the reigning Golden Monarch had retreated with
his entourage to a near-by fortress set inaccessibly at the centre
of a lake. His withdrawal only delayed his end. Mongol artificers
cut a channel from the lake to the Yellow river, and the level of
water round the fortress began to fall. Believing himself too

obese for further flight, the king handed his regalia to his son; and as the first of Subotei's troopers splashed across the dwindling lake, he hanged himself. Almost at the same moment the boy he had appointed in his place fell to the knife of a disaffected courtier. It was the end of the Kin regime and of the long, mortal struggle between Mongol and Jurchet.

But this moment of triumph only marked a stage in the Mongols' involvement in China. All the north was theirs at last. But the other China beyond – the huge teeming regions of the Yangtze basin and the farther south – was still ruled by the independent native dynasty of the Sung, seated at their magnificent capital of Hangchow. During Ogedei's campaign against the Kin, the Sung had been his allies. In the hope of receiving back part of the northern territories they had long since lost, they had sent a Chinese contingent to assist him at Kaifeng. But the Khaghan had proved niggardly; and in a fit of injured dignity the Sung emperor instructed his general on the spot to grab the city from the Mongol armies by force. The attempt was quickly frustrated: but the episode provided Ogedei, if he wanted it, with a perfect pretext for a full-scale invasion of central China.

At this point Ogedei paused. The idea of conquering central China was infinitely tempting. Its enormous native wealth, fostered by a long line of intelligent emperors, had been augmented by repeated influxes of skilled and moneyed men driven from the north by the successive invasions from Manchuria and Mongolia. The seizure of Sung China, the tapping of its accumulated, self-multiplying riches, would maintain the Mongol empire in affluence for all time. But the commitment such an ambition demanded might well prove total. Other states, other quarters of the world, might yield nearly as much for less risk and effort. It was time to consult, to establish priorities.

Two years after the destruction of the Kin, Ogedei called together an assembly of the Mongol leadership comparable to that which Chingis Khan had summoned in 1206. The setting was, however, different: Ogedei's gathering was held at the new city of Karakorum, on the Orkhon river in central Mongolia. For his people, much to their surprise, now possessed a capital of brick and stone. Its building had been started during Chingis's lifetime, at the insistence of Yelui ch'u ts'ai. There could not be an

empire, he had declared, without a focus. There must be a permanent point from which administration could radiate, to
which missions could bring their homage and tribute. The location he had chosen fitted these requirements: it was a traditional
place for the handling of caravan cargoes, and many steppe
tracks led to it. It had, moreover, been the site of the capital of
the Uighur Turks in the eighth century. By Ogedei's time Karakorum boasted a palace, audience-chambers, treasure-vaults and
warehouses – gaunt, static rectangles in a world of round, wind-
whipped tents and melting movement. Chingis had avoided it;
and succeeding Mongol generations seem to have regarded it
with an equal lack of enthusiasm. They graced its environs with
shifting suburbs of felt, leaving its rigid claustrophobic rooms to
the literate foreign officials – Uighurs, Persians, Khitans,
Chinese – who managed their empire for them.

At the Karakorum council of 1235 many proposals were put
forward. The idea again arose of a thrust into India. An army
should be dispatched to Khorasan for a further push into Iran.
A punitive column must be sent to suppress uprisings in Korea.
But these were subsidiary to a more crucial question: in which
direction should the main Mongol forces now be employed?
Should their objective be Sung China in the east? Or should
they strike into the far west to reap the fruits of the reconnaissance of the Black Sea steppes made by Subotei and Jebei
thirteen years before?

The case for a new campaign into China rested on the vast
rewards which were certain to attend success. But success could
not be assumed. No steppe empire had ever subdued central and
southern China. Only a hundred years previously the Jurchets,
then at the peak of their power, had tried and failed. They had
not been defeated by Chinese military strength but by the
human plethora of the Yangtze valley, its impregnable cities,
its maze of waterways. Ogedei's armies might be stopped in the
same way, and even engulfed.

But Subotei, cautious strategist though he was, had no doubts.
He believed that Mongol superiority was now such as to allow a
march on both China and the west at the same time. And he was
obsessed by the west. For beyond the Black Sea steppes lay
Europe; and all the information he had gathered on his expedition with Jebei had convinced him that Europe was as rich a

plunder-zone as China. His profound experience, his hard lucid arguments, won the day. The decision was taken to launch two mighty offensives simultaneously: one on central China, the other on Europe. To wage war on two fronts separated by some seventy degrees of longitude: Chingis Khan himself could scarcely have thought in terms bolder or more confident.

Within a year the Mongol armies of the east were pouring across the Sung frontiers. By that time Subotei, with every tou-man not required for China, was already on his way into the west.

The drive into Europe was Subotei's brainchild from the start. For years it had been taking detailed shape in his mind. The assaulting forces would assemble at the western limits of the empire, in the Aral-Ural-Volga zone. This was the region which Chingis had allotted to Juchi as his fief; and since Juchi's death its ruling prince had been his son, Batu. As Khan of the Mongol west, Batu would assume supreme command of the expedition, with Subotei as his chief adviser.

The first stage of the plan called for a show of strength against the Turkish frontier tribes along the Volga, and the incorpora-tion into the Mongol ranks of as many of their fighting men as force or persuasion could enlist. Their numbers thus augmented, the attackers would cross the river in winter and, using its frozen tributaries as roads through the forests, would fall upon the principalities of Russia. With Russian resistance crushed, the next objective would be the plain of Hungary; and from there Europe would be drained of its treasure. The whole campaign, Subotei reckoned, might take eighteen years.

By the winter of 1237 every frontier tribe of doubtful allegi-ance had been rendered harmless. The ancient khanate of Great Bulgary had been overrun and its capital, near the junction of the Volga and the Kama, destroyed. Beyond, on the Black Sea steppes, thousands of Kipchaks were dead, and others were again in flight towards the Danube. Droves of prisoners, drafted back to the base-camps in Batu's lands, had accepted service under Subotei. The Mongol army of the west had been doubled in size, largely from Turkish sources.

In December 1237 Subotei moved across the Volga to open the campaign proper. At his side rode Batu, with a galaxy of the

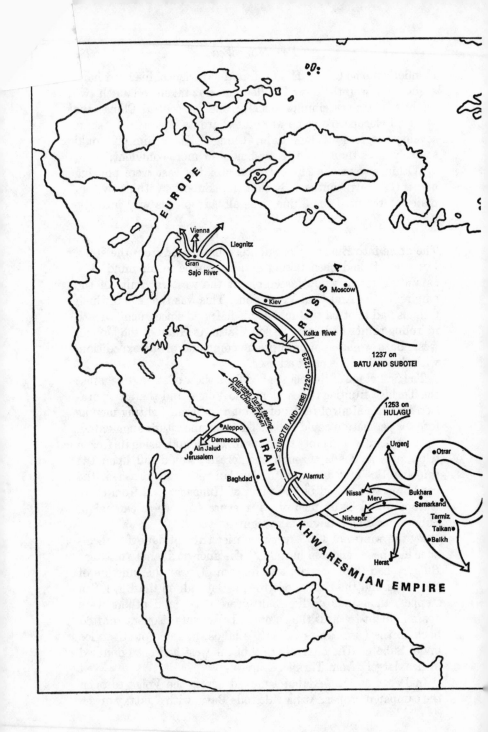

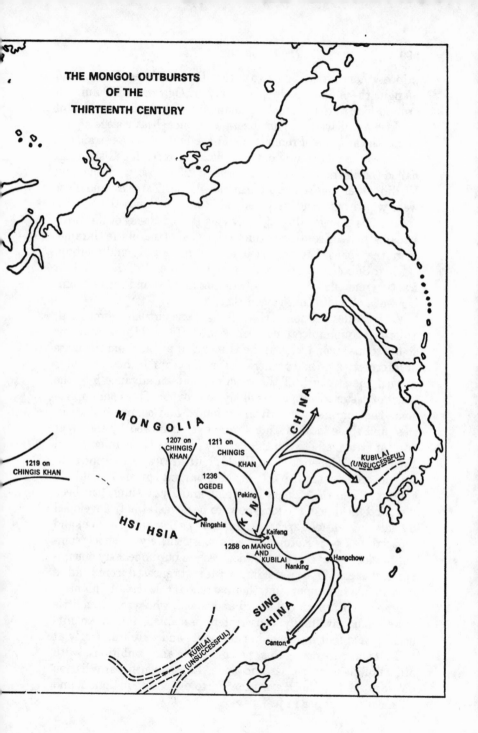

THE MONGOL OUTBURSTS
OF THE
THIRTEENTH CENTURY

MONGOLIA

CHINA

1207 on
CHINGIS
KHAN

1211 on
CHINGIS
KHAN

1236
OGEDEI

1219 on
CHINGIS KHAN

KUBILAI
(UNSUCCESSFUL)

Peking

K I N

HSI HSIA

Ningshia

Kaifeng

1258 on MANGU
AND
KUBILAI

Nanking

Hangchow

SUNG
CHINA

KUBILAI
(UNSUCCESSFUL)

Canton

princely house including two future Great Khans, Kuyuk and Mangu, the eldest sons respectively of Ogedei and Tului. All around him were the crack toumans from Mongolia, the host of Turkish auxiliaries, the engineers with their heavy siege equipment, the swarms of remounts and the endless wagon-trains.

Before the month was out, the flames enveloping Riazan signalled the alarm, too late. In February 1238 Moscow, Susdal and Vladimir were sacked and burnt. In March, Yaroslav and Tver were wiped out. And with central Russia in ashes the Mongol spearheads changed direction, leaving the ice-tracks of the forest streams, driving south-west on to the open plains of the Ukraine. Here they paused to rest their horses, to mop up and regroup.

Then Subotei struck again; and by the end of 1240 only a fraction remained of the stately domes of Kiev and the tall shining walls of white that ringed them.

With the destruction of Kiev, Russia was virtually eliminated. Subotei's communications were secure. He could now raise his sights to his second target: the Hungarian plain. From the mass of information he had gathered over the years, he had carefully gauged the strength of the reaction that an advance into the heart of eastern Europe was likely to provoke. It was unimpressive. The continent was riven by feudal and commercial rivalries; and these local divisions were overshadowed by the great current struggle between the Papacy and the German emperor, Frederick of Hohenstaufen. With political weakness went military incompetence. The arts of the mounted bowman, painfully acquired from the steppes by Rome and Byzantium, had been lost; and the day of the long-bow, to be devastatingly developed by the English foot-archers, had not yet dawned. Europe, and especially eastern Europe, relied almost entirely on shock combat at close quarters: on the picturesque but hopelessly encumbered clusters of lance-wielding aristocrats encased from head to foot in plate armour; on their attendant levies of infantry, equipped with spear and sword and shield, who were often little more than unwillingly conscripted peasants. Horsed knights usually held foot retainers in contempt; and were frequently at odds, owing to conflicting personalities and ambitions, with others of their own class and code. Consequently, any liaison between the two shock arms tended to evaporate in action, and alliances to founder in jealousy.

Nevertheless, since steppe blood flowed in their veins, stubborn resistance must be expected from the Hungarians themselves; and it was probable that neighbouring potentates would rally to their aid. Subotei therefore planned his attack on Hungary as a double movement. While he himself invaded the Hungarian plain with the main Mongol armies, a separate force under Kaidu, a young prince of Ogedei's house, would wheel through the country to its north and west to intercept any help approaching Hungary from central Europe.

From the Mongol concentration-point near Przemysl, on what is now the border between the Soviet Union and Poland, Kaidu's column clattered across the Vistula in February 1241. Almost at once it met and smashed the Polish army, then swept on through Cracow and Breslau, wrecking each city in turn. It was said that the woods of Poland were alive with pagan horsemen, passing like spectre riders none knew to what goal. Advancing into Silesia, Kaidu heard that the expected opposition was materializing. Prince Henry of Silesia and King Wenceslas of Bohemia were closing on him. But they had not yet joined forces. Before they could do so, on 9th April, Kaidu lured Prince Henry to battle at Wahlstadt, near Liegnitz. Coming upon a ragged mass of nomads apparently in hasty retreat, the Prince's chivalry gave chase in loose formation. Then, in silent response to quick-fluttering flags, the rabble on its little ponies was seen to turn, and to sort itself with startling precision into fighting order. While the Europeans were still without cohesion they were flailed by a fearful storm of armour-piercing arrows; and behind the whistling clouds the Mongol lancers charged. Henry himself disappeared in a welter of dying men and horses; and from the field of Liegnitz nine sackfuls of right ears cut from the slain – from German and Polish infantry, from Teutonic knights, from Templars and Hospitallers – were gathered up and sent back to Batu. Wenceslas sheered off to protect his own Bohemia from a like disaster; and Kaidu's men, resuming their wheeling march, severed the Hungarians from any hope of help from Austria.

At the same time Subotei had crossed the arc of the Carpathian mountains, and was racing across the plain of Hungary. For mutual protection his armies were moving in three widely separated columns: but their common destination was Budapest, or Gran as it was then called, the Hungarian capital on the

Danube where King Bela IV was concentrating nearly a hundred
thousand defenders. The speed of the advance was almost in-
credible; one of the Mongol columns covered 180 miles across the
plain, in deep snow, in less than three days. Outside Gran,
Subotei assembled his converging forces: but he made no attempt to invest the city. Instead he began a slow retirement to
the north-east whence he had come. The movement acted like a
magnet; Bela and his host emerged from Gran and followed him.
For six days the Mongols plodded back, retracing their steps
across the frozen grass, leading the Hungarians on. At length, at
the Sajo river in the wine-growing district of Tokay, they halted;
and on 10th April, the day after Kaidu's victory at Liegnitz,
they turned on their pursuers.

At a bridge across the river Batu delivered a frontal attack,
and Bela committed the bulk of his army to repulse it. But
Batu's assault was a feint, mounted with only a part of the Mongol strength. Unseen, Subotei forded the river with the remaining toumans, swept round behind the enemy, and surged upon
his flanks and rear. Surrounded, reduced to panic by the tem-
pests of arrows, Bela's formations strove to find a path of escape.
Deliberately the path was opened, and the trapped crowds
poured out through it. Waiting till they had streamed away into
open country, Subotei ordered a pursuit. For three days and
nights the horse-archers hounded them down, shot and sabred
them out of existence. When the Mongols finally pulled up
seventy thousand men – knights and infantry, Hungarians,
Croats, Germans, Frenchmen – were dead. 'You could see nothing along the roads but fallen warriors,' said an eyewitness.
'Their bodies were strewn everywhere like stones in a quarry.'

In little more than three years the power of the Russian
princes and the panoply of eastern Europe had been annihilated
by a marshal whose genius rivalled that of Chingis Khan. Once
more the advanced grazing-base of Hungary was in Heartland
hands; and from it the terror now began to feel its way into the
vitals of the continent. Gran was sacked; the farms of western
Hungary went up in smoke; the pall of destruction spread from
the Danube nearly to the Baltic. A Mongol column reached the
Dalmation coast. Another penetrated to Udine, within sixty
miles of Venice. A third, said to have been led by an English
knight in the Mongol service, pushed to Wiener Neustadt on the

outskirts of Vienna. Subotei was testing the gates of Italy and Germany. It seemed that nothing could save Europe from another Attila.

Then, in the spring of 1242, an arrow-messenger from Karakorum thundered into Batu's camp. Ogedei had died – of drink. The news had immediate significance for all the Mongol leadership. The election of a new Khaghan would follow; politics would run rife, and the presence of every prince and noble with interests to protect would be essential. To Subotei the prospect of an evacuation seemed of little moment. He had faced no enemies he could not rout, and he was convinced that any European coalition against him was likely to be ineffective. He could return at any time.

Within a few weeks every Mongol trooper had vanished into the eastern horizons. In all the territories west of Russia the miracle of deliverance was a reality. But for the Russian principalities there was no relief. With the utter ruin of its cities the old Kiev-Novgorod society had disappeared beneath the rule of the steppes. There was no need for the Mongols to abandon a region reduced to such helplessness; contiguous with Batu's lands, it could be held as a western extension of his fief. Henceforth, for more than two centuries, the overlords of Russia were to be Batu and his successors; its taskmasters the chieftains of their Turco-Mongol 'Golden Horde'.

Europe had been saved: but not by its own efforts. Accordingly, it became deeply necessary to rationalize the impotence it had displayed. The chroniclers asserted that the Mongols had not been men but fiends. They ate every human being they killed; and since they had a special relish for the female sex, their commissariat observed distinctions of rank in distributing the flesh of women. Rations prepared from skinny matrons went to the common troopers. Succulent young girls were the prerogative of the officers' messes; and their breasts, as the gourmet's delight, were served only in the princes' tents. Moreover, it was affirmed, they were giants; their enormous horses ate whole trees, and could only be mounted from ladders. Above all, it was their numbers that had rendered them so terrible; and though Subotei's armies had totalled one hundred and fifty thousand at most, the Mongol word *ordu*, meaning a grouping of families or tents, was inflated to suggest the uncountable hordes of the

Asian peril. Yet behind the compensating tales lingered an ugly unresolved truth, and a sense of failure. And though the Mongols were never to return, there settled across much of Europe the consciousness of an overhanging doom which has been compared to the pessimism born of the nuclear age, and which could only be averted by a higher deterrent. 'From the wrath of the Tartars, Lord deliver us.'

But the thrust of the Mongols into Europe, and their sudden withdrawal, also had a positive effect. The departure of their armies into the steppes acted like the undertow of a spent wave: it sucked Europeans into the Mongol empire.

The first stirring of this movement into the unknown world of the Heartland was due in part to the legend of Prester John. About a century earlier a Syrian bishop had informed the Pope that he had heard of a great realm in the farthest Orient ruled by an omnipotent king who, claiming descent from the Magi, was a fervent and militant Christian. The story may have contained a grain of truth, in that Nestorian Christianity had become fairly widespread on the steppes and a number of tribal rulers had embraced it. But in the mind of all concerned with the Crusades, Prester John assumed a stature far more important than that of a local tribal chief. In the Holy Land the Moslems were getting the upper hand, and the Crusaders sorely needed fresh help and inspiration. It followed that the Great Presbyter did indeed exist, and that his mighty armies would march to their aid beneath the banner of Christ. But who, and where, was he?

At first he was identified with the exiled Khitan prince who had established the Kara-Khitan empire in central Asia. This prince was known to have defeated the Seljuk Sultan Sanjar; and after this initial blow at Islam he would surely march through Iran to strike at the Turks in Mesopotamia. The hope proved vain. But with the rise of the Mongols another possibility appeared: Prester John was the new 'Emperor of the Tartars' – Chingis Khan. The Frankish East took heart again; for the formidable, mysterious figure who had broken the Moslem empire of Mohammed must undoubtedly be Christian. He would push on to the Mediterranean littoral and join hands with the Crusaders in Jerusalem.

The Mongols' incursion into Europe brought disillusionment.

Clearly their overlord was no friend of the West; and the Emperor Frederick, in describing his depredations to Henry III of
England, specifically stated his conviction that he was bent on
the extermination of the Christian faith. But the Vatican did not
abandon hope. Though the 'Tartar' king was not Prester John,
he might yet be endowed with the Prester's rumoured qualities.
If he could be converted to Christianity the Crusaders might
still benefit from his terrible power, and a repetition of his westward onslaught would be prevented. Accordingly, Innocent IV
dispatched a mission into the Heartland in the wake of the Mongol withdrawal. He chose as his envoy one John of Plano Carpini,
a Franciscan friar, and furnished him with two bulls addressed
to the reigning Khaghan. The first bade him listen well to the
friar, 'so that following his salutary instructions you may acknowledge Jesus Christ and worship His glorious name'; the
second reproached him for laying waste Christian lands and be-
sought him henceforth to 'desist entirely from assaults of this
kind'.[1]

In April 1245 Carpini set out, with one companion, on his
momentous journey into the Asian world. At the Russian borders Mongol outposts instantly challenged him. He was passed
on, through a series of local governors, to Batu's headquarters
on the Volga; and Batu, perplexed by the humble ambassador
who brought no presents worth accepting, sent him on to Karakorum. Carpini was sixty-five, pot-bellied, and in poor health.
Yet his escort, setting the pace, hustled him across the spaces of
the steppes at a smart trot. Day after day and sometimes far
into the night he was forced to ride, with never a break for rest,
covering the best part of 3,000 miles in less than four months.
That his elderly frame survived the endless jogging, his aching
thighs the perpetual rub of the saddle, suggests an unquenchable
spiritual zeal. And though his party changed horses three or four
times a day and traversed the grazing-grounds of tribe after
nomad tribe, not once does his account hint at a hitch in the
relay system or a threat of danger. From the Volga to Karakorum, Mongol rule had welded the Heartland into an ordered
whole.

At the capital the friar was not ill-received: though, owing to

[1] For the text of the two bulls, see Christopher Dawson, *The Mongol
Mission,* pp. 73–6.

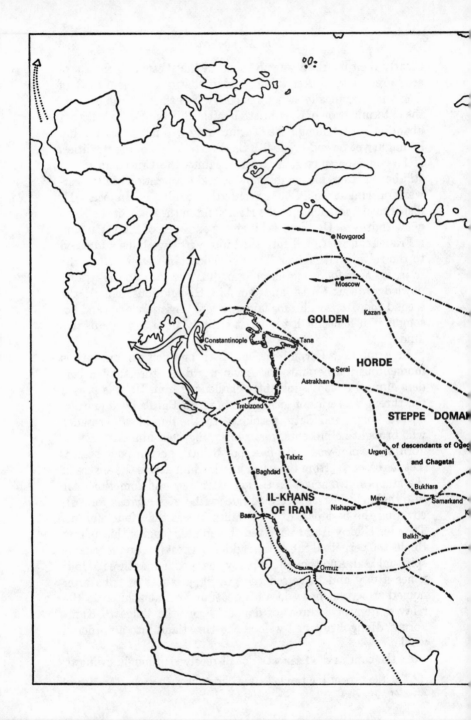

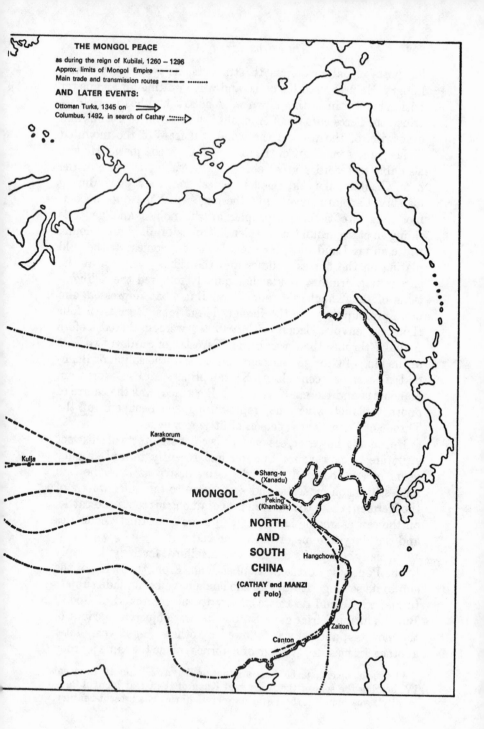

THE MONGOL PEACE

as during the reign of Kubilai, 1260 – 1296
Approx. limits of Mongol Empire ·—·—·
Main trade and transmission routes ——— ··········

AND LATER EVENTS:

Ottoman Turks, 1345 on ⟹
Columbus, 1492, in search of Cathay ⋯⋯⟹

Karakorum

Kulja

●Shang-tu
(Xanadu)

MONGOL

●Peking
(Khanbalik)

NORTH
AND
SOUTH
CHINA

(CATHAY and MANZI
of Polo)

Hangchow●

Zaiton●

Canton●

his hosts' usual meanness to strangers, he went perpetually hungry. He presented his bulls; and while waiting for an answer busied himself in setting down what he saw and heard. He described the fierce climate of Mongolia; the customs, virtuous and otherwise, of the people; the wonderful feats of the mounted archers, and something of the history of their conquests. He was also able to record a great occasion; for the investiture of the new Khaghan, Kuyuk, Ogedei's eldest son, took place during his stay. Carpini marvelled at the huge white marquee accommodating two thousand people; at the nobles and generals riding in state around it in splendid robes of different colours, white and red and blue, for each day's ceremonies; at the gold plating on the horses' saddles and the riders' armour; at the gargantuan drinking bouts that quickly followed the deliberations of the Khaghan's councillors. But what impressed him more profoundly were the foreign delegations. More than four thousand envoys, laden with tribute, were gathered before Kuyuk's throne: there was Prince Yaroslav of Susdal; two sons of the king of Georgia; the representative of the caliph of Baghdad; a dozen Saracen sultans, Khitan princes, ambassadors from Manchuria and Korea. Karakorum, it seemed, was the centre of another planet where he, representing the occupant of the Throne of Peter, was a person of little moment.

He did not, however, see one of the chief architects of this vast structure of power: for Subotei had recently retired. Eighty years of age, covered with glory, impassive as ever, he had modestly taken his leave and withdrawn to the quiet waters of the Kerulen; there to reflect in peace, among his tents and cattle, on the campaigns he had fought in more than thirty countries and the sixty-five major battles he had won.

Officially, Carpini's mission was a failure; for Kuyuk's reply to the Pope was hostile and unbending. 'From the rising of the sun to its setting,' it ran, 'all the lands have been made subject to me: who could do this contrary to the command of God?'[1] But the intrepid friar gave Europe its first objective account of the Mongols; and he was followed by others. Eight years later another Franciscan, William of Rubruck, made the same journey

[1] Dawson, op.cit., p. 85. The original of Kuyuk's letter to Innocent IV, bearing the seal of the 'Universal Khan of the Great Mongol Community', was found in the Vatican archives during the present century.

with the explicit aim of securing Mongol help for the Crusaders. He, also, failed in his purpose: but he amplified Carpini's narrative, and in particular brought Karakorum to vivid life. His description of its wondrous fountain, wrought by a Parisian goldsmith, and throwing simultaneous streams of koumiss, mead and rice wine into the air from the branches of a silver tree, seems to foreshadow the crude vitality of the organ that was to rob an English journalist of his night's sleep at Tomsk in 1901.

European missionaries, traders, travellers: one by one they were drawn into the empire that now stretched from the rising to the setting of the sun. Protected by the unity it had relentlessly imposed on the huge land-mass of the Heartland, they and their reports steadily transformed its inhabitants from shadowy fiends to living men.

Kuyuk died a year after his investiture. With his death a new line of Khaghans came to the fore; and this shift in the rulership marked the onset of a transformation of the Mongol empire.

The change at the summit was brought about by Batu. With the absorption into his domains of Russia, and of the Turkish tribes on the Black Sea steppes, his western fief had become so large and populous that its power began to rival that of Karakorum. Alarmed at Batu's swollen strength, Kuyuk had set out with a strong force to remind his cousin of his subordinate status; and it was during his march into the west that he succumbed, like his father Ogedei, to a chronic weakness for the wineskin. In the ensuing vacuum, Batu himself was offered the imperial throne: but being now orientated to his western interests, he refused it. Nonetheless, Batu was in a position to act as king-maker; and incensed by Kuyuk's march against him, he secured the exclusion of Ogedei's line from the succession. For the future, he insisted, the Khaghans should be chosen from the house of Tului.

Tului was already dead. But at Batu's dictate, three of his sons came to the forefront of the Mongol leadership. The eldest, Mangu, now became Khaghan in Kuyuk's place. Hulagu and Kubilai, his younger brothers, have already appeared briefly in this story: as little boys they had been initiated into the rites of the chase by Chingis himself as he returned in triumph from Khwaresmia. Hulagu, though he was to play a leading part during Mangu's reign, never became Great Khan. But Mangu and Kubilai, ruling successively, were to be the most illustrious of the later Mongol emperors. Inheriting the empire 'conquered from the saddle', they were to carry the legacy of conquest to its zenith. Statesmen as well as warriors, they came to couple the Mongol name not only with dread but with constructive, even liberal, government.

Not that either abandoned the policy of expansion pursued by their forebears. In 1253, within two years of his confirmation as Khaghan, Mangu launched his armies in Chingis's footsteps through Khwaresmia, to embark on a massive invasion of Iran and Mesopotamia. Acquisition of more wealth and territory was only a secondary object of this new campaign into the south-west. Mangu's real purpose was to eliminate what he conceived to be two sources of danger to himself and his regime: the Assassins, and the Baghdad caliphate.

The sinister order of the Assassins had been founded about 1090. It had centred originally round a band of Shi'ite Moslem adventurers wielding the weapon of political murder in the service of the Fatimid rulers of Egypt, with whom they had religious affiliations. They had mounted a ferocious underground resistance to the invading Sunni Seljuks, and had later struck repeatedly at the Christian Crusaders. With time, however, their sense of dedication – which often involved martyrdom – had become blurred: increasingly they killed to augment the power of their own order and of its Grand Masters. The almost legendary stronghold of Alamut, hidden in the inaccessible valleys of northern Iran and surrounded by a chain of subsidiary castles, formed their headquarters. There they grew the hashish which they used to dope and indoctrinate their young commandos, and from which their name of Hashishins derived; and from these mountain-shrouded eyries they terrorized the Middle East and even parts of Europe. Shortly after his accession, Mangu was warned that the Assassins intended to add him to their victims. He deemed the warning sufficiently credible to demand action.

If the new Khaghan believed his person to be threatened from Iran, he likewise considered his power to be under challenge from Baghdad. For the Abbasid caliphs still claimed to exercise spiritual authority over the entire Islamic world; and that world now included the Moslem-populated regions of the Mongol empire. In Ogedei's reign they had, indeed, gone so far as to declare a holy war against the Heartland oppressors of their religious subjects. To Mangu, a firm upholder of the secular nature of the Mongol state, such meddling was intolerable. The skill of the Seljuks in reducing caliphal pretensions by political means had evidently been wasted. Direct methods were now required. And any doubts he may have had as to their propriety were set at rest by his Nestorian Christian wife.

It was necessary to remove both dangers; and a single expedition under the Khaghan's brother Hulagu could achieve the double object. Circling the southern shore of the Caspian, Hulagu would first flush out the Assassins. That done, he would move on to Baghdad and bring the caliph to account.

Like his father Tului, Hulagu was an able, ruthless captain. Leading his toumans through Khorasan, he plunged into the fastnesses of the Elburz range and attacked the lairs of the Assassins. One by one they were overwhelmed: but despite the great batteries of siege equipment he brought against it, three years passed before Alamut itself was starved into surrender. On its final fall Hulagu applied their own methods to its occupants: all, down to infants in arms, were exterminated. Even so, the Assassins seem to have had the last word; for the Grand Master, spared as a prize of unique value and sent back to Mongolia under heavy guard, was murdered on the way – by an assailant who was never identified.

Hulagu now pressed on westward, sending ahead to Bahgdad to demand the submission of the caliph, al-Mutasim. Receiving a devious reply, he dispatched a second message. The caliph, it ran, was evidently as crooked as a curved bow: but he would soon be rendered as direct as the flight of an arrow. With that, Hulagu swept down through the Zagros mountains to the levels of the Tigris valley. Tumult rose around Baghdad. Terrified peasants, herding their families and animals, crammed their way into the shelter of the city. Outside, Hulagu's advance guards were seen massing before the gates; and the ominous sound of axes signalled the means to be used in the coming assault. The Mongol artillerists were felling the stands of date-palms along the river to feed their catapults.

For six days and nights the barrage of flying tree-trunks crashed against the walls, demolishing palaces and mosques.

Then al-Mutasim emerged with his long retinue, and gave himself up. Hesitating as to what course to take with him, Hulagu consulted his astrologers. Nothing untoward, they assured him, would result from stern measures; and in February 1258 the last of the Abbasid caliphs expired beneath the hooves of a Mongol execution squad. An orgy of looting and slaughter followed. The delicate mosaic of beauty spread along the winding Tigris – the glinting domes and cool courtyards from which the Arab influence had radiated for five centuries – was shattered. And the Mongol volleys, scourging the overcrowded streets, took a toll of nearly a million lives. Leaving a few regiments to guard the drained husk of the city, Hulagu escaped from the stench and pushed on west again, heading up the Euphrates into Syria.

Mangu's anxieties had been set at rest. And his brother's continued march was adding treasure and territory to the imperial estate. As Hulagu crossed the Syrian desert news arrived from Karakorum of his appointment as Il-Khan, or Viceroy, of Iran and of all the lands he was still conquering.

Along the Mediterranean coast the Crusaders were watching Hulagu's advance towards them with growing hope. Their previous attempts to secure a formal alliance with the Khaghan of the Mongol empire had failed; and accordingly their dream of crushing Islam between the millstones of east and west had faded. But suddenly, and in pursuit of strictly Mongol interests, the Khaghan's viceroy had silenced the religious voice of Baghdad; and beyond doubt he was now moving against the remaining Moslem stronghold of Egypt with its far greater military power. The vague, wishful figure of Prester John might have evaporated: but here, in the approach of the trotting toumans, razing mosques, emptying the Syrian towns of their Moslem populations, was the clear-cut reality of help from oriental Asia. For his part, Hulagu knew that he would soon be at grips with Egypt: he raised no objection to the Crusaders' eager offer of reinforcement for his columns. So Heartland shamanist and European Christian seized Aleppo side by side. Then, passing the vast bulk of Krak des Chevaliers looming above the gentle slopes of the Homs gap, Mongol archers and Frankish knights rode together towards the south: towards Damascus and Jerusalem.

.   .   .   .   .

At the time of these events – about the year 1258 – the Mongol empire was approaching the zenith of its power, its unity, and its extent. The domains owing allegiance to Karakorum reached from the Yellow Sea to the Black, and from the Arctic tundra to the Himalaya. No previous empire had ever encompassed so large a proportion of the earth's surface. To this day none has equalled its size.

Three enormous fiefs, each ruled by the descendants of one of Chingis Khan's sons, now formed the core of the Mongol realm. At its heart, stretching from the coast of Korea to the dry strait of Dzungaria, and including all northern China and Manchuria as well as the original homelands of Mongolia, lay the lands under the direct control of the Great Khan Mangu himself. To the west of this region, from the Tibetan plateau to the Aral Sea, from the Altai to Transoxiana, was the appanage of Chagatai and his line. And in the far west, enclosing the Volga basin, the Black Sea steppes and the forest zones of Russia, lay the vast sub-empire of the Golden Horde, partly Mongol and partly Turkish, which Juchi had bequeathed to Batu, and Batu, dying in 1256, to his sons.

And current campaigns of conquest were adding two further colonial spheres to the three great dominions already established. In the south-west Hulagu, having secured Iran and Mesopotamia, had nearly reached the Mediterranean. And in the south-east the drive into central China, initiated by Ogedei, was still in progress. It had been interrupted by the manpower requirements first of Subotei's European expedition, then of Hulagu's march. But it was now gathering momentum again – and under a leader of exceptional quality. For early in his reign Mangu had appointed his promising young brother Kubilai to the governorship of a large part of north China; and Kubilai, warming to his Chinese subjects, had for several years devoted himself – with a concern unprecedented for a Mongol warrior-prince – to the rehabilitation of the devastated areas round Kaifeng. By 1258, with more men becoming available, he was preparing for a decisive invasion of the Yangtze valley to oust the Sung regime and finish the war.

Between Hulagu's armies in the Syrian west and Kubilai's in the Chinese east, across the great fiefs bestriding the land-mass of Asia, there was order, stability, cohesion. On the pastures of the interior, tribal strife had been quelled. In the outer zones Mongol governors, assisted by native officials, held the conquered peoples of the littoral under a rule which, if arbitrary and always backed by force, was often no harsher than that they had known before the coming of the toumans. Over the steppes and deserts, over much of the fringe-regions between the Heartland and the oceans, the Pax Mongolica had settled. It was said that a girl with a pot of gold on her head could walk alone and unharmed from end to end of the Mongol lands.

Since the days of Chingis Khan regular contacts between the steppe regions and the coastal belt, between the nomadic and settled cultures, had been increasing. They had started with the herds of artisans transported to Mongolia during the first great outward thrusts. They had been enlarged, as the empire expanded, by the comings and goings of countless embassies renewing their submission and bringing their annual tribute. And in the steps of the missions, as military impact mellowed into imperial relations, had come distinguished men drawn by curiosity or invitation: Chinese scholars, Persian astronomers, Indian philosophers and mathematicians.

More important, long-distance trade burgeoned under the Mongol Peace. Exchange, as well as plunder, had always been vital to the nomad communities. Chingis Khan had hoped that in favourable circumstances it might offer an alternative to conquest: and though he had abandoned the hope, he had all along sought the goodwill of the merchants travelling his territories. By Mangu's time the extension of a single system of law and order to virtually the whole of inner Asia was having its logical economic effect. To the unprecedented fact of a strong unified administration on which they could rely, the merchants of the steppes responded by establishing a network of caravan-routes to serve the different sectors of the Mongol empire. And the adjacent settled zones were quick to take advantage of these internal routes. In the cities along the imperial frontiers exchange points sprang up for the trans-shipment of cargoes and the handling of import-export business. From something like a Heartland common market, a Eurasian world market was emerging. Not even in the heyday of the Silk Route had the interior distances seen so flourishing a web of international traffic, its presence welcomed by the Mongol authorities, its passage policed by the Mongol army. Not only the steppes, but every littoral region benefited: China, India, Iran – and Europe.

In Europe the great era of revelation – of the lifting of the veils upon the globe and its surrounding space – had not yet opened. But the European mind was already straining at the strait-jackets of secular anarchy and priestly dictation. If as yet in practice rather than principle, the Round-worlders were beginning to challenge the Flat-earthers. Strabo, Eratosthenes, Ptolemy, Herodotus, were being re-examined. Military necessity had forced the Crusaders to map the Near East with considerable accuracy. Carpini and those who followed him had penetrated the infinite to Karakorum; and among the latter William of Rubruck, on his return, had talked earnestly with Roger Bacon.

Moreover, commercial rivalry was sharpening between the city-republics of Italy. Pisa, Florence, Milan, Ancona, were jostling each other in the search for fresh markets and new sources of merchandise. Venice and Genoa, sea-going giants among the lesser landlocked fry, had long possessed trading-stations on the Black Sea – as Subotei had discovered to his advantage. The further east they could push into the Heartland, the wider they could cast their net for Asian goods, the better for their competitive positions. The supremacy of the Golden Horde in the western Heartland gave them their chance. For the Golden Horde, as part of the Mongol community, held the keys to the trade-routes from the Volga to the Indus and the Yellow. And its Khans, with six hundred thousand horse-archers at their call, and living comfortably on the fat squeezed from Russian agriculture, had time and inclination to think of their coffers; to re-create around themselves a trading state resembling that of their Khazar predecessors. At Serai, their capital on the Volga, Venetian and Genoese merchants found themselves well received. Soon they were dealing with the caravans from Iran and India and China, sending back their own wares, on-forwarding their purchases to Germany and France and England.

Through the decades of conquest the Mongol physical horizons had exploded in fury. And the mental outlook of the Khaghans had likewise expanded. In the wake of the armies, as the days of terror subsided into years of ordered calm, the difference between Chingis Khan and Yeliu ch'u ts'ai came to the fore; and in some respects Mangu's thinking was closer to that of his grandfather's subtle, humanitarian minister. The nomads had never been originators. But at this period of their omnipotence the Mongols fulfilled to an unsurpassed degree the special nomad function of transmission. Across its length and breadth their empire hastened people, ideas, objects, innovations, trade. And no outside community proved readier to seize the opportunity of Heartland trade than Europe.

But stresses existed within the mighty Mongol structure. Distance itself, and differing environments, produced distinctions of outlook between the ruling houses of the great component dominions; and these were exacerbated by the play of imperial politics. Batu's ruling at the time of Kuyuk's death had sparked off a lasting feud between the families of Ogedei and Tului. Hulagu's execution of the caliph aroused the resentment of the large Turkish Moslem element in the Golden Horde; and his appointment as Il-Khan of Iran suggested that he might cast ambitious glances at their territories north of the Caucasus.

At the same time a more general cleavage of interest was gradually dividing the empire against itself. Chingis Khan had postulated a 'closed tribute state': a central reservoir of nomad power, nourished and increased by the agriculture and industry of its littoral colonies, but remaining uncontaminated by their alien way of life. The unfinished nature of Chingis's own conquests outside Mongolia had limited his personal contact with the very real temptations offered to steppe-dwellers by the affluent world of the littoral; and he had steeled himself against such of its attractions as he had encountered. But by Mangu's reign the successive further thrusts had taken large numbers of Mongol soldiers and civilians into new peripheral colonies. Not only north China but Iran, Mesopotamia, and the eastern fringes of Russia were exerting their pull upon their conquerors, softening the hardy steppe fibre of the Mongol masters in their midst by their atmosphere of relative ease. And the tribute which, according to Chingis's concept, should have found its way back to the nomad interior was increasingly absorbed by the Mongol regimes occupying the Heartland's edges. As a result the inner regions of the empire, pursuing the old pattern of steppe life, found themselves becoming poorer than the outer conquered zones. A sense of separation set in between the 'unpolluted' traditionalists at the core, and those they came to regard as *nouveaux riches* living in luxury in the outlying lands. Political tension between centre and circumference was not the only effect of this imbalance. For the growing wealth and power of the outer regions meant that sooner or later one of them – Mongol China, Mongol Iran or the Mongol Russia of the Golden Horde – was likely to make a bid for the governance of the empire as a whole.

The push which was to shift the centre of gravity from the steppes to the periphery was given by Mangu's decision in 1258 to lend the full weight of the army, and of his own presence, to Kubilai's invasion of central China. The campaign was devised by the two brothers as a combined operation; and their plan resembled, on a far greater scale and stage, that by which Batu and Subotei had annihilated the Hungarians on the Sajo seventeen years before. While Kubilai pinned the Sung forces along the middle reaches of the Yangtze, Mangu swept down through the Ordos Loop and crossed the river higher up, in the neighbourhood of modern Chungking, to attack them in the rear. The jaws of the pincer had begun to close when, on 11 August 1259, the Khaghan, in true Mongol warrior style, prepared to lead an assault against the walls of a fortress. He suddenly collapsed, and within a few hours had died of dysentery.

Mangu's death was swiftly followed by events of critical significance. In May 1260 the Mongol army in China acclaimed Kubilai as his successor; and one of the first acts of the new Great Khan was to decree that Peking, instead of Karakorum, should henceforth be the capital of the empire. The reaction was immediate. The conservative chieftains of the central steppelands were, in any case, by no means unanimous in endorsing the choice of Kubilai; and in their eyes the removal of the imperial government to foreign soil smacked of treason. They raised a storm of protest.

Tidings of the crisis reached Hulagu as his armies, having captured Damascus, were moving on southwards towards Egypt. His hopes were at their height: he fully expected to defeat the Egyptian army, take Cairo, and extend his Iranian fief to the Nile. But despite the triumphant prospect, he concluded that his presence nearer home was imperative lest civil war should engulf the Mongol empire. Detaching a minimum force under his senior general, Kitboga, to hold Syria, he withdrew his main strength towards Iran.

In September 1260, near Tabriz, Hulagu received shocking news. Probing south into the Jordan valley, Kitboga had been surrounded at Ain Jalud, near the Sea of Galilee, by a huge army under the Egyptian Sultan Qutuz and his marshal Baibars. He had fought with furious courage: but his men, amounting to little more than a single touman with some Turkish and Crusader support, had been hopelessly outnumbered. They had been decimated, and Kitboga himself had been seized and beheaded on the spot.

For forty years no Mongol army had been seriously worsted in the field. Qutuz and Baibars had punctured a legend. More, they had underlined a turning-point in the Mongol destiny. Subotei had turned back from the west. Now Hulagu had done the same, and the door to the Mediterranean had been slammed behind him. At the other extremity of the empire Kubilai's bid for the imperial throne, and his audacity in declaring Peking the future seat of government, were tipping the balance. Control was moving decisively to the far east.

But Kubilai had to fight for the power he was pursuing from China. The situation in Mongolia was ugly, for the conservatives on the steppes had found a champion to whom they could rally. This was Arik Buka, 'the Little One', Tului's fourth son and Kubilai's younger brother. The Little One caused himself to be proclaimed Khaghan at Karakorum in opposition to his brother, and then began a series of damaging raids into Kubilai's Chinese territory. It was necessary to make a truce with the Sung in order to deal with him; and for a time the issue of the civil war which now broke out was in doubt. But Kubilai's Mongol forces were with him to a man, and he had trained his Chinese infantry to ride pillion into battle behind their mounted comrades. After four years of hounding and harrying, Arik Buka had had enough. He abandoned his claim and submitted to his brother.

With his throne secure, and now impatient to gather central China into his empire, Kubilai resumed his campaign against the Sung. The great prize, however, was not to fall easily into his lap. Under the pressure of the massing toumans the Sung

government at Hangchow showed itself faint-hearted: but the opposition put up by its armies was stubborn and continuous. Not until 1273 were the approaches to the middle Yangtze cleared. And although the Mongols were now under Bayan, as redoubtable a marshal as any of the old guard, it took them two further years to batter their way down the river to Nanking. But towards the end of 1275 Hangchow was surrounded, and after a short siege it capitulated. Bayan's entry into the magnificent capital was marked by a different attitude to that of the first-generation conquerors: Kubilai had forbidden slaughter and pillage, and his instructions were enforced on pain of death. Bayan took charge of the six-year-old boy who was then the Sung emperor; and Kubilai, receiving him kindly, sent him to be educated in a Buddhist monastery. Canton, in the far south, was the final Mongol objective; for fresh resistance was gathering there around another child, the former emperor's brother. As the city fell the youngster was taken on board a junk and spirited away to sea. For some months, in the sheltered inlets along the Cantonese coast, the vessel managed to dodge the craft searching for it: but eventually it was discovered and chased. As the pursuers ranged alongside, one of the officers took the child in his arms; and, exclaiming that an honourable death was better than surrender, leapt into the sea with him.

At last a vision had been realized which had fired and tormented the nomads of the eastern steppes since the inception of mounted archery. From the time when Chingis had first crossed from Mongolia into Hsi Hsia until the day in April 1279 when the South China Sea closed over the last of the Sung line, more than seventy years had elapsed. But a Heartland people now held China in its entirety, from the Great Wall to the Gulf of Tonkin.

As the first of the Yuan or 'Outland' dynasty, Kubilai the Mongol fulfilled the concern he had felt for China ever since Mangu had appointed him to a governorship in the north. To Chingis Khan's large thought and astute judgement the grandson added qualities of his own – liberalism, intellectual curiosity, affection for those beyond his immediate circle – which Chingis, forced to apply the brutal codes of his environment to achieve his ends, could seldom afford to show. Becoming virtually Chinese, Kubilai was China's triumph: he personified the absorption

which had always been her last bulwark against the nomads. He
also represented the triumph of Yeliu ch'u ts'ai: for Yeliu,
passionate in his hopes that China would eventually civilize
the Mongols, had always looked for the emergence of such a
figure.

Known to his Chinese subjects as the emperor Yuan Shih-
tsu, Kubilai set himself to resurrect a giant prostrated by
the miseries of war. Owing largely to the Jurchets and the
Mongols, the Chinese population had fallen from a hundred
million to sixty within a century and a half; and as a result
much good land was lying untilled in the midst of hunger.
Kubilai increased the size of peasant holdings, distributed seed
and tools to raise their productivity. As returning prosperity
allowed, he established reserves of food in the towns against famine years. He introduced public assistance for the needy, built
hospitals, opened homes for the old and lonely. Scholars, scien-
tists, theologians, could look to him for support: he encouraged
the compilation of dictionaries, accepted proposed revisions of
the calendar, permitted the practice of foreign religions. Peking
had never recovered from the devastation brought upon it by
Mukali: but in 1267 Kubilai began its reconstruction, laying out
the streets of the new Khanbalik – the Khan's City – to the
north-west of the old town, with his own vast palace at their
heart. Under him Hangchow, spared by his troopers, became the
busiest, the most fabled, and by far the largest urban complex
in the world. And between his capital in the north and the great
metropolis of the south he dug the Grand Canal – long stretches
of which are in active use today.

But perhaps his greatest achievement was the enlargement of
the pan-Eurasian economy of which the infrastructure had been
laid in Mangu's time. He joined the productive capacity of
southern China to the continental termini of the north, and so
lengthened the interior trade-routes and infinitely increased
their traffic. Silks and precious artifacts, exotic fruits, spices and
musk, travelled west to the branchings of the tracks in central
Asia: the returning caravans came back laden with the furs of
Russia and the wares of the Arab world. Engineering and administration perfected this great fabric of international movement. Desert paths became roads; bridges spanned the steppe
rivers; cuttings through steeply graded country eased the toil of

men and beasts. Mongol detachments patrolled the routes,
logged the progress of the caravans. In and out of the commercial traffic the Khan's messengers wove their galloping way; for
Kubilai systematized for purposes of civil government the
arrow-messengers of Chingis's armies. More than ten thousand
relay-stations stood along the highways, some keeping four hundred horses in readiness. Changing mounts every thirty miles,
the couriers could cover the Heartland at nearly three hundred
miles a day: a speed never subsequently equalled till the railway
age. At the post-houses accommodation was available for all passing on state business, and for travellers from whatever country.
And many of the latter were Europeans. 'Italian merchants
chaffered and Italian friars said Mass in the ports and cities of
India and China. The East and West for the first time came into
direct contact from end to end. And if it be asked how this came
about, the answer is that it was the result of the conquests of a
nomadic people which has come down in history with a reputation for unintelligent destruction equalled only by that of the
Vandals. They deserve to be judged as the power whose policy
towards commerce was so enlightened that they welcomed traders, lowered dues and protected roads throughout their dominions, maintaining free intercourse over the length and breadth
of Asia.'[1]

Kubilai surrounded himself with a splendour befitting his
omnipotence. He had begun the building of his summer retreat
of Shang-tu – the Xanadu of Coleridge's vision, set at the cool
southerly tip of the Khingan mountains – when he first arrived
in China; and the constant improvements to its marble palace,
to the park with its menagerie and its bamboo pavilion braced
against the wind by silken ropes, were his special pride. There he
'drank the milk of Paradise': koumiss, prepared from the yield
of the ten thousand pure white mares of the imperial herds and
served by cupbearers wearing masks over their mouths. Each
autumn his passage from Shang-tu to Peking was a progress of
state. 'He hath four armies of horsemen, one going a day's march
before him, one at each side, and one a day's march in rear, so
he goeth always, as it were, in the midst of a cross. The king

[1] Eileen Power, 'The Opening of the Land Routes to Cathay' in
Travel and Travellers of the Middle Ages, edited by A. P. Newton, pp.
125–6 and 155.

travelleth in a two-wheeled carriage, in which is formed a very goodly chamber, all of lign-aloes and gold, and covered over with great and fine skins, and set with many precious stones. And the carriage is drawn by four elephants, well broken in and harnessed, and also by four splendid horses, richly caparisoned. And alongside go four barons, keeping watch and ward over the chariot. Moreover, he carrieth with him twelve gerfalcons, so that if he sees any birds pass he lets fly his hawks at them.'[1]

For all this, Kubilai did not forget his background and his underlying isolation. He caused an area of his palace grounds to be planted with steppe grass as a reminder of his origins and their implications. He was well aware that in the last analysis his regime rested on a few thousand Mongols scattered through a population of sixty millions. For this reason he never allowed himself fully to trust the élite strata of Chinese society; and despite the resentment it caused, he made a practice of filling the higher posts in his government from foreign sources. It was in pursuit of this policy that he took into his service the European who was to paint for the western world its most vivid picture of the Great Khan and his empire.

Marco Polo belonged to a Venetian merchant family. His father and uncle, enterprising traders, travelled into Mongol territory; and while about their commerce in Bukhara they happened to meet a group of Kubilai's officials, who invited them on to Peking. Kubilai was anxious to foster relations with Europe at the highest Christian level, and in the Polo brothers he perceived men of substance who could further his aim. He charged them to return home, to enlist Papal cooperation, and to bring back to him a hundred persons of sufficient calibre to open fruitful discussions. The Polos did as the Great Khan asked: but it was only after two years' delay that they were able to set out again for Peking. For its part the Church sent with them, in place of the major delegation Kubilai had requested, two Dominican friars of no standing who quickly gave up when faced with the rigours of the journey. But Nicolo Polo now had with him his son Marco, then about twenty years of age; and on the party's arrival he presented Marco to Kubilai.

[1] From the account of Friar Oderic of Pordenone in *Cathay and the Way Thither,* translated and edited by Henry Yule, pp. 226–9.

The young man at once made a favourable impression on his illustrious host, not least because he had prepared himself to address the Great Khan in his own tongue. Before long he was virtually a member of the court entourage; and in 1277 he was appointed to an executive post under the privy council. Kubilai had need of such alert, intelligent foreign servants: but it was Marco's ability as a linguist that drew his special attention. Aliens could seldom acquire more than a few halting words of the countless languages and dialects spoken in his realm, and most of his Chinese officials were little better equipped. As a result Marco came to be entrusted with a series of confidential missions. He was to tour chosen regions, gather information on places, politics and opinion, and report his findings to the Great Khan personally.

No assignment could have appealed more to Marco's observant mind, or to the sense of wonder that was always excited in him as he approached the strange, often scarcely credible, sights he saw. Under imperial warrant, with all doors opening to him, he travelled through Hsi Hsia, visited Karakorum, penetrated the wild provinces of the Chinese south-west with their primitive peoples and their great rivers surging down from Tibet through the mountain gorges, toured southern India and the islands of the Bay of Bengal, and even served for a time as governor of the city of Yang-chow. After some twenty years in China, the Polos – for Marco's father and uncle had also remained in the country – sought leave to depart. The Great Khan was now an old man; and none could tell how foreigners, and especially foreign officials, would be treated at his death. Eventually, with great reluctance and after several refusals, they were allowed to go. But Marco's adventures were not finished. Three years after reaching home he was taken prisoner in a naval clash between the fleets of Venice and Genoa; and to while away the time in his Genoese gaol he dictated the story of his experiences in the Orient.

The Travels of Marco Polo has been described as one of the great books of history. Fifty years earlier Carpini and Rubruck had written, from the outside and for limited specialist circles, of a Mongol empire which was still in the making. Polo saw it at its pinnacle; and he described it from a position of inside privilege, and in a style so compelling that it could hardly fail to grip a wide public. He sketched the Mongol Heartland, its Chinese nucleus, and the Eurasian coasts encircling them: and he enriched his tremendous panorama with names that still evoke the smell of camel-dung in the scorching deserts, the bustling millions round the palaces and monuments and quays, the palm-fronds waving above white surf: Tauris and Yasdi; Cathay and Manzi; Kinsay, Cambulac and Chandu; Cipangu, Melibar, and the Two Islands called Male and Female. Between sober accounts of Kubilai's administrative system, his finances and foreign relations, he found time for vignettes of flashing detail: the 'glorious sight' of the royal hounds working; the methods of selecting the imperial concubines to weed out those who snored or suffered from halitosis. He was accused of wild exaggeration, and from his repeated references to millions was nicknamed 'Il Milione'. But it would be difficult to exaggerate the influence of his book. For it was read in succeeding generations by statesmen, bankers, geographers, explorers: the men of affairs and action who were shaking the foundations of the Middle Ages.

It was well that Polo observed the Mongol imperium when he did, for the glories of Kubilai's reign were in fact its sunset. Towards the end of his life he became obsessed with power. To engulf more territory or to avenge supposed insults he launched expeditions into Indo-China, Malaya and the Indonesian islands, Burma and Bengal. But his armies could not prevail against dank heat, deep jungle and poisoned arrows. And an attempted invasion of Japan ended in catastrophe: his men were thrown back from the beaches and a typhoon wrecked their ships. Heartland man had overreached his limits: geography and climate were forcing him back.

At the same time

> ... 'mid this tumult Kubla heard from far
> Ancestral voices prophesying war.

Beyond the magnificent façade he had erected in China, separatism and over-extension were gnawing away the vitals of the empire as a whole. At the opening of his reign he had scotched the pretensions of Arik Buka. But Kaidu, who had thrashed the Europeans at Liegnitz, soon reinspired the revolt of the central steppes against domination from China; and it proved necessary to send Bayan himself to drive the insurrectionaries back from the Chinese frontiers into the interior. Disaffected and frustrated, the Mongols on the inner grasslands began to lapse into their old ways, raiding each other for cattle and women, eroding the security of the trade-routes. When the Polos set out on their journey home in 1292 Kubilai had to route them by sea: it was no longer safe for travellers to cross the Heartland invoking the protection of the Great Khan.

The peripheral fiefs continued to absorb the empire's wealth and effort. And the Mongol governments and garrisons ruling them, handfuls of men holding down entire populations, progressively became assimilated by those they had conquered – with all the debilitating effects that Chingis Khan had instinctively foreseen. The Golden Horde grew steadily more Turkish, for its Mongol leaders were outnumbered by the Turks, mainly Kipchaks, they had recruited for Subotei's European campaign; and the more Turkish it became, the more it took to fighting within itself and to tightening the squeeze on captive Russia to make good the waste. The Il-Khans of Iran, Hulagu's descendants, succumbed to the delights of their settled environment; and like the Seljuks before them, allowed their realm to be parcelled into factious principalities.

Religion played its part in deepening discord and hastening absorption. Chingis and his immediate successors had been careful to inform themselves concerning the many faiths their conquests had incorporated into the empire: but they had preserved a sceptical neutrality towards them all, to their political advantage. Mangu had tried to compound them into a single creed to reinforce the universality of Mongol rule; but, realizing that his scheme was unworkable, had contented himself with reaffirming that since there was but one God above, there could only be one Khaghan below. After him, as the centrifugal pulls increased, religion became a catalyst of division. The emergence of a Turkish majority drove the Golden Horde into the arms of Islam; and by the end of the thirteenth century the Il-Khans had followed suit. By contrast, the Mongols in the Orient, taking their lead from Kubilai himself, accepted Buddhism – most of them in its lamaist, Tibetan, form; and it was due to this trend that the eastern Mongols, by their appointment of a lama to the regency of Tibet, prefigured the office of the Dalai Lama. Incompatible

religions at either extremity of the empire drove another wedge
between the fiefs of east and west.

Kubilai died in 1296 at the age of eighty. Although Mongolia
had become little more than a thorn in his flesh, his body was
carried back for burial to the holy mountain of Burkan-kaldun
where his grandfather lay. By this time the Golden Horde, its
eyes turned westward and its energies consumed by intrigues
with vassal Russian princes vying for its favour, had virtually
become a law unto itself; and a few years later Mongol Iran
formally renounced its allegiance to Peking. And though, early
in the fourteenth century, there was an attempt to reunite the
three great outlying dominions in the old spirit of cohesion, it
was too late. For in China itself the clouds of revolt were gathering.

The expense of Kubilai's splendid court, of his mighty works,
of his unrewarding campaigns towards southern Asia and Japan,
had been prodigious. In his later years the mint at Khanbalik
had staved off imperial bankruptcy by issuing paper money.
Polo, fascinated as he watched its manufacture from the bark of
mulberry trees, had averred that 'the Kaan causes every year to
be made such a vast quantity of this money, which costs him
nothing, that it must equal in amount all the treasure in the
world'.[1] But it was to cost his successors dearly. For Kubilai,
despite his enlightened measures of relief, had been unable to
dispel the poverty endemic among millions of Chinese; and after
his death inflation aggravated their hardships. Economic dis-
tress intensified sub-surface aversion to the Mongol occupiers
and their foreign aides. By 1340 hunger and hatred had burst
forth in riots.

Previous Mongol generations, resorting inexorably to arrows
and cold steel, and backed by the manpower reserves of the
entire eastern Heartland, might have turned the tide for the
time being. But no support could now be expected from Mongolia. And the detachment inherent in the Buddhist faith had
unstrung the taut sinews of the steppe governors of China; indeed, the zeal of the imperial house for lamaist practice had even
extended to a liking for its more comely yellow-robed exponents.
From the Cantonese south – the region farthest from the centres

[1] *The Travels of Marco Polo*, translated and edited by Henry Yule.
Vol. I, p. 424.

of such Mongol strength as was available – anarchy began to roll up into the Yangtze valley. It was hammered into military form by a passionate patriot, Chu Yuan-chang, himself a former Buddhist monk. Nanking declared for him; the wave of rebellion flowed on into the north; and in September 1368, with the mobs howling through the Peking streets and the forces of defiance at the gates, the tenth Yuan emperor, Toghon Timur, fled ignominiously to the steppes. The liberating troops instantly acclaimed Chu Yuan-chang. China was Chinese again. The Ming dynasty was in being.

The Mongols had ruled the whole of China for eighty-nine years; for little longer, that is, than they had spent in the struggle to overrun her. At a cost of suffering beyond assessment, lightened only by the reign of Kubilai, she gained from them one inestimable benefit: the national unity which has lasted to this day. But it proved to be a unity of seclusion: for as in earlier times she sought escape from the nomad terror by turning in upon herself, so she has never freed herself from the xenophobia that followed the Mongol evacuation.

Ming China was swift in revenge. Within a few decades she had taken the offensive, clearing the north-west frontiers, flinging her routed conquerors back across the Kerulen into the meadows and the plains of grass, summer-parched and winter-frozen, whence their power had sprung. There the Mongols of the east dissolved once more into the tribes from which Temujin had forged their singleness; and the tribes resumed their strife against each other as if the Nation of the Archers had never been.

Even while the Mongol empire was disintegrating, however, the shock-wave created by one of its early conquests was producing a delayed but momentous impact on the far west.

Chingis Khan's invasion of Khwaresmia in 1219 had dislodged a number of minor nomadic peoples then grazing at the central Asian borders of Iran – among them a group known as the Kayi, who were an offshoot of the Ghuzz Turks. This group fled before the Mongol advance, wandered across Iran, and found their way into Asia Minor. Here they came upon a confused scene, for Asia Minor at the time was divided between the rumps of two empires. Most of it was in the hands of remaining Seljuk sultans;

while its western tip, adjoining the Sea of Marmora, was still ruled from Constantinople as part of the shrunken empire of Byzantium.

The Seljuk sultan of Anatolia received the fugitives from Chingis's onslaught, and gave them the task of patrolling his border with the Byzantines. A few years later, while they were discharging this duty, their chieftain was converted to Islam. He assumed the name of Othman; and his people thereupon became the Othman or Ottoman Turks. The restless times suited the fierce Ottoman holders of the frontier. All the neighbouring sultans were preoccupied in striving to impose order on the mixture of wild Turkish tribes milling in their lands. Moreover, renewed waves of Mongol pressure on Iran, first during Ogedei's reign, then under Hulagu, drove other refugees westward: and from these the Ottomans built up their fighting strength. By the time of Kubilai's death in China in 1296 they had become a dominant presence among the Turks in Asia Minor, and were raiding into Byzantine territory.

For some two hundred years the Byzantine empire had been struggling against a chain of disasters. After Manzikert the Turks had overrun its eastern possessions. The Crusades had brought nothing but trouble; and the sack of Constantinople by the Fourth Crusade in 1204 had nearly extinguished the city. Since then the imperial provinces in Greece and the Balkans had been falling away one by one. Of the towering edifice of Eastern Rome only a rickety scaffolding was left. Faced with the threatening rise of Ottoman energy along their contracted frontier in Asia Minor, the Byzantines wearily resorted to the offer of pay.

The first Ottomans crossed the Dardanelles as Byzantine mercenaries about 1345. Finding little to restrain them, they soon threw off their subservient role. They spread northward through Bulgaria, reached the Danube, and then in 1371 – three years after the final Mongol collapse in China – won their first resounding victory in Europe by routing the Serbian army on the Maritsa river. Byzantium, with Constantinople at its weakening heart, was now an island in their rear. They turned back to finish it off.

Thus the scene was set for the cataclysm of 1453 when the ramparts of Constantine's city, so long enduring, crumbled for ever before invaders from the steppes. For Selim the Grim and

Suleiman the Magnificent, with their twenty-ton cannons, their élite Spahi lancer-bowmen and their matchless Janissary infantry recruited from captive Christian youths. For the overpowering plunder-gathering thrusts to the walls of Vienna, to Cairo, and through the Mediterranean. For the slide of the Ottoman empire into decadence as it became paralysed by Islamic conservatism and the increasing efficiency of European resistance. For the era of the Sick Man, of the Eastern Question, and of Gladstone's impassioned outburst against 'their Zaptiehs and their Mudirs, their Bimbashis and their Yuzbachis, their Kaimakams and their Pashas'.[1] For the national revival under Kemal Ataturk, when a people reborn in the twentieth century commemorated on their coins and stamps the ancient Turkish metal-workers of the Altai and the wolf's head carried into battle by the horse-archers from whom they stemmed.

All this was due to Chingis Khan: for the force that drove modern Turkey into being was the expanding march of his Mongol empire.

Within sixty years of its first tempestuous outsurge that empire had become a hollow husk. It had been magnetized to its constantly swelling perimeter, leaving a vacuum at its centre. And at the perimeter it had proved unable to fuse the pastoral with the sown. But, itself brought into being by armed revolution against the immemorial social structure of the steppes, it left behind the seeds of an infinitely wider and deeper revolution. For it set Europe on the road to an era of world domination that was to last until the Second World War.

In ancient times the balance between the littoral West and East, between Europe and the Orient, had been loaded in favour of the latter. Only at exceptional moments had the West been able to shake off its poverty and squalor sufficiently to rival the wealth and brilliance of the East. By the thirteenth century the balance was beginning to change; and the Mongols gave the scales a decisive push. Their destructive invasions affected only a small part of Europe: but in the East they ravaged economies already scarred by successive impacts from the steppes, and rigidified or threw back societies already static. The subsequent

[1] W. E. Gladstone, *The Bulgarian Horrors and the Question of the East,* 1876.

Mongol Peace benefited both East and West: but whereas it enabled the passage to Europe of traditional eastern goods, it carried into the East not only trade but the new objectivity, technology and enterprise which were stirring in the West. With these the Orient was unprepared to grapple; and the resources of the eastern world were thus laid open to superior powers of acquisition and extraction. It has been held that Chingis Khan and his descendants unwittingly set in motion that profound epochal shift of fortune, perhaps more predatory at its height than any of their own conquests, which has left Eurasia divided into haves and have-nots.

More. In the western Atlantic, at 2 a.m. on 12 October 1492, the report of a gun from the *Pinta* informed the Admiral on board the *Santa Maria* that land had been sighted. Columbus had read Marco Polo's book; and, placing it beside other studies, had concluded that by sailing westabout he would voyage in the direction of the realm once ruled by 'the great and wonderful magnificence of Cublay Kaan'. And in his description of the islands of the Bahama group that he had found and named, he wrote: 'When I came to Juana I followed its coast and found it to be so extensive that I thought it must be the mainland, the province of Cathay.'[1]

To Chingis Khan's grandson and his Venetian confidential agent, the New World owes the inspiration of its birth.

[1] From the 'Letter of Columbus describing the results of his first voyage'. *The Journal of Christopher Columbus*, translated by Cecil Jane, p. 191.

IO

Criminal Adventurers and Hideous Revisionists

Who rules the Heartland commands the World-Island:

Who rules the World-Island commands the World.

— HALFORD MACKINDER

BETWEEN the Mongol collapse and the opening of the Trans-Siberian Railway – where this story began – rather more than five centuries were to elapse. During that time the immemorial Heartland of the pastoral nomads was virtually to vanish; and its gigantic spaces were to be divided between two of the littoral peoples they had overrun. In that process a different inner Asia, extractive, industrial, agricultural, settled, was to appear in its place; and the frontiers between its new possessors were to become charged with the tension of dispute.

The old Heartland died slowly, making repeated attempts to revivify its traditional life-pattern of expansion, impact and conquest. With the break-up of the Mongol empire the disparate regimes of the Turks re-emerged across the western steppes, to resume their quarrelling and their endless attempts to despoil their neighbours. Among these meteoric short-lived outbursts was that of Tamurlaine – Timur-i-Lang, 'the Iron Limper'. Rising like a vulture from the cities of Transoxiana wrecked by Chingis Khan, he sought to re-create the imperium of the great Mongol, from whom he was descended in the female line.

It was a hopeless quest: for Tamurlaine, though possessed of much of Chingis's military genius, lacked all his forebear's qualities of political perception. In youth a bold and attractive adventurer, he became in maturity little more than a mass-murderer hounded on by a passion to secure immortal fame within a life-span he was convinced would be short. He seized Iran from the latter-day Il-Khans, ravaged Baghdad once again, attacked the Ottoman Turks in Asia Minor and so delayed their capture of Constantinople for some fifty years. He cut a swathe of ruin from the Black Sea steppes to Delhi; and after satisfying his largely mercenary armies from the loot, he removed the rest to Samarkand, turning that city into a fantastic museum-capital incongruously stuffed with the treasures of the lands he had laid waste. Adored by his henchmen, hated by the survivors of his campaigns, feared by all, he died in 1405 in a thunderstorm of exceptional violence while on his way to an intended conquest of Ming China. Perhaps his one action of lasting significance was his onslaught on the Turkish-Mongol domains in the Caspian-Volga area. For here, in two viciously fought battles, he permanently crippled the power of the Golden Horde; and this paved the way for the emancipation of Russia.

In the early sixteenth century the southern Heartland erupted again: but this time the results were almost wholly beneficial. A descendant of Tamurlaine, Babur, 'the Tiger', was forced from his homeland in Transoxiana by threatening nomadic movements in the region. Assembling a scratch army he passed down through Afghanistan, crossed the Indus, and in 1526 reached Delhi. His successor, Humayun, enlarged his conquests; and the third of the line, Akbar, brought the Moghul – 'Mongol' – empire in India to its summit. The Moghul emperors were men of mind as well as power. In 1570 Akbar began the building of his great palace at Fatepur-Sikhri, with its spacious quadrangles so reminiscent of the Great Court of Trinity College, Cambridge, with which they were contemporary; and from there he endowed northern and central India with a government as enlightened and a culture as splendid as those of Asoka. Enormously wealthy, autocratic and magnificent – he played chess with human pieces from a balcony overlooking a courtyard divided into squares – his essentially constructive outlook, bringing together Hindu and Moslem in the common cause of the public service, did much to close the rifts opened by previous waves of invasion from the Heartland. And it was on the administrative foundations laid by Akbar that the seaborne British, first appearing in India during his reign, subsequently erected the fabric of their rule.

But the most important recrudescence of Heartland power took place in the east. While the Moghuls were building their Indian empire, a nomad people related to the Jurchets were gathering strength in northern Manchuria. In 1583 the fortunes of this people, already promising, burgeoned further under a determined leader called Nurkhachi, who bound the tribes around him into a confederacy stronger than any since the days of the Mongols. To this confederacy he gave the name of Manchu.

To the Chinese, the presence of the formidable Manchus at their northern marches was a source of growing alarm, for by this time the energies of the Ming dynasty were waning; and before long China was seeking to mollify them with tribute. One day, however, a herdsman appeared before Nurkhachi and handed him an object he had found. It was the great jade seal of Chingis Khan, lost in the confusion of the last Mongol emperor's flight from Peking in 1368. Nurkhachi took the find as a good omen. In a few years he had swept the Chinese garrisons from southern Manchuria and set up his headquarters at Mukden, within striking distance of the Great Wall.

In 1644 a series of strange developments occurred in rapid succession in and around Peking. A Chinese brigand deposed the Ming sovereign and tried to usurp the imperial throne. The loyalist general in command of the forces defending the Wall appealed to the Manchus outside it to help him evict the rebel and restore legitimacy. Nothing loath, the Manchus swarmed through the Wall, set the general to chase the brigand, and themselves seized Peking and the reins of government throughout the country.[1] China had seen the last of native rule until the twentieth century; for the Manchu invaders, under the dynastic name of Ch'ing, were to govern until the revolution of Sun Yat Sen.

As former neighbours of China, the Manchus were partly sinicized before their arrival in Peking; and this ensured that their administration, wherever they might carry it, would be Chinese in character. But, like their predecessors from the Heartland wilds, they retained their tough martial fibre; and in the flush of their triumph and ambition they embarked on the enlargement

[1] For an entertaining account of this dramatic, and at moments hilarious, episode see Maurice Collis, *The Great Within,* Faber and Faber, 1941.

of their newly-won Chinese empire. By the end of the seventeenth century the Manchu emperor K'ang-hsi-ti had brought the Mongols of the Gobi region under his control, and had broken up an attempt by the tribes of the Altai district, farther west, to take possession of the pasturelands of Mongolia as a whole. In these campaigns of repression and expansion the Manchu armies were greatly assisted by the weakening influence that lamaism had spread across the eastern steppes, and by the mutual strife now intermittently dividing the Mongols who remained true to their warrior background. The decisive factor, however, was military and technical. Chinese firearms, in the form of wheeled cannon and primitive muskets, had become mobile and portable. Against stone and metal, and the terror of exploding gunpowder, the nomad archers and their ponies could not stand.

K'ang's grandson, Ch'ien-lung-ti, carried the banners of Manchu China still farther into the interior. In 1757 his artillery overwhelmed the western Mongols on the steppes of Lake Balkash, and the following year his forces occupied the Tarim basin. Great numbers of nomads between the Altai and the Pamir were systematically wiped out; their pastures were settled by colonists from metropolitan China; and the huge annexed areas of the southern Heartland were named 'the New Borderlands' – Hsin-chiang, or Sinkiang. Thus the westward drives under the ancient dynasties of Han and T'ang were once again repeated by the Manchus; and the Chinese empire, constantly fluctuating in extent through the ages, achieved in the eighteenth century the greatest size it had ever known.

Meanwhile, as the fortunes of the nomads dwindled, another growing nation at the Heartland's verges was staking its claim to the spaces of the Asian interior.

Their subjugation to the Golden Horde had not been entirely without advantage to the principalities of Russia. Partly to satisfy their masters' insatiable demand for food and fodder, the Russians had carved out large tracts of flourishing arable land from what had been virgin forest. And as time went on the khans of the Golden Horde, instead of levying cash tribute directly, had farmed out the collection of taxes to the Russian princes. This had had the effect of strengthening the princes' positions

vis-à-vis their own peasantries, and of providing them with rudimentary administrations of their own. Their rule was merciless; for as vassals of the Golden Horde their sub-governments were based on the absolutism of the Turkish-Mongol system. All were bound to the unquestioning service of an aristocratic despotism visiting vengeful punishment upon any guilty of deviation. And their regimes were made the harsher by a 'divide and rule' device practised by the khans. To the Russian princes offering the largest sums in tribute, the lords of the Golden Horde would frequently lend troopers – to be used against their less forthcoming neighbours; and in competing for such favours the princes squeezed their subjects without pity. If, under her nomad conquerors, Russia established the agricultural roots of her future power, it was also beneath their heel that she embraced the serfdom that was to distort her society until the nineteenth century.

Tamurlaine's fatal weakening of the Golden Horde in the 1390s not only created the conditions for a general revolt of the Russian princes: it also determined which principality should play the dominant part in the uprising when it came. For Toktamish, the reigning khan of the time, had been forced by Tamurlaine's onrush upon him to ask for help from his Russian vassals. Moscow, from its key position on the lucrative trade-route between Novgorod and the south, was already on the road to wealth and strength; and Vasili, the Prince of Muscovy, anticipating handsome reward, answered the call promptly. The move was not without peril: but Tamurlaine, far from his central Asian bases, had been unable to follow up his victories over Toktamish by an attack on his Russian ally. Thereafter, as the power of the battered Golden Horde diminished, that of Muscovy correspondingly increased – until in 1480 Ivan III, styling himself Tsar as a result of his ascendancy over his fellow princes, felt strong enough to renounce his allegiance to it.

Within a century formal repudiation of the Horde's suzerainty was followed by assertive action against its territory. In 1552 Ivan IV, the Terrible, taking advantage of the dissensions between the subordinate khans, seized Kazan; and in 1558, Astrakhan. With these conquests Moscow stood upon the Volga, poised at the Ural-Caspian gateway to the steppes.

Then came an event which was to set the pattern for the Russian drive into the farther Heartland. The grip of autocracy had not been clamped upon Russia without producing men who refused to bow to it. Some were individuals of spirit, others criminals and deserters, others again disaffected groups of younger peasants. Some were Russians, others nomadic tribesmen, yet others a mixture of both through intermarriage. These outlaws tended to drift away from the centres to the less heavily policed Russian borderlands, forming themselves into bands and living by their wits and their muscles. From their restless existence they became known as 'Wanderers' – Kazaks, or Cossacks. In 1581 a group of these rovers, under their headman Yermak, appeared to the north of the Kama river, moving towards the foothills of the Urals into the lands held by the powerful fur-trading, slave-dealing family of the Stroganovs. Their unruly arrival was not welcome: but it happened that the Stroganov properties were currently the target of a series of destructive raids by nomadic horse-archers from across the Urals. To rid themselves of both the Cossacks and the raiders, the Stroganovs gave Yermak the task of launching a punitive expedition into the nomads' territory.

Yermak crossed the mountains and followed the course of the Tura river down into Siberia. The Tura flows into the Tobol, and the Tobol into the Irtysh; and along these rivers his supplies accompanied him in boats. The khan of the region, Kutchum, mobilized all his bowmen throughout the Irtysh basin. Yermak had only eight hundred men behind him: but they had firearms.

In all probability gunpowder had been taken west from China by the Mongols, either during Subotei's European campaign or during the subsequent decades of the Mongol Peace. But the steppe-dwellers had never seized upon the secret they had carried. To fashion firearms in the grasslands was in any case virtually impossible. The materials required, when available, were localized; and at the point when contact between Russia and the Golden Horde grew close enough for the communication of ideas and skills, Tamurlaine had rounded up the Horde's best artisans and herded them off to Samarkand. Offered guns by travelling merchants, the nomads had usually declined to purchase them: the price was often too high, and the devotion of the steppes to the bow too strong. Only the Ottoman Turks, leaving the conservatism of the pastures behind tnem, and learning from the more advanced lands they were assaulting, had recognized the potential of powder and shot. But in Europe the steppe-transmitted invention, and the new weaponry to which it gave rise, had quickly spread. Writing about 1350, Petrarch noted that 'these instruments which discharge balls of metal with a most tremendous noise and flashes of fire were a few years ago very rare, and were viewed with the greatest astonishment and admiration: but now they are become as common and familiar as any other kind of arms'.[1] In 1376 Russia used cannon for the first time. By 1450 there were factories in Moscow and Tver for making lighter hand-guns as well. Now, in the advance into the Asian interior, muskets were all-important, for they reversed the balance of advantage between littoral and steppe. In smaller battles a resolute handful of infantry, their striking power multiplied many times over, could at last withstand the whirlwind charges of the fleetest steppe cavalry; and on the larger scale the superior numbers which the littoral peoples had always possessed were made effective against the hitherto overwhelming intensity of the nomad archers' arrow-storms. In 1582 Yermak smashed Kutchum's army on the Irtysh. And though he himself was later killed in a last-ditch affray mounted by the failing khan, the guns dragged and carried by his Cossacks had already assured their foothold in Siberia.

Cossacks, firearms – and rivers. These took expanding Russia across the Heartland. For the Cossacks were not, initially, the superb horsemen that they later became. In escaping from Tsarist absolutism many had taken to river piracy; and it was along the waterways that they now pushed east. The tributaries of the great rivers flowing to the Arctic run latitudinally; and these formed their roads. In canoes and shallow-draft boats, with their equipment following on rafts, they would coast down an eastward-flowing tributary to its junction with a main river, descend this river until they found a westward-flowing tributary debouching into it, then turn east again, working upstream against the current. Between the headwaters of the tributaries they portaged their lighter craft, hewing out new rafts from the forests to replace the heavier boats they had to leave behind. At strategic points along the way they built their *ostrogs* and *stanitzas* – log forts and hutted settlements to guard the water-roads and serve as centres from which occupation could radiate. Soon

[1] Petrarch, *De Remediis*. Lib. I, Dialog. 99.

river traffic was flowing to and fro along increasingly familiar, well-mapped routes; and always ahead of it, their firearms brushing nomad opposition aside, the half-wild river-hopping Cossacks, under Russian adventurers often no saints themselves, thrust their frontier forward in the name of a Tsar who had frequently placed a price upon their heads.

In 1609 they reached the site beyond the Ob where Tomsk was to rise. Twenty years later they were moving on from the Yenisei into the basin of the Lena, fortifying the settlement of Yakutsk on its bank, feeling their way down its lower reaches to the Laptev Sea. In 1636, less than sixty years after Yermak had crossed the Urals, a pioneer party was standing on the shore of the Sea of Okhotsk, staring out towards Kamchatka and the Pacific. And shortly afterwards a Cossack-captained ship sailed from the Arctic through the strait dividing Eurasia from America which was later to be navigated by the Danish explorer Bering.

The penetration of the southern steppes followed a similar pattern. Cossacks from the Dnieper, scattering nomad encampments north of the Black Sea, moved down into the Crimea and eastward to the Don – 'The Tsar reigns in Moscow, the Cossacks on the Don.' They probed the walls of the Caucasus, and so began an advance that in succeeding centuries was to set Russian vessels on the Caspian, send Russian occupying forces past the Aral Sea and Samarkand to the high ranges of Afghanistan skirting British India. And everywhere, behind the Cossacks, through the forests and over the boundless grass, came the apparatus of consolidation: governors and tax-collectors, fur-traders and sled-drivers, officers and priests, colonists and convicts; the great heterogeneous mass ranging from aristocrats to outcasts, heroic, selfless, greedy, cruel, whose lives and labours were eventually to form the roadbed for the longest railway in the world.

Caucasus, Elburz and Pamirs set bounds to Russian expansion towards the south. But in the east there were no such definite barriers: only the putative lines of demarcation afforded by the rivers. And it was along the Amur river that the collision came with the simultaneously expanding China of the Manchus. In 1650 the Russian frontiersman Khabarov, at the head of a Cossack posse, explored his way through the Yablonovy mountains to the upper Amur. The country was rich in sables, and he soon found himself embroiled with fur-trappers of the local tribes who accused him of poaching their preserves. Farther down the river, not far from where the city named after him now stands, Khabarov came upon some men dressed in silk. They were Chinese tax-collectors. The Manchu officials were quickly supported by troops, but Khabarov drove them off. In Peking, however, K'ang-hsi-ti was on the throne. He was in process of subduing Mongolia, and was not the man to underestimate the new threat at the borders of his growing empire.

At the most northerly point on the great curve of the Amur the Russians built and fortified a settlement which they named Albazin. A Chinese force, sent by K'ang to demand its evacuation, appeared before the little timber citadel; and faced by fifteen thousand men with two hundred guns, the Russians complied. The Chinese destroyed Albazin and, having restored the *status quo*, departed. When the coast was clear the Cossacks came back and began its reconstruction. Warned of this the Chinese returned as well, and laid siege to the rebuilt stronghold.

Tsarist Russia and Manchu China had been moving into the Heartland from west and east respectively, reducing to subservience the herdsmen-archers with their unchanging societies and outclassed weapons, shooting down resistance, allocating to the more docile nomads the lands they did not want for themselves, ordering and taxing their lives and livelihood. Both, as they rolled forward, were already remoulding in their own image the gigantic inner continent they were occupying, deepening across it their sedentary roots, beginning the first stages of the transformation that in our day was to open its mineral reservoirs, tap its latent energy, plough its pastures, set furnaces and factories from the tundra to the deserts. In the seventeenth century the advance guards at the tips of the converging spearheads might, as at Albazin, still be small. But behind these were nations of the first magnitude in the terms of the time: imperial states, centrally organized, with professional and formidably-armed military establishments, and with massive populations to defend and develop the spaces they were acquiring. Now, on the placid reaches of the Amur, the new Lords of the Ocean-Encircled Lands had met.

From the implications of the clash at Albazin the Russians

temporarily drew back. In 1689 they signed with China the
Treaty of Nerchinsk, abandoning by it all claim to both banks of
the Amur. And in 1727, reeling from the effects of Peter the
Great's reign – from his prolonged struggle with Sweden, from
the galvanic frenzy of his technological revolution – they recognized the hegemony of the Manchus in central Asia. And it was
largely these concessions of Peking's right to the sectors of the
Heartland adjoining China that for the time being deflected the
eastward momentum of Russia towards the north. With further
encroachment on China's *lebensraum* barred for the moment,
first Kamchatka then the chain of the Aleutian islands became
stepping-stones for Cossacks and fur-traders moving through
Alaska to the valleys of the Rockies, reaching California before
the settlers from the American Atlantic seaboard.

By the middle of the nineteenth century, however, the Manchu empire was threatened from a different quarter. Always,
China's defensive guard had been raised against inner Asia. Her
landward posture had enabled her to halt, or at worst to dissolve
into herself, the endless invasions from the steppes – as she had
so far contained the infiltrating Russians. Often, after an unusually catastrophic inburst upon her civilization, she had sought
comfort and forgetfulness by excluding the outer world and
drawing on her own past superiority – as, during the reaction of
the Ming period, she had tried to erase the memory of the Mongols. But the Opium War of 1840 with Britain, followed by the
forcing of her sea-gates by other nations of the maritime West,
marked the opening of an incursion of a totally new kind. Descended though they were from barbarian conquerors of China,
the later Manchu emperors were unable to deal with a new bar-
barism approaching from their sea flank and bringing an
ideology which retreat into isolation could not ward off. Nor had
they the political vigour left to dispel the internal questionings
which now began to challenge the adequacy of the imperial system itself in face of the revolution from without. From each
great dynasty in turn – Han and Sui, T'ang and Sung and
Ming – the Mandate of Heaven had been withdrawn as it became
exhausted: but, devolving upon a successor house, it had always
hitherto been renewed. In the circumstances of the Ch'ing
decline, it was becoming irrelevant.

As ever, China's incipient weakness gave the forces at her

landward frontier their chance. In 1847 Nicholas I appointed Muraviev governor-general of Eastern Siberia, with the ostensible task of preserving Russian interests in the region from encroachment by the European powers. Audacious and tireless, Muraviev first explored the lower Amur in detail; and then, under the guise of protecting China from her seaborne enemies, annexed long stretches of its northern bank, founding Khabarovsk, strengthening the outpost-town of Blagoveshchensk, and drafting in thousands of troops and immigrants to establish permanent settlement. The agreement of Nerchinsk, won by the forceful K'ang-hsi-ti, quickly became a dead letter. It was replaced in 1858 by the Treaty of Aigun, by which the Manchus, now beset from sea and land, renounced their title to all the territory north of the Amur. Two years later the Treaty of Peking – the second of the so-called 'unequal treaties' – confirmed Russia's gains and added to her Siberian empire the whole of eastern Manchuria between the Ussuri river and the coast, including the site of Vladivostok which the Cossacks had already occupied.

So Muraviev completed in 1860 the work begun by Yermak in 1581. The way was open for the railroad-builders to drive the Trans-Siberian from the Urals to the Pacific; for the tide of migration into the northern Heartland at the opening of the present century which the repeated counter-thrusts of Japanese ambition could not ultimately check; for the Soviet Union, inheriting one-sixth of the earth's land surface, to accelerate the shift of Russia's centre of industrial gravity towards the core of Asia; for her renewed confrontation, along some four thousand miles of mountain, steppe and river frontier, with the resurgent China of the People's Republic.

For the world outside its bleak skylines, the Heartland of the bygone ages held enduring mystery and fear. None could tell what stresses were at work within them, hidden beyond the howl of the steppe winds; or when these stresses, bursting into clash and combat, would send their waves of fury rolling over grass and desert to break upon the settled peoples of the coastal belt. The nomads are 'integrated' now; and the horse-archer, save in his pale image resurrected for ceremonial gatherings, is no more seen. But Lake Balkash reflects the arcing path of

Soviet rockets under trial; the Mongolian rivers, the passage of Russian armour. Around the Ordos Loop stand China's nuclear installations; in the sands of the Tarim basin, her nuclear testing sites. New issues stirring within the ancient cauldron of inner Asia. And for the external world, the old apprehensions in new terms.

Yet the Heartland of yesterday bequeathes to the giants poised across its corpse an aspect of itself. The mounted warriors of nomadic Asia, through the millennia when they held the greater part of mankind in fee, were striving to redress a basic imbalance of economic potential between the interior of the Eurasian continent and its oceanic rim. In that light the terror they spread and the tribute they exacted can be seen as a primitive attempt to abolish inequality; as the most stupendous and continuous programme of forced aid ever carried out. In return, for good or ill, the nomads imparted something of their own nature to the littoral peoples on whom their impacts fell. It has been said that the fusion of the qualities of steppe and sown has contributed to the emergence of what is now known as civilized man; that in his make-up are combined the peaceable, collaborative, reflective temperament of the cultivator, and the disciplined, competitive, warlike spirit of the herdsman fighting for his pasture-spaces and his plunder.

In Mongolia, once the springhead of the conquering hordes and now the buffer-state between their conquerors, a prophecy is still repeated. 'When that which is harder than the rock and stronger than the storm shall fail, when the White Tsar is no more and the Son of Heaven has vanished, then the camp-fires of Chingis Khan will be seen again, and his empire will stretch over the earth.'

Tsar and Emperor have gone. But it seems needless for Chingis to return. For in the tension within the Heartland of today, as in the conflict within each of us who have not yet subdued the urge to arms, he and all his like live on.

Works Consulted

ARMSTRONG, TERENCE. *Russian Settlement in the North.* Cambridge University Press, 1965.

BADDELEY, JOHN F. *Russia, Mongolia, China.* London: Macmillan, 1919.

BARCHAUSEN, JOACHIM. *L'Empire jaune de Genghis-Khan.* Paris: Payot, 1942.

BARROW, R. H. *The Romans.* London: Pelican Books, 1949.

BARTHOLD, W. *Turkestan down to the Mongol Invasion.* London: E. J. W. Gibb Memorial New Series V. 1928.

BEAZLEY, C. RAYMOND (Editor). *The Texts and Versions of John de Plano Carpini and William de Rubruquis.* London: Hakluyt Society, 1903.

—— *The Dawn of Modern Geography.* 3 vols. Oxford: Clarendon Press, 1906.

BOTTING, DOUGLAS. *One Chilly Siberian Morning.* London: Hodder and Stoughton, 1965.

BOULNOIS, LUCE. *The Silk Road.* London: George Allen and Unwin, 1963.

BUSSELL, F. W. *The Roman Empire from* A.D. 81 *to* A.D. 1081, Vol. 1. London: Longmans Green, 1910.

CASSON, LIONEL. *The Ancient Mariners.* London: Gollancz, 1959.

CH'ANG CH'UN. *Travels of an Alchemist.* Translated by Arthur Waley. London: George Routledge and Sons, 1931.

CIPOLLA, CARLO M. *Guns and Sails in the Early Phase of European Expansion.* London: Collins, 1965.

CLARK, REV. FRANCIS E. *A New Way Around an Old World.* New York and London: Harper and Bros., 1901.

COLES, PAUL. *The Ottoman Impact on Europe.* London: Thames and Hudson, 1968.

COLLEDGE, MALCOLM A. R. *The Parthians.* London: Thames and Hudson, 1967.

COLLIS, MAURICE. *The Great Within.* London: Faber and Faber, 1941.

COON, CARLETON S. *The History of Man.* London: Jonathan Cape, 1955.

CZAPLICKA, M. A. *The Turks of Central Asia*. Oxford University Press, 1918.

DALLIN, DAVID J. *The Rise of Russia in Asia*. Yale University Press, 1949.

DAWSON, CHRISTOPHER (Editor). *The Mongol Mission*. London and New York: Sheen and Ward, 1955.

FEDDEN, ROBIN and THOMSON, JOHN. *Crusader Castles*. Beirut: Khayat, 1957.

FOX, RALPH. *Genghis Khan*. London: John Lane, The Bodley Head, 1936.

FRASER, JOHN FOSTER. *The Real Siberia*. London: Cassell and Co., 1902.

FULLER, J. F. C. *Decisive Battles of the Western World*. 2 vols. London: Eyre and Spottiswoode, 1954.

GIBB, H. A. R. *The Arab Conquests in Central Asia*. London: Royal Asiatic Society, 1923.

GIBBON, EDWARD. *Decline and Fall of the Roman Empire*. London: edition of 1825, Vol. X.

GLUBB, JOHN BAGOT. *The Great Arab Conquests*. London: Hodder and Stoughton, 1963.

GRANT, MICHAEL. *The World of Rome*. London: Weidenfeld and Nicolson, 1960.

GROUSSET, RENE. *The Rise and Splendour of the Chinese Empire*. Translated by Anthony Watson-Gandy and Terence Gordon. London: Geoffrey Bles, 1952.

——*L'Empire des Steppes*. Paris: Payot, 1952.

——*Conqueror of the World*. Translated by Denis Sinor and Marian MacKellar. Edinburgh and London: Oliver and Boyd, 1967.

Guide to the Great Siberian Railway. Edited by A. I. Dmitriev-Mamonov and A. F. Zdziarski. Translated by Miss L. Kukol-Yasnopolski. St. Petersburg: Ministry of Ways of Communication, 1900.

HART, B. H. LIDDELL. *Great Captains Unveiled*. London: William Blackwood and Sons, 1927.

HERRMANN, PAUL. *Conquest by Man*. London: Hamish Hamilton, 1954.

HITTI, PHILIP K. *The Arabs*. London: Macmillan, 1948.

HOOSON, DAVID J. M. *A New Soviet Heartland?* Princeton: D. Van Nostrand Co. Inc., 1964.

——*The Soviet Union*. University of London Press, 1966.

HUNTINGTON, ELLSWORTH. *The Human Habitat*. Princeton: D. Van Nostrand Co. Inc., 1927.

——*Mainsprings of Civilization*. New York: John Wiley and Sons Inc., 1944.

IPSIROGLU, M. S. *Painting and Culture of the Mongols*. London: Thames and Hudson, 1966.

JOURNAL OF CHRISTOPHER COLUMBUS. Translated by Cecil Jane. London: Hakluyt Society, 1960.

JOYCE, T. A. 'The Physical Anthropology of the Oases of Khotan and Keriya', *Journal of the Royal Anthropological Institute*, Vol. XXXIII (London), 1903.

JUVAINI, ATA-MALIK. *The History of the World Conqueror*. Translated from the Persian by John Andrew Boyle. 2 vols. Manchester University Press, 1958.

KERNER, ROBERT J. *The Urge to the Sea*. University of California Press, 1942.

LAMB, HAROLD. *The March of the Barbarians*. London: Robert Hale, 1941.

——*Alexander of Macedon*. New York: Doubleday and Co. Inc., 1946.

LATTIMORE, OWEN. *Mongol Journeys*. London: Jonathan Cape, 1941.

——'The Geography of Chingis Khan', *Geographical Journal* 129, Part I (London), March 1963.

——'Chingis Khan and the Mongol Conquests', *Scientific American*, August 1963.

LLOYD, SETON. *Twin Rivers*. Oxford University Press, 1943.

LUM, PETER. *The Purple Barrier*. London: Robert Hale, 1960.

MACKINDER, HALFORD J. 'The Geographical Pivot of History', *Geographical Journal* 23 (London), 1904.

——*Democratic Ideals and Reality*. New York: Henry Holt and Co., 1919.

MAISKY, I. M. 'Jenghis Khan', *Anglo-Soviet Journal* (London), Autumn 1962.

MARTIN, H. DESMOND. *Chingis Khan and His Conquest of North China*. Baltimore: John Hopkins Press, 1950.

MCGOVERN, W. M. *Early Empires of Central Asia*. North Carolina: Chapel Hill, 1939.

MCNEILL, WILLIAM H. *The Rise of the West*. University of Chicago Press, 1963.

——*A World History*. New York: Oxford University Press Inc., 1967.

MEAKIN, ANNETTE M. B. *A Ribbon of Iron*. London: Constable and Co., 1901.

MONTAGUE, IVOR. *Land of Blue Sky*. London: Dennis Dobson, 1956.

NEEDHAM, JOSEPH. *Science and Civilisation in China*, Vol. I. Cambridge University Press, 1954.

NEWTON, A. P. (Editor). *Travel and Travellers of the Middle Ages*. London: Kegan Paul, Trench, Trubner and Co., 1926.

OMAN, C. W. C. *The Art of War in the Middle Ages.* Oxford: Blackwell, and London: T. Fisher Unwin, 1885.

PARKER, E. H. *A Thousand Years of the Tartars.* London: Kegan Paul, Trench, Trubner and Co., 1924.

PEISKER, T. 'The Asiatic Background,' *Cambridge Medieval History,* Vol. I. Cambridge University Press, 1911.

PFIZENMAYER, E. W. *Siberian Man and Mammoth.* London: Blackie and Son, 1939.

PHILLIPS, E. D. *The Royal Hordes.* London: Thames and Hudson, 1965.

PIRENNE, JACQUES. *The Tides of History.* Translated by Lovett Edwards. 2 vols. London: George Allen and Unwin, 1962.

POWER, EILEEN. *Medieval People.* London: Methuen, 1924.

PRAWDIN, MICHAEL. *The Mongol Empire.* London: George Allen and Unwin, 1940.

——*The Builders of the Mogul Empire.* London: George Allen and Unwin, 1963.

PROCOPIUS. *The Persian War.* Edited and translated by H. B. Dewing. London: Heinemann, 1914.

RICE, TAMARA TALBOT. *The Scythians.* London: Thames and Hudson, 1957.

——*The Seljuks.* London: Thames and Hudson, 1961.

RIDGEWAY, WILLIAM. *The Origin and Influence of the Thoroughbred Horse.* Cambridge University Press, 1905.

RUNCIMAN, STEVEN. *Byzantine Civilization.* London: Methuen, 1933.

——*A History of the Crusades.* 3 vols. Cambridge University Press, 1955.

SALISBURY, HARRISON E. *Orbit of China.* London: Secker and Warburg, 1967.

Secret History of the Mongols. Translated by Arthur Waley. London: George Allen and Unwin, 1963.

SEMYONOV, YURI. *The Conquest of Siberia.* Translated by E. W. Dickes. London: George Routledge and Sons, 1944.

SIMPSON, JAMES YOUNG. *Sidelights on Siberia.* London: William Blackwood and Sons, 1898.

SKELTON, R. A., MARSTON, THOMAS E., and PAINTER, GEORGE D. *The Vinland Map and the Tartar Relation.* New Haven and London: Yale University Press, 1965.

SKRINE, F. H. B. and ROSS, E. D. *The Heart of Asia.* London: Methuen, 1899.

STADLING, JONAS *Through Siberia.* London: Constable and Co., 1901.

STARK, FREYA. *The Valleys of the Assassins*. London: John Murray, 1934.

SYKES, PERCY. *A History of Exploration*. London: George Routledge and Sons, 1933.

THOMPSON, E. A. *A History of Attila and the Huns*. Oxford University Press, 1948.

THOMSEN, V. *Inscriptions de l'Orkhon*. Helsingfors: Mémoires de la Société finno-ougrienne V, 1896.

TREADGOLD, DONALD W. *The Great Siberian Migration*. Princeton University Press, 1957.

TUPPER, HARMON. *To the Great Ocean: Siberia and the Trans-Siberian Railway*. London: Secker and Warburg, 1965.

VAUGHAN, DOROTHY M. *Europe and the Turk*. Liverpool University Press, 1954.

VERNADSKY, GEORGE. *A History of Russia*. Yale University Press, 1929.

——*The Mongols and Russia* .Yale University Press, 1953.

VLADIMIRTSOV, B. Y. *The Life of Chingis Khan*. London: George Routledge and Sons, 1930.

VOLPICELLI, ZENONE ('VLADIMIR'). *Russia on the Pacific and the Siberian Railway*. London: Sampson Low, Marston and Co., 1899.

WALEY, ARTHUR. 'Lo-yang and its Fall', *History Today* (London), April 1951.

WALLACE-HADRILL, J. M. *The Barbarian West, 400–1000*. London: Hutchinson, 1952.

WELLS, H. G. *The Outline of History* London: Cassell, 1920.

WHITE, LYNN, Jnr. *Medieval Technology and Social Change*. Oxford University Press, 1962.

YAMADA, NAKABA. *Ghenko, The Mongol Invasion of Japan*. London: Smith, Elder and Co., 1916.

YULE, HENRY (Translator and Editor). *The Travels of Marco Polo*. 2 vols. London: John Murray, 1870.

——(Translator and Editor). *Cathay and the Way Thither*. London: Hakluyt Society, 1913.

Index